The British Constitution Resettled

Jim McConalogue

The British Constitution Resettled

Parliamentary Sovereignty Before and After Brexit

palgrave
macmillan

Jim McConalogue
Rickmansworth, UK

ISBN 978-3-030-25289-2 ISBN 978-3-030-25290-8 (eBook)
https://doi.org/10.1007/978-3-030-25290-8

Cover credit: mammuth/Getty Images

This Palgrave Macmillan imprint is published by the registered company Springer Nature Switzerland AG
The registered company address is: Gewerbestrasse 11, 6330 Cham, Switzerland

This book is dedicated to the memory of my late father Patrick and my mother Bernadette for their love, encouragement, humour and unwavering support.

Preface

This book—finished on the day Theresa May resigned as Prime Minister—sets out to argue that EU membership strongly 'unsettled' historically precedented understandings of UK parliamentary sovereignty. By adopting a broadly political constitutionalist view of the British constitution, this book first makes the case for an updated explanation of UK parliamentary sovereignty as the 'rule of the recognised helm'. It adapts H.L.A Hart's approach to sovereignty as the 'rule of recognition' while incorporating Bracton's medieval, political view of sovereignty as operating under the 'helm' of the ship of state, responsible for the government of the realm. The operation of such a 'rule of the recognised helm' in Britain is dependent upon a uniquely conditioned political history characterised by eight crucial precedented 'historical constitutional forms', defining parliamentary sovereignty, from the thirteenth century through the contemporary Parliament.

Britain's past and contemporary constitutional forms help to define the meaning and unsettling of parliamentary sovereignty. Throughout its history, Britain has experienced eight historical constitutional forms which explain its rule of parliamentary sovereignty. The first form, 'What the Crown-*with*-magnates enacts is law' (1200–1350) is divine in its claim to power and right but held in consultation with magnates. The second form is 'What the Crown-*with*-Commons enacts is law' (1350–1532). Fortescue's (1395–1477) then leading assessment of England's *dominium politicum et regale*, observes government as being both political and regal, signifying the essential character of the Crown needing to rule with the parliament to gain consent. The third form, 'What the Crown-*through*-Parliament enacts is law' (1533–1602) confirmed the assumption of legislative sovereignty by 1539–1540 and Parliament's omnicompetence—that no area involved in the government of realm was outside its authority. Fourth, the form 'What the Crown-*with*-disputed Parliament enacts is law' (1603–1687) reflect that in the first half of the seventeenth century, there were three disputed categories for those who made claims to sovereignty: the Crown; the Crown in Parliament, and; the law. The fifth form, 'What the Crown-*in*-regulating Parliament enacts is law' (1688–1689) reflects that since 1689, the great constitutional struggles of the seventeenth century meant that the royal succession could be regulated by parliament. The sixth form, 'What the Crown-*in*-mixed constitutional Parliament enacts is law' (1690–1790s) embodies Montesquieu's *The Spirit of the Laws* (1748) explaining the English 'power checks power' constitution in which the executive and the two branches of the legislative act as checks on one another yet the judicial power and tribunals of law are subordinate to legislation. Seventh, the form 'What the Crown-*in*-Parliamentary Cabinet enacts is law' (1800–1972) rests upon Bagehot's constitution in which the Cabinet marks the central institution of British government set within the fusion of legislative and executive powers. In the eighth contemporary form, 'What the Crown-*through*-Parliamentary political elite with external bodies enacts is law' (1973–present), the form of parliamentary elites ruling through Parliament transforms into the form that Government rules through Parliament or partially through external agency or bodies. A significant part of the transformation in the present constitutional form helps to explain the decision of the UK to leave the EU and thereby to resettle its parliamentary sovereignty.

The argument is critical of other approaches within strictly legal (neo-Diceyan), popular sovereigntist and common law paradigms which have accorded too little significance to the past historical precedents defining Parliament's sovereignty and its institutional inter-relationships. By overlooking historical constitutional forms, the gravity of the impact of EU membership on the UK constitution has often been misunderstood by those approaches.

My main contention is that under EU membership, successive governments, through Parliaments, have adopted practices which whilst preserving a fundamental legal and political rule, are at odds with past constitutional precedents. On the one hand, three key EU case studies—of the Financial Transactions Tax, of the freedom of movement of persons and of the Working Time Directive—affirm that the UK's recognised helm has, since 1973, incorporated EU institutions which *unsettles* those political precedents of parliamentary sovereignty. On the other hand, in the final chapter, Parliament's role since the UK's holding of the EU Referendum in 2016 and in scrutinising Theresa May's withdrawal agreement constitutes an enhanced, new constitutional *resettlement*, a realignment of Parliament with historical precedent and its sovereignty.

Rickmansworth, UK Jim McConalogue
May 2019

Acknowledgements

I would like to wholeheartedly thank Richard Heffernan and Georgina Blakeley (Open University) for their continued guidance and scrutiny of successive, earlier drafts of the chapters which formed the basis of this book. I am very appreciative of Andrew Gamble's (Sheffield) advice after my Ph.D. viva, which proved beneficial in refining earlier lines of argument. I am further grateful to Sarah Childs (at Birkbeck College) for facilitating an event at the Centre for Study of British Politics and Public Life at Birkbeck College, at which I presented my research on the British Prime Minister's constraint by parliament in the Brexit process, and also to Paul Evans (Clerk of Committees, House of Commons) for chairing the discussion. The feedback gained from exchanges with students, alumni, and members of the public was valuable to improving my understanding (and limitations) in recognising an enhanced parliamentary role throughout the Brexit process. Ambra Finotello and Anne Birchley-Brun at Palgrave, along with the anonymous reviewer, provided indispensable guidance which allowed this book to come to fruition.

I am especially grateful to my family—my wife Sarah, my parents, and to Helen and Thomas—mainly for putting up with me during the writing of this work. I am particularly thankful to Sheila for her editorial assistance.

Contents

List of Boxes

CHAPTER 1

The Impact of EU Membership on UK Government and Parliament's Sovereignty

The transition of Britain to its modern, post-war democratic form after two World Wars and the drawing to an end of an Empire brought about some significant changes to its political arrangements. It remains a 'settled polity' and it has been a full democracy for the past 100 years (Gamble 2016, 2019). Internally, within Westminster, Parliamentary sovereignty remains the supreme principle of the UK constitution. It makes Parliament the supreme legal authority in the UK, which can create or end any law; in that system, Acts of Parliament cannot traditionally be challenged in the courts. The Westminster system has been deeply embedded in the idea of accountability, which made it possible for the electorate collectively to hold the government of the day to account (King 2015, p. 19). The constitution as a whole continues to be expressed as "partly written and wholly uncodified" (UK Parliament 2019). Its representative institutions and political traditions stretch back to the seventeenth century (Gamble 2019).

Britain's place in Europe has formed, for many, a substantial part of its new post-imperial role. The role for Britain in Europe was ambiguous and difficult to express. To establish that role, politicians in Parliament passed the European Communities Act 1972, enabling the UK's entry to the European Union (EU) in 1973. It voluntarily limited the application of its parliamentary sovereignty (Smith 2017, p. 79). This and other laws reflected major political developments both within and outside the UK since the 1970s. Those laws have included:

J. McConalogue, *The British Constitution Resettled*,
https://doi.org/10.1007/978-3-030-25290-8_1

- the devolution of powers at Westminster to bodies like the Scottish Parliament and Welsh Assembly;
- the introduction of the Human Rights Act 1998 incorporating the European Convention on Human Rights into UK law;
- the decision to establish a UK Supreme Court in 2009, which ends the House of Lords function as the UK's final court of appeal.

With those changes, the UK has become less united by the activities of its multinational state than it was in the past. It has moved from being the most centralised state in Europe towards a more devolved system where the other nations of the UK are no longer subordinate to London, Whitehall and Westminster for their policies (Gamble 2016). Under EU arrangements, the constitution has potentially shifted away from the traditional Westminster model, in which ministers in government continue to lead their Departments through the executive and propose and draft Government bills for the UK population, with the consent of the House of Commons. With the Human Rights Act 1998 and the incorporation of the European Convention on Human Rights into UK law and the decision to establish a UK Supreme Court in 2009, it has widened the scope of a judiciary only previously required to give effect to the statutes of Parliament. Inside Westminster, the same two major parties, the Conservatives and Labour, who were the major parties in 1945, are still the same major parties (Bogdanor 2011), run along adversarial lines (King 2015, p. 18). As a subject, Europe split both of the major parties. For example, the Labour Party, in the 1980s, with a breakaway party of the Social Democratic Party; and then the Conservatives significantly in the 1990s (Bogdanor 2019, p. 12). Political events between 2016 and 2019 have highlighted how uneasy a subject it continues to be, including the holding of the EU Referendum of 2016, the majority vote to 'Leave' in that referendum, in addition to the vigorously scrutinised Article 50 negotiations and withdrawal agreement negotiated under Theresa May's Conservative-led Government. Britain had long failed and continues to dispute reconciling itself with being in Europe (Bogdanor 2011), neither being *of* Europe, nor run *by* Europe (Gamble 2016).

1.1 UK Membership of the EU

Britain's contemporary EU membership impacts upon its governmental competences only in so far as the EU has specific exclusive, shared, supporting or special competences to pursue certain actions or laws, in accordance only with the UK having shared or pooled those fields of legislative competence in certain policy areas through successive European treaties. It was to be the "most intimate and intense involvement" of foreign governments in the making of governmental decisions (King 2015, p. 25). In the post-war European political and economic landscape, the European Coal and Steel Community (ECSC), formed from a Treaty, possessed supranational characteristics with the objective of creating interdependence through a common market of coal, coke, iron ore, steel and scrap so that one country could no longer mobilise its armed forces without others knowing, which eased tensions after the Second World War (European Union 2014; Nugent 2006, p. 138). Britain was not a signatory to the Treaty establishing the ECSC, which was signed by six countries (France, West Germany, Italy, Belgium, Luxembourg, The Netherlands) on 18 April 1951. Later in the 1950s, Britain remained absent from signing the Treaties of Rome on 25 March 1957 with the objective to set up the European Economic Community (EEC) (and the European Atomic Energy Community, or Euratom). The EEC marked an extension of European integration to include general economic cooperation—which included the guidelines for establishing a common market in manufactured goods and a Common Agricultural Policy (CAP) (Dedman 2010, p. 82). It embodied a degree of supranationalism in decision-making (Nugent 2006, p. 47) and again, Britain was not a signatory to the EEC at that point. Britain was in general, opposed to a continental EEC, particularly through the establishment of supranational European institutions, and potentially detrimental to her export interests and undermining her claims of leading Europe (Berger 2013).

The intentional limiting of national sovereignty by Treaty for the purposes of enabling international cooperation was in line with a number of constitutional provisions set up after the Second World War (Chalmers 2013, p. 5; Kaplan 2018). In spite of Labour and Conservative Governments having no intention of being part of a supranational European organisation (Geddes 2013, p. 47), and during the time of the UK's original decision not to be part of the Treaty of Rome, it became recognisable to both Britain's leaders and people that economically the European Community was doing far better and being on the outside while high tariffs were "enormously disadvantageous" (Geddes 2013, p. 56; Wall 2008; King 2007, p. 92). Against the British favoured intergovernmental regional trade organisation, the European Free Trade Association (EFTA), the EEC "became the predominant organisation" (Geddes 2013, p. 53). A further Treaty, the merger Brussels Treaty, was signed on 8 April 1965. It led to the creation of a single Commission and a single Council to serve the then three European Communities (EEC, Euratom, ECSC) and was later repealed by the Treaty of Amsterdam.

In the meantime, the UK submitted its first application in 1961 to join the EEC, under Conservative Prime Minister Harold Macmillan, but the application had been vetoed by the French President, Charles de Gaulle (Geddes 2013, p. 54). The UK made a further, second application in 1967 under Labour Prime Minister Harold Wilson but had been blocked again by the French President (McLean 2009, pp. 184–185). Shortly after, a Conservative government was formed in Britain under Prime Minister Edward Heath in June 1970. Heath had been seeking for the right terms to be negotiated on the EEC and committed the UK to join in its long-term interest (Norton 2011, p. 55). It was eventually the European Communities Act 1972 under Heath which domestically permitted the UK specifically to join the EEC (McLean 2009, p. 184). The UK required the European Communities Act 1972 in its own domestic law in order to become a member. A series of significant new treaties and treaty amendments to the European Communities Act have been agreed since that Act and the changes in UK law necessary to give effect to the new treaties have been made under amending Acts. The result of the European Communities Act 1972 was that future Parliaments were, unless and until they expressly repealed it, bound by its terms (Goldsworthy 2013, p. 65). Politically, the original European Communities Act 1972 received public endorsement through a post-ratification referendum in 1975, with a two-to-one vote in favour of continued membership on a 64% turnout (Geddes 2013, p. 65). The UK only joined the European Communities on 1 January 1973, along with Denmark and Ireland, raising the then number of member states to nine.

It was not until the 1980s that the Single European Act (SEA) entered into force (1 July 1987), with the intention of deepening European integration. The Act sped up decision-making in preparation for the single market to be established by December 1992 and reforming the institutions in preparation for new members joining. It permitted the strengthening of EC institutional structures through the extension of qualified majority voting (QMV) over all internal market legislation in the Council—thereby undermining any one country's veto over proposed legislation—and the creation of co-operation procedure to give the European Parliament more influence (European Union 2014;

Geddes 2013, p. 70; Dedman 2010, pp. 114–115; Wall 2008, p. 49; Nugent 2006, p. 81). QMV carries with it the implication of a legitimacy deficit, because national parliaments lose credible power to influence EU-level decisions if their governments can be outvoted (Auel 2007, pp. 498–499; Dimitrakopoulos 2001, p. 405). The British view that the SEA sufficed to 'complete' the single market, and that further treaties were not required simply did not prevail in reality (Marshall 2013, p. 17). Treaty revision subsequently became a "virtual non-stop process since the mid-1980s" (Dedman 2010, p. 166).

Less than five years later, the Treaty on European Union (TEU), popularly known as the Maastricht Treaty, was signed on 7 February 1992 and entered into force on 1 November 1993. Its objective was to prepare for European Economic and Monetary Union (EMU) and introduce elements of a political union, including political features of citizenship and a common foreign and internal affairs policy. It established the "European Union" and introduced the co-decision procedure, giving the European Parliament more say in decision-making (Bux 2017; Hix and Høyland 2013, p. 172). New forms of cooperation developed between the UK and other EU governments, for example on defence and justice and home affairs (Novak 2017; European Union 2014). The Treaty itself was a milestone on the road to a potential federation (Gowland et al. 2010, p. 118) and the UK's political debate over the Maastricht Treaty demonstrated that popular and parliamentary groups increasingly contested the Crown and Parliament's powers assenting to the competences set out within the European Treaties. Accordingly, the UK's Conservative government under John Major secured two significant opt-outs on the Maastricht Treaty, including the deferral of a decision to participate in the final stage of economic and monetary union (EMU) and on the Social Chapter (Gowland et al. 2010, pp. 103–104).

Later, under Tony Blair's New Labour government, when the Treaty of Amsterdam entered into force on 1 May 1999 (Novak 2017), its purpose was to reform the EU institutions in preparation for the arrival of future member countries. It increased the use of the co-decision voting procedure. The EU's absence of appetite for reform at this stage reflected the reaction to Maastricht and its quest for deeper integration (Gowland et al. 2010, p. 151). The Treaty of Nice extended QMV to cover 90% of EU law, with national vetoes remaining only for a small core of articles (Dedman 2010, p. 173). That Treaty made "sufficient progress" to enable enlargement to occur in 2004, and 2007, but it was clear "even before the ink was dry that a further treaty reform would be required" (Smith 2012).

The EU had subsequently and painstakingly drafted a Constitutional Treaty establishing a single text document—a "constitution for Europe"—in 2004 (Nugent 2006, pp. 120–128) which was signed but never ratified. That non-ratification was, in part, a consequence of an increased division which emerged between the European bureaucratic elites and citizens over European integration who had no immediate access to an EU with a significant democratic deficit (Haller 2009). There remained nonetheless a series of momentum-building events in the search for political legitimacy (Walker 2005). Irrespective of the popular opposition in the UK to the subsequent Constitutional Treaty "as a massive step towards the creation of a federal superstate" (Gowland et al. 2010, p. 172), and the rejection of that Treaty by referendums in France (55%) and The Netherlands (62%) and the proposed pledge of a referendum in the UK, the Treaty establishing a Constitution for Europe was reworked through an "amending" treaty, the Treaty of Lisbon (see Smith 2012; Reh 2009).

The subsequent Lisbon Treaty was signed on 13 December 2007 with the objective of making the EU more democratic, more efficient and better able to address global problems. The Lisbon Treaty enhanced the power of the European Parliament, led to the change of voting procedures in the Council, provided a permanent president for the European Council, a new High Representative for Foreign Affairs and a new EU diplomatic service (European Union 2014; Dedman 2010, p. 177; Lisbon Treaty 2007). The EU gained 'legal personality' under the Lisbon Treaty, giving it rights under international law to adopt laws and Treaties. The Lisbon Treaty clarified powers and competences in the Treaties. It permitted an enhanced role of national parliaments, particularly with reference to an 'early warning system', whereby the national legislatures gained the right to monitor whether initiatives for EU decisions comply with the principle of subsidiarity (Auel and Neuhold 2017; Neyer 2014, p. 125; Miller 2012; Raunio 2009, p. 318; EU Committee 2008). All the EU Treaties are only effective in the UK by virtue of the European Communities Act 1972, which is amended by Parliament each time.

The single market is the EU's main economic foundation (Pelkmans 2016), enabling the free movement of goods, services, capital and labour. The trade within the single market, agriculture, environmental protection and competition policy are key areas in which the Union predominates and in which the competences of national governments have been substantially reduced or removed entirely (King 2007, p. 107; Department for Business, Innovation and Skills and Foreign and Commonwealth Office 2013; Department for Environment, Food and Rural Affairs 2013). In terms of the single market between the 28 European countries, the EU has become a major world trading power. The EU's economy, in terms of goods and services (expressed as GDP), is now bigger than that of the US.

The UK participates in the EU's other main objective which is to promote human rights both internally—through the introduction of EU citizenship—and around the world. Indeed, since the signing of the Lisbon Treaty in 2007, the EU's Charter of Fundamental Rights (annexed to the Treaty) brings all these rights together in a single text. The Charter dates back to a European Council meeting in Cologne in 1999 and agreement by Convention in 2000, aspiring for fundamental rights to be consolidated into a charter (Nugent 2006, p. 113). The EU's institutions and all EU governments are legally bound to uphold them when applying EU law. The Charter is indeed directly effective in the UK with supremacy over inconsistent national law, albeit it does not apply to all areas of national law (European Scrutiny Committee 2014).

The EU launched a single European currency, the euro, in January 1999. The euro is the common currency of most (19) EU countries—the UK has, again, very significantly, opted out of the euro, but the principle of which meant the UK was not required to participate in the third stage of European Economic and Monetary Union (EMU) and consequently introduce the euro (Gowland et al. 2010, p. 103). It is notable, however, that for the EU itself, the euro, which is used every day by some 340 million Europeans, is said by the European institutions to be the "most tangible proof" of cooperation between EU countries (European Union 2014).

The EU is a unique economic and political partnership currently between 28 European member states, albeit the UK is seeking withdrawal from the bloc. It possesses a unique institutional set-up. The EU's broad priorities and direction are set by the European Council, bringing together the UK and other national heads of state or government and the Commission President and Council President (European

Union 2014). The UK's directly elected Members of the European Parliament (MEPs) who represent European citizens are elected to the European Parliament along with those from all other member states. It is in the interests of the EU as a whole rather than of the UK alone, that objectives are promoted by the European Commission, whose commissioners are appointed by national governments. In basic terms, there are three main institutions through which the UK becomes directly or indirectly involved in EU legislation, namely: (i) the Council of the EU represents the UK and all EU governments of the member states whereby the Presidency of the Council is shared by the member states on a rotating basis; (ii) the European Commission, which represents the interests of the EU as a whole; and (iii) the European Parliament represents the UK's and the other EU's citizens and is directly elected by them. The UK participates in EU institutions through the "Ordinary Legislative Procedure" (once known as the 'co-decision' procedure) for policies and laws that apply within the EU. In principle, the Commission proposes new laws, and the Parliament and Council adopt them. The Commission and the UK and EU member countries then implement them, and the Commission ensures that those laws are properly applied and implemented (European Union 2014). The *acquis communautaire* is the whole body of EU law all member states including the UK must subscribe to, including the European Court of Justice decisions. Two other institutions play important roles, including the European Court of Justice which upholds the rule of European law and the Court of Auditors checks the financing of the EU's activities.

The powers and responsibilities of all of these institutions are laid down in the Treaties (see Box 1.1), which are the foundation of everything the EU does. They also lay down the rules and procedures that the EU institutions must follow. The Treaties are agreed by the Heads of Government of all the EU countries—in the UK's case, the Prime Minister—and ratified by their parliaments (and sanctioned by national populations through a referendum if necessary). The highest form of law is the Treaties themselves which not only set out the "constitution of the EU" and deal with substantive issues but a number of competences which provide for rights directly effective in the UK's and all other national legal systems in the EU (Bradley and Ewing 2010, p. 129).

Box 1.1: The EU Treaties

- Treaty of Lisbon (signed: 13 December 2007; entered into force: 1 December 2009) provided more power for the European Parliament, change of voting procedures in the Council, a permanent president of the European Council, a new High Representative for Foreign Affairs and a new EU diplomatic service.
- Treaty of Nice (signed: 26 February 2001; entered into force: 1 February 2003) provided for methods for changing the composition of the Commission and redefining the voting system in the Council.
- Treaty of Amsterdam (signed: 2 October 1997; entered into force: 1 May 1999) provided for amendment, renumbering and consolidation of EU and EEC treaties and increased use of the ordinary legislative procedure.
- Treaty on European Union (TEU)—Maastricht Treaty (signed: 7 February 1992; entered into force: 1 November 1993) provided for the establishment of the European Union and introduction of the co-decision procedure, new forms of cooperation between EU governments over defence and justice and home affairs.
- The SEA (signed: 17 February 1986; entered into force: 1 July 1987) provided for the extension of QMV in the Council (making it harder for a single country to veto proposed legislation) and; creation of cooperation and assent procedures.
- Merger Treaty—Brussels Treaty (signed: 8 April 1965; entered into force: 1 July 1967) provided for the creation of a single Commission and a single Council to serve the then three European Communities (EEC, Euratom, ECSC) and repealed by the Treaty of Amsterdam.
- The Treaties of Rome (EEC and EURATOM treaties, signed: 25 March 1957; entered into force: 1 January 1958) provided for the extension of European integration to include general economic cooperation.
- Treaty establishing the ECSC, the founding treaties being amended in 1973 when Denmark, Ireland and UK joined.

(European Union 2017; Novak 2017; Lisbon Treaty 2007)

The EU is based on the rule of law, but the rule of law, within the EU, only exists in so far as member states and the EU acts within the powers conferred on them by the legally-binding treaties that have been approved voluntarily and democratically by all EU member states, including the UK. For example, if a policy area is not cited in a Treaty, the Commission cannot propose a law in that area, including direct taxation, health provision in the NHS, defence and welfare. The Treaties set out supranational EU objectives, rules for EU institutions, how decisions are made and the relationship between the EU and its member countries.

1.2 EU Membership Impact on UK Governing Competences

The European Communities Act 1972, in practice, meant that EU law became part of UK law by virtue of that Act (Miller 2015). EU law takes precedence over existing UK law, which must be amended if it is found to conflict with EU law. The Act, as amended over time, allows EU specified instruments to become part of UK law without the need for separate enactment of each and every EU instrument. In one specific section—Section 2(1)—the Act gives the authority for Treaty provisions and directly applicable secondary legislation (e.g. regulations) automatically to have legal effect in UK domestic law without further enactment (Miller 2015). In terms of Westminster implementing EU law, in some areas, additional implementing measures are required, particularly in the field of agriculture, which for the UK means implementation by Statutory Instrument (SI). Directives and decisions which are not directly applicable can be enacted either by primary or secondary legislation in the UK.

The UK is wholly isolated in the EU in operating under the doctrine of parliamentary sovereignty and in which the constitution is interpreted as only "partly written and wholly uncodified" (UK Parliament 2019)—all other member states have adopted some form of written constitution.

The UK Parliament is and always has been well aware that when it joined the EC:

i. priority would be accorded to EC law where the EU has competence (Young and Gee 2016);
ii. it was inherent in the EC regime that functionally the priority must be given to EC law;

iii. the European Communities Act 1972 placed a duty on national courts to override national law in the event of a conflict (Craig 2011, p. 116);
iv. Parliament may still derogate from EU obligations expressly and the EU only maintains supremacy in areas of the law where it is applicable (Craig 2011, p. 118; Tabarelli 2013, p. 355).

Despite political controversies, or perceptions of 'awkwardness', the UK voluntarily belongs through the EU Treaties to the EU system of rules. The end result of the Treaties is that there is a division of competences with the EU. The Union therefore only has the competences conferred upon it by the EU Treaties. The Treaty of Lisbon (TFEU), which ended the European Community and replaced it with the EU, set out for the first time and very precisely, the division of competences between the EU and member states, by distinguishing between three main categories of competence: exclusive, shared and supporting competences (Rossi 2012).

The EU's 'exclusive competence' means that the Union—and therefore not the UK or other member states—have exclusive competence in the areas of, for example, the customs union, the monetary policy for the member states who share the euro currency and the common commercial policy (Article 3, TFEU). The EU alone is able to legislate and adopt binding acts in these fields. The UK and the other member states' role is therefore limited to applying these acts, unless the EU authorises them to adopt certain acts themselves. The 'shared competence' specifies that the EU has shared competence with the member states, including the UK, which applies in policy areas covering, for example: the internal market; social policy in certain respects; economic and social cohesion; agriculture, fisheries and environment; consumer protection; and the area of freedom, security and justice (Article 4, TFEU). As a shared competence, the UK may exercise its competence only in so far as the EU has not exercised, or has decided not to exercise, its own competence. In the EU's 'supporting competences', the Union is able to support and coordinate member state action on areas, for example, such as protection of human health; industry; culture; tourism; education, vocational training, youth and sport (Article 6, TFEU). The EU has no legislative power in those fields and may not interfere in the exercise of these competences reserved for member states, including the UK.

The EU also has some other 'special competences' in certain fields so that the UK and other member states coordinate their economic, social and employment policies within the Union. Member states whose currency is the euro are a special case within that field (Rossi 2012, p. 101). The common foreign and security policy (CFSP) (under Article 24, TEU) is in an unsettled position. On the one hand, the EU has competence in all fields connected with the CFSP, but subject to unanimity/veto, and goes as far as defining and implementing this policy through the High Representative of the Union for Foreign Affairs and Security Policy, whose roles and status have been recognised by the Treaty of Lisbon. Yet, on the other hand, the EU may not adopt legislative acts in this field and the European Court of Justice does not have competence to give judgement in this area. The specific reduction or extension of EU competences is a step which requires a revision of the Treaties, which domestically and institutionally carries with it its own crises.

EU membership influences the UK perhaps most importantly through the provisions and consequences of the single market (Pelkmans 2016), in which the EU's 'four freedoms' of goods, services, capital and people are guaranteed. In terms of intra-EU migration rules, EU nationals between member states do not require a visa to enter another member state, and no time limit may be placed on their stay (under the Free Movement Directive, EU Directive 2004/38/EC). Having ceded that competence, the inability of the UK to impose limits on immigration from the European Economic Area (EEA) remains a controversial aspect of EU membership in the UK, particularly since the expansion of the EU to Eastern Europe from 2004, which has driven a rise in net migration (Thompson and Harari 2013) and, played a significant role in the majority referendum decision of the British people to leave the EU in June 2016 (Curtice 2017; Sobolewska and Ford 2016; Hobolt 2016; Katwala 2019; Ford 2019).

The EU has a major exclusive competence to negotiate trade and investment agreements with countries outside the Union. It is a customs union with a common external tariff on imported goods and therefore the UK's membership of that union significantly affects the UK's trade relations with non-EU members throughout the world. The CAP affects consumer prices and membership impacts upon common external tariffs levied on imports. Single market law seeks to eliminate the differences in the way markets function between the UK and all EU member states—or creating a 'level playing field'—including on product standards for goods, and rules on consumer protection, to health and safety legislation, and competition policy. The UK does not operate with the euro currency and is not a member of the 19-member eurozone area. By sharing a single currency, those euro area countries must also coordinate their economic and fiscal policies much more closely than other EU countries such as the UK. Nonetheless, the EU is the largest economy in the world, although constituting only 7% of the world's population. The Common Fisheries Policy (CFP) is the EU's instrument for managing viable fisheries and aquaculture. Although mired in controversy for decades in the UK and which had largely "failed" as the health of fish stocks and fishing businesses deteriorated as bureaucracy increased, the CFP has been reformed in recent years.

In terms of the national competences over UK policy, Westminster does retain control over key areas of government—including direct taxation, health provision in the NHS, defence, welfare, and other vital areas:

- *Taxation*: competence on direct taxation remains primarily with the UK and other member states, although by indirect taxation, the UK is subject to Value Added Tax (VAT), excise duties and other indirect taxes and other issues, including the constraints on exercising their competence in line with the fundamental freedoms (HM Treasury 2013).
- *Public spending*: the UK's public spending is the responsibility of the Government and is expected to amount to £840.7 billion in 2019–2020 (Office for Budget Responsibility 2019). In the meantime, its net contribution to the EU budget in 2017 stood at £8.9 billion (Keep 2018) while the majority of EU funding received and spent by the UK is through the European Agricultural Guarantee Fund (EAGF), paying subsidies to farmers, and through European Structural Funds (Keep 2018; Department for Environment, Food and Rural Affairs 2013).
- *Labour and social law*: the UK maintains, unlike some other EU members, that member states regulate their labour market and their social systems according to their own needs and political priorities (Thompson and Harari 2013).
- *NHS*: the EU is generally limited to supporting the competence of improving health in the NHS and the EU has, for example, an extremely limited role in social care (Department of Health 2013).

- *International development*: the EU is only one of a number of multilateral organisations through which the UK channels its aid spending. In 2017, for example, the UK spent 37.4% of its aid budget through multilateral channels (including the United Nations) to address specific issues and spends the remainder of its aid budget bilaterally (Department for International Development 2018).
- *Foreign policy, defence and security*: common foreign security and defence policy decision-making is pursued by unanimity in the Council through member states' government ministers. Where all significant decisions are made by unanimity, each member state has a power of veto, particularly over the deployment of EU military operations and civilian missions. Each member state also retains full sovereign control of its troops, civilian personnel and other security assets (Foreign and Commonwealth Office 2013).
- *Education*: the UK, like other EU governments, has a "strong political desire" to make its own laws regarding education and training, externally entering into other bilateral and multilateral international agreements, provided it is not precluded by overriding EU competence in other areas (Department for Education 2014).

However, that does not mean UK parliamentary sovereignty is unaffected by EU membership. In particular, within a modern, multi-level polity, UK-EU institutional interaction combines different forms of policy governance (Bache 2012; Hooghe and Marks 2001) defined by:

- continuous negotiation among governments at multiple territorial tiers (Hooghe and Marks 2001; Marks 1993);
- supranational, national, regional and local governments existing within enmeshed territorially overarching policy networks (Marks 1993);
- previously national competencies moving away from central states up to the supranational level and down to the subnational level (Bache and Flinders 2004, p. 34).

In the multi-level polity, it remains legitimate to ask whether Britain, as a member state, can be considered sovereign (Aalberts 2004, p. 25) or democratically accountable (see Bache 2012, p. 11) if the locus of political control has shifted and is not exclusively at the state level any more. In contrast, the fundamental rules in the UK's legal and political system, which are nevertheless dependent on a uniquely conditioned political history, has defined the sovereignty of Parliament. Under EU membership, governments through Parliaments, have learned practices at odds with past constitutional forms, while not altogether abandoning the underlying fundamental rule.

1.3 The EU Challenge to Parliamentary Sovereignty

It is said that the doctrine of parliamentary sovereignty—or what the classical, iconic scholar of this concept, A. V. Dicey in 1885 referred to as "the very keystone of the law of the constitution" (Dicey 1964, p. 70), is defined as:

> The principle of Parliamentary sovereignty means neither more nor less than this, namely, that Parliament ... has, under the English constitution, the right to make or unmake any law whatever; and, further, that no person or body is recognised by the law of England as having a right to override or set aside the legislation of Parliament. (Dicey 1964)

Parliamentary sovereignty has, throughout the centuries, undergone major challenges and developments, which has left the UK with the Westminster Parliament it has today and another new (albeit, often similar) set of challenges. Those modern challenges—including devolution and human rights legislation consistent with the European Convention on Human Rights under the Human Rights Act 1998 and often understood generally as 'constitutional change'—affect parliamentary sovereignty and include the challenge posed by membership of the EU under the terms of the European Communities Act 1972 and its subsequent amendments. The sovereignty of parliament has been challenged, modified but far from overturned and continues to provide the touchstone of constitutional change (Walker 2014).

Given the understanding of the challenge posed by the EU to parliamentary sovereignty, examined widely across academic literature—crossing disciplines from constitutional law, political science and philosophy—what is necessary is to interrogate that definition of parliamentary sovereignty and then ask how it is interpreted in the context of EU membership affecting that doctrine. To do so can illuminate political and constitutional understandings of the UK's core constitutional doctrine of parliamentary sovereignty—and therefore how it has been *unsettled* by EU membership since the passing of the European Communities Act 1972, before being *resettled* in consequence of the repeal of that Act.

The European project began as a purely economic union, i.e. a common market as a customs union, but British reservations always existed on that very point alone, insisting that there was an obvious intention towards political union—and that supranational governance carried with it domestic consequences for the doctrine of the sovereignty of Parliament (see Geddes 2013, pp. 24–26). For example, the earliest legal attempts to challenge UK entry into the EEC in 1971 were made on the grounds that had been recognised by some groups as an abuse of treaty-making power by the executive thereby undermining the sovereignty of Parliament (Bradley and Ewing 2010, p. 117; *Blackburn v A-G* [1971]). In legislating for the European Communities Act 1972, the conception of sovereignty deployed in parliamentary debates was concerned with the power of political institutions (Young and Gee 2016). Sovereignty concerns were raised by MPs over the extent to which parliament would be able to enact legislation as it wished while impeded by EEC membership (Young and Gee 2016).

On the unique and very direct legal and political effects of the EU, there is a tension between the political exercise of the sovereignty of Parliament and the claimed supremacy of a complex EU legal and political order (Bogdanor 2019, p. 43; Tabarelli 2013, p. 344). The uniqueness of the EU institutional set-up, the primacy of EU law, and of direct effect for claimable EU rights in national courts (Nugent 2010, p. 213) characterise that order. Yet, Dicey's traditional definition provides for a principle whereby "...no person or body is recognised by the law of England as having a right to override or set aside the legislation of Parliament" (Dicey 1964). That is, in part, challenged under the European Communities Act 1972 (Loughlin and Tierney 2018, pp. 1009–1010)—and as set out later under the controversial *Factortame* [1990] case law (Tomkins 2003). The European Court of Justice does have a supreme right to override or set aside the legislation of Parliament. Parliament may still disapply, override or derogate from EU obligations if it wishes (Bingham 2010; Tomkins 2003; Tabarelli 2013, p. 355) and EU law only maintains supremacy in areas of the law where it is applicable, but the challenge to practical, everyday Westminster sovereignty doctrine is nonetheless present.

This book examines the way in which EU membership has unsettled historically precedented understandings of UK parliamentary sovereignty. By according insufficient significance and weight to previous historical understandings, the magnitude of the impact of EU membership on the UK constitution has often been misunderstood if not underestimated by other approaches. By adopting a broadly political constitutionalist position, and as a departure from Hart's (1997) rule of recognition, Chapters 2 and 3 propose an alternative explanation of UK parliamentary sovereignty, as the 'rule of the recognised helm'. It seeks to achieve that objective by adapting the approaches of the 'rule of recognition' while incorporating the medieval, political view of sovereignty as operating under the 'helm' of the ship of state, responsible for the government of the realm (particularly in McIlwain 1947, p. 86 on de Bracton 1235). Chapter 3 shows that the operation of the 'rule of the recognised helm' is dependent upon a uniquely conditioned political history characterised by eight crucial historically precedented 'historical constitutional forms' define UK parliamentary sovereignty, from the thirteenth century through to the contemporary Parliament of today. In the contemporary constitutional form under EU membership, successive governments, through Parliaments, have adopted practices which while not abandoning the fundamental rule, are at odds with those past constitutional precedents.

Some formal boundaries to this study need to be explained. It is possible that this text could become confused or left unanswered if the first question of European Union interaction is not first addressed. This priority is therefore to concentrate on how parliamentary sovereignty has been unsettled by EU membership and not its relationship to other important features of constitutional change, such as devolved bodies (particularly Scotland) within the UK and or the relevance of human rights legislation (particularly, the Human Rights Act 1998).

That relationship between parliamentary sovereignty and the EU is an entirely unique and very direct legal and political arrangement (Nugent 2010, p. 213). It has no true resemblance to the nature of the conflict between the sovereignty of Parliament vis-a-vis the devolved assemblies or human rights legislation as decided through the modern role of the courts. That is why the latter two issues are not the subject of this book. The debate over devolved assembly powers is not strictly a legal conflict in the first stage as much as a politically-led one which might be better understood as concerns over the trust between electors and their chosen/acknowledged Parliament. Devolution is often theorised as seemingly presenting a major practical challenge to parliamentary sovereignty (Blick 2012, p. 37; Bogdanor 2009, p. 112). At the same time, the British devolutionary settlement is in many ways continuous with previous arrangements in that administrative autonomy for the subnations has already been part of the Westminster system (Gifford 2010, p. 327). Westminster retains ultimate supremacy (specifically, Section 28(7) of the Scotland Act 1998), yet as an issue of political obligation will only legislate on devolved issues with the approval of the Scottish Parliament (Bradley 2011, p. 60; Tomkins 2003). Even following the Scottish independence referendum of September 2014—in which political independence was ultimately rejected—Bradley (2011) has been entirely accurate in demonstrating that under devolved arrangements, the claim to a political reality is more important than legal power—particularly if support for the Scottish Parliament as its main representative body develops to such a point, with political opinion and national sentiment putting it beyond the recognition of a mere 'subordinate legislature'. The central governing problem lies not necessarily in the law itself but in a form of political agreement to not legislate for Scotland in a domestic system devised by Westminster. That is unlike the European governing arrangements conceptualised by a voluntary, legal and political framework for collective action in which the UK is conjoined. The UK sovereignty-EU relationship cannot be understood in those terms and this book will not focus on devolution.

As for the doctrine of parliamentary sovereignty in relation to the Human Rights Act 1998, as Anthony Bradley writes, it "...has often been seen as a massive obstacle in the way of any significant increase in the formal protection given to human rights in UK law" (Bradley 2011, p. 61). However, the European Court of Human Rights is not part of the EU architecture—which is the key reason why it is not the subject of this discussion. There is some relevance however of the European Court of Human Rights because as well as strengthening the ability of courts to protect human rights, it empowered the courts to pursue judicial review with the power to strike down invalid legislation. In this book, there will be, through example, an examination of the European Court of Justice and the Charter of Fundamental Rights which will, in part, overlap with the power of the European Court of Human Rights and the European Convention on Human Rights (Chapter 6). However, the 1998 Act only allowed that subordinate legislation not compatible with

Convention rights could be quashed or disapplied. So primary legislation such as Acts of Parliament which were not compatible with Convention rights remained in force but the High Court would issue a 'declaration of incompatibility' where ministers would be expected to remedy or make amendments to remedy the Act in order to remove the incompatibility. Courts and tribunals had to act in accordance with Convention rights and must take into account Strasbourg Court decisions. Ministers in Parliament in charge of a government Bill must issue a statement of the Bill's compatibility with the European Convention on Human Rights (Bradley 2011, p. 64). So, whereas the courts cannot strike down Acts of Parliament in that context, EU legislation has direct legal supremacy and European institutions can politically act in accordance with that legal power. This book is inherently focused on the politics of sovereignty (or absence of it) and the feature of the European institutions as political actors relative to parliamentary sovereignty, which is both legally and politically direct. There is no requirement to refer to a 'declaration of incompatibility', nor that form of judicial review, in this sense because parliamentary sovereignty is considered in the context of the political power exercised by EU institutions in a unique and directly binding legal and political order.

The challenge of EU membership sets itself apart from other constitutional challenges. It entails government ministers delegating more powers to EU institutions with which it engages through the Council of the EU and European Council. It entails an elevation of national judicial architecture in its relationship with the Luxembourg court system. It entails perhaps most importantly a decline in the ability of national parliaments to scrutinise the executive branch of their national governments effectively (see Raunio 2009, 2011; O'Brennan and Raunio 2007; Raunio and Hix 2000). EU membership impacts upon Parliament's sovereignty because the European Parliament's effective powers can be understood in the context of the post-Lisbon Treaty provisions. Those Treaty articles have meant that national parliaments now operate within a new 'tricameral' model in which national parliaments constitute a lower order, third chamber in a reconfigured representative system for the EU (Cooper 2013, 2015; Miller 2012).

However, that does not equate to the UK parliamentary system, for almost without exception, "national parliaments are unequivocally considered the 'losers' in European integration because of their severe loss of competencies" (Sprungk 2013, p. 298, contra Rizzuto 2003). This book is only concerned, therefore, with the impact of EU membership—including the political supremacy of EU institutions, with the direct supremacy of EU law, direct effect in the courts, and with overarching jurisdictional power—relative to UK parliamentary sovereignty.

1.4 A Summary and Overview

The following chapter (Chapter 2) reviews the definition of UK parliamentary sovereignty by first recognising that classical descriptions of sovereignty suppose both that the concept is both intrinsically *historical* and also, it equates not only with law-making but a form of 'governing at the helm' of state (in which politics and law are historically co-dependent). On the other hand, constitutional thought inherits a neo-Diceyan tradition which questionably distances Parliament's sovereignty from its historical precedents and customs and detaches the highest law-making authority from the highest political authority (see Loughlin and Tierney 2018, p. 990). The legal rule recognising that a sovereign entity exists is separated out from the institutional location of power within the state in which it is said sovereignty must be located.

In this context, Herbert Hart's exposition of parliamentary sovereignty came very close to addressing the primary concern by framing a fundamental *social* 'rule of recognition' in the UK legal system—namely, 'What the Crown in Parliament enacts is law'. By modifying that rule of recognition to embrace the fuller form of sovereignty, it is possible to recognise the relevance of medieval sovereignty (as expressed in Bracton's view) in its assumption that the law and the law-making sovereign were "mutually conditioned", contingent, reciprocal and interdependent at the helm, even though the sovereign retained the power to govern the realm (Kantorowicz 1957, pp. 153, 155). By embracing an alternative political constitutionalist model—as the rule of the recognised helm—it becomes necessary to compare and refute other leading legal and political theories which place popular (Bogdanor 2009, 2012, 2016) and legal (e.g. Allan 2011, 2013) limitations upon legislative supremacy.

Those previous theories have opened the way both for inaccurate notions that the voluntary European Communities Act 1972 substantively limited Parliament (see Bogdanor 2012, pp. 184–186, contra Goldsworthy 2012), not to mention the neo-Diceyan weakness of simply equating parliamentary sovereignty with legal supremacy (Loughlin and Tierney 2018). Political constitutionalism, in this sense, offers an alternative explanation of Parliament's sovereignty in the UK constitution. The alternative formula expressed as 'the rule of the recognised helm' is both a fundamental rule of government and it is a helm which defines political actors, their uncodified relations and conventions between the executive, the legislature, the judiciary and the electorate in their tacit consent/recognition of a rule providing for sovereignty.

Chapter 3 follows up on the claim that a 'rule of the recognised helm' is essential to understanding parliamentary sovereignty by explaining how it has been made historically operable at different stages. As a social rule, a Hartian ultimate rule which enables the imposing of obligations as valid law and political settlement must also necessarily provide the historically precedented conditions of the rule. The third chapter is devoted to the innovative development and explanation of eight historical constitutional forms for that purpose:

i. 'What the Crown-*with*-magnates enacts is law' (1200–1350)
ii. 'What the Crown-*with*-Commons enacts is law' (1350–1532)
iii. 'What the Crown-*through*-Parliament enacts is law' (1533–1602)
iv. 'What the Crown-*with*-disputed Parliament enacts is law' (1603–1687)
v. 'What the Crown-*in*-regulating Parliament enacts is law' (1688–1689)
vi. 'What the Crown-*in*-mixed constitutional Parliament enacts is law' (1690–1790s)
vii. 'What the Crown-*in*-Parliamentary Cabinet enacts is law' (1800–1972)
viii. 'What the Crown-*through*-Parliamentary political elite with external bodies enacts is law' (1973–present)

Each historical constitutional form illustrates a different meaning attributed to the rule of the recognised helm, from its first form to its eighth contemporary form, in an episodical, partly-discontinuous approach. In the eighth, contemporary historical constitutional form, an executive-led Parliament partially delegates its law-making capacity to other institutions. Parliament constructs its sovereignty primarily because it is a historically institutionalised rule of the recognised helm which is dependent upon the customs, practices, conventions and politics of past historical precedents.

The incorporation of the EU into the recognised helm does not mean that the UK cannot voluntarily opt-out of other policies central to the EU. The Maastricht Treaty had incorporated a commitment to proceeding to European Economic and Monetary Union (EMU) by 1999 at the latest—but, as has been mentioned, for the UK's purposes, John Major negotiated an opt-out on this policy. Gamble (2012, p. 473) describes the Maastricht Treaty as part of "the new impulse to integration" during the 1980s, committing the European member states to ever-closer "European Union" and to the introduction of a single currency. The UK did not accede to the single currency and its opt-out clause was one of the conditions given which had to be met if the British government were to give its approval to the Treaty as a whole. The opt-out, though defended primarily on an economic (not constitutional) basis (Major 1994) was at least, in part, designed to assure that the UK's domestic incorporation of the Treaty respected the UK's parliamentary sovereignty (Adler-Nissen 2011, p. 1094). The UK therefore follows an independent monetary policy. It uses the pound sterling, not the euro currency. It maintains a floating exchange rate regime against the euro.

The UK's broader political debate over the Maastricht Treaty was an exemplary case in the history of the EU Treaties on the basis that the UK Parliament disputed the Crown-in-Parliament's own powers relative to the competences set out within the European Treaties. In Britain, this was met by widespread public opposition and parliamentary rebellion when the governing Conservative party was "torn apart by the civil war" over the Maastricht Treaty (Gamble 2012). In the course of events, the UK's 'awkwardness' had been accommodated through 'variable geometry' (Geddes 2013, p. 62), affirming that the UK proceeded with a form of 'flexible engagement' (Geddes 2013, p. 255). In this instance, the UK's Major government secured two opt-outs on the Maastricht Treaty: (i) deferring a decision on participating on the final stage of European Economic and Monetary Union (EMU); and (ii) the Social Chapter (Gowland et al. 2010, p. 103). They are often described as John Major's "negotiating triumphs" (Gamble 2012). The opting out of the single currency illustrates that Parliament retains a hand at the recognised helm, albeit it is not the only hand. The 45-year practice of incorporating the EU into the recognised helm does mean the UK can voluntarily and politically opt-out of other policies central to the EU, including the ability to opt out of the single currency.

Chapter 4 argues that Parliament's sovereignty has become practically unsettled because, since 1973, EU membership has led to a strong synthesising of the executive and judicial powers within the EU architecture at the expense of the dilution of the domestic legislature. That explanation of parliamentary sovereignty impacts upon the sixth of the eight historical constitutional forms, defined by the mixed constitution. The mixed constitution has generally been employed in relation to the British constitution, when it is said that the monarchic, aristocratic Lords and democratic Commons powers were able to check one another (Kors 2012; Jenkins 2011; Gagarin 2010; Lieberman 2006; Bellamy 1996, p. 441; Blythe 1992, p. 12), while retaining the benefits of each in a balanced constitution (Blackstone 1765, pp. 50–52; Lieberman 2006, p. 318). Focusing on the UK's interaction with the EU and by drawing contrasts with Bogdanor's (2009) constitutional state theory, or Martin Loughlin's (2010) 'ephorate' theory, it is proposed that the case study of the EU-level Financial Transaction Tax (FTT) demonstrates that the EU institutions led to an undoing of the historical precedented mixed constitution model, thereby unsettling parliamentary sovereignty. Long-standing historical principles establish for the House of Commons a sole right to authorise taxation to the Crown.

Chapter 5 develops the argument that Parliament's sovereignty has become unsettled because the recognised helm has had European Parliament-level parliamentary representation competing with it and specifically for its capacity to collectively represent its electorate. In the eighteenth century (sixth) constitutional form, the ultimate rule required balance against its political conditions, including collective representation, to support parliamentary sovereignty. The Westminster Parliament has grown unsettled due to the distorting of its capacity to collectively represent in contrast to the European Parliament exemplifying a high level of specialist 'functional' representation, a shared neo-corporatist emphasis with the central EU institutions, its reliance on 'constitutionalisation' as a means to strengthen its representative linkages and a role of party and management of political partisanship. The case study of the Working Time Directive illustrates that the UK recognised helm has had European Parliament-level parliamentary representation competing with its capacity to collectively represent. A form of inter-parliamentary competition in this sense produces an unsettling of Westminster's historically precedented capacity to secure the political representation of electors.

Such historical precedents were strongly embedded within previous historical constitutional forms, thereby diluting the strength of parliamentary sovereignty.

Chapter 6 goes on to argue that Parliament's sovereignty is effectively unsettled because the recognised helm has had EU-level fundamental rights schemes incorporated into it. Some early medieval precedents of Bracton (in the first historical constitutional form) present a constitution in which governing at the helm is presented as legally distinct but politically contingent upon its capacity to determine and respect fundamental rights. Under EU membership, EU fundamental rights schemes protected by the courts achieve a constitutional pre-eminence, entrenched in codes of written and legal form. As such, EU level rights are expressed as unchallengeable instruments above ordinary, parliamentary politics in distinction to the historically precedented and minimalist protection afforded by Parliament. The case study of the EU free movement right makes evident that the recognised helm has had EU rights incorporated into its constitution, leading to the elevation of the judiciary as a rights-adjudicating court system as it fuses ever-closer into the Luxembourg court system. This has meant the dilution of the domestic legislature as a rights-providing institution. The deep political claims made to the constitutional and legal entrenchment of the rights themselves, irrespective of political legitimacy, combined with the disappearing consensus between the arms of state and community in protecting rights, has progressed this continued legislative decline and judicial advance in the UK, unsettling parliamentary sovereignty.

Chapter 7 then holds that Parliament's sovereignty becomes unsettled, and thereby less sovereign, when the UK's recognised helm has incorporated EU-level decision-making into it. It directly reduces parliamentary ultimate decision-making power over political decisions as exercised by the Government-in-Parliament on behalf of its electors. Since the EU Referendum of June 2016, Parliament's ultimate power to decide on the UK's terms of withdrawal—notably on the withdrawal agreement—defines the executive's capacity to pursue a constitutional resettlement, if it so chooses, addressing the historical dilution of parliamentary powers. As the UK seeks to leave, credible evidence relating to the withdrawal agreement emerges, emphasising parliament's potential regaining of its ultimate decision-making power and which reaffirms Parliament as sovereign. This development affirms the realignment of Parliament with a historically precedented basis of government by consent. This suggests the holding of the 2016 referendum on the UK's membership of the EU and subsequent parliamentary episodes and votes has enhanced, not eroded, the principle of representative government (contra Bogdanor 2019; McKibbin 2017, p. 385) and parliamentary sovereignty.

So, the next chapter turns to a review of the definition of UK parliamentary sovereignty which can be better framed by reassessing the original definitions of sovereignty. It focuses on a notion of sovereignty in Parliament described as historical and in which politics and law are historically co-dependent. It seeks to consider UK parliamentary sovereignty as both a fundamental rule of government and a broader helm which defines political actors and their uncodified relations to enable the consent and recognition of that rule providing for sovereignty.

Bibliography

Aalberts, T. (2004). The Future of Sovereignty in Multilevel Governance Europe—A Constructivist Reading. *Journal of Common Market Studies, 42*(1), 23–46.

Adler-Nissen, R. (2011). Opting Out of an Ever Closer Union: The Integration Doxa and the Management of Sovereignty. *West European Politics, 34*(5), 1092–1113.

Allan, T. R. S. (2011). Questions of Legality and Legitimacy: Form and Substance in British Constitutionalism. *International Journal of Constitutional Law, 9*(1), 155–162.

Allan, T. R. S. (2013). *The Sovereignty of Law: Freedom, Constitution and Common Law*. Oxford: Oxford University Press.

Auel, K. (2007). Democratic Accountability and National Parliaments: Redefining the Impact of Parliamentary Scrutiny in EU Affairs. *European Law Journal, 13*(4), 487–504.

Auel, K., & Neuhold, C. (2017). Multi-arena Players in the Making? Conceptualizing the Role of National Parliaments Since the Lisbon Treaty. *Journal of European Public Policy, 24*(10), 1547–1561.

Bache, I. (2012). Multi-level Governance in the European Union. In D. Levi-Faur (Ed.), *The Oxford Handbook of Governance*. Oxford: Oxford University Press.

Bache, I., & Flinders, M. (2004). Multi-level Governance and the Study of the British State. *Public Policy and Administration, 19*(1), 31–51.

Bellamy, R. (1996). The Political Form of the Constitution: The Separation of Powers, Rights and Representative Democracy. *Political Studies, 44*(3), 436–456.

Berger, M. (2013). Motives for the Foundation of the ECSC. *The Poznan University of Economics Review, 13*(3), 55–90.

Bingham, T. (2010). *The Rule of Law*. London: Penguin.

Blackburn v Attorney-General. [1971]. EWCA Civ J0510-2 [1971] 1 WLR 1037.

Blackstone, W. (1765). *Commentaries on the Laws of England (1765–1769)*. Chicago, IL: University of Chicago Press (this edition 1979).

Blick, A. (2012). *Codifying or Nor Codifying the United Kingdom Constitution: The Existing Constitution*. London: Centre for Political and Constitutional Studies.

Blythe, J. M. (1992). *Ideal Government and the Mixed Constitution in the Middle Ages*. Princeton, NJ: Princeton University Press.

Bogdanor, V. (2009). *The New British Constitution*. Oxford: Hart Publishing.

Bogdanor, V. (2011). *Britain in the 20th Century: The Character of the Post-war Period*. London: Gresham College [Online]. Available at https://www.gresham.ac.uk/lectures-and-events/britain-in-the-20th-century-the-character-of-the-post-war-period. Accessed 12 February 2013.

Bogdanor, V. (2012). Imprisoned by a Doctrine: The Modern Defence of Parliamentary Sovereignty. *Oxford Journal of Legal Studies, 3*(1), 179–195.

Bogdanor, V. (2016). Europe and the Sovereignty of the People. *Political Quarterly, 87*(3), 348–351.

Bogdanor, V. (2019). *Beyond Brexit: Towards a British Constitution*. London: I.B. Tauris.

Bradley, A. (2011). The Sovereignty of Parliament—Form or Substance? In J. Jowell & D. Oliver (Eds.), *The Changing Constitution* (7th ed.). Oxford: Oxford University Press.

Bradley, A. W., & Ewing, K. D. (2010). *Constitutional and Administrative Law* (15th ed.). Harlow: Longman.

Burke, E. (1774). Speech to the Electors of Bristol. In E. J. Payne (Ed.). (1999), *Select Works of Edmund Burke* (Vol. 4). Indianapolis, IN: Liberty Fund. Available at http://oll.libertyfund.org/titles/burke-select-works-of-edmund-burke-vol-4. Accessed 17 December 2013.

Bux, U. (2017). *The European Parliament: Historical Background* [Online]. Available at http://www.europarl.europa.eu/ftu/pdf/en/FTU_1.3.1.pdf. Accessed 12 March 2017.

Chalmers, D. (2013). European Restatements of Sovereignty. In R. Rawlings, P. Leyland, & A. Young (Eds.), *Sovereignty and the Law: Domestic, European and International Perspectives* (pp. 186–212). Oxford: Oxford University Press.

Conway, G. (2011). Retrieving a Separation of Powers in the European Union. In *The Limits of Legal Reasoning and the European Court of Justice* (pp. 172–200). Cambridge: Cambridge University Press.

Cooper, I. (2013). Bicameral or Tricameral? National Parliaments and Representative Democracy in the European Union. *Journal of European Integration, 35*(5), 531–546.

Cooper, I. (2015). A Yellow Card for the Striker: National Parliaments and the Defeat of EU Legislation on the Right to Strike. *Journal of European Public Policy, 22*(10), 1406–1425.

Craig, P. (2011). Britain in the European Union. In J. Jowell & D. Oliver (Eds.), *The Changing Constitution* (7th ed., pp. 104–133). Oxford: Oxford University Press.

Curtice, J. (2017). Why Leave Won the UK's EU Referendum. *Journal of Common Market Studies, 55*(Suppl. 1), 19–37.

de Bracton, H. (1235). *De legibus et consuetudinibus Angliae* [On the Laws and Customs of England] [Online]. Available at http://bracton.law.harvard.edu. Accessed 17 January 2013.

de Montesquieu, C. (1748). *The Spirit of the Laws* (A. M. Cohler, Ed.). Cambridge: Cambridge University Press (this edition 1989).

Dedman, M. J. (2010). *The Origins and Development of the European Union, 1945–2008*. Oxford: Routledge.

Department for Business, Innovation and Skills and Foreign and Commonwealth Office. (2013). *Review of the Balance of Competences Between the United Kingdom and the European Union: The Single Market* [Online]. Available at https://www.gov.uk/government/uploads/system/uploads/attachment_data/file/227069/2901084_SingleMarket_acc.pdf. Accessed 28 November 2013.

Department for Education. (2014). *Review of the Balance of Competences Between the United Kingdom and the European Union Education, Vocational Training and Youth* [Online]. Available at https://www.gov.uk/government/uploads/system/uploads/attachment_data/file/388092/2903012_BoC_Education_acc.pdf. Accessed 28 July 2015.

Department for Environment, Food and Rural Affairs. (2013). *Review of the Balance of Competences Between the United Kingdom and the European Union Animal Health and Welfare and Food Safety Report* [Online]. Available at https://www.gov.uk/government/uploads/system/uploads/attachment_data/file/227367/DEF-PB13979-BalOfComp-HMG-WEB.PDF. Accessed 28 November 2013.

Department for International Development. (2018, November). Statistics on International Development, Final UK Aid Spend 2017.

Department of Health. (2013). *Review of the Balance of Competences Between the United Kingdom and the European Union: Health* [Online]. Available at https://www.gov.uk/government/uploads/system/uploads/attachment_data/file/224715/2901083_EU-Health_acc.pdf. Accessed 26 November 2013.

Dicey, A. V. (1885/1964). *An Introduction to the Study of the Law of the Constitution*. London: Macmillan.

Dimitrakopoulos, D. G. (2001). Incrementalism and Path Dependence: European Integration and Institutional Change in National Parliaments. *Journal of Common Market Studies, 39*, 405–422.

EU Committee. (2008, March 13). *The Treaty of Lisbon: An Impact Assessment* (HL Paper 62-I) [Online]. Available at https://publications.parliament.uk/pa/ld200708/ldselect/ldeucom/62/62.pdf. Accessed 8 August 2015.

European Scrutiny Committee. (2014, April 2). *The Application of the EU Charter of Fundamental Rights in the UK: A State of Confusion* (HC 979) [Online]. Available at https://publications.parliament.uk/pa/cm201314/cmselect/cmeuleg/979/979.pdf. Accessed 8 August 2015.

European Union. (2014). *About the EU* [Online]. Available at http://europa.eu/about-eu/index_en.htm. Accessed 2 August 2014.

European Union. (2017). *EU Treaties* [Online]. Available at https://europa.eu/european-union/law/treaties_en. Accessed 1 February 2017.

Factortame: *The Queen v Secretary of State for Transport, ex parte: Factortame Ltd and Others*. [1990]. Judgment of the Court of 19 June 1990. Reference for a Preliminary Ruling: House of Lords—United Kingdom. Case C-213/89. Available at http://eur-lex.europa.eu/legal-content/EN/TXT/?uri=CELEX%3A61989CJ0213. Accessed 21 June 2014.

Ford, R. (2019, January 22). Immigration: Is Public Opinion Changing? In The UK in a Changing Europe, *Brexit and Public Opinion 2019* [Online]. Available at https://ukandeu.ac.uk/wp-content/uploads/2019/01/Public-opinion-2019.pdf. Accessed 5 February 2019.

Foreign and Commonwealth Office. (2013). *Review of the Balance of Competences Between the United Kingdom and the European Union: Foreign Policy* [Online]. Available at https://www.gov.uk/government/uploads/system/uploads/attachment_data/file/227437/2901086_Foreign_Policy_acc.pdf. Accessed 28 November 2013.

Gagarin, M. (Ed.). (2010). *The Oxford Encyclopaedia of Ancient Greece and Rome*. Oxford: Oxford University Press [Online]. Available at Oxford Reference. Accessed 10 February 2014.

Gamble, A. (2012). Better Off Out? Britain and Europe. *The Political Quarterly, 83*(3), 468–477.

Gamble, A. (2016). What's British About British Politics? In R. Heffernan, C. Hay, M. Russell, & P. Cowley (Eds.), *Developments in British Politics 10* (10th ed., pp. 1–19). London: Palgrave.

Gamble, A. (2019). A Hundred Years of British Democracy. *Political Quarterly, 90*(S1), 152–163.

Geddes, A. (2013). *Britain and the European Union*. London: Palgrave Macmillan.

Gifford, C. (2010). The UK and the European Union: Dimensions of Sovereignty and the Problem of Eurosceptic Britishness. *Parliamentary Affairs, 63*(2), 321–338.

Goldsworthy, J. (2012, March 9). *Parliamentary Sovereignty's Premature Obituary.* UK Constitutional Law [Blog]. Available at https://ukconstitutionallaw.org/2012/03/09/jeffrey-goldsworthy-parliamentary-sovereigntys-premature-obituary/. Accessed 1 July 2012.

Goldsworthy, J. (2013). Parliamentary Sovereignty and Constitutional Change in the United Kingdom. In R. Rawlings, P. Leyland, & A. Young (Eds.), *Sovereignty and the Law: Domestic, European and International Perspectives.* Oxford: Oxford University Press.

Gowland, D., Turner, A., & Wright, A. (2010). *Britain and European Integration Since 1945: On the Sidelines.* London: Routledge.

Haller, M. (2009). Divisions in Europe Between Elites and Citizens. In A. Gamble & D. Lane (Eds.), *The European Union and World Politics: Consensus and Division* (pp. 118–136). Basingstoke: Palgrave Macmillan.

Hart, H. L. A. (1997). *The Concept of Law* (2nd ed.). Oxford: Clarendon Press.

Hix, S., & Høyland, B. (2013). Empowerment of the European Parliament. *Annual Review of Political Science, 16,* 171–189.

HM Treasury. (2013). *Review of the Balance of Competences Between the United Kingdom and the European Union: Taxation* [Online]. Available at https://www.gov.uk/government/uploads/system/uploads/attachment_data/file/224710/2901087_Taxation_acc.pdf. Accessed 28 November 2013.

HM Treasury. (2016). *Budget 2016* (HC901) [Online]. Available at https://www.gov.uk/government/uploads/system/uploads/attachment_data/file/508193/HMT_Budget_2016_Web_Accessible.pdf. Accessed 4 March 2017.

Hobolt, S. B. (2016). The Brexit Vote: A Divided Nation, A Divided Continent. *Journal of European Public Policy, 23*(9), 1259–1277.

Hooghe, L., & Marks, G. (2001). *Multi-level Governance and European Integration.* Oxford: Rowman & Littlefield.

Jack, M., Hutton, M., Johnson, C., Millar, D., Patrick, S., & Sandall, A. (Eds.). (2011). *Erskine May: Parliamentary Practice* (24th ed.). London: LexisNexis Butterworths.

Jenkins, D. (2011). The Lockean Constitution: Separation of Powers and the Limits of Prerogative. *McGill Law Journal, 56*(3), 543–589.

Kantorowicz, E. H. (1957). *The King's Two Bodies: A Study in Medieval Political Theology.* Princeton, NJ: Princeton University Press.

Kaplan, Y. (2018). (Re)considering Sovereignty in the European Integration Process. *Journal of German and European Studies, 3*(1), 1–11.

Katwala, S. (2019, January 22). Immigration: A Polarised Debate? In The UK in a Changing Europe, *Brexit and Public Opinion 2019* [Online]. Available at https://ukandeu.ac.uk/wp-content/uploads/2019/01/Public-opinion-2019.pdf. Accessed 5 February 2019.

Keep, M. (2018, November 23). *The UK's Contribution to the EU Budget* (House of Commons Briefing Paper CBP 7886).
King, A. (2007). *The British Constitution*. Oxford: Oxford University Press.
King, A. (2015). *Who Governs Britain?* London: Pelican.
Kors, A. C. (2012). *Encyclopaedia of the Enlightenment*. Oxford: Oxford University Press [Online]. Available at Oxford Reference. Accessed 10 February 2014.
Lieberman, D. (2006). The Mixed Constitution and the Common Law. In M. Goldie & R. Wokler (Eds.), *The Cambridge History of Eighteenth-Century Political Thought* (pp. 317–346). Cambridge: Cambridge University Press.
Lisbon Treaty. (2007, December 17). Amending the Treaty on European Union and the Treaty Establishing the European Community. *Official Journal of the European Communities, C 306, 50*, 1.
Loughlin, M. (2010). *Foundations of Public Law*. Oxford: Oxford University Press.
Loughlin, M., & Tierney, S. (2018). The Shibboleth of Sovereignty. *The Modern Law Review, 81*, 989–1016.
Mabbett, D. (2017). Parliamentary Sovereignty and Brexit. *Political Quarterly, 88*(2), 167–169.
Major, J. (1994, April 25). Interview. *Der Spiegel*.
Marks, G. (1993). Structural Policy and Multi-level Governance in the EC. In A. Cafruny & G. Rosenthal (Eds.), *The State of the European Community: The Maastricht Debate and Beyond* (pp. 391–411). Boulder, CO: Lynne Rienner.
Marshall, P. (2013). Forty Years on: Britain in the EU, the Round Table. *The Commonwealth Journal of International Affairs, 102*(1), 15–28.
McIlwain, C. H. (1947). *Constitutionalism: Ancient and Modern*. Ithaca, NY: Cornell University Press.
McKibbin, R. (2017). In the Shadow of the Referendums. *The Political Quarterly, 88*(3), 382–385.
McLean, I. (2009). *What's Wrong with the British Constitution?* Oxford: Oxford University Press.
Miller, V. (2012). *National Parliaments and EU Law-Making: How Is the 'Yellow Card' System Working?* (House of Commons Library Standard Note SN06297).
Miller, V. (2015). *EU Obligations: UK Implementing Legislation Since 1993* (House of Commons Library Standard Note SN07092).
Neyer, J. (2014). Justified Multi-level Parliamentarism: Situating National Parliaments in the European Polity. *The Journal of Legislative Studies, 20*(1), 125–138.
Norton, P. (2011). Divided Loyalties: The European Communities Act 1972. *Parliamentary History, 30*(1), 53–64.

Novak, P. (2017). *The Maastricht and Amsterdam Treaties* [Online]. Available at http://www.europarl.europa.eu/atyourservice/en/displayFtu.html?ftuId=FTU_1.1.3.html. Accessed 23 June 2017.

Nugent, N. (2006). *The Government and Politics of the European Union* (6th ed.). Basingstoke: Palgrave Macmillan.

Nugent, N. (2010). *The Government and Politics of the European Union* (7th ed.). London: Palgrave.

O'Brennan, J., & Raunio, T. (2007). *National Parliaments Within the Enlarged European Union: From 'Victims' of Integration to Competitive Actors?* London: Routledge.

Office for Budget Responsibility. (2019). *A Brief Guide to the Public Finances* [Online]. Available at https://obr.uk/forecasts-in-depth/brief-guides-and-explainers/public-finances/. Accessed 4 April 2019.

Pelkmans, J. (2016). Why the Single Market Remains the EU's Core Business. *West European Politics, 39*(5), 1095–1113.

Peters, G., & Pierre, J. (2004). Multi-level Governance and Democracy: A Faustian Bargain? In I. Bache & M. Flinders (Eds.), *Multi-level Governance* (pp. 75–89). Oxford: Oxford University Press.

Raunio, T. (2009). National Parliaments and European Integration: What We Know and Agenda for Future Research. *The Journal of Legislative Studies, 15*(4), 317–334.

Raunio, T. (2011). The Gatekeepers of European Integration? The Functions of National Parliaments in the EU Political System. *Journal of European Integration, 33*(3), 303–321.

Raunio, T., & Hix, S. (2000). Backbenchers Learn to Fight Back: European Integration and Parliamentary Government. *West European Politics, 23*(4), 142–168.

Reh, C. (2009). The Lisbon Treaty: De-constitutionalizing the European Union? *Journal of Common Market Studies, 47*(3), 625–650.

Rizzuto, F. (2003). National Parliaments and the European Union: Part of the Problem or Part of the Solution to the Democratic Deficit in the European Constitutional Settlement? *Journal of Legislative Studies, 9*(3), 87–109.

Rossi, L. S. (2012). Does the Lisbon Treaty Provide a Clearer Separation of Competences Between EU and Member States? In A. Biondi, P. Eeckhout, & S. Ripley (Eds.), *EU Law After Lisbon*. Oxford: Oxford University Press.

Smith, J. (2012). The European Dividing Line in Party Politics. *International Affairs, 88*(6), 1277–1295.

Smith, J. (2017). National Parliaments and the European Union—A View from Westminster. In D. Jancic (Ed.), *National Parliaments After the Lisbon Treaty and the Euro Crisis: Resilience or Resignation?* Oxford: Oxford University Press.

Sobolewska, M., & Ford, R. (2016). The Politics of Immigration: Old and New. In R. Heffernan, C. Hay, M. Russell, & P. Cowley (Eds.), *Developments in British Politics 10* (10th ed., pp. 221–243). London: Palgrave.

Sprungk, C. (2013). Legislative Transposition of Directives: Exploring the Other Role of National Parliaments in the European Union. *Journal of Common Market Studies, 51*(2), 298–315.

Tabarelli, M. (2013). The Influence of the EU and the ECHR on "Parliamentary Sovereignty Regimes": Assessing the Impact of European Integration on the British and Swedish Judiciaries. *European Law Journal, 19*(3), 340–363.

Thompson, G., & Harari, D. (2013, September 17). *The Economic Impact of EU Membership on the UK* (House of Commons Library Standard Note SN/EP/6730) [Online]. Available at http://researchbriefings.parliament.uk/ResearchBriefing/Summary/SN06730. Accessed 5 November 2014.

Tomkins, A. (2003). *Public Law*. Oxford: Oxford University Press.

Tomkins, A. (2010). *Written Evidence to the European Scrutiny Committee, Clause 18 of the Bill: Parliamentary Sovereignty and EU Law*. The EU Bill and Parliamentary Sovereignty. Available at https://publications.parliament.uk/pa/cm201011/cmselect/cmeuleg/633ii/633we02.htm. Accessed 5 December 2010.

UK Parliament. (2019). *Parliamentary Sovereignty* [Online]. Available at https://www.parliament.uk/about/how/role/sovereignty/. Accessed 11 April 2017.

Walker, N. (2005). Europe's Constitutional Momentum and the Search for Polity Legitimacy. *International Journal of Constitutional Law, 3*(2–3), 211–238.

Walker, N. (2014, July). Our Constitutional Unsettlement. *Public Law*, 529–548.

Wall, S. (2008). *A Stranger in Europe: Britain and the EU from Thatcher to Blair*. Oxford: Oxford University Press.

Young, A., & Gee, G. (2016). Regaining Sovereignty, Brexit, the UK Parliament and the Common Law. *European Public Law, 22*(1), 131–147.

CHAPTER 2

Making Sense of Sovereignty, Parliamentary Sovereignty and the 'Rule of the Recognised Helm'

The central argument of this chapter begins by reviewing the definition of parliamentary sovereignty and examining the locating of the ultimate rule permitting the *steering*, *direction* or *control* of the powers of the Crown to govern the realm. The definition and explanation of parliamentary sovereignty can be better understood by turning to five classical and original definitions. Sovereignty, in this sense, can be understood as intrinsically *historical* and means not only law-making but a form in which politics and law are historically co-dependent. Parliament's sovereignty in the UK constitution is approached as 'the rule of the recognised helm'. It is both a fundamental rule of government and as a helm which defines political actors, their uncodified relations and conventions between the executive, the legislature, the judiciary and the electorate in their tacit recognition of a rule providing for sovereignty.

Legal and political theory inherits in the contemporary mainstream, a neo-Diceyan tradition. Such a framework has responded precisely to the requirement for an axiom of legal supremacy—to make or unmake any law—as understood by the common lawyer and the courts. It has however retained a silence on the foremost role of political institutions, including parliament's primacy and consequently, divorces Parliament's sovereignty from its historical precedents and customs. What is absent in Dicey and what is required in a theory of Parliament's sovereignty is the assumption of an ultimate rule *directing* and *steering* government, through Parliament, and which can be recognised by others as providing

J. McConalogue, *The British Constitution Resettled*,
https://doi.org/10.1007/978-3-030-25290-8_2

the capacity to enable government. Hart came close to that understanding by asserting that 'What the Crown in Parliament enacts is law' is a 'rule of recognition' in the UK legal system (Hart 1997). Yet, even where Hart argues for a rule of recognition, it becomes almost purely a legal rule for validating law even though it is referred to as social (Perry 2015, p. 284), thereby eliminating the role of the helm of state in making Parliament sovereign. Hart's rule of recognition requires some political modification. Such an amendment must seek to embrace a form of sovereignty which is both intrinsically historical and in which politics and law are interdependent 'at the helm'.

This is to refute other leading legal and political theories, not merely the neo-Diceyan inheritance of the English lawyers. Constitutional state theory, under Vernon Bogdanor's (2009) approach, for example abandons rule-recognition in favour of a rearranged, modern, popular constitutional state, affirming 'popular sovereignty'. The need for a 'political' theory also develops out of the refutation of radical common law constitutionalism which assumes that parliamentary sovereignty is founded on a common law foundation. It suggests the proposition that parliamentary sovereignty has been limited by EU law (Allan 2013) and that the power of the law of the courts has explicitly made parliament sovereign.

Political constitutionalism can help to reframe an alternative explanation of Parliament's sovereignty in the UK constitution. In the constitutional network, 'the rule of the recognised helm' refers to both a fundamental rule of government and a helm which defines political actors and their uncodified inter-relationships in their recognition of a rule providing for sovereignty. Why should legal and political theory otherwise seek to equate the recognition of the rule of Parliament's sovereignty with *only* the law of Parliament i.e. statute (Dicey 1964), or increasingly the recognition of statute by the common law of the courts (Allan 2011, 2013), or increasingly by the people (Bogdanor 2009)? The central place of representative, parliamentary government which affirms the ultimate rule adequately expresses the supreme role of the legislature, as elected and *steered* by the people, but also a subsidiary role of the judiciary, and their elected government, in providing recognition to the rule. Such a model reaffirms the essential and elective nature of political institutions, including Parliament, acting through very ordinary political and legislative processes to determine its sovereignty.

2.1 The Five Principles of the Meaning of Sovereignty

The meaning of sovereignty itself is important to unbundle before one can begin with the meaning of parliamentary sovereignty. If sovereignty could be generally conceived of as the continued supremacy to rule over a given territory, there are identifiable features of that sovereignty formula that have occupied a primacy within that concept. The five following concepts are fundamental to my unbundling of the concept of sovereignty. The narratives of sovereignty are found within a rich interweaving of its medieval and modern forms, usually to provide political stability and anchorage.

Firstly, *supremacy* is central because what legal and political theorists such as Hart have attempted to identify is the ultimate rule, where assessing the 'rule of recognition' will provide the criteria by which the validity of all other rules are judged. That ultimate rule expresses a rule of recognition providing the criteria by which the validity of other rules in the legal system are assessed (Hart 1997, pp. 102–103). Supremacy, in a general sense, has simply meant "the state or condition of being superior to all others in authority, power, or status: the supremacy of the king" (*Oxford English Dictionary* 2017). Theories of sovereign authority have long rested upon the claims of supreme and absolute authority in the polity (Bartelson 2011).

Secondly, specific priority in understanding sovereignty is also given to the meaning of government at the recognised helm. With reference to Henry de Bracton's medieval constitutionalism, he essentially divided the total act of the Crown's government as *gubernaculum* from the claims of fundamental law, *jurisdictio* (McIlwain 1947, p. 86). That is, government is separated from law. As Vile argues, the limitations placed upon the Crown by subjecting him to a fundamental law which he did not himself make provided the basis for a legislative power which was independent of the will of the King. That went hand in hand with the idea of an executive power in the King, to ensure that the law was put into effect (Vile 1967, p. 23). While the distinction made by McIlwain has often been thought of as less than convincing (Corwin 1941, p. 535), it is the *gubernaculum* that is primary feature. It is the Crown's helm of the ship of state, which steers, directs and controls that which is necessary for the governance of the realm. It is often overlooked that the proper classical concept of *gubernātiō* is "steering; direction, control" and most importantly, *gubernaculum* is seen as the "helm" of the 'ship of state' (Morwood 2005)—it is raw political sovereignty. That 'taking of the helm' is often recognised as government being exercised by a given political actor or set of actors—be it the Crown, officials or governments—and irrespective of Hart's narrow contemporary emphasis on law (as opposed to habit, obedience, coercion, etc.), focused on how they are seeking to maintain that position. Sovereignty becomes a necessary feature of politics, in principle and as exercised.

Thirdly, one of the classical and Roman forms of sovereignty (*Imperium*) has been that the power of government to legislate and execute laws (Fellmeth and Horwitz 2009) and ultimately, the "Latin word for a command, which grew to signify the right to give orders, and so to mean supreme power..." (Morwood 2005). *Imperium* of the Roman Empire is characterised as the unlimited discretionary authority to issue commands carrying the binding, statutory force of law (Lee 2016, p. 18). For Hobbes, *imperium* itself is rule (Hoekstra 2013, pp. 1095–1096). When observing the capacity to make law in the transformation of the sovereign structure in England, then the UK, in the past seven hundred years, constitutional theorists are attempting to indicate the structure of office and institutions of the sovereign, for example, from the Crown-consulting-Parliament, the Parliament-rules-with-the-Crown, or the Parliament-rules-through-Parliament and external bodies.

It only tells us about the nature of office. But detailed analyses of sovereignty require more than that. How have they maintained their sovereignty, as exercised—as edict, norms, moral guidance or laws? Modern sovereignty came to rest not on law generally or the legal order itself (as Allan 2010, p. 27, maintains) but legal sovereignty established through Parliament and its enactments. It is possible to concede—with Bodin (1576) and Hobbes (1651)—that in that modern form, law is the major requirement. The notion of sovereignty invariably depends upon supreme authority combined with a supreme law and a supreme law-making capacity (i.e. a parliament). Lords Scarman and Hailsham's questioning over the modern executive-in-Parliament's total control over law (Scarman 1992; Hailsham 1976) are even approached as the problematic "*imperium* of Executive Government" (Kirby 2006, p. 466). So strong is the claim to law-making as the basis of sovereignty that legal theorists (for example, Law and Martin 2009) tend to define sovereignty merely in terms of that which has ultimate authority to impose law on everyone else in the state and to alter any pre-existing law.

Fourthly, the role of sovereignty as continuation, or succession of political authority, is of relevance since in contemporary legal and political theory, Hart's 1961 legal exposition of sovereignty, *The Concept of Law*, provides a necessary explanation of legal sovereignty on the assumption that it must be characteristic of a legal system to possess a continuity of law-making power by a set of rules bridging the succession from one law-giver to another law-giver in advance (Hart 1997, p. 53). Where a new Parliament begins to legislate, it is clear that there is a definite and established rule providing him or her—as a (new) line of persons—the right to do this when it is their turn. It is often recognised that a fundamental aspect of the rule of sovereignty, including for Dicey (1964) and Hart (1997), is that 'no Parliament can bind its successors'. The Crown-in-Parliament is preserved throughout changes of successive legislators—by it resting on generally accepted fundamental rules. That general acceptance is dispersed between officials and ordinary citizens. In doing so, they collectively affirm the continuation of sovereign power.

Fifthly, sovereignty is also defined with strong reference to territorial boundaries (Bartelson 2011; Holland 2010; Ruggie 1993). One of the foundational claims to sovereignty is that of the concept of territory, or *dominium*, meaning the state's claim to all the territory where it is located (Grant and Barker 2009). Dominium has been defined as "the power of a state to exercise supreme authority (absolute sovereignty) over all persons and things within its territory" (Law 2017). The state possesses the only legitimate voice, diplomatic influence and arms for the community within its territory to assert its sovereignty.

It is a thorny problem to explicate a complete and parsimonious theory of sovereignty in the abstract when assessing parliamentary sovereignty but it might aid the explanation of parliamentary sovereignty to accept in general terms the criterion set out in Box 2.1.

Box 2.1: Sovereignty

The concept of sovereignty:

i. implies *supremacy as a ranking of principle*;
ii. confers *gubernaculum as steering, direction and control over the governance of the realm*;
iii. consists of *imperium, the commanding power of government to legislate and execute laws*;
iv. relates to *its continuation/ successors*;
v. relates to *territory, or dominium*.

The sovereignty of Parliament is, in this sense, a ranking of principles and, in which the fundamental/ultimate rule located at the helm trumps all others on a continuing basis to permit the steering, direction or control of the powers of the Crown to govern the realm by the power of law-making and ensuring the execution of the laws it has made, within the territory of the Government of the UK.

The working definition is conditional and dependent upon the five features of sovereignty discussed above. The features themselves reflect the assumption that one form of sovereignty should not be viewed as operating linearly from antiquity to medieval and modern forms. The features explain both that:

- Sovereignty is intrinsically historical. Sovereignty is predicated on a competition between rules in which a more supreme ultimate rule (or set of rules) permits government and which can be recognised by others, including its competitors, as providing that capacity to enable government.
- Sovereignty requires a form of 'governing at the helm' of the ship of state to steer, direct and control the realm. Sovereignty requires a power of government to legislate and execute the laws, an authority buttressed by a supreme law. It is also identified that the succession of law-making power and definition of territorial boundaries are instrumental political features in defining sovereignty and understanding its parameters. More concisely, the definition of sovereignty prioritises both the provision of a fundamental rule of recognition, in addition to government at the helm, in which law and politics are historically co-dependent.

2.2 The Meaning of Parliamentary Sovereignty: The Right to Make or Unmake Any Law

It is to Dicey's credit and his long-serving definition that it dealt so precisely with the axiom of legal supremacy as understood by the common lawyer and the courts. Yet, by dismantling the power of command behind law-making as well as government of the realm, as the political, institutional arrangement at the 'helm of state', Dicey (1964) often discarded political sovereignty (see Loughlin and Tierney 2018). It is a framework which offered only a barebones theory of legal supremacy, not parliamentary sovereignty. On a legal basis, the doctrine of parliamentary sovereignty is defined by:

- A positive limb, expressed as the "... right to make or unmake any law whatever" and;
- A negative limb, expressed in the feature "that no person or body is recognised by the law of England as having a right to override or set aside the legislation of Parliament" (Dicey 1964, pp. 39–40).

Dicey (1964) confusingly refers to the doctrine as both the "dominant characteristic of our political institutions" and yet it is only "a legal fact, fully recognised by the law of England" (Dicey 1964, p. 39). He accepts it as the unlimited legislative authority of Parliament, although by practicality and common sense, he affirms that there are some tyrannical laws which could not pass (Dicey 1964, p. 41). For Dicey, the supremacy over any competing legislative power in his definition applies only to the Crown, each House of Parliament, the constituencies and the law courts in the English constitution—certainly, not the European Communities or Union, which did not exist in Dicey's age.

For Dicey, all judicial legislation is subordinate (Tabarelli 2013, p. 344) and cannot be considered to be inconsistent with the supremacy of Parliament primarily because judges, following precedents, do not claim to exercise any power to repeal a statute whilst Acts of Parliament on the other hand may override the law of judges (Dicey 1964, p. 60). Moral law cannot limit it because morality cannot invalidate an Act of Parliament before a court. For Dicey, even Royal prerogative powers can be regulated or abolished by Acts of Parliament (Dicey 1964, p. 64). One central feature of parliamentary sovereignty on his terms is that one Parliament, by its enacted laws, cannot bind its successors. Dicey accepts the sovereign power is invested in Parliament but is critical and dismissive of sovereignty's political dimension, as opposed to its strict legal sense (Dicey 1964, p. 73). Even though Dicey is strongly considerate of representative government, and that the will of the electors will always in the end "assert itself as the predominant influence in the country", he considers this only as a "political, not legal fact" (Dicey 1964, p. 73). The courts take no notice of the will of the electors in making judicial decisions (Dicey 1964, pp. 73–74). It is notable, however, that Dicey assigns a sort of convenient, symbiotic, equivalence between the sovereignty of

Parliament and the "the rule or supremacy of law" securing the rights of the individual (Dicey 1964, p. 184, Chapter XIII), which can leave legal theory in some confusion in the modern context.

Dicey's principle presents legal supremacy under the form of parliamentary sovereignty. It is not coincidental that most contemporary, neo-Diceyan legal scholarship refers to parliamentary sovereignty as legal supremacy of the Acts of Parliament. Dicey is critical of the doctrine's political legitimacy dimension (Loughlin and Tierney 2018, p. 993) because despite his embracing approach toward representative government and the rule of law, it cannot consider politics as relevant to Parliament's sovereignty. That is chiefly because any constraint upon it must be recognised by the courts only, otherwise on Dicey's terms, it does not exist. The elimination of politics and conventions helps to explain the confusing parity Dicey provides for parliamentary sovereignty and the supremacy of the rule of law (Francis and Morrow 1994). To its credit, Dicey's theory affirms an ultimate rule—the Crown in Parliament's right to make or unmake any law—in the legal system (positive limb) and as supreme to other bodies (negative limb) in the eyes of the law of England. It is dismissive however of Parliament's sovereignty enabling a co-dependence between law and the politics of commanding and governing, because it is simply not concerned with government at the helm, merely the role of politics in its service to statute.

Parliament does retain the theoretical power to make or unmake any law, consistent with the positive limb of Dicey's definition, even if it runs contrary to Community law and even where there may be political difficulties in pursuing that path. However, the negative limb provides that nobody may override or set aside an Act of Parliament. The difficulty here is that although that remains true in English law, the EC case law of the Court of Justice has since the early 1960s established that wherever there is a conflict between national law and Community law, EC law would prevail. It is therefore questionable as to whether, in all circumstances, a political body in England could not set aside an Act of Parliament. Parliament can still make or unmake any law whatsoever but it is only under English law (not EC law) that nobody may override or set aside a statute (Tomkins 2010). To reclaim the 'fullness' of its sovereignty, its ultimate sovereignty, it could choose to repeal or further amend the European Communities Act 1972 (see also Goldsworthy 2013, p. 65; Smith 2017, p. 79; Tabarelli 2013, p. 346). There are in fact historical examples of draft parliamentary Bills and amendments in

Westminster which expressly negate the effect of the EU rule, although none have until recently been enacted (Tomkins 2010). The European Union (Withdrawal) Act 2018 under Theresa May's post-2017 Conservative Government legislated to end that supremacy of EU law in the UK by repealing the European Communities Act 1972.

The modern British constitution's rule of parliamentary sovereignty with respect to EU law—as expressed through the ongoing judgements of the courts—such as Lord Denning in *Macarthys Ltd. v Smith* [1980], Lord Diplock in *Garland v BR Engineering* [1983], Lord Bridge in *Factortame* [1990], and Lord Justice Laws in *Thoburn v Sunderland City Council* [2002]—all confirm the 'entirely voluntary' nature of the UK entering into that arrangement under the European Communities Act 1972. One considerable reservation might be Laws in *Thoburn* holding, problematically, that the ECA is, by nature of the common law, a constitutional statute (see Laws contra Goldsworthy 2013, p. 65). The courts, however, only act in such a way because Parliament, through its legislative authority, told them to—if Parliament under that same authority told them not to do so, then they would obey that too (Bingham 2010, p. 164). That entirely voluntary nature describes a pooled sovereignty which can be reclaimed. The theory demonstrates the quandary of the neo-Diceyan definition—it accurately accepts on the one hand the voluntary nature of Parliament in making or changing European arrangements via Acts of Parliament, whilst also, on the other hand, enabling the dilution of the role of national institutions and politics (including Parliament) and the politics of people as part of that.

The neo-Diceyan definition has enabled the national Parliament, judges, and courts to inhabit a sphere of quasi-silence on the primacy of its political institutions, including parliamentary primacy itself, and deeper arrangements inhabiting the national constitutional character in the structure between the executive, the legislature, the judiciary and the electorate. Of considerable interest is one ECJ case confirming the supremacy of EU law in relation to principles of national fundamental rights and national constitutional character, *Internationale Handelgesellschaft v Einfuhrhund Vorratsselle fur Getreide und Futtermittel* [1970] (see also Bradley and Ewing 2010, p. 127). While it confirmed, perhaps unsurprisingly, that "the law stemming from the Treaty, an independent source of law, cannot because of its very nature be overridden by rules of national law, however framed, without being deprived of its character as Community law and without the legal basis of the Community itself being called into question", it also made a deeper political point about national constitutional character in relation to fundamental rights and the EU. It said of constitutional structure that "the validity of a Community measure or its effect within a member state cannot be affected by allegations that it runs counter to either fundamental rights as formulated by the constitution of that state or the principles of a national constitutional structure" (*Internationale Handelgesellschaft v Einfuhrhund Vorratsselle fur Getreide und Futtermittel* [1970]). Respect for fundamental rights, in other words, is not only integral to the principles of EU law protected by the Court of Justice but precedes consideration of the constitution of a state.

Dicey knowingly divorced constitutional law from customs and conventions because the latter were not enforced by the courts (Allan 2013; Dicey 1964). Although Dicey accepted certain political customs, principles and rules as "the conventions of the Constitution" which regulate relationships, he subverted them as non-legal additions to the constitution (see Loughlin and Tierney 2018, pp. 1006–1007). For example, that the Prime Minister cannot remain in office without the support of a majority in the House of Commons is a constitutional convention only. The neo-Diceyan view suffers from seeking to divorce Parliament's sovereignty from its historical precedents (Loughlin and Tierney 2018). It attempts to divorce the highest law-making authority from the highest political authority. The nineteenth century constitution was less focused on establishing clear links between sovereign power and individual rights (Francis and Morrow 1994, p. 23). In other words, the consensual ultimate rule recognising that a sovereign entity exists is divorced from the very 'helm' of the state in which it is said to be located. Of course, law and law-giving are undeniable features but parliamentary sovereignty has no sovereign aspect if it does not first accept that its sovereign power is lodged within its entrenched, widely recognised and organised pattern at the helm of the governing state.

2.3 The Meaning of Parliamentary Sovereignty: The 'Rule of Recognition'

Sovereignty can be predicated on a competition between rules in which a more supreme, ultimate rule permits government and which can be recognised by others as providing the capacity to enable government. Given the limitations of the neo-Diceyan view, it becomes important to move towards Hart's view which, like Dicey before him, refuted the earlier approach of John Austin that law consists of orders backed by threats. The legal system consists of social rules, according to Hart (1997), but it is important that Hart is held to account on how those rules are genuinely social (Perry 2015). He discards of sovereignty as explained by Hobbesian or Austinian habit of obedience because he believes that cannot explain rules themselves (see Shapiro 2001, p. 156). Yet Hart does assert that 'What the Crown in Parliament enacts is law' is a 'rule of recognition' in the UK legal system because it states the conditions any rule must satisfy in order for that rule to impose obligations as valid law (Hart 1997). Because of uncertainty, the static character of rules and inefficiency as basic defects in the primary rules of obligation, they are necessarily supplemented by secondary rules (Hart 1997, p. 94). Hart's reductionism is attributable to his distinct legal positivist approach which by its very definition, is a doctrine which holds not only that that what counts as law in any particular society is fundamentally a matter of social fact, rule or convention but that there is no necessary connection between law and morality (Leiter and Coleman 2010). In the US, the rule is the constitution itself. Instead of using moral or political benchmarks for assessing the validity of law, it is assessed and consensually accepted that private persons and officials are given the authoritative criteria for identifying primary rules of recognition (Hart 1997, p. 100), although some legal theorists assume the rule of recognition is upheld only by senior law-applying officials (see Shapiro 2001, contra Postema 2008, p. 49; Goldsworthy 1999). The rule of recognition affirms something fundamental about the operation of Parliament's sovereignty.

Hart argues for a rule of recognition. This becomes almost purely a legal rule for validating law even though it is referred to as social (see Perry 2015). It thereby eliminates the role of the recognised helm directing and commanding law-making. In a complex legal system, for Hart, law requires the union of primary and secondary rules—whereas primary rules impose obligations, secondary rules provide rules through which we can introduce, modify or end those primary rules. Within the scheme of secondary rules, Hart argues for a 'rule of recognition'—which is the rule that states the conditions any rule must satisfy in order for that rule to impose obligations as valid law (Hart 1997, p. 94). That rule of recognition will provide some features which by that rule are a "conclusive affirmative indication" that it is a rule of the group to be supported by the social pressure it exerts; even though in Hart's words, little is said of the social pressure it exerts.

By avoiding Hart's legal reductionism, it seems reasonable to defend the operation of legal rules as social rules (Perry 2015), requiring the consensus of state officials and private persons (Sciaraffa 2011; Galligan 2006, p. 65; Goldsworthy 1999, 2010; Hart 1997). In spite of Hart acknowledging the rule of recognition as a social rule, it is then treated as anything but social or political. In this specific sense, Tucker (2011) made a similar observation but it is not obvious that the acknowledging of the social results in an indeterminacy of the rule of recognition. It appears less credible that contested norms/conventions result, as Allan (2013, p. 54) proposes, in Hart's ultimate rule being viewed as indeterminate. It is plausible to share Hart's preoccupation with law as a social rule (Perry 2015) and that a complex legal system requires a rule of recognition maintained by officials and private persons. It is possible therefore to accept his expression of the rule of recognition while not sharing the neglect of parliamentary structure of law and state, which underpins the rule.

Legal and political theory should strive to explain the broader political and legal space and boundaries within which law is made and constrained, not merely law per se. While Hart's amended version of legal positivist doctrine in terms of its normative and systematic assumptions of law does recognise law as social fact, that equally means acknowledging facts as social. The rule of recognition is an apolitical abstraction in explaining parliamentary government if it is not a rule of the recognised helm. A recognised helm enables some primacy to be accorded to the role of precedents and conventions existing within previous historical constitutional forms. The rule of recognition otherwise implies an abstract rule recognised as sovereign rather than the collective institutional framework of the state which operates within the rule.

It is reasonable to assume that Hart's rule of recognition can be modified politically. Such an amendment must seek to embrace a form of sovereignty which recognises and determines the ultimate rule. Hart's original formula is one that requires recognition because in parliamentary terms it requires consent. It cannot exist as a standalone definition. Hart's rule as 'What the Crown in Parliament enacts is law' is a "rule of recognition" in the UK legal system which confirms that 'recognition' is vital. On recognition, Postema (2008, p. 49) acknowledges that Hart himself recognised both that the fundamental rule of recognition must be accepted and practiced by law-applying officials, and also, that "the behaviour of most of the population governed by these norms must be in broad conformity with the system of legal norms traceable to the rule of recognition". Postema (2008) also observes that Hart was 'silent' about the status of the second condition and the relationship between the two 'recognition' conditions. It is a central point in recognising the political legitimacy of legal norms. By accepting Hart's ultimate rule, it can be assumed that the secondary condition or sub-rules relate to recognition of rules by others which Hart did not consider or allude to.

The silence however on legitimately expressing 'recognition' as consent by Parliament, public and officials explains the problem of understanding rules as social. Recognition is complex but it is meaningful to maintaining sovereignty (both internally and externally). It is broadly more constitutive of statehood and fulfils an inherently conservative function where it presupposes a world populated by distinct and bounded political communities (Bartelson 2016, pp. 313, 319).

Fundamentally, when fully expressed, the Hartian rule of recognition does strongly help to clarify the meaning of parliamentary sovereignty. It affirms the sovereignty conferred by an ultimate rule in an order of legal rules but in the absence of the power to command or govern—a power through which the state organises its structure between the executive, the legislature, the judiciary and the electorate. What Hart had in fact acknowledged, but did not express, is a rule of the 'recognised helm', which addresses the political and legal space and boundaries within which law is made and constrained. The rule of the recognised helm combines the features of two existing theories—one of them is contemporary (Hart) and the other is traceable to a medieval understanding of sovereignty (Bracton).

The legal assertion that there is 'sovereignty in Parliament' implies specific steps are taken by Parliament to act and to legislate, namely Hart's rule, 'What the Crown in Parliament enacts is law'. Although the contemporary Parliament has broad functions in politics—to provide the government and thereafter support it, to scrutinise the work of government and to enable the government to raise taxes, not merely debating and passing all laws—it nonetheless returns to, and pursues Hart's rule, in providing for a parliamentary process. In that process, a proposal for a new law, a Bill, that is presented for debate in Parliament can be introduced by the House of Commons or House of Lords first (except in the case of Finance Bills) and when both have agreed on its content, then the reigning Crown approves it—it receives Royal Assent and becomes an Act of Parliament (UK Parliament 2019). Understandably, the powers of the House of Lords are, to an extent, limited by the Parliament Acts. Since the monarch in modern time retains an important symbolic role—after administration of justice was removed from 1689 onwards and subsequent depoliticization—the everyday practical implementation of the Act of Parliament is the responsibility of ministers and their relevant government departments. The 'Crown' powers previously exercised by the reigning monarch have meant, in the present day, that ministers of the executive now exercise the majority of those powers. The powers of the Crown are in present times exercised by the executive through and on the advice of ministers accountable to Parliament (Jack et al. 2011). In other words, the executive exercises powers only in so far as it retains the confidence of the legislature. That is what makes statute *law*. With the assertion of the authority to legislate also comes the capacity to take that law away i.e. by repeal, so that Parliament at all times retains a right to legislate as well as the reflexivity to take away that legislation without losing its successive and inherent function to make law.

2.4 The Meaning of Parliamentary Sovereignty: The 'Rule of Recognition' and the Contemporary British State

There have been serious and substantive attempts by British constitutional theorists to describe the advanced, modern, political state architecture as eliminating the existence of the rule of recognition. On Bogdanor's (2009) argument by drawing a distinction between the old, traditional parliamentary sovereignty and the transition toward popular sovereignty, he asserts that there is a new British constitution with the Human Rights Act at its heart, EU membership since 1973, Scottish, Welsh, Northern Irish and regional devolution and the formation of a quasi-federal (rather than unitary) state, with a reformed House of Lords as primary features of the new constitution. In the view of constitutional state theorists like Bogdanor, parliamentary sovereignty is questionably being consigned to history, the next step being a central written constitution (Bogdanor 2009). The rule of recognition has been swept away. Bogdanor adopts a similar perspective to other 'messy constitutionalists', again, combining many of the features of the above, such as Anthony King, arguing there is a new British constitution under which "the British parliament is no longer sovereign", it is "a legal fiction … far more fictive than legal", but accepting we have ended up with a constitutional 'mess', often citing the development of the EU (King 2007, p. 99; see also Mabbett 2017).

However, although Bogdanor's primary argument asserts that the Human Rights Act has created a 'cornerstone' of a new constitution (Baranger 2010), by giving more power to courts vis-a-vis Parliament, he displaces the old principle of parliamentary sovereignty, a keystone of a framework underpinning the 'old' constitution. From Bogdanor's 'popular sovereignty' perspective, the modern theory of a popular constitutional state directly seeks to affirm the primacy of electors as delegating their representatives in the representation process at the expense of the doctrine of parliamentary sovereignty. Rather than viewing the electorate as steering and directing the exercise of parliamentary sovereignty in the recognised helm, it makes the people themselves sovereign. For Bogdanor, on the British model, those who enjoy the right to make political decisions are empowered to do so by virtue of the representative mandate they have received from the electorate. The direct 'popular sovereignty' representation attempts to misconstrue the parliamentary relationship between electors and trustees.

The next step in moving away from Hart's rule of recognition in Bogdanor's (2009, 2019) constitutional state is towards an entrenched and written constitution. A substantive aspect however of this move is "a quasi-federal territorial separation of powers between Parliament and the European Union" (Drewry 2012, p. 533). While it is clear that Parliament has delegated a swathe of law-making powers to the EU, the suggestions of steps toward a written constitution seem unproven. It appears that the entrenchment of EU law has not led to an ultimate decaying of parliamentary sovereignty, as Bogdanor holds, in line with the radical version of the common law tradition. He argues EU law has become entrenched and not merely incorporated (Bogdanor 2012, p. 184) but that has remained significantly contested. Parliament can only impose upon itself, not substantive limits, but limitations of "manner and form" i.e. courts only accept as law that which has been made in the proper legal form. The constitutional state view has, in other words, led to an exaggerated view of the binding nature of EU obligations. For Parliament to impose substantive limits upon itself it would have to alter its wider rule of recognition (see Goldsworthy 2012, contra Bogdanor 2012). An alternative view worth some consideration is that the existence of the Hartian rule of recognition is dependent upon historical precedents. While it is disputed that the European Communities Act is viewed as directly affecting the Hartian rule of recognition in the UK, as Bogdanor asserts, how can that occur by the legal entrenchment of that Act? It was a voluntary Act, passed by Parliament in 1972, and amended in similar vein, all perfectly consistent with the rule of recognition. So equally would its repeal by parliamentary enactment, for example, through the EU (Withdrawal) Act 2018. It might be accepted that a rule of recognition can be indirectly changed, but only by a change in the underlying historical precedents which determine the UK constitutional structure. The Hartian rule of recognition is as much political as legal. The fundamental point about parliamentary sovereignty is that the restriction and extension of powers which enable that form are not an exercise in the recognition of other, deeper, more fundamental principles of morality or common law principles which Bogdanor (2009) strongly relies upon. As Loughlin (2010) notes, those factors may mediate the sovereignty claim but the claim itself is rooted in deep-seated political conditions (Loughlin 2010, pp. 236–237).

2.5 The Meaning of Parliamentary Sovereignty: The 'Rule of Recognition' and the Common Law

Radical common law constitutionalism has provided a rationale for the abandonment of a rule of recognition when explaining parliamentary sovereignty and a brief response to that theory is necessary. In the law court system itself and legal constitutionalist circles, the meaning of the Diceyan definition has in recent years been widely questioned by common law constitutionalist radicals, including at the highest level by Government ministers (Foreign and Commonwealth Office 2010, p. 40; European Scrutiny Committee 2010; Goldsworthy 2010, pp. 14–15). Senior judges such as Lord Steyn maintain that "…the supremacy of Parliament is still the general principle of our constitution. The judges created this principle …" (Lord Steyn, *R v Secretary of State for the Home Department, ex parte Pierson* [1998]). Lord Hope states, "Step by step, gradually but surely, the English principle of the absolute sovereignty of Parliament which Dicey derived from Coke and Blackstone is being qualified … The rule of law enforced by the courts is the ultimate controlling factor on which our constitution is based …" (*Jackson v Attorney General* [2006]). The radical common law tradition holds parliamentary sovereignty is founded on a common law foundation (Holdsworth 1937; Goldsworthy 2010, p. 14)—and this has a strong relationship with the proposition that parliamentary sovereignty has been limited by EU law (see Young and Gee 2016). Notably, if legal and political theorists seek to claim that directly effective EU law derives its effect from the common law, then this generates the possibility that even a statute repealing the European Communities Act would not fully enable parliament to legislate contrary to EU law. The courts could in theory refuse to recognise the repealing statute as valid law (Young and Gee 2016).

It mistakenly asserts that legal supremacy in the British constitution is understood as a rule of the common law (Loughlin and Tierney 2018, pp. 1008–1009) which was created and may be altered by the courts. It assumes that the judges become superior to Parliament (Goldsworthy 2010, p. 15). This "minority" view held among a "small handful of judges" (Young and Gee 2016, p.15) explicitly asserts, however incorrectly, the power of the courts in making Parliament sovereign. This argument must be scrutinised because:

- the law of judges is not a substitute for politics;
- it is a view which misinterprets the historical foundation(s) of parliamentary sovereignty as having singular common law roots and;
- political decisions in a parliamentary democracy ought to be made by representatives who can be removed (Tomkins 2010; Griffith 1985).

Rather than consider a broader 'rule of the recognised helm' in explaining parliamentary sovereignty, common law radicalism asserts that Parliament's sovereignty is to be treated as a product of, or controlled by, judge-made common law (Allan 2013; Foreign and Commonwealth Office 2010, p. 40; *Jackson v Attorney General* [2006]; Lord Steyn [1998]; Goldsworthy 2010, p. 16). Dicey's definition of parliamentary sovereignty and the contemporary employment of that definition in the neo-Diceyan tradition is accepted in the mainstream, albeit with increasing reservation in law and legal theory and "hotly contested" by the jurisprudence common law arguments of TRS Allan (2013). Common law interpretation to this extent only fails in its understanding that ultimate parliamentary sovereignty has not ever historically been comprehensively understood as the creation of that system (Tomkins 2010; Goldsworthy 1999, pp. 247–248).

While a narrow band in the legal literature on the subject appears to accept some form of limitations as undermining the ultimate rule in its very character, it is not obvious that all those conditions merely become limits or boundaries upon legal or political supremacy (contra Allan 2013, p. 140). As with Bogdanor (2012), there is an amplification of 'manner and form' limits, in which courts only accept as law that which has been made in the proper legal form, as substantive limitations upon legislative supremacy. This has opened the way both for inaccurate notions of the voluntary European Communities Act 1972 substantively and legally limiting Parliament, not to mention the neo-Diceyan weakness of simply equating parliamentary sovereignty with legal supremacy (e.g. Bradley 2011; Allan 2010). The Act, it is claimed, enabled Parliament to bind its successors (Allan 2010; Wade 1996). Given Hart's understanding of the official consensus to maintain the rule, it is not credible, or at least, very radical, to suggest that all the various contested norms, customs and connections should result in the ultimate rule being viewed as 'indeterminate' (e.g. Allan 2013, p. 154; Tucker 2011). Most historically precedented, political conditions or constitutional conventions have a reflexive, not necessarily conditional or causal role, in altering the rule (see Jaconelli 2005). Furthermore, there is little to no evidence to suggest that there has been a contemporary, measurable change in the consensual intra-state understandings of British legal officials that judges do not have the authority to declare a statute invalid (Goldsworthy 1999, p. 253). That challenge to a form of judicial sovereignty is, however, not to deny the role and status of political sovereignty, or understanding how historical precedents have shaped parliamentary sovereignty.

The rule of recognition does not derive its validity from *judicial* interpretation of the underlying principles of a political theory, as Allan maintains. Such an assumption would place judges in a politically superior place to Parliament in the constitution. It derives its validity from its capacity to express the conditions which will enable all other rules to impose obligations as valid law, consistent with its historically precedented political conventions. The assertions by judges of deeper principles of political morality behind the rule of recognition, including principles derived from EU case law, represents the discourse of judicial supremacy (see Goldsworthy 2010, p. 53), as against parliamentary sovereignty. It also conflates common law principles (e.g. liberty and justice) as being more fundamental than the most ultimate rule. As Tomkins suggests, legal constitutionalism has viewed law as an activity that is not only distinctive from but also superior to politics (Tomkins 2005, pp. 11–14). That 'politics bad, law good' approach favours the courts. It has failed to acknowledge 'the political', or its supremacy. The arguments of Loughlin (2010), Tomkins (2005, 2013), Griffith (1979, 1985), and Bellamy (2007) and others are crucial to political theory for different reasons but primarily because they address the centrality of politics—of contestation, of parliamentary dispute, of wider disagreement—in the UK's constitutional regime.

This approach will not address the specific debate about the direct legal issues implied in the UK legal sovereignty-EU debate, focusing on the repeal or invalidating of one Act of Parliament with another (Craig 2011, pp. 112–113). That problem in itself is more aligned to the question of the role of judicial decision-making in the interpretation of Acts of Parliament and the doctrine of 'implied repeal', which will only be considered here as secondary. These debates have been widely represented by the traditionalists such as H. W. R. Wade (1996) in contrast to the 'New View' of Sir Ivor Jennings (1957), RFV Heuston (1964), and G. Marshall (1957).

It should be briefly considered that the school of common law radicalism with its questionable abandonment of rule of recognition asserts that Parliament's sovereignty is to be treated as a product of, or controlled by, judge-made common law and has advanced several arguments originally introduced by the moral constitutionalist tradition. 'Moral constitutionalists' such as Ronald Dworkin (1977, p. 24) and neo-Dworkinian theory have asserted that Hart's ultimate rule of recognition, as a rule, does not exist in an 'all or nothing' fashion; the legal system instead consists of legal principles which should be assigned a metaphorical weight relative to other principles, on the basis of broadening the scope of judicial interpretation. Allan's interpretation is 'broadly consistent' with Dworkin's view of interpreting law in balance with its moral justification (Allan 2013, pp. 20, 340; Loughlin and Tschorne 2016, pp. 13–14). It thereby subverts parliamentary sovereignty by mischaracterising the pre-existing Hartian relationship which exists between rules and conditions. Although an attempt will be made to respond throughout to Allan's (2013) arguments, I depart from Dworkin's theory, which unlike Hart's, believes that legal principles rather than rules (Hart 1997) and rather than sovereigns (Hobbes) are the foundations of the legal system. Dworkin's theory holds that judges must look to how they interpret principles, including value judgements, rather than simply obey rules when applying the law. Dworkinian theory generally takes a substantive leap in divorcing principles (moral or political) from the ultimate rule. It has been adapted for example to explain parliamentary sovereignty more as a principle than a rule, to be balanced against competing principles (McGarry 2012) as if it were some flexibly-based principle balanced against higher justifying moral principles (Dworkin 1977; see Loughlin and Tierney 2018, pp. 1008–1009). It has subsequently been connected with the common law position, through its assertions that courts do not judge Acts of Parliament simply in balance against any other principles but on the basis of judge-decided competing principles derived from the common law (McGarry 2012, p. 598). Nevertheless, Dworkin helpfully recognised Hart's concession that an ultimate rule can impose obligations as law enacted by particular institutions e.g. parliament, but rules established by custom also (Dworkin 1977, p. 41). Customs can count as law even before the courts recognise it (Dworkin 1977, p. 43). In theory, then, certain political conditions and customs, that is, previous historical precedents, which are not necessarily legally binding, could then provide the conditions for the ultimate rule.

The Dworkin conviction that a fundamental rule derives its legal validity from a broader, underlying political theory is entirely plausible. However, it is a leap to then adopt a theory which requires a look beyond constitutional rules to judge-decided deeper underlying principles when applying the law. It is an even greater leap still to reject the rule of recognition (i.e. parliamentary sovereignty) for being inconsistent with those deeper principles. Politically, the UK constitution does not designate judges (unelected) to cherry-pick supposedly deeper underlying principles of the rule of law to diminish the rule of parliamentary sovereignty and with it, the selective weakening of the capacity to represent the wishes of the electorate. They have not constitutionally had the power conferred upon them and are not likely to at any future point; but in practice, the incorporation of EU procedure into the UK constitution has enabled the judiciary to at least attempt to achieve such powers.

But ultimately Dworkin cannot accept a reconsideration of the rule of recognition. Loughlin (2010) emphasises that the parliamentary sovereignty form and the restriction and extension of powers which enable that form demonstrate that it is not an exercise in legal logic or the recognition of fundamental principles of morality, according to moral theory, as those legal considerations may sometimes mediate the sovereignty claim but the claim itself is rooted in political condition (Loughlin 2010, pp. 236–237). Dworkin's theory is no doubt useful to common law judges assessing interpretation, but it is less helpful for political theory to have dismissed the role of the rule of recognition according Parliament its sovereignty simply on the basis that the rule must be exercised in balance, or mediated, with other deeper, moral principles.

2.6 Political Constitutionalism: Returning to the Rule of the Recognised Helm

The rule of the recognised helm is necessary because it is a fundamental rule of government which is recognised and practised by persons serving a purpose in the institutions of the state architecture. It is not fundamental because it simply exists—it must be recognised by them as providing for valid law and political settlement. It is not fundamental because it is recognised by only the parliament, courts or people or government but consensually recognised and steered by all of them. As a departure from Hart's (1997) rule of recognition, it is a helm which defines the relationship of political actors, and those of the executive, the legislature, the judiciary and the electorate, in their tacit consent or recognition of a rule providing for sovereignty.

Why should it be necessary to equate the recognition of the rule of sovereignty with *only* the law of Parliament (Dicey 1964) or increasingly the recognition of statute by the common law of the courts (Allan 2013) or increasingly by the people (Bogdanor 2009)? The central place of representative, parliamentary government which affirms the ultimate rule of 'What the Crown in Parliament enacts is law', at the very least, begins to express the supreme role of the legislature, as elected by the people, but also a subsidiary role of the judiciary, and their elected government, in providing recognition to the rule. Why put substantive limits on the institutional location which parliamentary sovereignty is recognised by, given that:

- Dicey (1964) recognised Parliament as foundational, but only in so far as it made law, and not in terms of its political primacy.
- Allan (2013) overstates the courts as having a leading role in establishing Parliament's sovereignty.

- Bogdanor (2009) describes the people under the Human Rights Act 1998, through ever-growing local government and regional, devolved and federal units, as holding the key to where sovereignty is located.

It is unnecessary to hold one sole actor as key to recognising the rule of Parliament's sovereignty, when the executive, the legislature, the judiciary and the electorate must each play their part in upholding the rule. The rule of the recognised helm ought to express a more fundamental rule to be practised by persons possessing a purpose in the institutions of the state.

The conceptualisation of politics, historical conventions, precedents and political conditions in relation to the rule of the recognised helm is vital to an alternative, new approach and the content of my argument. Loughlin (2010) recognises that importance when concluding that in the British system, an investigation into constitutional understanding requires an investigation into the constitution of the state. The quest for constitutional understanding requires both analysis of the rules of positive law within an appreciation of the conditions of *droit politique* (Loughlin 2010, p. 272). It is possible to understand the constitution of the state as *droit politique* (Loughlin 2010, pp. 231–237) in which the constituent elements of the public sphere embedded in historical customs, precedents and practices sustain the ordering of the state. The *droit politique* has a generative function in which the directing ideas sustain the institutions of government and institutions make legal and constitutional rules (Loughlin 2010, p. 233, in citing the French public lawyer Hauriou's idea, although Hauriou denies legal rules can make institutions). It provides the key to understanding the constitution of the state. Understanding parliamentary sovereignty in terms of a political constitutional model enables it to be viewed through an explanatory framework within which to make sense of our constitutional self-understandings (Gee and Webber 2010), be it political or legal.

To move towards a rule of the recognised helm, Hart's ultimate rule of parliamentary sovereignty must consider the positive and political nature of the rule of persons within the helm of the state. The medieval state, which will be interpreted in Chapter 3, examines how in Henry de Bracton's view, sovereignty at the helm was bound to moral duty. Ultimately, the law and the law-making sovereign remaining mutually conditioned, reciprocal and interdependent at the helm, even though sovereignty equates to the power to govern the realm (Kantorowicz 1957, pp. 153, 155). This has a deeper relevance to a modern constitution with multiple actors, including agencies and the EU through to enhanced judicial bodies. In contemporary political theory, Richard Bellamy (2007) persuasively makes the point that whereas government is the agency authorised by law to issue laws, the rule of law can then barely constrain the rule of persons. For Bellamy, at some point, some body of persons, judges or politicians, must decide for example if a government has breached rules (Bellamy 2007, p. 56). After all, Parliament in the form of the Commons reflects the people. On the one hand, Bellamy's view is certainly attractive because it addresses the presence of the political in a theory of political constitutionalism. On the other hand, it overlooks Hart's ultimate rule as a fundamental rule on which it is assumed there is already an acknowledged consensus between officials or persons within those different institutional parts (as described by Goldsworthy 1999, p. 253; 2010, pp. 53–54; Hart 1997).

In the demotion of the commanding power over the law and of governing at the helm, many factors are being dismissed which help to explain how parliamentary sovereignty exists in the political constitution. This book reaffirms the relevance of the political constitution to parliamentary sovereignty because the legal definition of parliamentary sovereignty, in effect:

- Marginalises those who exercise political power to hold to account through political institutions, namely, Parliament.
- Is dismissive of that which is 'political' characterised by divisive debate, conflict, disagreement, messiness, and as-yet unresolved chaos.
- Gives great weight to judicially enforceable limits on the legislature which fail to recognise the deeper politics of rights claims, nor see that law is neither separate nor superior to politics (Griffith 1979).
- Is dismissive of the procedures in which political decisions should be taken by politicians as responsible and accountable representatives, not judges, simply because they are electable and removable at the ballot box and are accountable to Parliament throughout their tenure (Griffith 1979).
- Provides insufficient recognition that both law and politics are to be understood by deference to 'the circumstances of politics', so that there is a common framework or decision or course of action on a

disputed matter, despite disagreement about what the best possible decision might be (Waldron 1999).

- Overlooks the role of political life in the British often adversarial, political system and political party competition, and the use of majorities to provide settlement and/or agreement, as more defining features of the political constitution, explained by theorists such as Bellamy (2007) and Tomkins (2013).

The centrality of the political constitution proposed by Bellamy (2007), Tomkins (2013) and to an exaggerated degree, Griffith (1979), is a fundamental point because at the heart of UK parliamentary sovereignty is the capacity of voters at free and fair general elections to elect their chosen representatives to the elective part of Westminster, the House of Commons. They thereby choose to have MPs decide on the laws and policies by which they are to be governed. In pursuance of that task, electors primarily affirm that stabilising Hartian social rule of the constitution within the wider political system. Directly and practically, in polling stations, they enable constituency representatives to represent their general wishes in accordance with manifestos, as open to all UK voters. In that exercise, they also affirm their individual freedom of choice within the political system to choose their representatives and the policies and laws which will affect their everyday lives, and ultimately answer the question of who governs the UK. It is their power to choose and send to Westminster an elected representative (and therefore perhaps remove an incumbent one) to make law in accordance with their general wishes. That sovereignty adheres to older, medieval understandings of the state particularly where it relates to stability and the maintenance of the balance of power as well as more modern ideas of parliamentary democracy and of guaranteeing individual and political freedom.

Whereas Tomkins (2013) puts ministerial responsibility to Parliament at the heart of the political constitution, it is Bellamy's emphasis on the legislature's law-making function, legislative votes by majorities, and institutionalised party competition (Bellamy 2007) which is more fundamental to the political constitution in which parliamentary sovereignty operates. The claims Bellamy (2007) makes to that being a democratic constitution or reinforcing 'political equality' can be more difficult to justify. It does reaffirm the essential and elective nature of political institutions, including Parliament, acting through very ordinary political and legislative processes to determine its sovereignty. Finally, by recognising both that there is a legal rule of recognition and that it exists within a deeply political helm of the state, I share Loughlin's (2010) and to a degree, Tomkins' (2013) concern for a 'polarised opposition' between a political and legal constitution and by developing the idea of a rule of the recognised helm also intend to move beyond that concerning dualism.

The following chapter (Chapter 3) will develop the claim that a 'rule of the recognised helm' is essential to understanding parliamentary sovereignty by explaining how it has been made historically operable in different historical constitutional forms. It follows the constitutional logic that if there is to be a Hartian ultimate rule which provides the conditions another rule must satisfy in order for that rule to impose obligations as valid law (Hart 1997) and political settlement, it must be necessary to provide the historically precedented conditions of the social rule. The third chapter is devoted to the innovative identification and explanation of eight historical constitutional forms for that purpose, beginning with 'What the Crown-*with*-magnates enacts is law' (1200–1350) through to today's constitutional form, 'What the Crown-*through*-Parliamentary political elite with external bodies enacts is law' (1973–present). Today's Parliament retains its theoretical sovereignty—expressed as the power to terminate or change that membership by repealing or amending the European Communities Act 1972—while the 45-year practice of not terminating or changing substantial aspects of its Parliament-diminishing EU membership has been thought to have left the doctrine intact. Parliament is sovereign not because of a general Prime Ministerial, judicial or popular 'say so' but because it is a historically institutionalised rule of the recognised helm which is dependent upon deeper customs, conventions and politics of past historical precedents.

Bibliography

Allan, T. R. S. (2010, December 7). *'Evidence (26)' in House of Commons' European Scrutiny Committee* (The EU Bill and Parliamentary Sovereignty, HC 633-I) [Online]. Available at https://www.publications.parliament.uk/pa/cm201011/cmselect/cmeuleg/633/633i.pdf. Accessed 12 December 2013.

Allan, T. R. S. (2011). Questions of Legality and Legitimacy: Form and Substance in British Constitutionalism. *International Journal of Constitutional Law, 9*(1), 155–162.

Allan, T. R. S. (2013). *The Sovereignty of Law: Freedom, Constitution and Common Law*. Oxford: Oxford University Press.

Baranger, D. (2010). The New British Constitution by Vernon Bogdanor. *The Modern Law Review, 73*(2), 331–334.

Bartelson, J. (2011). Sovereignty. In B. Badie, D. Berg-Scholsser, & L. Morlino (Eds.), *International Encyclopedia of Political Science*. Thousand Oaks, CA: Sage [Online]. Available at http://dx.doi.org/10.4135/9781412959636.n573. Accessed 17 April 2017.

Bartelson, J. (2016). Recognition: A Short History. *Ethics & International Affairs, 30*(3), 303–321.

Bellamy, R. (2007). *Political Constitutionalism: A Republican Defence of the Constitutionality of Democracy*. Cambridge: Cambridge University Press.

Bingham, T. (2010). *The Rule of Law*. London: Penguin.

Bodin, J. (1576). *Six livres de la république*. Lyon: Imprimerie de Jean de Tournes.

Bogdanor, V. (2009). *The New British Constitution*. Oxford: Hart Publishing.

Bogdanor, V. (2012). Imprisoned by a Doctrine: The Modern Defence of Parliamentary Sovereignty. *Oxford Journal of Legal Studies, 3*(1), 179–195.

Bogdanor, V. (2019). *Beyond Brexit: Towards a British Constitution*. London: I.B. Tauris.

Bradley, A. (2011). The Sovereignty of Parliament—Form or Substance? In J. Jowell & D. Oliver (Eds.), *The Changing Constitution* (7th ed.). Oxford: Oxford University Press.

Bradley, A. W., & Ewing, K. D. (2010). *Constitutional and Administrative Law* (15th ed.). Harlow: Longman.

Coke, E. (1610). *Dr. Bonham's Case*, 8 Co. Rep. 114 (Court of Common Pleas).

Corwin, E. S. (1941). Book Review. *Harvard Law Review, 54*(3), 533–535.

Craig, P. (2011). Britain in the European Union. In J. Jowell & D. Oliver (Eds.), *The Changing Constitution* (7th ed., pp. 104–133). Oxford: Oxford University Press.

de Bracton, H. (1235). *De legibus et consuetudinibus Angliae* [On the Laws and Customs of England] [Online]. Available at http://bracton.law.harvard.edu. Accessed 17 January 2013.

Dicey, A. V. (1885/1964). *An Introduction to the Study of the Law of the Constitution*. London: Macmillan.

Drewry, G. (2012). The Coalition and the Constitution. *Journal of Legislative Studies, 18*(3–4), 533–534.

Dworkin, R. (1977). *Taking Rights Seriously*. London: Gerald Duckworth.

European Scrutiny Committee. (2010, December 7). *The EU Bill and Parliamentary Sovereignty* (HC 633-I) [Online]. Available at https://www.publications.parliament.uk/pa/cm201011/cmselect/cmeuleg/633/633i.pdf. Accessed 12 December 2013.

Factortame: *The Queen v Secretary of State for Transport, ex parte: Factortame Ltd and Others*. [1990]. Judgment of the Court of 19 June 1990. Reference for a Preliminary Ruling: House of Lords—United Kingdom. Case C-213/89. Available at http://eur-lex.europa.eu/legal-content/EN/TXT/?uri=CELEX%3A61989CJ0213. Accessed 21 June 2014.

Fellmeth, A. X., & Horwitz, M. (2009). *Guide to Latin in International Law*. Oxford: Oxford University Press [Online]. Available at Oxford Reference. Accessed 9 October 2012.

Foreign and Commonwealth Office. (2010, December 7). *Written Evidence from the Foreign and Commonwealth Office to the European Scrutiny Committee Inquiry on Clause 18 of the EU Bill* (The EU Bill and Parliamentary Sovereignty, HC 633-II). European Scrutiny Committee [Online]. Available at https://www.publications.parliament.uk/pa/cm201011/cmselect/cmeuleg/633/633i.pdf. Accessed 12 December 2013.

Francis, M., & Morrow, J. (1994). *A History of Political Thought in the Nineteenth Century*. London: Duckworth.

Galligan, D. (2006). *Law in Modern Society*. Oxford: Oxford University Press.

Garland v BR Engineering. [1983]. 2 AC 751, HL(E).

Gee, G., & Webber, G. C. N. (2010). What Is a Political Constitution? *Oxford Journal of Legal Studies, 30*(2), 273–299.

Goldsworthy, J. (1999). *The Sovereignty of Parliament: History and Philosophy*. Oxford: Clarendon Press.

Goldsworthy, J. (2010). *Parliamentary Sovereignty: Contemporary Debates*. Cambridge: Cambridge University Press.

Goldsworthy, J. (2012, March 9). *Parliamentary Sovereignty's Premature Obituary*. UK Constitutional Law [Blog]. Available at https://ukconstitutionallaw.org/2012/03/09/jeffrey-goldsworthy-parliamentary-sovereigntys-premature-obituary/. Accessed 1 July 2012.

Goldsworthy, J. (2013). Parliamentary Sovereignty and Constitutional Change in the United Kingdom. In R. Rawlings, P. Leyland, & A. Young (Eds.), *Sovereignty and the Law: Domestic European and International Perspectives*. Oxford: Oxford University Press.

Grant, J. P., & Barker, J. C. (Eds.). (2009). *Encyclopaedic Dictionary of International Law* (3rd ed.). Oxford: Oxford University Press [Online]. Available at Oxford Reference. Accessed 10 February 2014.

Griffith, J. A. G. (1979). The Political Constitution. *Modern Law Review, 42*(1), 1–21.

Griffith, J. A. G. (1985). *The Politics of the Judiciary* (3rd ed.). London: Fontana.

Hart, H. L. A. (1997). *The Concept of Law* (2nd ed.). Oxford: Clarendon Press.

Heuston, R. F. V. (1964). *Essays in Constitutional Law* (2nd ed.). London: Stevens & Sons.

Hobbes, T. (1651). *Leviathan, or the Matter, Form, and Power of a Commonwealth Ecclesiastical and Civil*. London: Crooke.

Hoekstra, K. (2013). Early Modern Absolutism and Constitutionalism. *Cardozo Law Review, 34*(3), 1079–1098.

Holdsworth, W. (1937). *A History of English Law* (2nd ed.). London: Methuen and Sweet & Maxwell.

Holland, B. (2010). Sovereignty as Dominium? Reconstructing the Constructivist Roman Law Thesis. *International Studies Quarterly, 54*(2), 449–480.

Internationale Handelgesellschaft v Einfuhrhund Vorratsselle fur Getreide und Futtermittel. [1970]. Case 11/70.

Jack, M., Hutton, M., Johnson, C., Millar, D., Patrick, S., & Sandall, A. (Eds.). (2011). *Erskine May: Parliamentary Practice* (24th ed.). London: LexisNexis Butterworths.

Jackson v Attorney General. [2006]. UKHL 56.

Jaconelli, J. (2005). Do Constitutional Conventions Bind? *Cambridge Law Journal, 64*(1), 149–176.

Jennings, I. (1957). *Constitutional Laws of the Commonwealth.* Oxford: Oxford University Press.

Kantorowicz, E. H. (1957). *The King's Two Bodies: A Study in Medieval Political Theology.* Princeton, NJ: Princeton University Press.

King, A. (2007). *The British Constitution.* Oxford: Oxford University Press.

Kirby, M. (2006). Law Reform and Human Rights: Scarman's Great Legacy. *Legal Studies, 26*(4), 449–474.

Law, J. (Ed.). (2017). *A Dictionary of Law* (8th ed.). Oxford: Oxford University Press [Online]. Available at Oxford Reference. Accessed 10 July 2017.

Law, J., & Martin, E. A. (2009). *The Concise Oxford Dictionary of Politics* (3rd ed.). Oxford: Oxford University Press [Online]. Available at Oxford Reference. Accessed 10 February 2014.

Lee, D. (2016). *Popular Sovereignty in Early Modern Constitutional Thought.* Oxford: Oxford University Press.

Leiter, B., & Coleman, J. L. (2010). Legal Positivism. In D. M. Patterson (Ed.), *The Blackwell Companion to Philosophy of Law and Legal Theory* (2nd ed., pp. 228–248). Oxford: Wiley-Blackwell.

Lord Hailsham. (1976). *Elective Dictatorship* [Online]. Available at http://www.bbc.co.uk/programmes/p00fr9gh. Accessed 5 September 2015.

Lord Scarman. (1992). *Why Britain Needs a Written Constitution.* The Fourth Sovereignty Lecture. London: Charter 88 Trust.

Lord Steyn. (1998). *R v Secretary of State for the Home Department, ex parte Pierson,* AC 539.

Loughlin, M. (2010). *Foundations of Public Law.* Oxford: Oxford University Press.

Loughlin, M., & Tierney, S. (2018). The Shibboleth of Sovereignty. *The Modern Law Review, 81,* 989–1016.

Loughlin, M., & Tschorne, S. (2016). Public Law. In M. Bevir & R. A. W. Rhodes (Eds.), *Routledge Handbook of Interpretive Political Science* (pp. 324–337). Abingdon: Routledge.

Mabbett, D. (2017). Parliamentary Sovereignty and Brexit. *Political Quarterly, 88*(2), 167–169.

Macarthys Ltd. v Smith. [1980]. Case 129/79, ECR 1275.
Marshall, G. (1957). *Parliamentary Sovereignty and the Commonwealth*. Oxford: Oxford University Press.
McGarry, J. (2012). The Principle of Parliamentary Sovereignty. *Legal Studies, 32*(4), 577–599.
McIlwain, C. H. (1947). *Constitutionalism: Ancient and Modern*. Ithaca, NY: Cornell University Press.
Morwood, J. (Ed.). (2005). *Pocket Oxford Latin Dictionary: Latin-English* (3rd ed.). Oxford: Oxford University Press [Online]. Available at Oxford Reference. Accessed 10 February 2014.
Oxford English Dictionary. (2017). Oxford: Oxford University Press [Online]. Available at Oxford Reference. Accessed 7 May 2017.
Perry, A. (2015). The Internal Aspect of Social Rules. *Oxford Journal of Legal Studies, 35*(2), 283–300.
Postema, G. J. (2008). Conformity, Custom, and Congruence: Rethinking the Efficacy of Law. In M. H. Kramer, C. Grant, B. Colburn, & A. Hatzistavrou (Eds.), *The Legacy of H.L.A. Hart: Legal, Political, and Moral Philosophy* (pp. 45–66). Oxford: Oxford University Press.
Ruggie, J. G. (1993). Territoriality and Beyond: Problematizing Modernity in International Relations. *International Organization, 47*(1), 139–174.
Sciaraffa, S. (2011). The Ineliminability of Hartian Social Rules. *Oxford Journal of Legal Studies, 31*(3), 603–623.
Shapiro, S. J. (2001). On Hart's Way Out. In J. L. Coleman (Ed.), *Hart's Postscript: Essays on the Postscript to the 'Concept of Law'* (pp. 149–192). Oxford: Oxford University Press.
Smith, J. (2017). National Parliaments and the European Union: A View from Westminster. In D. Jancic (Ed.), *National Parliaments After the Lisbon Treaty and the Euro Crisis: Resilience or Resignation?* Oxford: Oxford University Press.
Tabarelli, M. (2013). The Influence of the EU and the ECHR on "Parliamentary Sovereignty Regimes": Assessing the Impact of European Integration on the British and Swedish Judiciaries. *European Law Journal, 19*(3), 340–363.
Thoburn v Sunderland City Council. [2002]. EWHC 195 (Admin). Available at http://www.bailii.org/ew/cases/EWHC/Admin/2002/195.html. Accessed 5 September 2014.
Tomkins, A. (2005). *Our Republican Constitution*. Oxford: Hart Publishing.
Tomkins, A. (2010). *Written Evidence to the European Scrutiny Committee, Clause 18 of the Bill: Parliamentary Sovereignty and EU law*. The EU Bill and Parliamentary Sovereignty. Available at https://publications.parliament.uk/pa/cm201011/cmselect/cmeuleg/633ii/633we02.htm. Accessed 5 December 2010.

Tomkins, A. (2013). What's Left of the Political Constitution? *German Law Journal*, *14*(12), 2275–2292 [Online]. Available at http://www.germanlawjournal.com/index.php?pageID=11&artID=1604. Accessed 12 December 2013.

Tucker, A. (2011). Uncertainty in the Rule of Recognition in the Doctrine of Parliamentary Sovereignty. *Oxford Journal of Legal Studies, 31*(1), 61–88.

UK Parliament. (2019). *Information* [Online]. Available at www.parliament.uk. Accessed 3 February 2019.

Vile, M. J. C. (1967). *Constitutionalism and the Separation of Powers* (2nd ed.). Indianapolis, IN: Liberty Fund [Online]. Available at http://oll.libertyfund.org/titles/vile-constitutionalism-and-the-separation-of-powers. Accessed 12 March 2013.

Wade, H. W. R. (1996, October). Sovereignty: Revolution or Evolution? *Law Quarterly Review*, *112*, 568–575.

Waldron, J. (1999). *Law and Disagreement.* Oxford: Oxford University Press.

Young, A., & Gee, G. (2016). Regaining Sovereignty, Brexit, the UK Parliament and the Common Law. *European Public Law, 22*(1), 131–147.

CHAPTER 3

Eight Historical Constitutional Forms: Defining the Rule of the Present Day 'Recognised Helm'

In making the claim that a 'rule of the recognised helm' is essential to understanding parliamentary sovereignty, as both a legal and political concept, it is necessary to also draw conclusions on how that essential sovereignty deferred to Parliament has been made workable at different stages. After all, since there is a Hartian ultimate rule which provides the conditions another rule must satisfy in order for that rule to impose obligations as valid law and political settlement, it must also be necessary to provide the historical conditions of the social rule. Below, it is briefly set out how a series of eight historical constitutional forms describing prominent historical features help to frame multiple forms of the rule providing for parliamentary sovereignty:

i. 'What the Crown-*with*-magnates enacts is law' (1200–1350)
ii. 'What the Crown-*with*-Commons enacts is law' (1350–1532)
iii. 'What the Crown-*through*-Parliament enacts is law' (1533–1602)
iv. 'What the Crown-*with*-disputed Parliament enacts is law' (1603–1687)
v. 'What the Crown-*in*-regulating Parliament enacts is law' (1688–1689)
vi. 'What the Crown-*in*-mixed constitutional Parliament enacts is law' (1690–1790s)
vii. 'What the Crown-*in*-Parliamentary Cabinet enacts is law' (1800–1972)
viii. 'What the Crown-*through*-Parliamentary political elite with external bodies enacts is law' (1973–present)

J. McConalogue, *The British Constitution Resettled*,
https://doi.org/10.1007/978-3-030-25290-8_3

This chapter innovatively identifies eight historical constitutional forms for that purpose. Each form illustrates the different meanings attributed to the rule of the recognised helm. From its inception to its contemporary context, its historical meaning(s) have shifted in a partly episodical, occasionally tangential but gradually evolving development. The 'Crown' powers previously exercised by the reigning monarch have been passed, in the present day, to the ministers of the executive who now exercise most of those powers. The Crown powers are now exercised by the executive through, and on the advice of, ministers accountable to Parliament (Jack et al. 2011) and in so far as the executive retains the confidence of the MPs in the House of Commons.

In terms of sovereignty involving the modern Crown in Parliament, law and the political community, it is then argued that the modern concept of parliamentary sovereignty has been left with an entrenched quandary in the meaning of today's eighth historical constitutional form. An executive-led Parliament often delegates a part of its law-making capacity to other bodies and institutions. Those institutions then impose external control, steerage and direction upon that law. In that ordering, MPs who are elected to the House of Commons by voters to make law forego that practical capacity. MPs' everyday capacity or competency, but not ultimate right, was voluntarily ceded under the European Communities Act 1972. An elective, delegated Parliament is paradoxical in a political sense. Parliament retains its ultimate sovereignty because it has the power to terminate or change that membership by repealing or amending the European Communities Act 1972 (Tomkins 2010). In practice, despite the growth of popular and parliamentary British Euroscepticism (Geddes 2016, p. 265; Gifford 2014), the 45-year practice of not terminating or changing substantial aspects of its Parliament-diminishing EU membership has been imagined to have left that doctrine of parliamentary sovereignty intact.

Finally, the recognised helm can better be understood, by adapting Bracton's view, according to which the sovereignty to govern in the medieval state in relation to the law remains "mutually conditioned", reciprocal and interdependent at the helm (Kantorowicz 1957, pp. 153, 155). Historical constitutional forms provide for precedent, by which it is meant that the fingertips of past, historical precedents are pressed into the old, dry sponge of UK constitutional history by past political customs, traditions and constitutional conventions, to be compressed, reshaped and reconfigured in reflecting those precedents. Historical constitutional forms characterise features of sovereignty and parliamentary sovereignty which are not simply accrued or aggregated—they thrive, survive, part-survive or completely decay or die, but nonetheless they all provide precedent and convention. The historical conditions of the ultimate rule of the recognised helm can be understood, on Locke's grounds, as customs which are reasonable. On that basis, customs support the authority of reasonable legal rules where there are good reasons for them (Grant 2012). The rule of the recognised helm therefore exists on the basis that the powers of the executive, the legislature, the judiciary and the electorate are incorporated through their precedented inter-relationships. Those accustomed features, as conditions, give the rule existence providing for valid law and political settlement. The conditions are therefore crucial, but by no means causal or restrictive, to the rule. Parliament is sovereign not because it is a principle to be weighed against others via judicial interpretation but because it is an institutionalised rule of the recognised helm which is dependent upon the customs, conventions and politics of past historical precedents.

The specific periodisation of the historical constitutional forms have not been inherited from any one political or constitutional theorist, or historian, in particular. It is however notable that historiographers, political theorists and genealogists have often and similarly, for example, distinguished between 'parliamentary' sovereignty in the early Stuart period and post-1688 settlement, between and after the 1530s or even between the pre- or post-European Communities Act 1972 explanations, as each has been bound by substantive and observable constitutional changes. The historical constitutional form conveys the inter-relationships between different types of historical interpretations and the ways in which specific 'new' understandings evolve, however unevenly, tangential, episodic or discontinuous from older notions. The historical constitutional forms provide the features in the recognised helm which exist in that cohesive structure. The powers of the executive, the legislature, the judiciary and the electorate are incorporated through those historically precedented inter-relationships. The arms of government exist with different roles and functions but the overlapping relationships between the institutions help to explain the sovereignty formed in Parliament. Accustomed inter-relationships can help to explain how the legislature incorporates the closeness or distance between the executive, the judiciary and the electorate at different times.

Historical constitutional forms are employed to explain the changing, dislocated forms of parliamentary sovereignty which enable further exploration of the relationship between different types of historical interpretations and the ways in which specific 'new' understandings evolve—progressively, unevenly or tangentially—from older notions. Each historical form itself summarises features within broad historical thresholds insofar as a 'threshold' itself does not denote a prescribed teleology. It is not accepted that those conditions or the ultimate rule itself represents an accrual, or aggregation, or cumulative end-point of a teleological process. It is far more significant than that—the conditions of the ultimate rule provide legal and political precedent.

It has been generally indicated, but never formally established by legal and political theorists or historians that sovereignty can be understood as a historical constitutional form as a cluster of positive powers, which themselves can be contested in definition during a defined period. By focusing upon 'unbundling' the historical conditions and conventions that parliamentary sovereignty adheres to and performs within a historical form, the classical divide between European centralisation versus Westminster centralism can be called into question (see Prokhovnik 2007) and will, in subsequent chapters, help to later understand parliamentary sovereignty in relation to EU membership.

Consistent with Quentin Skinner's contextualism (Perreau-Saussine 2007, p. 118), the analytical features contained within the historical constitutional forms are only true for the historically situated political actors within the immediate circumstances in which they hold those beliefs or ideals. This contextualism can liberate political theory from the strictly legal hegemonic account of parliamentary sovereignty and how it *should* be understood (see Lane 2012, p. 74 on Skinner; Perreau-Saussine 2007, p. 107; Skinner 1965). The philosophical ideas are inseparable from the historical context in which they occur (Skinner 2002, contra Clarke 2013) and by subscribing to a hermeneutic approach, the purpose is to attain an objective truth of a given feature in relation to texts (see Burns 2011). The historical constitutional forms explain what practical work the concept is doing and it thereby underpins the historical normative basis and political contingency upon which its authority is often based. It is an ever-changing work in progress. The constitutional forms contain a conceptual system of discourses, which are open-ended and open to the possibility of constant modification (consistent with Prokhovnik 2008). The forms permit contestability between the features and other forms, the unexpected, the unintended and malleable political formations. The features of the constitutional forms, partially identified by historians, constitutional and political theorists, are at the same time irretrievably bound to the understanding of the present (see Bartelson 1995). An attempt to embrace a more favourable innovative, hermeneutic approach which views historical forms as providing for past historical precedents, can remain relevant to the present. The approach can provide a more formal and deeper level of theoretical explanation to both the historical and contemporary forms of parliamentary sovereignty.

In understanding historical precedents expressed as conventions, those 'constitutional conventions' are, as Jaconelli (1999) observes, social rules which govern the relationships between institutions of government, Parliament and political parties. They are constitutional in character, non court-enforced and form the interrelationships of the constitution. One the one hand, it is not always obvious that we can simply ascertain the binding status or power of a convention on a rule simply via their legal status before the courts, as Jaconelli (1999, 2005) argues. On the other hand, it can be assumed that the relevance and powers of historical political precedents—otherwise understood in the neo-Diceyan tradition as constitutional conventions or non-binding, political constraints—to socio-legal rules does rely on the changing nature of customs and historical circumstances.

In focusing on the organisation of the constitution, the historical constitutional forms also seek to answer the question—what is sovereignty and where is it located in each historical form? What is its function? The constitutional form conveys the relationship between different types of historical interpretations and the ways in which specific 'new' understandings evolve, however unevenly or tangential, from older notions. For example, in seeking a historical understanding of sovereignty in Early Stuart England, as a set of discernible constitutional forms of themes and values, the historian Alan Orr (2002) assesses sovereignty in terms of a practical definition, as a historical cluster of positive or 'state' powers, which themselves can be contested in definition (Orr 2002, p. 475). Orr himself does so to reconsider the concept of sovereignty at the centre of discussion on the origins of the English Civil War. In the following narrative, parliamentary sovereignty can be understood through historical constitutional forms, recast in eight unique narratives. Each form can be characterised as having internal conceptual connections between its meanings during a defined period. That does not infer a comfortable relationship. The forms can often reflect the political contradictions and dilemmas within a contested political environment.

The historical constitutional forms respond to Bogdanor's (2009) claim that constitutions have the objective of 'providing organisation' (Bogdanor 2009, pp. 53–54), and to that extent forms specify the organisational and relational features of the English or British 'constitution' during different historical periods. They clarify the functions of the institutions of government and the relationship between them. In each historical form, we specify the interactions within the British constitution which confirms the sovereign powers and relationships between political actors, particularly in relation to the institution of Parliament.

While theories of the British constitution should seek to understand parliamentary sovereignty relative to the whole constitution, as the common law tradition maintains (see Allan 2013, p. 23), the constitution might better be understood more widely in this sense as a *palimpsest.* The idea of the 'palimpsest' in its general understanding is one of "a manuscript written on a surface from which an earlier text has been partly or wholly erased" (Baldick 2008). In the times before paper, it was common in the Middle Ages given the high cost of parchment and vellum. The notion of a reuse of parchment in which the original script was reworked can appeal to analysts and critics of the British constitutional form—it has never been destroyed, introduced in a whole new form, but merely rewritten, redrafted and reworked. The constitutional palimpsest conveys a process of paradigm-shifting political change, just as Thomas Kuhn's theory of scientific revolutions in *The Structure of Scientific Revolutions* understands how normal science, as the rule, is undermined by revolutionary science, as the exception, after enquiries and realities expose anomalies in the normal science (Kuhn 1970). The shift in paradigms results from anomalies undermining normal science and revolutionary science becomes the normal science. When David Marquand (1999) assesses Britain's apparent move away from its "old constitution", it is asserted that it never was "the crystalline monolith of Dicey's imagining" but instead, it "… was a palimpsest of sometimes discordant myths, understandings, and expectations, reflecting the changing values and preoccupations of succeeding generations" (Marquand 1999, p. 3). In so far as critics can accept that understanding of change being reworked in a palimpsest, the concept has some validity. Marquand holds that the Crown-in-Parliament has proceeded in several forms in the older forms of the constitution, reflecting Dicey's "monolithic" view.

In contrast, in the following scheme, it is proposed that historical forms are simply passing, in the palimpsest into another new phase (the eighth constitutional form). The Crown-in-Parliament formulation therefore never really belonged *only* to the old constitution or to Dicey's monolithic view which, for all its faults (discussed in Chapter 2), appeared overwhelmingly practical for judges and common lawyers and utilised throughout the legal and political establishment. Most importantly, the eight constitutional forms, including the most recent historical form, reinforce Marquand's view of the constitution as a palimpsest. The principles and features of each of the eight constitutional forms described below illustrate the textual redrafting—the political pacts and major legislative and political precedents between each of the features within the forms—which in many ways help to grapple with the historical development of the constitutional forms.

3.1 The Making of the Present: Historical Transitions in Constitutional Conventions and Form

3.1.1 Constitutional Form One: 'What the Crown-with-Magnates Enacts Is Law' (1200–1350)

The understanding of sovereignty as *gubernaculum*, government through the helm of the ship of state, can first be understood from the vantage point of the period of medieval kingship in the centuries preceding the Reformation in the thirteenth and fourteenth centuries (Harding 1993; Kantorowicz 1957; McIlwain 1947), if not more broadly to the reign of Anglo-Saxon monarch Athelstan (924–939) (History of Parliament Trust 2015, p. 12). That characterisation is expressed as divine monarchical sovereignty-with-magnates—*divine* in its claim to power and right but in consultation with magnates in council. In simple terms, the unequal theory of the 'Crown rules' model only ever really existed as an alternate model of unequal power—'the Crown rules by consulting with magnates' (Box 3.1). The Crown's sovereignty within the helm of the ship of state is checked by barons (originally, the 'Curia Regis'). The ultimate rule sat in equilibrium with that particular political condition to bolster the rule.

Sovereignty provides a ranked ultimate rule, conferring supremacy on the acknowledged God-ordained power of the Crown, which existed within an embracing condition—the elevating of the magnates to create a more powerful authority than the Crown could possess alone. The word 'parliament' is itself first used in England in the thirteenth century to describe the broad meetings of the monarch's counsel with barons, bishops and prominent royal servants, advising the Crown on law-making, administrative matters and to assist in judicial decisions (Payling 2013; Jack et al. 2011). The divine power behind the Crown-magnate power concept described in this historical constitutional form can be explained, in the writings of the judge Henry de Bracton (1210–1268). In this tradition, the Crown is held under God and under the law, understood as moral duty (on that point, see Goldsworthy 2010, p. 24), consistently pursued in accordance with his own goodwill, reinforced by baronial counsel, but importantly acted upon under the threat of divine retribution (see Van Duffel 2004, pp. 157–158; Goldsworthy 1999; Nederman 1988; Wyclif 1378 in Nederman and Forhan 1993, p. 223; see Le Van Baumer 1940, p. 57; McIlwain 1910, p. 97). The capacity to govern through the Crown's sovereignty at the helm of the medieval state, was only bound to natural and divine law as moral duty—but "above the law" in his status as Crown, by prerogative power, unconstrained by positive law (Goldsworthy 1999; Kantorowicz 1957, p. 149). Ultimately, for Bracton, the law and the law-making Crown were "mutually conditioned", reciprocal and interdependent at the helm, even though the Crown retained the power to govern the realm (Kantorowicz 1957, pp. 153, 155).

The Crown was the undoubted pinnacle of a legal system, the heart and essence of the English political system—and his law "eternal like the stars" (Van Duffel 2004, p. 156; Bradford 2011)—but it is with the combined role of the earls that his power is really buttressed. As Donald Hanson maintains, "... the answer of the great twelfth and thirteenth century law books to fundamental questions was that such matters lay with the monarch and the magnates of the realm" (Hanson 1970, p. 180; Loughlin 2010, p. 246). Parliament developed out of the medieval convention of baronial counsel, it was the 'Crown's Parliament', the Crown being forced to accept its importance (on the former point, see Goldsworthy 1999, p. 28; on the latter point, see Bradford 2011). Sovereignty had already developed through political institutions, depersonalised from the physical persons embodying political authority (Bartelson 2011; Loughlin and Tierney 2018, p. 997). That 'royal' power exercised by the sovereign which allowed the Crown to do as she pleased insofar as it was consistent with fundamental law, was an earl-reinforced power of the Crown, not any 'joint' parliamentary power as such. Such a view does not conform to a divine-right theory of the Crown because under medieval kingships, it was only possible to affirm a ranked ultimate rule, conferring supremacy not merely on the Crown, as such, but the buttressing of the Crown's ultimate authority by the earls. Magna Carta of 1215 began to codify the means by which the Crown should seek counsel (Nelson 2015a). Simon de Montfort's parliament of 1265 shows knights and townspeople could be called upon to advise on questions of the realm in the Crown's name (Nelson 2015b; History of Parliament Trust 2015, p. 21). This reflected a broader structure of authority and not solely with the Crown, nor sovereignty within Parliament per se.

Sovereignty performed a function within the helm of the ship of state. Sovereignty was exercised through the use of baronial counsel to raise taxes for 'defence' of territory and pass law to dispense justice (Bradford 2011). The sense of sovereignty as the power of the Crown to command and make law, is not given primary status because the conditioned Crown-earl sovereignty is primarily achieved through the instrumental control of wealth and nobility and political actors within that realm. That control is pursued in order to defend or gain territory and achieve war through taxation and only secondarily, enable law to satisfy those assenting barons from the shires and boroughs. Sovereignty did require the perceived claim to 'unified' representation (not democratic) and was developed by the 1260s into the 'quid pro quo' principle of the Crown maintaining broader consent and representation from localities because of the necessary taxation for Crown revenues and war (Loughlin 2010, p. 251; Payling 2013; Norton 2013, p. 18; Bradford 2011; see also Payling 1999, p. 241).

The formula in the first constitutional form of 'What the Crown-with-magnates enacts is law' (1200–1350) in balance with political powers, is at odds with the neo-Diceyan view. It is overtly concerned with political power. The sovereignty is affirmed by a ranked ultimate rule, that is a supremacy of the acknowledged Crown-with-magnates. Sovereignty performed a function within the helm of the ship of state—it was exercised through the consent of baronial counsel to raise taxes for defence of territory and pass law to dispense justice (History of Parliament Trust 2015, pp. 12–17). The 'rule at the helm' required the perceived claim to representation for the governance of the realm. In the first constitutional form, the understanding of the commanding power of the Crown to make law is not given primary status. That is because sovereignty is achieved through other means and only in its finale, to give law to satisfy those assenting barons from the shires and boroughs.

Box 3.1: Constitutional Form One: 'What the Crown-with-Magnates Enacts Is Law' (1200–1350)

- Thirteenth and fourteenth century constitutional form of sovereignty defined by the Crown with magnates.
- Sovereignty exercised by the Crown as divine power, increasingly subject to fundamental law, moral duty and baronial counsel.
- The helm of the ship of state governed by the Crown advised by counsel.
- Perceived claim to representation necessary for generating taxation for Crown revenues.
- Sovereignty is overtly political, not legal, albeit increasing codification of means through which the Crown should seek counsel.
- Crown's power to govern is mutually conditioned by fundamental law/rights understood as moral duty.

3.1.2 Constitutional Form Two: 'What the Crown-with-Commons Enacts Is Law' (1350–1532)

In the second constitutional form, by the mid-fourteenth century, the characterisation of parliamentary sovereignty which developed in the pre-Reformation period is geared towards a petitionable Crown in Parliament with representatives. The ultimate rule that the Crown rules with an occasional and separate counsel transforms into a Crown ruling with an increasingly relevant Commons. It became the high crossroad of power networks, an unparalleled rendezvous point, where Crown and Parliament could barter in interests, power and money. Fortescue's (1395–1477) then leading assessment of England's *dominium politicum et regale*, as government being both political and regal, signifies the essential character of the Crown needing to rule with the parliament to gain consent (Koenigsberger 1978, 1989). The ultimate rule required particular political features, including the representation by petition and impeachment of officers (History of Parliament Trust 2015, p. 20; Loughlin 2010, p. 256), to make the rule a reality.

The meaning of sovereignty as the ultimate rule expressing the legitimate authority gained through the conditional exercise of a petitionable sovereign was already well-formed in the first constitutional form or by 1341 at least (see Norton 2013, p. 18), and developed under extended modes of representation. Those steps tipped the balance from monarchical sovereignty to the Reformation's conditions necessary for some degree of parliamentary rule. In this constitutional form, defining parliamentary sovereignty in terms of the Crown relative to the fast-developing but poorly-attended Parliament meant a fuller Commons and Lords having developed from substantial political changes, including the widening basis of county- and town-representing (see Quinault 2012; Goldsworthy 1999). Shire representatives 'represented' those in 1430 with an annual income of at least 40 shillings and with freehold land (History of Parliament Trust 2015, p. 24; Payling 1999, p. 244). Although not in the English tradition, Marsiglio of Padua's *Defensor Pacis* in the fourteenth century is a European example of law-making by a loose quasi-representation—it provides a basis for the singular authority for the creation, alteration and revision of law as the *legislator humanus,* which is composed of the whole body of citizens (Lee 2009; Nederman 1991, p. 23).

Sovereignty existed in the sense that Parliament marginally began to exercise its own power and influence, for example, through the depositions of monarchs (History of Parliament Trust 2015, pp. 20, 22). In that context, factions of magnates from the realm arranged for validation of the removal of a monarch (such as Richard III in 1485) by parliamentary assent (Jones 2012, p. 24). During the constitutional upheavals of the fifteenth century involving the depositions of monarchs, leading to fifteenth century monarchs desiring parliamentary validation of the title to the throne, there is a great deal of evidence testifying to the highest authority attributed to a Parliament representing the entire community (Goldsworthy 1999, p. 31). In discourse, however, neither Parliament nor Crown sought to guarantee claims to 'exclusive sovereignty' (Le Van Baumer 1940, p. 3).

There is an acceptance of the condition that the Crown, within the Parliament, stood equated with the highest law-making authority, signifying the equalising of government with the ability to legislate. The supremacy of the English Parliament in making the highest law continued to be accepted and expressed among the essentially conservative political, royal and lawyerly elite of the period (Le Van Baumer 1940, p. 3). The prevalence of natural or fundamental law also meant that there was no theory of 'absolute monarchy' (Le Van Baumer 1940, p. 6). Fortescue who served as a Member of Parliament, Chief Justice of England and Lord Chancellor, saw that the entire body of the realm according to the laws of England was represented in Parliament (Goldsworthy 1999, p. 41). England enjoyed *dominium politicum et regale*, not merely *dominium regale*, the government being both political and regal and the Crown by himself unable to change the law of the land (Le Van Baumer 1940, p. 10).

The formula in the second constitutional form of 'What the Crown-with-Commons enacts is law' (1350–1532) in balance with particular political conditions and constitutional conventions (Box 3.2) is inconsistent with the neo-Diceyan view. Sovereignty as an ultimate rule expressing the legitimate authority gained through the conditional exercise of a petitionable sovereign was acknowledged. It is founded around the extension of representation to the 40 shilling per annum landowners. Parliament had developed its own power, influence and independence, albeit not as an exclusive power. The relationship signifies the increasing alignment of government with the power to legislate, realised as the Crown located within a politically subordinate Parliament as the highest legal authority.

Box 3.2 Constitutional Form Two: 'What the Crown-with-Commons Enacts Is Law' (1350–1532)

- A constitutional form of the late fourteenth century to the Reformation in which sovereignty is defined by Crown with the Commons.
- The Crown rules with the Commons but increasingly bound, not only advised by, the Commons activity.
- Widening representation through the use of petitions, county- and town-representing, and impeachment of officers.
- Equalising of power at helm of state with capacity to pass law i.e. *dominium politicum et regale.*
- Parliamentary validation of the title to the throne.
- The Crown's power to govern continues to be mutually conditioned by fundamental law/rights understood as moral duty.
- Electorate of men with freehold estate of 40 shillings or more from the shires.

3.1.3 *Constitutional Form Three: 'What the Crown*-Through-*Parliament Enacts Is Law' (1533–1602)*

Although in the Reformation period, the real fundamental question that remained, given that the rival Crown *versus* Church supremacies had been addressed after 1533 was that England had been left with a self-regulating Church separated from a Parliament which is sovereign (Bogdanor 1997, p. 225). It confirmed the assumption of legislative sovereignty by 1539/40 (see Keir 1968, p. 117; Goldsworthy 1999, p. 55). That stage also confirms Parliament's omnicompetence (Loughlin 2010, p. 254)—that no area involved in the government of realm was outside its authority. The sovereign working through the omnicompetent Parliament of the sixteenth century helped to define the meaning of parliamentary sovereignty. The omnicompetence is important because it conveys how close the Parliament was coming to independence and a wide stable of functions, in the service of the power it sought.

In the third constitutional form, the ultimate rule that the Crown rules with a Commons transforms into a Crown needing to rule through Parliament. The ultimate rule of 'What the Crown-*through*-Parliament enacts is law' (1533–1602) required equilibrium with the political features, including that omnicompetence, to make the rule a reality. It was maintained widely by the political elite of the period that the Crown in Parliament indisputably had legal omnicompetence (e.g. Keir 1968, p. 135; Le Van Baumer 1940, p. 1). While sovereignty as government became reducible to the principle of legal competence, there was still a strong sense of its operation outside legal controls and therefore, despotic. Under the Reformation Parliament, Parliament was considered the supreme legislator and not held back by other laws or types of law-makers, overriding both the crown and the courts (Seaward 2013). St German's 'Doctor and Student', first published in 1523, argued that the Crown in Parliament was omnicompetent, able to legislate on both temporal and spiritual matters under the dictum, *jus regale politicum*—and represented the Church. As a defender of parliamentary sovereignty, St German also held that human law was subordinate to natural law (as in medieval political theory, and also, Fortescue, Blackstone and Austin) which was preserved on the basis that Parliament would never seek to violate natural law (Goldsworthy 1999, pp. 71–72; Le Van Baumer 1940, pp. 150–151). The UK Parliament (2014) asserts that the omnicompetence meant that "no area involved in the government of the realm was outside its authority" (see also Elton 1986, p. 36) and that is viewed as a wholly "unexceptional" view (see also Roskell 1993; Denton 1981, p. 88). Sovereignty in this constitutional form is invested in an omnicompetent Parliament, wide in its functions to the extent that Parliament could do anything except the impossible—an issue which Blackstone (1765) reiterates in his later definition in the eighteenth century.

There was an obvious contestation in the interpretation because—despite an absence of a "deep-seated quarrel" about the supremacy of the Crown and Parliament in general, as Le Van Baumer argues—there remained significant division about the nature of authority. Royalist theories supporting Crown-sanctioned statute with the advice and assistance of the Lords, Commons and High Court of Parliament conflicted with parliamentarian theories in which the Crown, Lords and Commons in Parliament shared supreme legislative power and in collectively representing the community (Le Van Baumer 1940, pp. 143–163). Nonetheless, sovereignty was exercised as authority on the tacitly accepted principle of the lawful taxation by common consent, in addition to the Crown requiring consent for the validity of legislation (latterly, see Le Van Baumer 1940, p. 143). Even in parliamentarian theories of the fifteenth and sixteenth century, it was widely assumed that all members of the community were represented in Parliament and the consent of Parliament was equated with the consent of every man (see John Hooker and Thomas Smith, in Dean 1998, p. 8). The division and competition in Royalist and Parliamentarian arguments, nonetheless, strongly suggests that sovereignty as supremacy was not a question of primacy of the Crown (ruling)-*through*-Parliament, but on the different ranking of all other principles relative to the ultimate rule.

Parliament's sovereignty was predicated upon a basic acknowledgment of the Crown, Lords and Commons in a mixed constitution, combining elements of monarchy, aristocracy and democracy. It was an avoidance device against an excessive concentration of power which would undermine freedom. The argument owes some debt to the language offered by the Greco-Roman theory of the mixed constitution, particularly the second-century BC, Polybius (Gagarin 2010), as a checking power of the political body (Bellamy 1996, p. 441). It also emphasises a re-interpretation of Aristotle which produced an equating of political rule with a mixed constitution (Blythe 1992, p. 12). The constitutional conventions of the Lords, Commons and Crown within a mixed government polity of monarchical, aristocratic, and democratic aspects, was a fundamental point in the sixteenth century constitution (Goldsworthy 1999, p. 75).

The third constitutional form defined by 'What the Crown-*through*-Parliament enacts is law' (1533–1602)—reflected the events and Tudor rule during the Reformation, and stood in contrast to the rule and Parliament under the Early Stuarts. The rule in the third constitutional form in equilibrium with its constitutional convention of legislative omnicompetence, is not a neo-Diceyan view. The Crown-through-Parliament had legal omnicompetence and while sovereignty as government was viewed through the lens of legal competence, there was a strong sense of its operation outside strict legal controls i.e. a royal despotic power (see Box 3.3). The supremacy of the ultimate rule exists but the ranking of principles relating to the Crown, Lords, Commons and the consenting community as a source of power is questioned. There is a wider acknowledgement of Parliament's sovereignty as predicated upon the Crown, Lords and Commons in a mixed constitution, the three estates being responsible for the governance of the realm.

Box 3.3 Constitutional Form Three: 'What the Crown-through-Parliament Enacts Is Law' (1533–1602)

- Sovereignty defined after the Reformation is increasingly derived from the Crown through Parliament (Parliamentarian theory), not simply the Crown with Parliament (Royalist).
- An assumption is made of legislative sovereignty after 1539/1540.
- Reformation Parliament is said to gain omnicompetence e.g. *jus regale politicum*, in which no area involved in the government of the realm is outside of its authority, but royal despotic power is exercised.
- The Crown did require consent for lawful taxation and legislation.
- The Crown, Lords and Commons exist within a mixed powers constitution.
- The Crown's power to govern is mutually conditioned by fundamental law/rights understood as moral duty.
- An assumption is made of parliamentary representation of the political community as the consent of every man. Electorate of men with freehold estate of 40 shillings or more from the shires.

3.1.4 Constitutional Form Four: 'What the Crown-with-Disputed Parliament Enacts Is Law' (1603–1687)

The fourth constitutional form's parliamentary sovereignty, formed from great instability and uncertainty during the Early Stuart period, reflected the immense turmoil of the country at large during the period (see Keir 1968, p. 231). The ultimate rule operated in balance with often irreconcilable political conditions of a 'divine right' theory Crown, the argument that sovereignty rested with the immemorial, ancient common law constitution (Pocock 1987), and that sovereignty rested with the Crown-in-Parliament, in order to make the rule a reality. The sovereignty expressed in the constitutional form of the 'unappealable' parliament by the Crown, by common law, or by community, in Early Stuart England and throughout the English Civil Wars is perhaps more divided against itself than under any other form. Under constitutional form four, the ultimate rule that the Crown rules *through* Parliament, because of civil war challenges to sovereignty, develops tangentially into the Crown attempting to rule only *with* a disputed Parliament. However, it is not until the issue is so substantively contested under the fifth form that the principle of the Crown-*in*-Parliament is proven so fundamental.

First, in this constitutional form, given the dispute over supremacy and ranking of principle, there was a practical (though widely disputed) reassertion of parliamentarian theory (Goldsworthy 1999). It made the assertion that God conferred powers of government on the community as a whole—rather than directly on the Crown (Royalist) or that there was some ancient common law constitution (common law) (Pocock 1987, p. 124). In turn, the community had delegated them to the Crown in so far as he made laws and imposed taxes through the consenting Parliament (e.g. Goldsworthy 1999, pp. 79–124). The argument for the supremacy of the Crown with Parliament had prevailed after the English Civil War and Cromwell's death although great uncertainty remained in the competing Royalist, Parliamentarian and common law narratives. The English Civil War involving the replacement of the monarch with the Commonwealth of England followed by the Protectorate under Oliver, then Richard Cromwell, demonstrated an important facet of the constitution: the Crown could no longer govern without parliamentary consent. Even within those narratives, there remained disagreement, for example, on whether Parliament was infallible, or final, or unappealable, and whether religious tension was still itself the basis of the tensions over the Crown with Parliament (Orr 2002).

Second, the competition in political ranking of principle perseveres between the three categories for those who made claims to sovereignty. The political theories explaining the sovereignty of Parliament in early Stuart England, which are by no means mutually exclusive, can be characterised by three different schools. Theorists such as Maitland (1908, p. 298) held that in the first half of the seventeenth century, there were three categories for those who made claims to sovereignty, namely, the Crown, the Crown in Parliament, and the law. Those three different schools are essentially elaborated upon in this period as (i) Royalist; (ii) Parliamentarian; and (iii) common law defences. In the latter, confusingly, both Crown and Parliament were said to have derived powers from a supposed ancient constitution, consisting of fundamental principles of common law, which regulated the balance between the two and was legally superior to both (Goldsworthy 1999, p. 78; Somerville 1986).

Third, Sir Edward Coke in *Dr. Bonham's* case undermined the previously acknowledged ultimate rule by upholding in 1610 that statute could be invalidated by the courts on the basis of the common law, right and reason. It is a judgement often used to support common law theorists (Goldsworthy 2010, p. 18). Coke stated,

> [I]t appears in our books, that in many cases, the common law will controul Acts of Parliament, and sometimes adjudge them to be utterly void: for when an Act of Parliament is against common right and reason, or repugnant, or impossible to be performed, the common law will controul it, and adjudge such Act to be void. (Sir Edward Coke, *Dr. Bonham's Case* [1610])

The radical common law theorists of early Stuart England incorporated Roman law doctrine in which the sovereign's absolute powers were claimed to be derived from primitive acts of a sovereign people (*lex regia*) and, therefore, sovereignty need not exist or belong to one holder along monarchical lines (Lee 2016, pp. 289–290).

Within this fourth constitutional form, the understanding of Parliament is extremely divided in the interpretations of the foundational powers underlying the sovereign, of common law and the community in

Early Stuart England. The unworkable formula is expressed in the fourth constitutional form of 'What the Crown-with-disputed Parliament enacts is law' (1603–1687) (Box 3.4). The form required extreme balance with its competing political conditions of Crown, common law or Crown with Parliament, overwhelming the legalistic, neo-Diceyan definition. There was a dispute over the ranking of principle of Crown and common law in relation to the supremacy of parliament but parliamentarian theory prevailed in practice following the Civil War and the Restoration. Competing claims to sovereignty were made for the Crown, the Crown in parliament or the law.

In contemporary legal and political thought, the recent "renaissance" in those divisions between common law theorists (e.g. Allan 2013; on that renaissance, see Tomkins 2010) and traditional legal sovereignist views (e.g. Goldsworthy 1999; Hart 1997; Tomkins 2003) continue to feed through into the defence of, and challenges to, Dicey's traditional definition.

Box 3.4 Constitutional Form Four: 'What the Crown-with-Disputed Parliament Enacts Is Law' (1603–1687)

- Sovereignty defined in the early Stuart period and the Restoration is less derived from Crown-through-Parliament, increasingly by the Crown-with-Parliament.
- The Parliament rules with the Crown but disputed foundations of Crown, ancient common law or consenting community.
- A distinct emphasis, however erroneous, is placed on the common law constitution as a foundation of sovereignty.
- The Crown's power to govern is bound, it is claimed, by the assertion of an ancient common law, now understood as legal (not moral) duty.
- With no consensus, the monarchy was finally restored and with the assumption of legislative authority of the monarch with Parliament.
- Continued assumption is made of parliamentary representation of the political community.
- Electorate of men with freehold estate of 40 shillings or more from the shires.

3.1.5 *Constitutional Form Five: 'What the Crown-in-Regulating Parliament Enacts Is Law' (1688–1689)*

Since 1689, the monarchy has owed its title to parliament and the great constitutional struggles of the seventeenth century that meant that the royal succession could be regulated by parliament (Bogdanor 1997, p. 43). Against the Royalist-absolutist schools was an account of parliamentary sovereignty provided in the post-Restoration, pre-Revolution political situation. The fifth constitutional form is an unbundling of 'What the Crown-in-regulating Parliament enacts is law' theorised before the Revolution and crystallised in 1688/1689 and the political structures which developed out of that 'first modern revolution' (Pincus 2009). The settlement of 1688 and 1689 resolves the dispute of Crown with Parliament to the Crown embedded in and regulated by Parliament. Before the Revolution of 1688, the conflict between monarchists, Parliamentarians, the Whigs and of the latter, John Locke's view of parliamentary sovereignty—including the supreme legislative within the separation of powers and strongly reliant upon the consent of the political community—illustrates the redefining of that concept and the political arguments up to 1688 and well beyond (Goldsworthy 1999, p. 50). Locke and the English revolutionaries of 1688 "created a new kind of modern state"—it did not set a precedent for future politics, but following calls for a free Parliament, "merely reasserted parliamentary sovereignty" (Pincus 2009, pp. 28, 238–253).

This definition and the previous constitutional form are about the omnipotency of Parliament and Locke's legislative is a deliberate attempt to unite the *trust* of the community with that Parliament via a balanced and mixed constitution (on the mixed constitution, see Lieberman 2006, p. 319; Weston and Greenberg 1981; Weston 1965); a mix which had been an impossibility under a Hobbesian sovereign unity, centred upon the requirement for the finality of sovereign authority (Hoekstra 2013, pp. 1080–1081; Bourke 1999, p. 108). The Crown is finally under the powers of the legislature (Wade 1955), the courts are denied the power to limit Parliament's sovereignty (Bradley 2011; Bradley and Ewing 2010) and the representative claim to Parliament has developed its own independence. The ultimate rule was balanced against the political conditions and constitutional conventions, including that elective trust relationship, in making the rule a reality. That rule-based view of legislating within Locke's *Second Treatise of Civil Government*, complements his approach toward a Westphalian state (Prokhovnik 2008, p. 82; Locke 1988), governed through the supremacy of the legislature. Contemporary Lockean scholars have not always accepted on the whole the contribution of Locke's view to parliamentary sovereignty (e.g. Franklin 1981). However, Locke's Parliament is a people-sanctioned ruling legislative power which is consensual, elective, representative, majoritarian and in which the electorate publicly participate on the basis of trust. Accordingly, his view of sovereignty in action is the entrusting of parliamentary law-making by majority representation (*Second Treatise* 1988, pp. 154, 157, 158).

The creation of the fundamental rule resolved the conflict between the Crown and Parliament protecting the succession and prerogatives of the Crown from statute which crystallised into the Bill of Rights of 1689 and limited the powers of the Crown in relation to parliament, and thereby established a parliamentary monarchy (Bogdanor 1997, p. 5). Locke's understanding of the supremacy of the legislative in the *Second Treatise*—which, in England's case, he presented as the Crown, Lords and Commons assembled together—had been predicated on several important assumptions. At its core, the trust that electors placed in representatives to sit in the legislature means that those representatives must duly act in accordance with the consent given to them.

The Lockean and wider liberal tradition referred to sovereignty as being refocused through the tighter definition of a people-sanctioned, law-making legislature. Previously, greater ruler sovereignty had been equated with the older tyranny. Subsequently, law was required to replace the possibility of tyrannical forms of extra-legal decision-making. By permitting an understanding of parliamentary sovereignty within a framework which accounts for those conditions, it may allow us to focus on Raia Prokhovnik's critical observation that "The liberal tradition in implicit ways redefines political sovereignty in terms of legal sovereignty, reduces politics to the implementation of law, and so works with a depleted notion of what might be called ruler sovereignty" (Prokhovnik 2008, p. 2).

The fifth constitutional form evidenced an omnipotent Parliament operating on trust with the sovereign during the events of 1688/1689. The formula in the fifth constitutional form of 'What the Crown-in-regulating Parliament enacts is law' (1688–1689) requires balance with key political conditions, and new constitutional conventions (Box 3.5). As such, this form both affirms and reviews the neo-Diceyan definition. The sovereignty is affirmed by an ultimate rule-based view of legislating through a Westphalian state governed by the supremacy of the legislative. John Locke's Parliament is theorised as a people-sanctioned ruling legislative power which is elective, representative and majoritarian and in which people participate on the basis of trust. The creation of the ultimate rule at the helm establishes a parliamentary monarchy. Broad political sovereignty is refocused through the lens of institutionalised, legislative law-making because ruler sovereignty is associated with a tyrannical past. A people-sanctioned legislative power, with its laws, replaces the extra-legal decision-making inherent to tyranny.

Box 3.5 Constitutional Form Five: 'What the Monarch-in-Regulating Parliament Enacts Is Law' (1688–1689)

- Theorised before the revolutionary events of 1688/1689.
- Sovereignty is established in the form of a parliamentary monarchy.
- The Crown is brought under the powers of the omnipotent legislature.
- The Courts are thereby denied the power to limit Parliament's sovereignty.
- The Crown power to govern continues to be mutually conditioned by fundamental law, understood however as moral duty, not as a legal duty. The claimed supremacy of an ancient common law constitution is limited by the settled supremacy of Parliament.
- The representative claim to gaining consent through a consensual, elective, representation and majoritarian Parliament develops its own independence.
- Broad political sovereignty is tied to a tighter definition of legal sovereignty.
- An electorate of men with a freehold estate of 40 shillings or more from the shires.

3.1.6 *Constitutional Form Six: 'What the Crown-*in*-Mixed Constitutional Parliament Enacts Is Law' (1690–1790s)*

The status of sovereignty as it was stated in the ultimate rule in the eighteenth century reflected the 1688/1689 settlement, the 1707 Union and the rivalling of popular sovereignty with Parliament's sovereignty. The ultimate rule required balance and accommodation of its changing political conditions (Loughlin and Tierney 2018, p. 992), including a mixed constitution, to support the rule. The Whiggish ultimate rule that the Crown is embedded in and regulated by Parliament prevails and is justified increasingly by the balance of monarchical (Crown), aristocratic (Lords) and democratic (Commons representing people) powers.

The Revolution of 1688 is said to have vindicated the parliamentarian theory of the Whigs and, with it, the view that sovereignty was entrusted to the Crown in Parliament rather than only the Crown (Quinault 2012; Goldsworthy 1999, p. 159; Williams 1962, p. 3; Clark 1956, p. 150). Eighteenth century theorists appear to be forced to either endorse or reassess that premise. The supremacy conferred by the ultimate rule over the legislative power, as a power which had been derived from the Crown, was generally accepted by legal and political theorists. The most recognised voice on the concept of parliamentary sovereignty in the eighteenth century in relation to the laws of England is Blackstone (1765). In 1765, he wrote of Parliament that it has sovereign and uncontrollable authority. It was an absolute despotic power entrusted by the constitution, and could do anything unless of course it was naturally impossible (Lubert 2010; Goldsworthy 1999, p. 202; Blackstone 1765). Blackstone adopted from Montesquieu (1748) the idea of a balanced tripartite constitution of mixed, separate-but-coordinated powers between the executive, legislature and judicial elements (Lieberman 1999, p. 22; 2006, pp. 318, 335). In the eighteenth century, it is said that "… the Whig conception of a sovereign Parliament had hardened into an orthodoxy given its classic formulation by Sir William Blackstone in 1765" (Jezierski 1971, p. 96). An Act of Parliament was the execution of the highest authority of the kingdom. It could bind every subject, including the Crown, and could not be repealed, amended, altered or dispensed with unless Parliament chose to do so. Constitutionally close to Blackstone, Montesquieu's *The Spirit of the Laws* (1748) has a section dealing with the English 'power checks power' constitution (Bellamy 1996, p. 443) in which the executive and the two branches of the legislative act as checks on one another yet the judicial power and tribunals of law are subordinate to the legislation (Lubert 2010; Goldsworthy 1999, contra Jenkins 2011, p. 577; de Montesquieu 1748). Again, Adam Smith's jurisprudence lectures in the 1760s emphasise parliamentary sovereignty—laying with the Crown and Parliament—"The authority of the Parliament in some things, of the King and Parliament in others" and "in whatever place there is a sovereign, from the very nature of things the power must be absolute" (Bourke 1999, p. 109). In terms of parliamentary representation, however, during this period and up to 1832, the voter is only essentially a yeoman with a freehold estate with a value of 40 shillings who collectively formed an electorate of a shire (Baskerville 1998, p. 48; Dean 1998). The acknowledging of the Whiggish constitutional rules resulted from an elite political consensus. The 'formalised conflict' between Whig and Tory parties (Loughlin 2010, p. 265; Loughlin and Tierney 2018, p. 994) depends on the Tories accepting that legislative sovereignty belonged to the Crown in Parliament (not the Crown alone) and the Whigs accepting that the people could not be trusted beyond a limited political role (Goldsworthy 1999, p. 176).

Another important condition, or convention, for parliamentary sovereignty in this context is the idea of a mixed constitution, to preserve political freedom by preventing and checking arbitrary acts of power (see also Kors 2012; Lieberman 2006, p. 317), initially discussed in relation to the third constitutional form in the sixteenth century. Blackstone, Burke and many other key political figures in eighteenth century England described the British constitution as being a well-balanced combination of different forms of government—monarchical, aristocratic and democratic—each balancing out the other (Lieberman 2006, p. 318; Blackstone 1765, pp. i, 50–52). The meaning of the sovereignty of Parliament for Edmund Burke, like Locke, is located within a balanced constitution configured around a triangulated trust between the Crown and Parliament (see Craig 2012, pp. 106–108). The mixed constitution was important to Burke, in the 1760s, because "What mattered most to him were the chains of trust that existed between these elements and that were crucial to the effectiveness of government" (Craig 2012, p. 108). The constitution was not perfect and historical political circumstances generally reflected a ramshackle system held together by a poorly integrated composite state (O'Gorman 2012). The Prime Minister and Cabinet also first appeared (Norton 2013, p. 20) as an early sign of the growth of government. Nonetheless, both Court Whigs and Tories boasted of the equilibrium between the Crown, Lords and Commons (Goldsworthy 1999, p. 200). Judicial review was in this context not considered necessary for a system in which the Commons claimed to represent the electors and the Crown and the Lords checked that relationship.

A reform movement in the last few decades of the eighteenth century attempted to challenge parliamentary sovereignty, including the arguments of John Wilkes, Thomas Paine and radical Whigs. They had maintained that the people and not parliamentary sovereignty prevailed, until this notion itself was discredited by the actions of the French Revolution and the fears of a French invasion of England by Napoleon. Nonetheless, European conceptions of sovereignty came to rest upon the will of the people (Bartelson 2011).

The ultimate rule in the sixth constitutional form of 'What the Crown-*in*-mixed constitutional Parliament enacts is law' requires balance against its political conditions of the mixed constitution to support the rule (Box 3.6). The neo-Diceyan approach gives no direct credit to the mixed constitution in understanding parliamentary sovereignty. The ultimate rule conferred supremacy upon the unlimited and absolute power of Parliament. The rule was fixed by a Tory-Whig consensus, agreeing on the Crown-in-Parliament, but with a limited role of the people. Power was exercised within the mixed constitution of the Crown, Lords and Commons. For theorists such as Edmund Burke, a partition of the mixed governmental powers was perfectly consistent with the indivisibility of sovereign authority (Bourke 1999).

Box 3.6 Constitutional Form Six: 'What the Crown-in-Mixed Constitutional Parliament Enacts Is Law' (1690–1790s)

- The eighteenth-century formulation of sovereignty bolstered by a mixed, balanced constitution.
- Parliamentary oligarchy has an uncontrollable, despotic sovereign power combined with a commitment to limited government.
- A balanced and mixed, 'power checks power' constitution of the monarchical (monarch), aristocratic (Lords) and democratic (Commons representing people) powers.
- Tories concede that legislative sovereignty belongs to the Crown in Parliament.
- Whigs concede that people cannot be trusted beyond a limited political role.
- The power to govern continues to be mutually conditioned by fundamental law understood as moral duty (not legal) duty. The claimed supremacy of an ancient common law constitution figures heavily in dialogue but is closed off in practice by the supremacy of Parliament.
- Reform movements to undermine parliamentary sovereignty are discredited by the activities of the French Revolution.
- An electorate of men with a freehold estate of 40 shillings or more from the shires.

3.1.7 Constitutional Form Seven: 'What the Crown-in-Parliamentary Cabinet Enacts Is Law' (1800–1972)

By the nineteenth century, the doctrine of parliamentary sovereignty had been taken for granted by lawyers and political theorists. The ultimate rule that the Crown is embedded *in* and regulated by Parliament prevails and is justified increasingly by the efficient leadership of ministerial Cabinet powers at the centre of the House of Commons. It is conceptualised as an aristocratically elite representative Parliament making law without external direction. The ultimate rule requires balance against its political conventions, including its representative function and the absence of external direction of government, to support the rule. Sir Thomas Erskine May—whose guidelines continue to be utilised today in Parliament in an updated form—reported in his first edition of the 'Treatise on the Law, Privileges, Proceedings and Usage of Parliament' (May 1844) the legislative authority of Parliament was not subject to limits. There were no limits other than when the people should no longer wish to obey and therefore resist (Dicey 1964; Loughlin and Tierney 2018, p. 995). More straightforwardly, even with a limited franchise, the people could elect a different parliament. The context to the supremacy and ranking of an ultimate rule in this constitutional form is one of a mixed, fluid constitution, with a "plastic power of self-amelioration", yet whose Whig reformers thought of their reforms "on a trajectory towards democracy" (Saunders 2011, p. 9). They were, by its fluidity, explaining a seemingly stable constitution against the background of major revolution in Europe in 1848.

John Stuart Mill in 1885 expressed a more liberal, representative, community-bearing, majoritarian-led, Commons-focused theorising of sovereignty. Mill held that the ideal form of government which Britain retained is that in which sovereignty as the supreme controlling power is held by the aggregate of the community (see Turner 2010, p. 29; Begby 2003; see also Goldsworthy 1999, p. 226). The strong claims to the representative Parliament presupposes a process of internal, domestic representation and thereby an absence, or limitation, on external direction of government.

Walter Bagehot's Victorian study of what he called the English constitution recognised the ultimate power within the legislative as the single ultimate authority. His executive-in-Commons theory meant that he endorsed legislative sovereignty achieved through fused Cabinet-legislative powers as efficient (Bagehot 2001). In the English context, the mixed constitution characterised an 'equilibrium' or 'balance' in the constitution and summed up an essential feature of the seventeenth and eighteenth-century constitution by a diverse number of political theorists including Montesquieu (1748), Blackstone (1765), and Burke (1774). However, for all its sworn primacy, Walter Bagehot, his disciples and many other theorists in the nineteenth century insisted not on the antiquated doctrine of the mixed constitution (Francis and Morrow 1994, p. 10). Instead, Bagehot argued that within the constitution, the Cabinet was the central institution of British government, set within the fusion of legislative and executive powers, and not their separation or mix (Bagehot 2001; Loughlin 2010, p. 267). Bagehot's Commons had that efficiency and despotic formality to conclude an issue without external requirement/obligation and internationally sovereignty was exercised through quietism and restraint (see Clinton 2003). The interest in efficiency made Bagehot and others less concerned with any notion of a balanced, mixed constitution of checks and balances or the claims to liberties delivered through an ancient constitution (Francis and Morrow 1994, pp. 10, 23). Internally, Bagehot maintained that the executive and legislative powers were not separate: the role of the Cabinet as ministers meeting along with Members of Parliament in voting legislation through under minister-instructed party lines meant a fusion of centralised powers at the heart of the legislative (Bagehot 2001). At least the British had stable and efficient government (Colls 2007, p. 518) and he underlined the requirement of popular assent and fresh election to establish the absolute nature of parliamentary sovereignty. In general terms, the major justification for the doctrine of parliamentary sovereignty was Parliament's democratic purpose which was essentially expressing the will of 'the people' via representation. That mantra of its democratic and representative purpose survived in Dicey's concept. In reality, Government, Cabinet, Party and Whips dominated the parliamentary agenda.

In terms of its emphasis on representation, by loosening the grip of the aristocracy, essential nineteenth and early twentieth century reforms radically altered the franchise for the Commons—but not the Lords. In particular, the Reform Acts of 1832, 1867 and 1884 abolished the 40 shilling franchise and broadened the electorate to establish a more uniform franchise throughout the country (UK Parliament 2019a; Norton 2013, p. 20). The extension in terms of representation meant that changes in 1918 and 1928 enabled the female franchise to be brought into line with the standards for men (Norton 2013, p. 22).

Like mass industrialization itself, parliamentary sovereignty acquired a 'cog in a machine' efficiency, acknowledged widely by the political and legal elite. The formula in the seventh constitutional form of 'What the Crown-in-Parliamentary Cabinet enacts is law' (1800–1972) in balance with its political conditions and constitutional conventions, naturally supports the neo-Diceyan view (Box 3.7). Dicey and his contemporaries confirmed the primacy of the Crown-in-Parliament formula, as the supremacy and ranking of the ultimate rule. The characterisation of its development can be described as serving the purposes of increasingly efficient government-in-parliament. It therefore had a heighted relevance along its previous eighteenth century path of reconciling popular and representative sovereignty to parliamentary sovereignty based on a legal definition. The intervention of Cabinet-style Government, the reliance on party voting among the electorate, adopting the party line and ensuring votes in Parliament and the imposition of party discipline through the Whips system mediated the role of representatives. It thereby emphasised the executive's leadership in their making law through Parliament although technically, without external direction. Those constitutional changes presented Parliament as possessing a Bagehotian technical efficiency. Internally, parliamentary institutions were restructured, for example in 1911, and in line with the previous constitutional form of the nineteenth century, to give the Commons primacy and Lords subordination under the principle of asymmetrical bicameralism. Until the early years of the twentieth century, the House of Lords had the continued power to stop legislation. However, following a crisis in which the House of Lords refused to pass David Lloyd-George's 'people's budget' of 1909, the budget was then passed after a general election in 1910, followed again by a second general election on the reform of the Lords. The resulting Parliament Act 1911 removed from the Lords the power to veto a Bill, but permitted them to delay Bills for two years. A further Parliament Act of 1949 further reduced the Lords' delaying powers to one year. The political reality of the concept meant that it was at first dependent upon coherent and powerful parliamentary parties in the Commons to make policy, as initiators, without the Crown, to govern the country and choose the executive. That is a practice which seems to have predominated in law, the Cabinet and the Prime Minister's office throughout the eighth constitutional form of the twentieth century, including the passing of the European Communities Act 1972, Human Rights Act 1998 and the devolution legislation.

Box 3.7 Constitutional Form Seven: 'What the Monarch-in-Parliamentary Cabinet Enacts Is Law' (1800–1972)

- The nineteenth century formulation of sovereignty as largely exercised by the Crown and parliamentary political elite.
- The aristocratic elite rule through an increasingly more representative Parliament.
- The capacity of Parliament to make law without external direction upon the nation.
- The fusion of ministerial Cabinet powers at the heart of the Commons—the Commons having primacy over the Lords, and no preoccupation with the balanced or mixed constitution.
- Stable and efficient government, requiring popular assent and fresh elections.
- Altering of the franchise, significantly and incrementally broadening the electorate and ending of the 40 shilling freeholder.
- Almost solely defined through law, less through politics.
- Cabinet government's efficient power to govern provides no settled legal relationship between sovereign power as being mutually conditioned by the rule of law and fundamental rights. The serious claim to the supremacy of an ancient common law constitution does not prevail.

*3.1.8 Constitutional Form Eight: 'What the Crown-*Through*-Parliamentary Political Elite with External Bodies Enacts Is Law' (1973–Present)*

The meaning of parliamentary sovereignty in the late twentieth and twenty-first century's confronts specific historical challenges which have arisen, domestically and externally, within the recent context of post-war European political and economic development and against a historic backdrop of its inheritance. The principle that parliamentary elites rule through Parliament transforms into the principle that Government rules through Parliament or partially through external agency or bodies. The ultimate rule is balanced against its political conditions supporting the rule. The ultimate rule that the Crown is embedded in and regulated by Parliament prevails but justified increasingly and paradoxically by the leadership of the Government through Parliament and partially through external bodies (Box 3.8).

In 2019, the UK Parliament website states publicly of the principle of parliamentary sovereignty and its general definition:

> Parliamentary sovereignty is a principle of the UK constitution. It makes Parliament the supreme legal authority in the UK, which can create or end any law. Generally, the courts cannot overrule its legislation and no Parliament can pass laws that future Parliaments cannot change. Parliamentary sovereignty is the most important part of the UK constitution. (UK Parliament 2019b)

The constitution is explained as "partly written and wholly uncodified." The UK Parliament's own account is notably frank on the issue of Parliament passing legislation which it describes as limiting the application of parliamentary sovereignty, including the devolved bodies (of the Scottish Parliament, the National Assembly for Wales and the Northern Ireland Assembly), the Human Rights Act 1998, the UK's entry into the EU in 1973 and the decision to establish a UK Supreme Court in 2009. It carefully adds that those developments do not undermine the principle of parliamentary sovereignty on the basis that 'in theory', Parliament could repeal any of the legislation underpinning those changes (on repeal and disapplication of EU law, see European Scrutiny Committee 2013, p. 97; 2014; Tomkins 2003; Lord Denning in *Macarthys Ltd. v Smith* [1980]).

Parliamentary sovereignty was conditioned by ongoing internal reforms guaranteeing the primacy of an executive-led House of Commons, complete with a dominating Cabinet and Whips possessing greater primacy. The increasing professionalisation of representatives, albeit with greater independence (Norton 2013, p. 27), the nineteenth century realities of Cabinet-style Government with the reliance on party voting inside and outside Parliament exerted ever-heightened leadership over Parliament, even during the substantial constitutional changes of the late twentieth century.

In terms of the balance of powers between the Crown in Parliament, law and the political community, the concept of parliamentary sovereignty has been left with an entrenched quandary. An executive-led Parliament delegates its law-making capacity in certain regards to other bodies and institutions. The officials within those institutions then impose external control, steerage and direction upon statute, so that representatives elected to the House of Commons by the political community to make law no longer have that practical capacity. Their practical ability, but not ultimate right, was voluntarily ceded under the European Communities Act 1972. An elective, delegated Parliament is in a deeper, political sense a contradiction. Yet, as legal theorists and lawyers have tended to oversee the ownership and terms of that debate (Loughlin and Tierney 2018, p. 989), it has focused purely on the law and the European Communities Act. Since it is only a voluntary Act, it is assured that parliamentary sovereignty has remained virtually untouched by EU membership. That conclusion seems both legally accurate but institutionally myopic.

Theoretically, Parliament retains its ultimate legal sovereignty because it has the power to repeal or amend the European Communities Act 1972 (Tomkins 2010). In practice, the 45-year political practice of choosing not to terminate or change substantial aspects of its Parliament-diminishing EU membership within a multi-level polity has been said to have left that doctrine intact. The crisis in the absence of 'the political' is misinterpreted. The tension is in the restructuring of the state and in electoral representation to Parliament—the displaced political conditions and conventions which form the historical precedents. The legal definition of sovereignty is provided but often without a satisfactory account of a deliberative politics and the institutions of the modern polity, upon which parliamentary sovereignty depends.

Parliament has voluntarily established a higher set of European rules by which its legislation can be indirectly reviewed or overridden by higher law of a delegated body or agency. The neo-Diceyan definition which the UK has retained now possesses a meaning exhausted by previous constitutional struggles. The contemporary debate is not because of faults that lie at Dicey's door but it is to a great extent impoverished by the absence or a failure to engage with the historical precedents discussed in those eight constitutional forms.

Box 3.8 Constitutional Form Eight: 'What the Monarch-through-Parliamentary Political Elite with External Bodies Enacts Is Law' (1973–Present)

- The twentieth and twenty-first century formulation of sovereignty exercised by Government through the political elites in Parliament and with external bodies, particularly the EU.

- An increased strength for Government ruling through Parliament and when applicable, external agency and bodies.
- A political elite of ministers elected by a full franchise of the people governs through an asymmetrical, bicameral elected Parliament in which the Commons decides and the Lords advises.
- The EU, the devolved bodies, the Supreme Court and the Human Rights Act can each claim to enhance executive and judicial institutions but limit the application of parliamentary sovereignty.
- Practical primacy is accorded to executive leadership in House of Commons through the increased power of Cabinet and Whips.
- Government's power to dominate prevails but is now mutually conditioned by fundamental rights and under certain legislation, even bound as a legal duty. The claimed supremacy of the rule of law and a common law constitution features heavily in dialogue although is largely closed off in practice by the supremacy of Parliament.

3.2 The Making of the Recognised Helm: Placing Present Hands on the Wheel

Having reviewed those eight constitutional forms alongside the neo-Diceyan legacy, it is crucial to understand where the current assessment stands. For all its critics, Dicey's definition remains in contemporary legal and political usage 132 years later (Loughin and Tierney 2018, p. 990). It is strictly interpreted as the legal supremacy of statute, which means that there is no source of law higher than or more authoritative than an Act of Parliament, even if it violates international law or changes a principle of judge-made, common law (Tomkins 2010, para. 6).

With the advent of significant constitutional changes, there has been a great deal of research which in one short phrase appears to throw out the constitutional baby, that is parliamentary sovereignty, with the political bathwater. There are various reasons given for doing so—namely on the role and interpretation of the European Communities Act 1972 (e.g. Norton 2011), Human Rights Act 1998 (e.g. Feldman 2011) and post-1998 devolution legislation (e.g. Tomkins 2007). On Vernon Bogdanor's argument, for example, the old British Constitution is expressed as Hart's rule of recognition—'What the Crown in Parliament enacts is law' (Bogdanor 2009, pp. 13, 73–74), with the author rejecting its relevance and role in the modern context. However, major political changes—now including the Human Rights Act 1998, the European Communities Act 1972 and significant devolution—have not simply meant an end to the ultimate rule in any previous constitutional form, and there is therefore no reason why it should be the case in the eighth form.

Both Vernon Bogdanor (2009) and Anthony King (2007) make a substantive leap from their understanding of a heavily delegated, mixed political and parliamentary structure. King's constitutional 'mess' and Bogdanor's mixed, quasi-federal constitution, both of which cite the development of the EU, have led them to conclude, as King maintains, that there is a new British constitution under which "the British parliament is no longer sovereign" (King 2007, p. 99). The contradiction in brief (in my view) in the final constitutional form is that the ultimate rule is preserved in theory, and yet the executive-led Parliament makes law in practice with external steerage and direction. One major example of that steerage has been the EU, which is not itself the creation of an Act of Parliament. Representatives are elected by the political community to Parliament to make law in an executive-led assembly that has voluntarily ceded, by legislation, to delegate that law-making capacity to the EU among other bodies.

In a multi-level polity, the notion of 'steerage' means the inner governing centre often finds new ways to steer and coordinate newly found governance arrangements (Bache and Flinders 2004, p. 47). A strength can be found in directing attention to how the state reinvents itself and develops new strategies to retain power in the modern context. Multi-level arrangements carry with it the objective of "…the steering of a society … towards some common goals…" (Peters and Pierre 2004, p. 86) The relevance of steerage to parliamentary sovereignty, the executive and other core UK constitutional structures can be interpreted as helpful. The most recent contemporary constitutional form under EU membership operates from the viewpoint in which an executive-led Parliament makes law in practice with a strong degree of external steerage and direction from the European Union.

Overall, it is briefly summarised above in Boxes 3.1–3.8, how those series of eight constitutional forms, describing prominent historical features, help to frame the multiple constitutional forms of parliamentary sovereignty. Each of those constitutional forms chart the different historical meanings attributed to the rule of the recognised helm, from its inception to its contemporary context. They evolve in a partly episodical, partly tangential but partly continuous succession. Only eight substantive events triggered an alteration of the fundamental rule to produce a new constitutional form: (i) the codification of the Crown seeking counsel from magnates; (ii) a petitionable Crown seeking approval from the House of Commons; (iii) the initiation of the Reformation; (iv) the overstatements of divine monarchical power and of common law rights relative to the legislature in the Early Stuart period, then Restoration period; (v) the revolution and settlement of 1688/1689; (vi) the settlement of a mixed power checks power constitution; (vii) the vast extension of the franchise (under the Reform Acts) with an efficient Cabinet-led Commons; and (viii) the vast extension of agencies and bodies, namely the EU, in providing government.

The ultimate rule credits the actors in the recognised helm. The nature of being 'at the helm' is the description of the leading, traditional, composite parts of the state. Throughout the constitutional forms, there is a Crown, whose prerogative powers are today conducted through the powers of the ministers in the executive. They each inherit various descriptions throughout different constitutional forms. It is a recognised helm because there is an acceptance or consent for those participating actors to fulfil a given purpose within their constitutional boundaries. In the first medieval constitutional form, the Crown and magnates are, constrained only marginally at the helm by codified, fundamental law (e.g. the Magna Carta). In the late fourteenth century to the Reformation of the second form, the Crown and the Commons are at the helm, constrained and conditioned only partially by fundamental law and in some limited manner by concerns of the 40 shilling freeholder constituents and county- and town-representing. The third constitutional form of sovereignty after the Reformation, defers strongly to the Crown and Parliament at the helm to govern in every area of the realm, but particularly for lawful taxation and legislation. The constraining actors at the helm, again, could only be understood in terms of fundamental law and the concerns of the 40 shilling freeholder constituents.

The fourth form defines the Crown and Parliament at the helm but more strongly—potentially, legally—constrained by: (i) the judges and the perceived ancient common law constitution, and; (ii) the binding claims of the consenting community as foundational to sovereignty and in some cases, with (iii) the competing claim of the Crown reigning supreme over Parliament. The fifth form emphasises the settlement between the Crown, the Parliament directly linked as representative of the people and in particular, through the political parties. The claims of the judicial element over the common law are importantly recognised but regulated, unable to exceed the limits of Parliament's claim to sovereignty. The sixth form identifies the Crown (Royal), Commons (democratic), Lords (aristocratic) and the judiciary as actors participating and checking within a balanced constitution. The seventh form of sovereignty recognises the Crown and the parliamentary, aristocratic, political elite of the Cabinet in government as the main constitutional powers. They are increasingly conditioned and constrained by the electorate through major changes to the franchise under the Reform Acts, but there is no realistic limitation to the Cabinet in parliament by common law claims. The eighth constitutional form adopts the Crown powers and the parliamentary political elite of ministers at the centre of the recognised helm. Only more recent claims by the EU, the devolved bodies, the Supreme Court, the European Court of Human Rights seeking to enhance executive and judicial institutions have limited the objectives of ministerial Crown powers and assented to by the governing parliamentary elite. The ministerial power to dominate Parliament's agenda prevails but it is bound by fundamental rights doctrines under certain legislation, namely, the Human Rights Act and the European Communities Act. Parliament is bound even to the point it is obliged as a legal duty to follow or consider that legislation where inconsistent with its own national legislation (Craig 2011, p. 116).

The recognised helm is therefore the acknowledged and recognised legal and political space defining what is permitted to steer, direct and control new or novel *inter-relationships*. It is the helm of state which has permitted the incorporation of new inter-relationships, for example, between the Crown and the magnates of the realm; between Papal interference and the Crown, the Church and the community; between the EU and the executive, the legislature, the judiciary and the electorate; between the Magna Carta's listed rights and the Crown, the magnates and the people. In each case, competing historical claims often insist that sovereignty in or involving Parliament has been lost, qualified, eroded, altered or destroyed, with others claiming it is preserved or enhanced. However, with the proposition of a recognised helm, there is a more reflexive model. It is less prescriptive. It does rely on the acknowledgement, or recognition, of participating actors within the constitution.

The first constitutional form of 'What the Crown-with-magnates enacts is law' (1200–1350) is a Crown whose sovereignty only makes sense with reference to this inter-relationship with the counsel of magnates. The exercise of sovereignty is increasingly and formally politically bound by a counsel of magnates but more loosely and morally bound by fundamental law. The second form of 'What the Crown-with-Commons enacts is law' (1350–1532) is a form of sovereignty defined by the petitionable Crown with the Commons. The exercise of sovereignty is increasingly bound, not only advised by, the Commons activity through use of petitions and county- and town-representing. It is also only minimally and mutually conditioned by morally binding fundamental law. The third form of 'What the Crown-through-Parliament enacts is law' (1533–1602) is sovereignty derived from a Crown *through* Parliament, not simply a Crown *with* Parliament. The exercise of sovereignty depended upon a Parliament in which no area involved in the government of the realm was outside of its authority. A form of Royal despotic power continued to be exercised, since it remained only minimally and mutually conditioned by morally binding fundamental law. The fourth form 'What the Crown-with-disputed Parliament enacts is law' (1603–1687) moves towards a sovereignty formula in which it is less derived from Crown-through-Parliament, increasingly by Crown-with-Parliament. Parliament is devalued. The exercise of sovereignty is increasingly bound, it is claimed, by the judges' prominent assertion of a mythical ancient common law constitution but now comprehended as legal (not moral) duty. In the fifth constitutional form, 'What the Crown-in-regulating Parliament enacts is law' (1688–1689). The Crown is brought under the powers of a regulating, sovereign omnipotent legislature. The courts were thereby denied the power to limit Parliament's sovereignty. The claims to the binding nature or supremacy of an ancient common law constitution is now limited by the settled supremacy of Parliament. In the sixth form, 'What the Crown-*in*-mixed constitutional Parliament enacts is law' (1690–1790s), is an inherited sovereignty of a supreme Parliament bolstered by a mixed, balanced constitution of the monarchical (monarch), aristocratic (Lords) and democratic (Commons representing people) powers. The parliamentary oligarchy has uncontrollable power balanced with the Crown and the judges and checked by a much-discussed supremacy of an ancient common law constitution which is closed off in practice. In the seventh form, 'What the Crown-in-Parliamentary Cabinet enacts is law' (1800–1972), sovereignty is mostly legislative, largely exercised by the Crown and parliamentary political elite through the Cabinet, bound increasingly by the broadening franchise. The efficient ministerial powers to govern provided no settled link or bind on the sovereign power whatsoever by the rule of law of the courts. The eighth constitutional form, 'What the Crown-through-Parliamentary political elite with external bodies enacts is law' (1973–present) considers sovereignty exercised by political elites in Parliament and through external bodies bound increasingly by the EU within a multi-level polity which can both steer and limit the practical exercise of parliamentary sovereignty. The mutually conditioning of sovereignty by fundamental law and rights can under certain legislation now be constrained by compliance with a legal duty.

The recognised helm carries with it a substantive implication about the nature of power sharing and of sovereignty. Sovereignty assumes that there are recognised actors and a recognised set of inter-relationships (Loughlin and Tierney 2018, p. 999). When those actors and relationships between the executive, the legislature, the judiciary and the electorate are recognised, there is an assumption of jointly, and however competitively, bolstering sovereignty at the helm (see Loughlin and Tierney 2018, p. 1000). They wield substantive power in the state and parts of their roles and functions are shared. Therefore, it is not necessary to assume that all the constraints of fundamental rights charters or of popular power upon sovereignty should be understood merely as limitations. Both in the case of respecting fundamental rights and expressions of popular power, each can be properly understood as steering and bolstering parliamentary sovereignty. Equally, the full exercise of executive power, under the full consent of Parliament, bolsters not limits parliament's sovereignty. Therefore, not all power-sharing at the helm ought to be understood as somehow a limitation. Where limitations upon parliamentary sovereignty are enacted or created, it can often be understood through the altering of, or introduction of, new actors and their inter-relationships (consistent with Tabarelli 2013, p. 362) at the helm, to the extent that they transgress the precedented relationships as understood through previous constitutional forms. The significance of power-sharing need not be overstated because, as has already been described, actors at the recognised helm can steer and direct other central actors i.e. namely the Government acting through Parliament. The steering and directing power does not necessarily equate to the sharing of power. It is mainly the executive, the legislature, the judiciary and the electorate who have a hand at the wheel of the ship of state, sometimes having their power strengthened while at other points weakening their power in comparison to other state powers.

The concept of 'steering' is familiar to 'multi-level governance' (MLG) approaches in understanding how EU institutions have had a distinct impact on the traditional Westminster model and specifically, where new UK-EU level processes have been absorbed to provide steerage in UK policy-making process. At the heart of this model, where the process of governing is less uniform and more strongly defined by the nature of the policy problem and sector, a focus on steerage towards policy process and outcomes and in which the model of governing largely defies structure (Peters and Pierre 2004, p. 84) can prove valuable to understanding the impact of EU decision-making in steering at the recognised helm.

In the case of the EU within the recognised helm, limitations upon parliamentary sovereignty are created through the altering and introduction of new EU institutional actors and their inter-relationships with the EU (Tabarelli 2013, p. 362) and national courts, the legislature and member state governments and the people. The alteration has been created at the point that the constitutional 'unsettling' transgresses the precedented relationships as understood through previous constitutional forms. The broad powers of the UK state exist within an EU "constitutionally disputed polity", characterised by an open and unsettled relationship with states (Walker 2012, p. 11). The EU contributes, with its competitive hand on the helm, to steering and directing the Government and Parliament, giving it a greater role in navigating state policies. At the recognised helm, successive governments, through Parliaments, have adopted practices which whilst preserving the fundamental rule, are at odds with past historical precedents. This process has led to an altering of the relationships between the executive, the legislature, the judiciary and the electorate with the EU machinery of government (Jack et al. 2011, p. viii), unsettling those historical precedents of parliamentary sovereignty. Walker (2014) has previously identified the UK as existing within a state of 'constitutional unsettlement'—a theory both prescient and increasingly relevant since the European Union referendum held in June 2016. Multipolar arrangements of EU membership, devolution and human rights protection have become normalised, at least regularised, subject to continuous contestation. It is an unsettled state because its end-phase offers neither a return to a settled constitution nor arrival to a newer one. The existing constitutional unsettlement has come to enshrine precedented agreements no longer held in practice. Young and Gee (2016) refer further to that unsettlement, given the increasing doubts about the relevance of parliamentary sovereignty in a multi-polar state and the contested understandings of EU membership. Simultaneously, Walker's view, to some degree, displaces what Loughlin and Tierney (2018) describe as the way in which rules of parliamentary sovereignty and of the constitution are held by institutions which evolve through deeply historical political conditions. After all, the precedents embedded within historical constitutional forms offer a sense of continuity; other features suggest a break with previous constitutional understandings. Walker clearly does proceed to ask the fundamental question, "How, if at all, do we periodize across such a vast historical expanse of the unwritten constitution, both pre-and post-parliamentary sovereignty?" But the research literature has not responded to the question of periodising the historical development of that sovereignty. It is hoped this chapter has gone some way to begin to remedy that question by offering a deeper understanding of both periodising and incorporating historical developments into the construct of parliamentary sovereignty.

In the creation of (and breaking of) each constitutional form, parliamentary sovereignty and the formation of the constitution has been unsettled—and yet through the creation of a qualitatively different *Brexicated* form, parliamentary sovereignty is potentially being resettled. In the eighth contemporary phase and a potential transition towards Brexit, the UK is presented with a terminus which has offered neither a return to a settled constitution nor arrival at a new constitutional settlement. Whereas EU membership has defined the eighth contemporary form, 'What the Crown-through-Parliamentary political elite with external bodies enacts is law' (from 1973 to the present), the Brexit process has begun to symbolise a breaking from, and resettling of, the traditional powers in which for 45 years it had been deemed 'normalised' for Government to rule partially through external agencies or bodies.

When there is friction or conflict between past constitutional forms of the UK constitution, it is possible to consider the friction or unbalancing of past constitutional conventions as 'unsettling'. After all, the UK has steadfastly relied on its historical constitutional conventions to regulate government (McHarg 2008, 2018). In particular, when a modern constitutional form of the constitutional understanding in the eighth stage is in conflict with the previous seven historical constitutional forms, an 'unsettling' occurs which centres on:

- A shift from one constitutional form to a newer or different one, particularly a past historical form and the contemporary eighth constitutional form.
- The experience of disturbing historically precedented interrelationships (for example, Jack et al. 2011, p. viii; Tabarelli 2013, p. 362) between the executive, the legislature, the judiciary and the electorate.
- A shift away from or toward a qualitatively and uniquely different constitutional form in which one of the defining features (e.g. bringing the executive under a more formal accountability to the legislature or bringing the legislative under a uniquely new form of accountability to its electorate) has been altered or swept away.
- When there is a shift in one major feature of a constitutional form, it necessitates an impact on all or most other powers in the constitution e.g. the Reformation and the creation of an omnicompetent Parliament or the incorporation of the EU in 1973.
- The most substantive form of 'unsettling' derives from a change in the fundamental rule which underpins the contemporary constitutional form of parliamentary sovereignty, for example, after the Reformation, and the events of 1688.

The less substantive form of unsettling, including changes induced by the European Communities Act 1972 and its subsequent amendments and post-1997 constitutional reforms, derive from the change in some of the features from previous historical constitutional forms. The eighth constitutional form deviates strongly from past historical forms, particularly through its emphasis on fundamental rights charters adjudicated upon by courts in Luxembourg and Strasbourg, the independence and elevation of the national judiciary in respect of the legislature and executive, and a body of government derived from EU institutions.

In describing legal and political settlement, if there is to be a Hartian ultimate rule of the recognised helm which must provide the conditions another rule must satisfy in order for that rule to impose obligations as valid law and settlement, the requisite historical conditions of the social rule must be given. The composite parts of parliamentary sovereignty which have been provided for in the eight historical constitutional forms have provided the rule with its criteria. The helm can be defined, in Bracton's view, by sovereignty at the helm of the medieval state being bound to moral duty. Ultimately, the law and the law-making sovereign remaining "mutually conditioned", reciprocal and interdependent at the helm, even though the sovereign power retains the capacity to govern the realm (Kantorowicz 1957, pp. 153, 155). Each defining moment of parliamentary sovereignty's historical meaning have a share in the criteria provided by the ultimate rule. In a constitution prone to silence and which therefore affords creative solutions to political crises regarding the scope and limits of constitutional authority of different actors (McHarg 2018, p. 953), it is not maintained that all conditions have an equal share. Primarily, historical events and the flexible relevance that precedents have to contemporary politics, as balanced within the unique historical forms, determine the relevance of, for example, omnicompetence or fundamental rights provision to the current meaning of parliamentary sovereignty. The conceptualisations of parliamentary sovereignty as described within the eight historical constitutional forms find their expression, however latent or however pronounced, in that ultimate rule. Without them, the rule of the recognised helm is an internal vacuum, an apolitical, legal abstraction and not 'ultimate' in any sense. The rule of the recognised helm attempts to respond to both the requirements of legal positivists in insisting upon rules which provide valid law (e.g. Hart 1997) and also to constructivist and poststructuralist assumptions of sovereignty as historically contingent upon political conditions.

The conditions of the ultimate rule provide for historically precedented constitutional forms of the constitution by explaining the relationship between institutions, rules and customs. By precedent, it might be conceived that the fingertips of past, historical precedents are pressed into the old, dry sponge of UK constitutional history by political customs and constitutional conventions, to be compressed, reshaped and reconfigured in reflecting those precedents. On the interaction between rules and precedented historical customs, even though classical liberal thought, particularly in the approach of John Locke, conceived of custom in the negative—as inhibiting individual reason—his view on liberal culture was one where customs were reasonable. This means customs support the authority of reasonable rules where there are good reasons for them (Grant 2012, p. 621). Hart himself, however, rejected habitual obedience or accustomed belief in the sovereign in the view of political theorists such as Austin and Hobbes, or custom, or obedience, or habit, etc., as the basis for laws as social rules. However, on the basis that Hart assumes laws are rules and therefore social, his fuller theory was not as parsimonious as first might seem. Some place must be given to custom and political precedent otherwise there is really no such thing as Hart's own proposition of laws as social rules.

In terms of custom, Edmund Burke, for example, critiqued the brutality of the French revolutionaries' determination to transform political life by their having removed historical tradition and constitutional custom (Berkowitz 2013, p. 52)—custom thereby embodied the nation's inherited and accumulated wisdom relating to their organisation and institutions (see also, Pocock 1987, p. 242). For Burke, sovereignty and the business of governing were a matter of convention, customised by inheritance, prescription and simple necessity (Radasanu 2011, p. 18). Locke and Burke are rarely mentioned together in the classical orthodoxy of political theory, but they do help us in this context because historical constitutional forms which we employ to characterise features of sovereignty and parliamentary sovereignty are not simply accrued or aggregated—they thrive, survive, part-survive or completely decay or die, but nonetheless they all provide precedent and convention. They are the conditions of the ultimate rule of the recognised helm contained within Locke's liberal culture in which customs are reasonable. They support the authority of reasonable legal rules and that there can be good reasons for them. Such a view is not as custom-based as Burke suggested the constitution might be simply because he did not accept that sovereignty, law and the business of governing are rule-based (Radasanu 2011). Nevertheless, those rules and the ultimate rule are themselves buttressed by historical precedent, as conventions and customs upheld, for example, by inheritance.

In understanding the rule of the recognised helm, historical customs, conventions and practices contained within the eight constitutional forms are pertinent. Parliament is sovereign not because it is a principle to be weighed against others via judicial interpretation but because it is an institutionalised rule of the recognised helm dependent upon the customs, conventions and politics of past historical precedents. To that extent, historical customs, as political precedents written into the UK's constitutional history, bolster the legal rule of parliamentary sovereignty.

For that reason, it is certainly plausible and valuable to argue that sovereignty acquires the status of a 'shibboleth'. It can be "...a widely held politico-cultural belief about the necessity of maintaining ... political power and legal authority at the centre" (Loughlin and Tierney 2018, p. 996), bearing in mind that the shibboleth(s) are carried by evolving historical precedents which both politically underlie, but are different from, the fundamental legal rules in the system.

The following chapter (Chapter 4) will set out that Parliament's sovereignty, since 1973, has become unsettled because the fusion of the executive with EU machinery, the dilution of the domestic legislature and the fusion of the judiciary with the Luxembourg court system, impacts upon and unsettles a past constitutional form of parliamentary sovereignty. A consideration of the case study of the EU-level Financial Transaction Tax (FTT) provides some evidence that the UK's recognised helm has, through a distancing from the historical precedented mixed constitution model, unsettled parliamentary sovereignty. Chapter 5 then goes on to argue that Parliament's sovereignty has become practically unsettled because of the distorting by the European Parliament to collectively represent its electors. The case study of the Working Time Directive illustrates that the recognised helm has had European Parliament-level functional representation competing with the Westminster Parliament to produce an unsettling of the historically precedented capacity to collectively represent its electors as strongly embedded within precedented political historical constitutional forms. It thereby unsettles the political strength of parliamentary sovereignty. Chapter 6 proceeds to describe Parliament's sovereignty characterised by unsettlement in part because the recognised helm has had EU-level fundamental rights schemes, protected by the courts, incorporated into it. The case study of the free movement right has illustrated the dilution of the domestic legislature as a rights-providing institution, which combined with the disappearing consensus between the arms of state and community in providing rights, has progressed a continued legislative decline and judicial advance in the UK, impacting indirectly upon the stabilisation of parliamentary sovereignty. Chapter 7 then argues that Parliament's sovereignty becomes characterised by unsettlement when the recognised helm has had EU-level decision-making incorporated into it, directly reducing the Government-in-Parliament's ultimate decision-making power over political decisions. Since the EU Referendum of

June 2016, Parliament's ultimate power to decide on the UK's terms of EU withdrawal can permit, amend (or reject) the executive's pursuit of a constitutional resettlement, if it voluntarily wishes, addressing the historical dilution of parliamentary powers. That step illustrates the realignment of Parliament with a historically precedented basis in which government operated by the consent of parliament's ultimate decision-making power over political decisions.

Bibliography

Allan, T. R. S. (2013). *The Sovereignty of Law: Freedom Constitution and Common Law*. Oxford: Oxford University Press.

Bache, I. (2012). Multi-level Governance in the European Union. In D. Levi-Faur (Ed.), *The Oxford Handbook of Governance*. Oxford: Oxford University Press.

Bache, I., & Flinders, M. (2004). Multi-level Governance and the Study of the British State. *Public Policy and Administration, 19*(1), 31–51.

Bagehot, W. (2001). *The English Constitution*. Oxford: Oxford's World Classics.

Baldick, C. (2008). *The Oxford Dictionary of Literary Terms* (3rd ed.). Oxford: Oxford University Press [Online]. Available at Oxford Reference. Accessed 10 July 2014.

Bartelson, J. (1995). *A Genealogy of Sovereignty*. Cambridge: Cambridge University Press.

Bartelson, J. (2011). Sovereignty. In B. Badie, D. Berg-Scholsser, & L. Morlino (Eds.), *International Encyclopedia of Political Science* [Online]. Thousand Oaks, CA: Sage. Available at http://dx.doi.org/10.4135/9781412959636.n573. Accessed 17 April 2017.

Baskerville, S. W. (1998). Elections and the Yeoman: The Changing Identity of the English County Voter, 1700 to 1850. *Parliamentary History, 17*(1), 48–57.

Begby, E. (2003). Liberty, Statehood and Sovereignty: Walzer on Mill on Non-intervention. *Journal of Military Ethics, 2*(1), 46–62.

Bellamy, R. (1996). The Political Form of the Constitution: The Separation of Powers, Rights and Representative Democracy. *Political Studies, 44*(3), 436–456.

Berkowitz, P. (2013). *Constitutional Conservatism: Liberty, Self-Government, and Political Moderation*. Chicago, IL: Hoover Institution Press.

Blackstone, W. (1765). *Commentaries on the Laws of England (1765–1769)*. Chicago, IL: University of Chicago Press (this edition 1979).

Blythe, J. M. (1992). *Ideal Government and the Mixed Constitution in the Middle Ages*. Princeton, NJ: Princeton University Press.

Bogdanor, V. (1997). *The Monarchy and the Constitution*. Oxford: Clarendon Books.

Bogdanor, V. (2009). *The New British Constitution*. Oxford: Hart Publishing.

Bourke, R. (1999). Sovereignty, Opinion and Revolution in Edmund Burke. *History of European Ideas, 25*(3), 99–120.

Bradford, P. (2011). A Silent Presence: The English King in Parliament in the Fourteenth Century. *Historical Research, 84*(224), 189–211.

Bradley, A. (2011). The Sovereignty of Parliament—Form or Substance? In J. Jowell & D. Oliver (Eds.), *The Changing Constitution* (7th ed.). Oxford: Oxford University Press.

Bradley, A. W., & Ewing, K. D. (2010). *Constitutional and Administrative Law* (15th ed.). Harlow: Longman.

Burke, E. (1774). Speech to the Electors of Bristol. In E. J. Payne (Ed.). (1999), *Select Works of Edmund Burke* (Vol. 4). Indianapolis, IN: Liberty Fund. Available at http://oll.libertyfund.org/titles/burke-select-works-of-edmund-burke-vol-4. Accessed 17 December 2013.

Burns, T. (2011). Interpreting and Appropriating Texts in the History of Political Thought: Quentin Skinner and Poststructuralism. *Contemporary Political Theory, 10*(3), 313–331.

Clark, G. (1956). *The Later Stuarts, 1660–17* (2nd ed.). Oxford: Oxford University Press.

Clarke, M. T. (2013). The Mythologies of Contextualism: Method and Judgment in Skinner's Visions of Politics. *Political Studies, 61*(4), 767–783.

Clinton, D. (2003). 'Dash and Doubt' Walter Bagehot and International Restraint. *Review of Politics, 65*(1), 61–81.

Coke, E. (1610). *Dr. Bonham's Case*, 8 Co. Rep. 114 (Court of Common Pleas).

Colls, R. (2007). After Bagehot: Rethinking the Constitution. *The Political Quarterly, 78*(4), 518–526.

Craig, D. (2012). Burke and the Constitution. In D. Dwan & C. J. Insole (Eds.), *The Cambridge Companion to Edmund Burke* (pp. 104–116). Cambridge: Cambridge University Press.

de Bracton, H. (1235). *De legibus et consuetudinibus Angliae* [On the Laws and Customs of England] [Online]. Available at http://bracton.law.harvard.edu. Accessed 17 January 2013.

de Montesquieu, C. (1748). *The Spirit of the Laws* (A. M. Cohler, Ed.). Cambridge: Cambridge University Press (this edition 1989).

Dean, D. (1998). Introduction: Parliament and Locality from the Middle Ages to the Twentieth Century. *Parliamentary History, 17*(1), 1–11.

Denton, J. H. (1981). The Clergy and Parliament in the Thirteenth and Fourteenth Centuries. In R. G. Davies & J. H. Denton (Eds.), *The English Parliament in the Middle Ages* (pp. 88–108). Manchester: Manchester University Press.

Dicey, A. V. (1885/1964). *An Introduction to the Study of the Law of the Constitution*. London: Macmillan.

Elton, G. R. (1986). *The Parliament of England, 1559–1581*. Cambridge: Cambridge University Press.

European Scrutiny Committee. (2013, November 28). *Reforming the European Scrutiny System in the House of Commons* (HC 109-I) [Online]. Available at https://publications.parliament.uk/pa/cm201314/cmselect/cmeuleg/109/109.pdf. Accessed 12 December 2013.

European Scrutiny Committee. (2014, April 2). *The Application of the EU Charter of Fundamental Rights in the UK: A State of Confusion* (HC 979) [Online]. Available at https://publications.parliament.uk/pa/cm201314/cmselect/cmeuleg/979/979.pdf. Accessed 8 August 2015.

Feldman, D. (2011). Extending the Role of the Courts: The Human Rights Act 1998. *Parliamentary History, 30*(1), 65–84.

Francis, M., & Morrow, J. (1994). *A History of Political Thought in the Nineteenth Century*. London: Duckworth.

Franklin, J. H. (1981). *John Locke and the Theory of Sovereignty: Mixed Monarchy and the Right of Resistance in the Political Thought of the English Revolution*. Cambridge: Cambridge University Press.

Gagarin, M. (Ed.). (2010). *The Oxford Encyclopaedia of Ancient Greece and Rome*. Oxford: Oxford University Press [Online]. Available at Oxford Reference. Accessed 10 February 2014.

Geddes, A. (2016). Britain Beyond the European Union? In R. Heffernan, C. Hay, M. Russell, & P. Cowley (Eds.), *Developments in British Politics 10* (10th ed., pp. 264–286). London: Palgrave.

Gifford, C. (2014). The People Against Europe: The Eurosceptic Challenge to the United Kingdom's Coalition Government. *Journal of Common Market Studies, 52*(3), 512–528.

Goldsworthy, J. (1999). *The Sovereignty of Parliament: History and Philosophy*. Oxford: Clarendon Press.

Goldsworthy, J. (2010). *Parliamentary Sovereignty: Contemporary Debates*. Cambridge: Cambridge University Press.

Grant, R. W. (2012). John Locke on Custom's Power and Reason's Authority. *The Review of Politics, 74*(4), 607–629.

Hanson, D. (1970). *From Kingdom to Commonwealth: The Development of Civic Consciousness in English Political Thought*. Cambridge: Harvard University Press.

Harding, A. (1993). *England in the Thirteenth Century*. Cambridge: Cambridge University Press.

Hart, H. L. A. (1997). *The Concept of Law* (2nd ed.). Oxford: Clarendon Press.

Hoekstra, K. (2013). Early Modern Absolutism and Constitutionalism. *Cardozo Law Review, 34*(3), 1079–1098.

Jack, M., Hutton, M., Johnson, C., Millar, D., Patrick, S., & Sandall, A. (Eds.). (2011). *Erskine May: Parliamentary Practice* (24th ed.). London: LexisNexis Butterworths.

Jaconelli, J. (1999). The Nature of Constitutional Convention. *Legal Studies, 19*(1), 24–46.

Jaconelli, J. (2005). Do Constitutional Conventions Bind? *Cambridge Law Journal, 64*(1), 149–176.

Jenkins, D. (2011). The Lockean Constitution: Separation of Powers and the Limits of Prerogative. *McGill Law Journal, 56*(3), 543–589.

Jezierski, J. V. (1971). Parliament or People: James Wilson and Blackstone on the Nature and Location of Sovereignty. *Journal of the History of Ideas, 32*(1), 95–106.

Jones, C. (Ed.). (2012). *A Short History of Parliament: England, Great Britain, the United Kingdom, Ireland, and Scotland.* Woodbridge: Boydell Press.

Kantorowicz, E. H. (1957). *The King's Two Bodies: A Study in Medieval Political Theology.* Princeton, NJ: Princeton University Press.

Keir, D. L. (1968). *The Constitutional History of Modern Britain, Since 1485* (9th Ed.). London: A & C Black.

King, A. (2007). *The British Constitution.* Oxford: Oxford University Press.

Koenigsberger, H. G. (1978). Monarchies and Parliaments in Early Modern Europe—Dominium Regale or Dominium politicum et regale. *Theory and Society, 5*(2), 191–217.

Koenigsberger, H. G. (1989). Composite States, Representative Institutions and the American Revolution. *Historical Research, 62*(148), 135–153.

Kors, A. C. (2012). *Encyclopaedia of the Enlightenment.* Oxford: Oxford University Press. [Online] Available at Oxford Reference. Accessed 10 February 2014.

Kuhn, T. (1970). *The Structure of Scientific Revolutions.* Chicago: University of Chicago Press.

Lane, M. (2012). Doing Our Own Thinking for Ourselves: On Quentin Skinner's Genealogical Turn. *Journal of the History of Ideas, 73*(1), 71–82.

Lee, A. (2009). Roman Law and Human Liberty: Marsilius of Padua on Property Rights. *Journal of the History of Ideas, 70*(1), 23–44.

Lee, D. (2016). *Popular Sovereignty in Early Modern Constitutional Thought.* Oxford: Oxford University Press.

Le Van Baumer, F. (1940). *The Early Tudor Theory of Kingship.* New Haven, CT: Yale University Press.

Lieberman, D. (1999). *The Mixed Constitution and the Common Law, UC Berkeley Public Law and Legal Theory* (Working Paper No. 99-4). Available at http://dx.doi.org/10.2139/ssrn.184708. Accessed 18 January 2018.

Lieberman, D. (2006). The Mixed Constitution and the Common Law. In M. Goldie & R. Wokler (Eds.), *The Cambridge History of Eighteenth-Century Political Thought* (pp. 317–346). Cambridge: Cambridge University Press.

Locke, J. (1988). Second Treatise. In P. L. Laslett (Ed.), *Two Treatises of Government, Student Edition* (pp. 137–428). Cambridge: Cambridge University Press.

Loughlin, M. (2010). *Foundations of Public Law.* Oxford: Oxford University Press.

Loughlin, M., & Tierney, S. (2018). The Shibboleth of Sovereignty. *The Modern Law Review, 81,* 989–1016.

Lubert, H. L. (2010). Sovereignty and Liberty in William Blackstone's Commentaries on the Laws of England. *The Review of Politics, 72*(2), 271–297.

Macarthys Ltd. v Smith. [1980]. Case 129/79, ECR 1275.

Maitland, F. W. (1908). *The Constitutional History of England: A Course of Lectures Delivered.* Cambridge: Cambridge University Press.

Marquand, D. (1999). *Populism or Pluralism? New Labour and the Constitution.* UCL Mishcon Lecture [Online]. Available at https://www.ucl.ac.uk/political-science/publications/unit-publications/46.pdf. Accessed 5 August 2017.

May, T. E. (1844). *A Treatise Upon the Law, Privileges, Proceedings and Usage of Parliament.* London: Charles Knight.

McHarg, A. (2008). Reforming the United Kingdom Constitution: Law, Convention, Soft Law. *Modern Law Review, 71*(6), 853–877.

McHarg, A. (2018). Navigating Without Maps: Constitutional Silence and the Management of the Brexit Crisis. *International Journal of Constitutional Law, 16*(3), 952–968.

McIlwain, C. H. (1910). *The High Court of Parliament and Its Supremacy: An Historical Essay on the Boundaries Between Legislation and Adjudication in England.* New Haven: Yale University Press.

McIlwain, C. H. (1947). *Constitutionalism: Ancient and Modern.* Ithaca, NY: Cornell University Press.

Nederman, C. J. (1988). The Royal Will and the Baronial Bridle, the Place of the Addicio de Cartis in Bractonian Political Thought. *History of Political Thought, 9*(3), 415–429.

Nederman, C. J. (1991). Knowledge, Consent and the Critique of Political Representation in Marsiglio of Padua's Defensor Pads. *Political Studies, 39*(1), 19–35.

Nelson, J. (2015a, June 15). *Magna Carta and Counselling the King.* History of Government [Blog]. Available at https://history.blog.gov.uk/2015/06/15/magna-carta-and-counselling-the-king/. Accessed 15 June 2015.

Nelson, J. (2015b, January 20). *Simon de Montfort's 1265 Parliament.* History of Government [Blog]. Available at https://history.blog.gov.uk/2015/01/20/simon-de-montforts-1265-parliament/. Accessed 15 June 2015.

Norton, P. (2011). Divided Loyalties: The European Communities Act 1972. *Parliamentary History, 30*(1), 53–64.

Norton, P. (2013). *Parliament in British Politics* (2nd ed.). London: Palgrave Macmillan.
O'Gorman, F. (2012, November 22). *British Politics in the Long Eighteenth Century: A Defense of Political History.* Institute of Historical Research [Podcast]. Available at http://www.history.ac.uk/podcasts/franco-british-history-external/british-politics-long-eighteenth-century-defense-political. Accessed 25 November 2012.
Orr, D. A. (2002). Sovereignty, Supremacy and the Origins of the English Civil War. *History, 87*(4), 474–490.
Payling, S. J. (1999). County Parliamentary Elections in Fifteenth-Century England. *Parliamentary History, 18*(3), 237–259.
Payling, S. J. (2013). *Middle Ages—Parliament and Politics Before 1509.* London: History of Parliament Trust [Online]. Available at http://www.historyofparliamentonline.org. Accessed 20 March 2013.
Perreau-Saussine, E. (2007). Quentin Skinner in Context. *Review of Politics, 69*(1), 106–122.
Peters, G., & Pierre, J. (2004). Multi-level Governance and Democracy: A Faustian bargain? In I. Bache & M. Flinders (Eds.), *Multi-level governance* (pp. 75–89). Oxford: Oxford University Press.
Pincus, S. (2009). *1688: The First Modern Revolution.* New Haven, CT: Yale University Press.
Pocock, J. G. A. (1987). *The Ancient Constitution and the Feudal Law: A Study of English Historical Thought in the Seventeenth Century.* Cambridge: Cambridge University Press.
Prokhovnik, R. (2007). *Sovereignties: Contemporary Theory and Practice.* Basingstoke: Palgrave Macmillan.
Prokhovnik, R. (2008). *Sovereignty: History and Theory.* Exeter: Imprint Academic.
Quinault, R. (2012, November 20). *Westminster as the Seat of National Government: The Long View.* Institute of Historical Research [Podcast]. Available at http://www.history.ac.uk/podcasts.
Radasanu, A. (2011). The Modern Foundations of Burke's Conservatism. *Perspectives on Political Science, 40*(1), 16–26.
Roskell, I. (1993). The Place of Parliament in the King's Government. In J. S. Roskell, L. Clark, & C. Rawcliffe (Eds.), *The History of Parliament: The House of Commons 1386–1421* [Online]. Available at http://www.historyofparliamentonline.org/volume/1386-1421/survey/ii-place-parliament-kings-government#footnote1_ai79k3f. Accessed 10 July 2014.
Saunders, R. (2011). *Democracy and the Vote in British Politics, 1848–1867: The Making of the Second Reform Act.* Aldershot: Ashgate.
Seaward, P. (2013). *Stuarts—Parliament and Politics from 1603 to 1714.* The History of Parliament Trust [Online]. Available at http://www.historyofparliamentonline.org/periods/stuarts. Accessed 20 March 2013.

Skinner, Q. (1965). History and Ideology in the English Revolution. *The Historical Journal, 8*(2), 151–178.

Skinner, Q. (2002). Meaning and Understanding in the History of Ideas. In Q. Skinner (Ed.), *Visions of Politics, Volume 1: Regarding Method* (pp. 57–89). Cambridge: Cambridge University Press.

Smith, T., & Dean, D. (1998). Introduction: Parliament and Locality from the Middle Ages to the Twentieth Century. *Parliamentary History, 17*(1), 1–11.

Somerville, J. P. (1986). *Politics and Ideology in England 1603–1640*. London: Longman.

Tabarelli, M. (2013). The Influence of the EU and the ECHR on "Parliamentary Sovereignty Regimes": Assessing the Impact of European Integration on the British and Swedish Judiciaries. *European Law Journal, 19*(3), 340–363.

The History of Parliament Trust. (2015). *The Story of Parliament: Celebrating 750 Years of Parliament in Britain*. London: History of Parliament Trust/St James's House.

Tomkins, A. (2003). *Public Law*. Oxford: Oxford University Press.

Tomkins, A. (2007). The Rule of Law in Blair's Britain. *University of Queensland Law Journal, 26*(2), 255–291.

Tomkins, A. (2010). *Written Evidence to the European Scrutiny Committee, Clause 18 of the Bill: Parliamentary Sovereignty and EU Law*. The EU Bill and Parliamentary Sovereignty. Available at https://publications.parliament.uk/pa/cm201011/cmselect/cmeuleg/633ii/633we02.htm. Accessed 5 December 2010.

Turner, B. (2010). John Stuart Mill and the Antagonistic Foundation of Liberal Politics. *The Review of Politics, 72*(1), 25–53.

UK Parliament. (2019a). *Information* [Online]. Available at www.parliament.uk. Accessed 3 January 2014.

UK Parliament. (2019b). *Parliamentary Sovereignty* [Online]. Available at https://www.parliament.uk/about/how/role/sovereignty/. Accessed 11 April 2017.

Van Duffel, S. (2004). Natural Rights and Individual Sovereignty. *Journal of Political Philosophy, 12*(2), 147–162.

Wade, H. W. R. (1955). The Basis of Legal Sovereignty. *Cambridge Law Journal, 13*(2), 172–197.

Walker, N. (2012). The European Union's Unresolved Constitution. In M. Rosenfeld & A. Sajó (Eds.), *The Oxford Handbook of Comparative Constitutional Law*. Oxford: Oxford University Press (Chapter 59).

Walker, N. (2014, July). Our Constitutional Unsettlement. *Public Law*, 529–548.

Weston, C. C. (1965). *English Constitutional Theory and the House of Lords 1556–1832*. London: Routledge & Kegan Paul.

Weston, C. C., & Greenberg, J. R. (1981). *Subjects and Sovereigns: The Grand Controversy over Legal Sovereignty in Stuart England*. Cambridge: Cambridge University Press.

Williams, B. (1962). *The Whig Supremacy, 1714–1760*. Oxford: Oxford University Press.

Wyclif, J. (1378). In C. J. Nederman & K. L. Forhan (Eds.) (1993), *Medieval Political Theory: A Reader: The Quest for the Body Politic, 1100–1400*. London: Routledge.

Young, A., & Gee, G. (2016). Regaining Sovereignty, Brexit, the UK Parliament and the Common Law. *European Public Law, 22*(1), 131–147.

CHAPTER 4

Parliamentary Sovereignty, the Precedent of the Mixed Constitutional Model and the UK's Membership of the EU

Parliamentary sovereignty rests on the historically precedented constitutional form of the mixed constitution in which the executive, the legislature and the judiciary are intermeshed as functionally separate but practically inter-related. That sovereignty is unsettled because, since 1973, the UK's constitution has had the EU institutions incorporated into it, through a fusion of the executive with EU machinery. This has led to the dilution of the domestic legislature and the fusion of the judiciary with the Luxembourg court system, which unsettles the political strength of parliamentary sovereignty. Contemporary explanations of parliamentary sovereignty rest upon precedented constitutional forms. The eighteenth century's constitutional form (the sixth of the eight forms) illustrates the meaning of the mixed constitution attributed to parliamentary sovereignty.

Parliamentary sovereignty during the eighteenth century, stated as 'What the Crown-*in*-mixed constitutional Parliament enacts is law' (1690–1790s), reflected the 1688/1689 settlement of powers, the 1707 Union and the emerging rivalry of popular sovereignty with Parliament's sovereignty. The ultimate rule in the sixth historical constitutional form requires balance against its political custom of the mixed constitution to support the rule. It is the sixth episodical moment within a historically discontinuous approach of eight potential historical constitutional forms describing parliamentary sovereignty. It is a balanced constitution which depends upon government through the mixed monarchical (monarch), aristocratic (Lords) and democratic (Commons representing people)

J. McConalogue, *The British Constitution Resettled*,
https://doi.org/10.1007/978-3-030-25290-8_4

powers, broadly in the interests of a parliamentary oligarchy. This historically precedented constitutional form responds to Bogdanor's (2009) claim that constitutions have the objective of 'providing organisation' (Bogdanor 2009, pp. 53–54). To a large degree, the historical forms of the mixed constitutional model specify the organisational and relational features of the British 'constitution'.

For modern purposes, as the contemporary classical guide to parliamentary practice and procedure, *Erskine May*, prefaced by the former Clerk of the House of Commons, Sir Malcolm Jack, states "The flexibilities inherent in the United Kingdom's constitutional arrangements mean that the relationships between the principal elements, the Crown, the legislature, the executive and the judiciary, are not immutable, but even so the rate and extent of change, particularly in respect of the relationships between the legislature and the executive and the legislature and the judiciary … has been remarkable. Some of that change—for example law emanating from the European Union — occurs outside but greatly influences the workings of Parliament" (Jack et al. 2011, p. viii). In other words, the contemporary, changing relationships between the executive, the legislature and the judiciary have been remarkable because of the interaction with the EU. It unsettles the political precedents of parliamentary sovereignty. Parliament is practically unsettled because EU membership has unsettled prior historical constitutional forms in which the powers of the executive, the legislature and the judiciary must now be joined by the EU. To adapt Blackstone's terms, the arrangement impels the machinery of government in a direction different from which either acting by itself would previously have done.

It is not unusual to refer to, or imply, that the contemporary British constitution is a mixed constitution. Tomkins (2013) proposes that the contemporary British constitution is indeed now a "mixed constitution", but does not seek to employ the term with reference to historical precedent but in the sense of referring to the contemporary mix of politics and law (Tomkins 2013, p. 2275). The mixed constitution possesses elements of both a political constitution and a legal constitution in explaining how the modern executive is held to account; and the distinction between the legal and political can often be seen as a false choice. Yet, in doing so, it resists references to the mix of monarchy, aristocracy, and democracy that eighteenth century legal and political scholars had described. Tomkins adds that the concept does not take us very far. In his view, "It matters less that the constitution is mixed than what the balance of the mix is, and should be" (Tomkins 2013, p. 2276). However, it matters both that the constitution is mixed and what the balance of the mix is, because that is precisely how EU membership has affected the underlying political custom of the mixed constitution, underpinning parliamentary sovereignty. Although far from unusual, constitutional theorists such as Turpin and Tomkins (2011), to some degree, overlook the relevance of the separation of powers doctrine in relation to buttressing contemporary parliamentary government and sovereignty. To some extent, that is partly due to their focus being limited to an analysis of parliamentary government after the Reform Act of 1832 as not having been formally based on the separation of powers doctrine (Turpin and Tomkins 2011, p. 129).

4.1 Parliamentary Sovereignty and the Historical Mixed Constitution

The mixed constitution has an inherent place in the historical development of the British constitution. The most preeminent authority on parliamentary sovereignty during the eighteenth century is Blackstone, who in 1765, wrote of Parliament that it has sovereign and uncontrollable authority (Blackstone 1765), an absolute despotic power entrusted by the constitution and was able to do anything unless of course it was naturally impossible (Lubert 2010; Goldsworthy 1999, p. 202). Blackstone characterises such sovereign power as located within a tripartite, neo-Montesquieuan mixed constitution (Lieberman 2006, pp. 318, 335; de Montesquieu 1748), although Lieberman questionably rejects parliamentary sovereignty as impermissible in that constitution. For Blackstone, England historically enjoyed a mixed constitution founded on the Crown, Lords and Commons—as "distinct powers" which jointly impel the machinery of government in a direction different from what either one acting by itself would have done and thereby in a direction formed from each part (Blackstone 1765). Close to Blackstone, Montesquieu's view of the English 'power checks power' constitution (Bellamy 1996, pp. 443–444) is one in which the executive and the two branches of the legislative act as checks on one another yet the judicial power and tribunals of law are subordinate to the legislation (Lubert 2010; Goldsworthy 1999; de Montesquieu 1748). The sovereignty of Parliament, for Edmund Burke, is located within a balanced constitution configured around a trust between the Crown and Parliament's chambers (Craig 2012, pp. 106–108).

Blackstone, Burke and many other leading political and constitutional theorists in eighteenth century England described the British constitution as being a well-balanced combination of different forms of government—monarchical, aristocratic and democratic—each balancing out the other (Lieberman 2006, p. 318; Blackstone 1765, pp. i, 50–52). The constitution generally reflected a ramshackle system held together by a poorly integrated composite state (O'Gorman 2012). Nevertheless, judicial review was in this context not considered necessary for a system in which the Commons claimed to represent the electorate and the Crown and the Lords checked that relationship (Goldsworthy 1999). Parliament essentially decided what the law was which was then enforced by the courts. The organising principle for the English eighteenth-century constitution was that it could preserve political freedom by effectively preventing arbitrary or tyrannical acts of power (Lieberman 2006, p. 317). The ultimate rule in the sixth historical constitutional form of 'What the Crown-*in*-mixed constitutional Parliament enacts is law' requires balance against its political convention of the mixed constitution to support the rule.

Although Dicey in the nineteenth century accepted principles and rules as "the conventions of the Constitution" which regulate relationships, he subverted those conventions of Blackstone (1765), Burke (1774), and Montesquieu (1748) in theory as non-legal, additions to the constitution, rather than having political primacy. The later Diceyan approach provided no direct credit to the mixed constitution as a political custom (Francis and Morrow 1994, p. 10) in understanding parliamentary sovereignty. In the eighteenth century constitution (the sixth historical constitutional form), as described in Chapter 3, however, the ultimate rule conferred supremacy upon the unlimited and absolute power of Parliament. The rule is constructed by political conventions, including a Tory-Whig consensus with the Crown-in-Parliament, but limited role of the people, and exercised within an intermeshing mixed constitution of the executive, legislature and the judiciary.

Government at the helm of state—involving the mixed constitution of the executive, the legislature and the judiciary—has since 1973 incorporated the EU institutions into its structure. Given that the sovereign Parliament has so often been nested within the mixed constitution, it can be helpful in demonstrating the EU's institutional impact on the UK's rule of the recognised helm. The conceptualisation of parliamentary sovereignty as emanating from the mixed constitution of Blackstone (1765), Montesquieu (1748), and Burke (Craig 2012; Bourke 1999) in the sixth historical constitutional form finds its expression, however latent or however pronounced, in that ultimate rule. After all, the construction of the ultimate rule provides for constitutional custom and legal and political precedent. Parliamentary sovereignty is an ultimate rule of the recognised helm because, as a rule, it provides those political conditions, including the mixed constitution, which other rules must satisfy in order for the rule to impose obligations as valid law, affirming political settlement. The rule works because the executive initiates law and policy, the legislature accepts or rejects them, and the judiciary applies the law of that executive, assented to by the legislature, without substantial external interference. The conditions are therefore crucial, but by no means causal or restrictive, to the rule because of the flexibility inherent to past, political precedent. A mixed constitution which places limits on government does not necessarily challenge the sovereignty of Parliament. Blackstone's (1765) notion that the mix of Commons, Lords and Crown would jointly impel the machinery of government was derived from the notion that Parliament as a whole had sovereign authority. On the basis the ultimate rule of parliamentary sovereignty must provide its conditions in order to impose obligations as valid law and political settlement, the requisite conditions of the rule must be properly described. That task will enable a better understanding of the role of the EU institutions as it impresses upon the organised, historical precedent of the mixed constitutional model.

4.2 Parliamentary Sovereignty and the Contemporary Mixed Constitution

It is imperative to recognise the contemporary relationship between parliamentary sovereignty and the mixed constitutional model—particularly in contrast to ideal types underlying features of either a republican model or a constitutional state which undermine that connection and never wholly explain parliamentary sovereignty or its relationship to the mixed constitution, unsettled by EU membership. Bogdanor (2009) in his central argument in *The New British Constitution*, argues that the post-2007 era of constitutional reform, together with Britain's entry in 1973 into the European Communities has had the effect of replacing one constitution—that is the Diceyan doctrine of parliamentary sovereignty and Bagehot's proposed fusion of the legislative and executive powers—with a new constitution. The main elements of the new constitution include: post-European Communities Act arrangements; the Human Rights Act, the cornerstone of the new constitution; the devolution legislation, which has turned Britain from a unitary into a quasi-federal state; reform of the House of Lords, radically altering the role of the upper House; and the employment of referendums to validate constitutional reforms. He suggests those reforms strengthened the likelihood of Britain adopting a written or codified constitution and the potentiality for a popular constitutional state (Bogdanor 2009, pp. i–xiii). However, the emergence of a popular constitutional state, based on those features, is not evident. The old constitution, he theorises, was based on the sovereignty of Parliament; the new constitution is based on a constitutional state with an enhanced separation of powers (Bogdanor 2009, p. 285). In describing the complex mix of the new constitution, Bogdanor (2009) recognises it but views the rule of law as superseding Hart's rule along with other more novel features and reforms at the forefront of the constitution. However, it has never been a zero-sum game as Bogdanor assumes: the UK has both parliamentary sovereignty and a pragmatically organised, partial separation of powers (on the latter, see Masterman 2011) which ultimately have a directing capacity at the helm. Bogdanor's theory is antithetical to recognising the contemporary connection between parliamentary sovereignty and the separation of powers, as the tripartite basis of mixed government.

The traditional mixed constitution of the executive, the legislature and the judiciary is practically inter-related in the sense that under the Westminster model, ministers in government leading their departmental Bill teams (including legal advisers) and policy officials of the executive exist within a recognised helm. By proposing and drafting conventional Government Bills, ministers in turn require consent of the House of Commons and application of the law by the judiciary. As a 'reactive' legislature, the House of Commons is the means for a Government's dominant, partisan parliamentary majority to support, amend or reject the executive's legislation and their wider governing objectives, but not propose alternatives on their own (Norton 1984, 1994; Mezey 1979). The 1689 Bill of Rights established for the House of Commons a sole right to authorise taxation and the level of financial supply to the

Crown. The Westminster model assumes the Prime Minister and members of the Cabinet are mostly drawn from the Commons (especially the more senior members), mostly from within a dominant Government, built upon a partisan Commons majority. In practice, a Government, with a strong majority, rules through Parliament (which has led many to view parliamentary sovereignty itself as only a vehicle for the will of the Government). The House of Lords has limited powers in the form of a legitimising and scrutinising body for proposing revisions to the Commons. The heightened democratic basis of the House of Commons secures its primacy over the House of Lords and the Crown within Parliament. The judiciary are then required to give effect to the statutes of Parliament or interpret their meaning where complexity and uncertainty arises as to how the law applies in a given situation. The judiciary is the branch of government responsible for interpreting the law and for resolving legal disputes, albeit under the Human Rights Act 1998, courts are able to make decisions through interpretation of legislation in a way which preserves European Convention rights (Bradley 2011, p. 64; Bradley and Ewing 2010, pp. 401–407). Those functionally separate institutions of the executive, the legislature and the judiciary are practically interrelated by procedures and flexible relationships which underpin the rule of parliamentary sovereignty.

The contemporary recognised helm has historically experienced the incorporation of EU institutions into that helm. The effect has been a fusion of the executive with EU machinery, the dilution of the domestic legislature and the fusion of the judiciary within the Luxembourg (and Strasbourg) court system. Each has impacted upon parliamentary sovereignty. As such, EU obligations dilute and unsettle Blackstone's (1765) understanding of the mixed constitution, existing as historical precedent. To adapt Blackstone's thinking, the Crown and legislature are now joined by the EU at the helm in jointly impelling the machinery of government in a direction different from what either one acting by itself would have done and thereby a direction formed from each part. Bogdanor (2009), in line with many contemporary legal theorists, chiefly and questionably designates the constitutional reforms implemented since 1997 as having fundamentally altered the balance between the executive, the legislature and the judiciary—and enhancing a separation of powers. Such an assumption provides little credit to the much earlier EU membership itself as having enhanced, affected or distorted that separation. In broad terms, the tendency in the research literature on the British constitution has often been to look at constitutional unsettlement, if not a renewed moment of constitutional fluidity, as resulting from Britain's own post 1997-constitutional reforms and its asymmetrical devolution arrangements (Bogdanor 2019, p. 260; Walker 2014) rather than a consequence of the elephant in the room: the impact of EU membership. It has meant, for Bogdanor (2009), that the idea of parliamentary sovereignty has been replaced (not enhanced) by that of the separation of powers—a key feature in Britain's move towards a constitutional state. This assumption comes at the expense of considering a state which in practice operates on the rule of parliamentary sovereignty bolstered by the historical precedent of a mixed constitution, which is subsequently unsettled by EU membership.

There is a partial separation of powers (see Masterman 2011), particularly between the executive and the legislature and the extent of that separation depends upon the extent to which Parliament asserts itself against the government of the day. The EU has in many ways reinforced and enhanced that separation. As Bogdanor (2009) perceptively observes, the traditional British constitution, in line with Bagehot's view, supposes that there is no separation of powers at all, only a fusion between the executive and legislature, between Cabinet and Parliament, through the Cabinet. Bogdanor holds, contrary to Bagehot, however, there had always been a partial separation of powers given that not every MP is a minister, there is a separation of powers between Cabinet and Parliament. He also holds the extent of that separation depends upon the extent to which Parliament asserts itself against the government of the day which depends upon political vicissitudes (Bogdanor 2009, p. 285), although ministers *must* collectively support the government and backbench government MPs only *ought* to. The separation of government and Parliament has also been intensified by the removal of the hereditary peers from the House of Lords (Bogdanor 2009, p. 288); with peers chosen specifically for the purpose rather than by birth being more prepared to challenge, or assert a position, against the government of the day. It is through Bogdanor's separation of powers, not Bagehot's unity of the executive and legislature, under which the defined powers of the Commons are unsettled under EU membership. Unsettlement occurs because the governing weight of the national executive is grafted onto EU governmental machinery, creating uncertainty between the executive and legislature.

There is ample evidence that the constitutional strengthening of the UK executive occurs through a fusion with EU governmental machinery. The Prime Minister, with other Heads of Government and respective Presidents of the European Council and Commission interacting to make decisions at the highest political level in the European Council (Kassim 2016a). The ministers for the executive integrate with the Council of the EU and the other 27 executives to negotiate and make EU laws and take economic, trade, foreign and security policy decisions (Kassim 2016b, c). Ministerial meetings are prepared in detail by diplomats from the executive through the 'Committee of the Permanent Representatives of the Governments of the member states to the EU' (Coreper) and national civil servants perform official functions for Council working groups and committees (Kassim 2016d). EU legislation is eventually implemented by the UK executive (through Departments, agencies and local authorities) with national-level bodies administering 90% of the EU Budget (Kassim 2016c). The EU institutions are fused to the executive because they were created by member state executives to help them achieve the objectives described in the EU Treaties (Kassim 2016c). The legislature cannot be said to have any kind of equivalent connection as the executive within EU-level institutional decision-making through the European Council, European Commission or Council of the EU. The legislature is reported to by the UK executive. It usually decides, due to partisanship in Parliament, to scrutinise but not oppose what the executive has done.

Conceptually, the traditional ultimate decision-making power of Parliament defines a Westminster model of MPs taking ultimate political decisions over policy and laws on behalf of the electorate whose interests and concerns they seek to represent. One common, leading assumption in the research, however, proposes a deparliamentarisation thesis in which EU integration has led to an erosion of Parliament's regulating of the executive (Raunio and Hix 2000; Schmidt 1999), generating a broad executive-legislature accountability gap. The 'deparliamentarisation thesis' expresses that the development of European integration has led to the erosion of parliamentary accountability over the executive branch, based both on constitutional rules and the political dynamics of the EU policy process (Raunio 2009, 2011; O'Brennan and Raunio 2007; Raunio and Hix 2000). As national governments represent their countries in EU negotiations, this tends to create "informal asymmetries" between the executive and the legislature (Raunio 2011). In those circumstances, the historical precedent of Montesquieu's (1748) 'power checks power' constitution, in which primarily the executive and the two branches of the legislative act as checks on one another, becomes partly anachronistic.

Bogdanor (2009, 2019) wrongly dismisses the ultimate rule, 'What the Crown in Parliament enacts is law' as a rule of recognition in the UK legal system. He does so because the underlying theory cannot conceive of sovereignty invested in a legislative power yet where the state maintains a distributed network of sub-powers (Bogdanor 2019, p. 43). It also assumes that the ultimate, contemporary rule does not state the historically precedented conditions the rule must satisfy in order for it to impose obligations as valid law providing for political settlement. The settlement works because the historical precedent of the mixed constitutional model configures the internal executive, legislature, judicial relations to validate the rule, but Bogdanor (2009) does not examine this as a form of historical precedent, nor its ***unsettling*** under EU membership.

It is not evident that a UK rule-based constitutional structure, including the rule of parliamentary sovereignty, within a tripartite constitution, has completely disappeared or given way to complex arrangements of other executive bodies. Loughlin (2010) considers that:

> … in place of a clear, symmetrical, rule-based constitutional structure, we are obliged to examine a complex arrangement of government in which local and non-public bodies play important roles and where knowledge and other flows are no longer linear but recursive. (Loughlin 2010, p. 416)

The author therefore assumes a lesser role for the activity of governing which takes shape within a tripartite structure of the executive, the legislature and the judiciary—and instead it occurs through an elaborate administrative network of persons, institutions, practices and processes involving a mixture of public roles (Loughlin 2010, p. 416). It is not clear that a rule-based structure such as the rule of the recognised helm necessarily gives way to complex arrangements of other public bodies—rather they confirm it. The convention of the tripartite structure likewise does not dissipate, but can often permit, an elaborate administrative network.

The growth and magnitude of EU administrative powers in the UK's recognised helm does raise concerns over the limits and dilution of the traditional separation of powers doctrine. This is particularly acute given the influence of EU administrative powers on the supremacy of the executive, the dilution of the domestic legislature and the strengthened basis of administrative law in the judiciary. Those effects unsettle and destabilise parliamentary sovereignty. As Loughlin argues, the emergence of a separate system of administrative law and administrative powers of government has been tied to governmental modernisation and centralisations (Loughlin 2010, p. 436). The system of administrative law that emerged in Europe during the eighteenth and nineteenth centuries was antithetical to English ways of governing consistent with the common law tradition (Loughlin 2010, p. 444), the principles of parliamentary sovereignty and the rule of law (Loughlin 2010, p. 441). It is an overstatement of the position however to adopt more radical analysis such as that of Rubin, in which the mixed constitutional model is reduced to 'heuristic' or 'metaphor' and the three branches of government "exist only in our minds" (Rubin 2005, p. 2995; Loughlin 2010, p. 447). The growth in scale and complexity of contemporary government through administrative arrangements has made the recognition of a mixed, tripartite structure particularly acute.

For Loughlin, the growth of administrative power raises doubts about whether we can continue to work within the understanding of a separation of powers (Loughlin 2010, p. 448)—although it might be more helpful to consider the influence EU administrative powers have had on the increased concentration of mixed powers than to abandon its role in a multi-level polity. Loughlin credibly proceeds to argue for the rise of elaborate networks (or ephorate, as he refers to it), in which ministers at the apex of the system are being replaced by differentiated arrangements, domestic and European, with elaborate service networks and public bodies (some 650, including the BBC) which operate at some remove from electorally authorised sources of authority (Loughlin 2010, p. 448; Conway 2011, p. 184; Bache and Flinders 2004, pp. 43–44). This does not mean, as Loughlin indicates, that unaccountable bodies are now emerging to constitute a new fourth power but that they help inform parliamentary sovereignty. Yet it can mean, as Loughlin suggests, that public bodies do not generally exercise governmental power but they have a major impact on policy decision-making (Loughlin 2010, p. 450). It is not necessary to view the network as a new branch of government comprising office-holders who possess the type of expertise and specialised knowledge that has enabled the basis of effective governmental decision-making. An interpretation of Edmund Burke's view that the sovereignty of Parliament is located in a balanced constitution configured around a triangulated trust between the Crown and Parliament's chambers (Craig 2012, pp. 106–108) now incorporates the EU into that constitution. This dilutes the trust and balance necessary for the inter-relationships in the mixed constitution and its dislocating of the sovereignty of Parliament.

The nature of the EU's interaction with the mixed constitutional model in the UK parliamentary sovereignty structure occurs in the context of the rise of the administrative machinery. In that machinery, the network bodies realise their potential through an original, not delegated authority. It is an original, not delegated, authority because the delegating authority from the Commons' is diluted under EU membership, the authority of the executive is preserved, if not enhanced, and judicial power is further enhanced through decision-making over competencies or competition in the administrative machinery. The evolution of the EU has meant the rise of the administrative machinery where EU functions relate to the acquisition of technical knowledge in specific regulatory fields, assisting intergovernmental institutions e.g. Council of the EU, to make policy decisions (Loughlin 2010, p. 463). The extent of the development of the modern EU has meant it has become increasingly greatly more supranational than Loughlin might observe. The EU could hardly be depicted as an entity that merely assists intergovernmental institutions. It has its own supranational political powers and institutions also.

It is conceivable in the EU context that the growth of administrative agency power (Egeberg and Trondal 2017) threatens to 'unbalance' the separation of powers doctrine, particularly where bodies realise their potential through a newly developed and original, not delegated authority. It is not completely proven, however, that there is a fourth branch of government of increasingly complex, specialised, expert public bodies, or that it proposes completely breaking the tripartite structure. It need not be certain either that the new paradigm creates an alternative image of government as network—there are many agencies, domestic and European, and with a plurality of functions and purposes. In the domestic context, it is worth bearing in mind the domestic Coalition Government's (2010–2015) policy of the 'bonfire of the quangos', or 106 non departmental public bodies which closed, drastically reducing their number (*The Guardian* 2012), meaning those elaborate networks not only extend but contract. Furthermore, Theresa

May's post-referendum government, in pursuit of a potential UK withdrawal from the EU, entails a potential, deliberate shrinking of the UK's participation in extensive and elaborate European networks. An administrative apparatus, largely an extension of governmental institutions and which mostly execute policy, are a layer of executive agencies which need not be viewed as a cumbersome complex network, overriding the tripartite structure, but rather changing its relationships. It can occur simply because, as Egeberg and Trondal (2011) argue, EU level agencies become building blocks in a multilevel union administration, partly bypassing, for example, national executives (see also Egeberg and Trondal 2017).

By recognising that parliamentary sovereignty both accommodates and creates the tripartite mixed constitutional model and that the mixed constitution informs parliamentary sovereignty, the crisis of Bogdanor's zero-sum game is averted. The UK can have both parliamentary sovereignty and a pragmatically organised, partial separation of powers. The recognised helm incorporating EU institutions entails the fusion of the executive with EU machinery, which unsettles parliamentary sovereignty. To his credit, Bogdanor (2009) recognises that there is a partial separation of powers, particularly between Cabinet and Parliament and that the flexibility and extent of that separation depends upon the extent to which Parliament asserts itself against the government of the day.

Political theorists such as Richard Bellamy (1996) have credibly argued that the classically mixed government model is historical, or of the past. However, to diverge from Bellamy's work, it also remains important to capture that past historical constitutional form as relevant to parliamentary sovereignty's historical meaning. Such political precedent has a share in the composite parts provided by the ultimate rule of 'What the Crown in Parliament enacts is law'. Whether we examine Hart's (1997) ultimate rule, Bellamy's (2007) consideration of the rule of persons including Hobbes' primacy of a political body of persons to decide on rules of law, all share an assumed or acknowledged consensus between officials within the different institutional parts of the state. That is relevant because the ultimate rule rests upon the sharing of the space at the recognised helm with institutional executive, legislature and judicial powers where there is an assumed or acknowledged consensus between persons in those institutional arms (see Sciaraffa 2011; Galligan 2006; Goldsworthy 1999; Hart 1997). When parliamentary sovereignty co-exists in the modern constitution with at least a partial separation of powers, the purported existence of a wider plurality of competing public and private agencies does not make an efficient check, as might be thought, but presents a problem for those distinct parliamentary powers governing at the helm.

EU institutions and agencies incorporated into government exert an influence through the supremacy of executive agencies (Egeberg and Trondal 2011, 2017) as above domestic legislative-scrutiny powers. It is not evident however that a UK-rule based constitutional structure, including the rule of parliamentary sovereignty, within a tripartite constitution, has given way to complex arrangements of local or non-public bodies, as Loughlin indicates. Rather, the rule-based structure confirms and provides for the complex administrative arrangements, even though at the institutional level European administrative bodies (e.g. the European Banking Authority, European Food Safety Authority and the European Defence Agency) compete at the recognised helm. The nature of EU interaction with the mixed constitutional model in the UK parliamentary sovereignty structure occurs in the context of the rise of the administrative machinery and where network bodies realise their potential through an original, not delegated, authority (e.g. Egeberg and Trondal 2017; Wonka and Rittberger 2010; Gilardi 2002). It is an original, not delegated, authority because the delegating authority by the Commons' is diluted under EU membership, the authority of the executive is enhanced since it evolves to a degree on its own terms (i.e. without delegated instruction) and the judicial power is fused into the Luxembourg court system. The case of the Financial Transactions Tax (FTT) makes clearer the role of EU institutions in unsettling parliamentary sovereignty.

4.3 Parliamentary Sovereignty and the Contemporary Mixed Constitution Under EU Membership: The Case of the Financial Transactions Tax (FTT)

The European Commission's proposal for an EU-wide tax on transactions in financial instruments, including 0.1% for standard transactions on stocks and bonds and a 0.01% tax for transactions in derivatives, was first set out for member states in 2011. It was initially described as a measure to recover cost of the financial crisis from banks (Council of the EU 2013; EU Committee 2013). It was a partly popular measure in the light of the global financial crisis in which banks were deemed responsible for failures leading to the crisis. The tax was to be payable not by individuals but financial institutions located within a member state participating in the tax measure. The rationale for the tax was also grounded in regulators reducing risk, to level the playing field value-added tax (VAT) and EU tax harmonization. At the time, France and Italy had already introduced national financial transaction taxes. The proposed tax is to be imposed on a wide range of financial transactions where at least one party to the transaction is a financial institution established in a member state participating in the FTT. After six years, it began to appear "highly questionable" whether the tax would be implemented at least as originally conceived (Kastner 2017). In that form, it subsequently led to a "less ambitious", watered-down, narrow-based tax on a limited number of transactions (Kastner 2017). The proposal then found itself stuck in stalemate in the EU Council working group meetings with significant differences remaining among the ten participants (see Moscovici 2017; Barbière 2017). Only in December 2018 and March 2019 have Germany and France again sought to (re)outline a joint proposal for the tax, based on a nationally tested model developed in France (Euractiv 2018).

4.3.1 *Changing the Inter-related Pragmatically Organised, Partial Separation of Powers*

A consideration of the FTT demonstrates precisely how the recognised helm has incorporated the EU institutions into its sphere through an influence on the executive, the legislature and the judiciary, indirectly unsettling parliamentary sovereignty. There are other financial services legal disputes in which a similar argument could be made. Other legal disputes preceding the UK's EU referendum of June 2016 include the Advocate-General to the ECJ dismissing the arguments of the UK Government in its attempts to block proposed EU restrictions in banker bonuses as a ration of salary (see Barker 2014a; Freshfields Bruckhaus Deringer 2013; Euractiv 2013). Separately, the ECJ also dismissed the UK Government's and parliamentary arguments to attempt to retain its national power over short selling in the markets, as compared with the new powers given to the EU-level European Securities and Markets Authority (ESMA) (Barker 2014b; House of Commons 2011; BBC News 2014). This chapter will focus exclusively on the FTT.

The FTT notably centres upon a contested EU-derived policy which invokes responses from across the executive, legislature, judiciary and the electorate.

An unsettlement occurs despite the UK agreeing to the powers of the European institutions through the EU Treaties. In particular, the "genuinely supranational" European Commission (King 2007, p. 103) has the complete 'right of initiative' in policy areas covered by the Treaties—it can propose new laws in accordance with the subsidiarity principle, meaning, in theory, it deals only with issues that cannot be dealt with effectively at national, regional or local level (European Union 2019) and only in policy areas where the Treaties provide for action. The Commission is the administration as well as providing a degree of policy and political direction (Hooghe and Kassim 2012). It drafts proposals for new European laws and manages the day-to-day business of implementing EU policies.

The FTT is an example of taxation which itself classically falls under the remit of policies in which Parliament is deemed sovereign. What will become clear is that Vernon Bogdanor's zero-sum game that the UK cannot have parliamentary sovereignty but instead an enhanced separation of powers is expressed differently: the UK retains its rule of parliamentary sovereignty, but has altered its strongly inter-related pragmatically organised, partial separation of powers through EU obligations. Neither does Hart's ultimate rule need to be consigned to the past, as Bogdanor (2009) assumes, because the direct challenge by the FTT to the ultimate rule does not occur. A brief consideration of the EU-level FTT demonstrates those key inter-relationships.

The European Commission explained its original FTT proposal as a transaction tax that would avoid fragmentation of the internal market for financial services and ensure that financial institutions make a fair contribution to covering the costs of the financial crisis (see the House of Lords EU Committee 2013). An earlier proposal by the Commission had the grander aim of creating a new revenue stream which could gradually displace national contributions to the EU budget, thereby lessening the burden of national treasuries. It is because of the UK (and Sweden's) objections that the original Commission-led EU-wide proposal for a FTT in 2011 was blocked—and was thereby permitted to be adopted as an amended version of the tax through the 'enhanced cooperation' method with 11 (Council of the EU 2013), then subsequently, only 10 member states (Barbière 2017). The 'enhanced cooperation' is an EU procedure in which EU members (a minimum of 9) can jointly pursue a policy of advanced integration or cooperation within EU structures, but without all the other EU countries being involved (EUR-Lex 2017). However, as the proposal was subsequently pursued and amended by 10 member states under enhanced cooperation, such a move made it unlikely that the tax could be used as a stream of revenue for the EU budget.

Traditionally, under the mixed Westminster model, it is the House of Commons as an institution which provides the means for a Government's dominant, partisan parliamentary majority to provide financial supply and support the executive. Under that model, the 1689 Bill of Rights established for the House of Commons a sole right to authorise taxation and the level of financial supply to the Crown. And it is historically the executive which initiates the taxation measures, not the European Commission. So, paradoxically, the scope of weakened, minister-led, executive-sanctioned EU decision-making powers exerted through the Council of the EU widens significantly into the sphere of legislative consent-providing powers. Under contemporary EU membership, the Commission however has the complete 'right of initiative'—it can propose new laws in accordance with the subsidiarity principle and in policy areas where the Treaties provide for action. Domestically, the role of ministers in government and policy officials are unsettled in an executive scenario where they might normally expect to propose and draft Government Bills. In this instance, they do not 'initiate' the proposed tax. Constitutional unsettlement occurs despite the European Commission being subject to *scrutiny* by the national executive and those of the 27 EU members (Kassim 2016b). The legislature however has no comparable connection to that of the Prime Minister and Cabinet in the executive within European Commission-level institutional decision-making. National legislatures have therefore, in this process, lost traditional legislative powers of initiative to hold to account, to amend and subsequently approve all final measures (Raunio 2009, 2011; Schmidt 2005; Raunio and Hix 2000).

4.3.2 *Judicialisation of the Parliament-Sanctioned Executive*

Executive and judicial powers are clearly separated at the recognised helm, but judicial decision-making moves ever closer into the scope previously defined by executive decision-making. This process occurs as national judiciaries become more independent of the executive as a consequence of their EU-related roles (Schmidt 2005). On 17 April 2013, the UK Government made an application to the ECJ for the annulment of the Council Decision authorising enhanced cooperation in the area of the FTT (*UK v Council of the EU* [2014]). The application focused on the extraterritorial elements of the tax. In that form, the FTT Directive would infringe the rights and competences of non-participating member states by departing from accepted international tax norms. The UK Government were concerned about the 'deemed establishment principle' (House of Lords EU Committee 2013, p. 11), where, for example, a UK bank would be deemed to be established in a participating member state (e.g. Germany) by virtue of their transactions involving bonds in that participating state.

The scope of judicial decision-making overreaches into the sphere of legislative and executive decision-making. The ECJ was able to dismiss the arguments of the Crown-in-Parliament in its attempts to block the tax on financial trades, and despite a UK veto at the EU level in the legislative process (Barker 2014c; *UK v Council of the EU* [2014]). The Council, as an EU institution, enables the overarching objective of the UK and all other members to articulate and consolidate their national interests by representatives of each of the national governments by legislating jointly with the European Parliament (Hayes-Renshaw 2012, p. 68). The law is to be applied by judges but the political sphere is divided and the open-ended politics over the tax remained contested. It has nevertheless been the case that the UK entry into the EU brought about a significant expansion of judicial power, not least because of the supremacy of EU law (Blauberger and Schmidt 2017; Tabarelli 2013, p. 346; Weiler 1991, 1994). A judiciary once obliged to merely give effect to the statutes of Parliament under the Westminster model overlaps at the recognised helm. It specifically did so with the proposing of taxation usually reserved for the executive, consolidated further by judicial overlapping with the dominant, partisan, Government majority in the House of Commons who legitimately expect to sanction the tax.

A substantial body of literature explains how European integration tends to encourage such a judicialisation of politics (Weiler 1991, 1994) and spreads a juridified mode of governance, or 'Eurolegalism' (Kelemen 2012, p. 55). This assumes that judicial institutions can answer deeply political questions, such as those on taxation. Compared to legislatures, unaccountable courts tend to do more to serve the interest of powerful economic actors and vested interests (Hirschl 2004; Bellamy 2008). At the European level, there is a widespread consensus that the ECJ has played a major part in the progress towards European integration (Easson 1989)—"an indispensable role" as a motor of European integration (Kelemen and Schmidt 2012), particularly as its substantive role ensures that the law is observed in the interpretation and application of the Treaties. The court has for many decades been accused of "being an excessively activist judiciary" (see reports by de Waele 2010, p. 3). Such a judicialisation of politics in Europe has led courts to become involved in nearly every major political and policy dispute imaginable (Kelemen 2012, p. 59), including that of the FTT.

4.3.3 EU Cooperation, Indirect Taxation and the Absence of Parliamentary Consent

Although the court dismissed the UK's challenge because their view was directed at elements of a future tax which was yet to be agreed, the tax continued to be pursued by a Eurozone grouping of 11 (Council of the EU 2013), and subsequently 10 member states, through enhanced cooperation (after Slovenia later withdrew) (Moscoivici 2017; Barbière 2017). The ruling also confirms the UK had limited power to block the Eurozone from pursuing joint policies under enhanced cooperation that potentially damage UK interests, even in the field of taxation where the UK retained its vetoes on EU rules (Barker 2014c). The recognised helm has judicial EU institutions incorporated into its government through a direct competitive overreach, and dilution, of the executive powers. Its consequence is the comparative weakening of legislative powers in the Commons to 'have its way' vis-a-vis the ECJ and thereby an unsettling of parliamentary sovereignty.

The balance of parliamentary scrutiny powers as contrasted with those of the executive remain distinct and yet executive decision-making dilutes the House of Lords powers of scrutiny and the role of the legislature in general at the recognised helm. In terms of assessing specific impacts of the EU on the UK, prior to 2016, Parliament itself, as distinct from the executive, had two special committees (one in each House of Parliament) which exercise scrutiny functions for Parliament in assessing the impact of EU legislation and activity (Bradley and Ewing 2010, p. 136). The UK Parliament has a European Scrutiny Committee and three European (standing) Committees in the Commons, and an

EU Committee with (currently, six) sub-committees in the Lords. The House of Lords' EU Committee were highly critical of the measure and the Government's treatment of the tax on an ongoing basis (EU Committee 2012). The committee insisted that there was a substantial risk that financial institutions would relocate outside the EU if a FTT was introduced, with serious consequences for the City of London and for the EU economy as a whole (EU Committee 2013, p. 7). The Committee were consistently critical of the measure, referring to the proposal as clearly having "a significant adverse impact" on financial institutions established in non-participating member states, specifically "making them liable for the FTT under either the deemed establishment or issuance principles" (EU Committee 2013, p. 86).

The Committee condemned the process as being "divisive", "significantly detrimental to the UK's interest" and "deliberately contentious in such a controversial area". They were strongly critical of the Government in their approach to negotiations at an EU Economic and Financial affairs Council (ECOFIN) vote on 22 January 2013. The vote authorised the use of enhanced cooperation. The Government merely abstained rather than voting against the authorising decision. Ministers had not encouraged other non-participating member states to vote against, particularly given that fewer than one half of member states advocated the tax (EU Committee 2013, p. 10). It is often reported the UK votes more often than other EU member states against EU measures, but even so, rarely votes against proposals (Thompson and Harari 2013; Van Aken 2012).

The committee played a significant part in contesting not only the FTT but more importantly, the Government's overall approach to the tax. The committee were very concerned of the potential damage caused by a FTT introduced by a smaller group of EU member states but found only a "marked complacency" within the UK's HM Treasury as to the potential deleterious impact, a serious underestimation of the political will amongst supporting member states and an inadequate response to the committee's report (EU Committee 2013). The committee even viewed the Government's initial assessment to be based on the assumption that the UK stood to benefit from a FTT imposed by other member states. Nonetheless, the Government declined sufficiently detailed responses or negotiations with the committee and finally pursued a legal challenge with the court—rather than adhere to Lords' suggestions and proposals throughout the legislative process. The government subsequently lost their legal challenge. The recognised helm has incorporated EU institutions such as ECOFIN which reciprocate the strength of the executive role in EU government machinery. This is particularly the case in a minister's power to act by qualified majority vote at the Council. Of course, the UK, through the European treaties and its regular practices, have agreed that through the intergovernmental Council of the EU (previously known as the Council of Ministers), its own representative national ministers and those from all member states meet to adopt laws and coordinate policies (see Bradley and Ewing 2010, p. 120). That process leads to a direct dilution of Lords' and Commons' scrutiny and voting powers (House of Commons' European Committee B [2013]) and to the weakening of legislative scrutiny powers and of parliamentary sovereignty.

During the EU policy process, executive decision-making powers shift away from their traditional role of accountability to the House of Commons' consent-providing powers (Raunio 2009, 2011) in the field of taxation. While the power to levy taxes remains central to the sovereignty of UK and other EU member states, there is some agreed limited UK competence for the EU in this area—outside of personal direct income taxes—which enable the smooth running of the single market, the harmonisation of indirect taxation (e.g. VAT, excise duties, import levies, and energy and other environmental taxes), fighting tax evasion and avoidance, tax challenges to fair competition and money laundering, and the potential proposal for a common consolidated corporate tax base (Paternoster 2016).

It is widely debated in the literature that almost without exception, "national parliaments are unequivocally considered the 'losers' in European integration because of their severe loss of competencies" (Sprungk 2013, p. 298) and it has been briefly discussed how the executive experiences the loss of the 'right of initiative'. The executive voluntarily shorn of its initiative at the helm, but which integrates its functions as a qualified majority voting stakeholder in the Council of the EU—ECOFIN in this case—effectively bypasses the scrutiny system in the Lords' and Commons' (House of Commons' European Committee B [2013]). That tension in multi-level governance (MLG), expressed as a "Faustian bargain" means the claimed advantages of accommodation and consensus, for example, in ECOFIN, are exchanged for an authority that seeps away from institutions where accountability is exercised (Peters and Pierre 2004, p. 85). In that process, the executive retains a significant degree of discretion over policy-making where Parliament is made partially absent as an actor.

This process occurs as the elevation of the executive through its fusion with EU governmental machinery is strongly maintained, chiefly in its relationship with the Council of the EU. The ministerial executive integrates with the Council of the EU and the other 27 executives to negotiate (Kassim 2016d) their respective positions in creating such taxation measures. The ministers, diplomats and civil servants belonging to the UK executive attend the meetings of the Council of the EU (Kassim 2016d) to set out their support, rejection or amendments on the tax. Specialised EU decisions are taken by those ministers. The legislature has no comparable connection to that of Cabinet ministers in the executive within Council-level institutional decision-making.

As one tax adviser told the House of Lords EU Economic and Financial Affairs and International Trade Sub-Committee, when providing evidence on the measure:

> A substantial part of the tax paid to Brussels would therefore be at the cost of the British taxpayer, simply transferring revenue from the UK budget subject to Parliamentary scrutiny (and a National Audit Office which is allowed to be effective) to Brussels where there are no such safeguards. (Chown 2011, p. 108)

More broadly, the development of the EU's quasi-institutional structures has significantly affected all member states' accountability structures by altering the traditional power and authority of national governments (Schmidt 2005).

The Commons consenting to indirect taxation in the precedented, historical convention of the mixed constitution is highly relevant to parliamentary sovereignty's historical meaning. Where EU membership enables a strengthening of executive decision to make law for the whole of the EU within a Council arrangement, decisions are shifted away from a national sphere of legislative consent-providing powers. As such, it dilutes the relevance of that historical precedent.

Given the tense debate between Conservative MPs during the period of Coalition Government, there is initially both a uniting and contesting, rather than strict separation, of powers between the executive and legislature because the majorities of each were all in opposition to the tax (to differing degrees). Subsequently, despite the later fact that at the original ECOFIN vote on 22 January 2013, the Government merely abstained rather than voted against the authorising decision for the use of enhanced cooperation, the Lords' committee then strongly criticised the decision (EU Committee 2013).

The dispute did not terminate at this stage. The political cleavage between Government and Parliament re-opened and deepened the debates at Westminster between 2013 and 2015 for more urgent referendum legislation on EU membership. The urgency had been fuelled by the failure of the Government's legal challenge at the ECJ, a challenge which the Commons majority had indirectly supported. An unregulated, political and irregular division opens up between Government and Parliament because (i) the Government has no 'initiative' in this case, as compared with the Commission and European Parliament; (ii) the Government's reciprocity, engagement and trust through ECOFIN, the European Parliament and the court proved ineffective; and (iii) traditionally, the House of Commons is the means for the Government's dominant, partisan majority to provide financial supply but in this case, their vote against the tax is partly opposed and bypassed at the EU-level.

4.3.4 The Rule of the Recognised Helm Preserved?

It is relevant to acknowledge that the upholding of the ultimate rule of parliamentary sovereignty is notably dependent upon an acknowledged consensus between Government and Parliament and even at the EU-level within the different institutional parts. For example, when the Government abstained against the authorising decision, ministers did so on the basis (however paradoxical) that if they attempted to block others from proceeding, they would have undermined the broader EU consensual principle of national sovereignty over taxation matters. Again, the then Financial Secretary to the Treasury, Greg Clark, reflecting the House of Commons' European Scrutiny Committee view, observed that the measure raised questions relating to parliamentary sovereignty and primacy (House of Commons 2013). Although proceeding in fundamentally different ways, both Government and Parliament openly acknowledged a rule of sovereignty in the protection of taxation measures.

Furthermore, within the EU itself, the Legal Service of the Council on 10 September 2013 played a significant part in the political discourse by identifying several critical aspects of the revised FTT (Barker 2013).

It argued that the 'deemed establishment principle'—affecting financial institutions established in non-participating member states—did not comply with the Treaty conditions through enhanced cooperation because: (i) it exceeded member states' jurisdiction to impose tax extraterritorially; (ii) it infringed the competences of non-participating member states (e.g. UK); and (iii) it was discriminatory and likely to lead to lead to distortion of competition to the detriment of non-participating member states (e.g. UK) (Barker 2013). In the opinion of the Legal Service of the Council, there would be insufficient connection between the taxpayer and the member state imposing the tax (Barker 2013). It would fail to respect the competence of non-participating member states as the FTT would be imposed on institutions resident in their territory by and to the benefit of the participating member state despite the fact that the primary competence for taxation lies with the non-participating member state (EU Committee 2013, p. 16). The Commission immediately rejected this opinion (House of Lords' EU Committee 2013, p. 8). The opinion of the Legal Service of the Council, in short, while not specifically referring to the problems as relating to sovereignty, inferred strong concerns over taxation sovereignty when the tax exceeded member states' jurisdiction to impose tax extraterritorially and that there would be insufficient connection between the taxpayer and the member state imposing the tax (Barker 2013). While the recognised helm has incorporated EU institutions into its government—and although the ECJ marginalised the Opinion of the Legal Service of the Council, there was ultimately a dilution of the executive powers impacting upon the comparative weakening of legislative powers in the Commons. Despite this trend there remained a wider acknowledged consensus, both domestic and European, on the UK's ultimate rule as protecting domestic, territorial, budgetary sovereignty. This suggests that the EU will not always as a whole transgress more fundamental principles of territorial, budgetary sovereignty over taxation—applicable not just to the UK but all member states. Equally, where the EU can potentially gain voluntary consent, such as through enhanced cooperation, it can by gradual developments accrue that power.

So far, despite the presentation of proposals, the EU has had difficulties accruing such power to construct the tax (Kastner 2017; Euractiv 2018); leaving tax sovereignty and parliamentary sovereignty broadly intact. The recognised helm with its limited legislative-sanctioned power and through the exercise of executive power can voluntarily choose to not participate in, and therefore not incorporate, specific EU measures which might impact upon its claims to sovereignty.

4.3.5 *Fracturing Executive-Legislative Relations and Opening the Door to Parliamentary and Popular Political Campaigns*

Through political contestation, the subsequent impasse in which the Government had not yet realised the policy it had set out, or to have reformed or blocked the measure in the EU legislative process, and having further lost their legal challenge, the outcome heightened the fracturing of executive-legislative relations arising from EU policy. The dispute drove the policy into a deeply contentious political debate and the UK Government's proposed high-level EU renegotiation with other member states. The tax, by nature of the executive-legislature division in the Commons became part of the deeper, political EU treaty renegotiation agenda being sought by the then UK Prime Minister, David Cameron (Parker and Barker 2015) preceding the 2016 referendum on EU membership. It is often in the House of Commons where the division of powers are most observable. In the past, post hoc Prime Ministerial statements in the Commons' on the European Council meetings or the Chancellor's announcements on ECOFIN meetings have long been perceived to be weak guarantees of Westminster accountability for ministerial decisions made at the EU-level. The government's own backbench MPs disaffection in Parliament, in reaction to the Government's impasse in its European policy and strategy, drove a deeper political wedge in executive-legislative relations. The unregulated political division is created when the Government demonstrates reciprocity, comity and trust in the Council and court system of the EU at the expense of comity and trust with the House of Commons as the means for the Government's dominant, partisan majority to provide their ultimate consent to a tax. The process confirms Bogdanor's political intervention on Bagehot: there is a partial separation of powers, particularly between Cabinet and Parliament and the degree of that separation depends upon the extent to which Parliament asserts itself against the government (Bogdanor 2009, p. 285). Neither Parliament, nor its dominant, partisan majority found a need to strictly assert itself against the government of the day because the Government were already in opposition to the measure. However, as a 'new phase' opened up, following the initial ECJ legal challenge which had failed, the separation of power between executive and the elected legislature further deepened. The deepening separation is evidenced by MPs pushing for ever more urgent EU referendum legislation and the Prime Minister pledging a renegotiation of the UK-EU relationship (see Parker and Barker 2015).

By nature of the contested political, open-ended situation of possibilities, including the then potential outcomes of the EU referendum and Prime Ministerial renegotiation, and despite the ECJ judgement, the disagreement within the UK of accepting the FTT continued to proceed within the political sphere. The fracturing of executive-legislative relations creates an open door for parliamentary and popular politics. Historical constitutional forms contain a conceptual system of discourses, which are open to the possibility of ongoing modification (consistent with Prokhovnik 2008). Contestability occurs between the present constitutional form and other historical forms. The historical custom of the mixed constitution conflicts with the modern customs and assumptions of modern parliamentary sovereignty.

The Government's approach to the FTT was contested by a parliamentary opposition and a popular opposition organised by several campaign groups. Those national and sub-national groups and minority political groups seeking support for the FTT who found their views underrepresented in the Commons' subsequently found a greater collective representative capacity in the European Parliament. The European Parliament strongly voted for and supported the tax. By its nature, this produces a negative or poor stature of the Westminster Parliament in the eyes of minority political groups. The European Parliament's competition at the recognised helm directly distorts the representative capacity of the Commons. The Commons, without a willing executive-led majority to support the proposed tax, remains in the eyes of minority and sub-national groupings, less trusted than the EU parliamentary and court system for giving them the tax/right they desired. The 'deparliamentarisation' of the system partially occurs under the rise of the executive branch and notably a Westminster submission to a "legislative powerhouse" (Kohler 2014) of the European Parliament. The Government won its parliamentary votes on Motions sceptical of the tax, although the Government won those votes through the whippable support of dominant, partisan majorities in Parliament. But this was not all unopposed. The strength of public anger directed against the financial sector and the view that those who contributed to the financial crisis should contribute to its costs resonated in popular political and mainstream opposition

Labour Party discourses and in proposals for some form of transactions tax (House of Lords' EU Committee 2013, p. 7), indicating support for the FTT (Labour Party Manifesto 2017; Labour Party EU Manifesto 2014; House of Commons 2013). In the UK itself, 65% were in favour of (while 25% opposed) a FTT (Eurobarometer 2011).

As against the Conservative-led Coalition Government's position, the FTT proposal followed a historically strong socialist origin in Europe and there have been many testimonies from those who campaigned for the tax (Ford 2012). The recognised helm has since 1979 had a directly elected European Parliament incorporated. It has resulted in an influence on the balance of the executive, and judiciary, along with a dilution of the domestic legislature by a European legislative body, which impacts indirectly upon parliamentary sovereignty. The Lisbon Treaty in late 2009, brought further law-making powers to the European Parliament that put it on an equal footing with the Council and which further diluted the position of the domestic legislature. The executive and judiciary receive a deep engagement in the EU system—through ECOFIN votes, the European Parliament involvement in the legislative process and a court challenge through the ECJ (Barker 2014c; EU Committee 2012, 2013). However, the domestic legislature, in which the Commons has primacy, receives virtually no equivalent form of engagement. To make this observation is to acknowledge the relationship between the precedented, historical constitutional form of the mixed constitution in the sixth of the eight historical forms as relevant to parliamentary sovereignty's historical meaning. Ultimately, EU membership results in the scope of EU-integrated Prime Ministerial (European Council) and executive decision-making powers (ECOFIN) moving into the remit of Commons' consent-providing powers through reciprocity and engagement at the EU-level, which unsettles that precedent.

4.3.6 *Tax-Collecting Powers Diluting Mixed Government: The Role of Non Westminster-Delegated Authority*

It stands contrary to some aspects of Loughlin's (2010) work when it is considered that a UK rule-based constitutional structure, including parliamentary sovereignty within a tripartite constitution, has not completely disappeared or given way to complex arrangements of local and non-public bodies. But Loughlin, it seems, may be justified in arguing for the rise of the elaborate networks. The objectives of ministers at the apex of the system are being diluted at the recognised helm by differentiated arrangements with elaborate service networks. Her Majesty's Revenue & Customs (HMRC) and other public bodies, when sanctioned by the EU, for such explicit EU purposes, operate at some remove from electorally authorised sources of authority.

Furthermore, the nature of the EU's interaction with UK parliamentary sovereignty occurs in the context of Loughlin's purported rise of the administrative machinery. It strengthens the hand of the executive at the helm and where network bodies realise their potential through an original, not delegated authority (e.g. Wonka and Rittberger 2010; Gilardi 2002), it dilutes the Commons' historic capacity to sanction tax-collection. The growth of administrative powers threatens to unbalance the legislative as against heightened executive, tax-collecting powers. Their modern development has diluted the basis of mixed government, particularly where EU-sanctioned bodies realise their potential through a newly developed, original, and not Westminster-delegated authority.

The primacy of steerage and coordinating processes and outcomes pursued by executive bodies are often considered to be central to MLG approach(es). Governance necessarily involves understanding steering multiple agencies, institutions, and systems that can be operationally autonomous and yet structurally coupled through reciprocal interdependence (Jessop 2004, p. 65). In contemporary governance, a great deal of attention has been paid to the way in which some entities take a greater responsibility for "steering" (Bache 2012; Skelcher 2005), with a specific focus on steerage by EU-institutional level entities such as the Commission, the Council of the EU, and the European Parliament. The role of institutions in the FTT suggests outcomes-focused steerage at multiple levels has been incorporated. The role of Commission, Council of the EU and HMRC agencies all feature as inputs of potential steerage for governing at the helm.

It has been importantly suggested in the course of events that by implementing The Mutual Recovery Directive in relation to the FTT, if one of the parties to that financial transaction was established in the UK then the tax authorities of the FTT member state would be able to request the UK's HMRC to collect and account for them when the tax is imposed directly or indirectly (EU Committee 2013). The issue had been heavily scrutinised because the involvement of the HMRC to collect the tax is of notable relevance when the employment of executive agencies for European purposes again fuses the national executive into an administrative order where the rules are separate and differently incorporated.

While it might be accepted parliamentary sovereignty co-exists in the modern constitution with at least a 'partial separation of powers', the contemporary existence of a wider plurality of competing public and private agencies can present difficulties for those distinct but diluted powers in governing at the helm. The HMRC is not operating with normal domestic tax-collecting circumstances in this case. The HMRC operates within a plurality of competing public and private agencies which do not overcome the anxiety that checking might subvert the independence of a branch of government or institution, but rather unsettle the operation of other branches of government.

The elevation of executive agency powers occurs as EU legislation is eventually implemented by the UK executive. In this case, the recognised helm has incorporated EU-sanctioned national executive agencies into its government notably through an influence on the elevation of executive agency powers. This produces a limited involvement of the legislature-sanctioned power, unsettling parliamentary sovereignty.

4.4 Conclusion

The complexity of MLG tends to blur the lines of accountability and decision-making (Bache and Flinders 2004, p. 43) and the literature often recognises that traditional sovereignty and the separation of powers are thereby considered outmoded, redundant normative concerns (see Conway 2011, p. 174). EU interaction has unsettled prior historical constitutional forms in which the powers of the executive, the legislature and the judiciary are organised, now joined by the EU. The EU jointly impels the machinery of government in a unique direction different from that pursued under the Westminster model. Traditionally, the theoretical explanation of parliamentary sovereignty had accommodated the sixth of the eight historical forms, illustrating the meaning of the mixed constitution attributed to parliamentary sovereignty. Contemporary, changing relationships between the executive, the legislature and the judiciary have been clearly impacted by their interaction with the EU.

The consideration of the FTT demonstrated that the recognised helm, with those deeply intricate inter-relationships, had been disturbed and this experience unsettled parliamentary sovereignty. The scope of judicial decision-making widens into the sphere of legislative and executive decision-making at the recognised helm. The ECJ fenced off the arguments of the Crown-in-Parliament in its attempts to block the tax on financial trades, and despite a UK veto at the EU level in the legislative process. A constitutional unsettlement occurs because the Commons-consenting-of indirect taxation between the precedented, historical convention of the mixed constitution in the sixth of the eight historical constitutional forms had previously been relevant to parliamentary sovereignty's historical meaning. Where EU membership results in broadening the scope of executive decision-making powers relative to the sphere of legislative consent-providing powers, it unsettles and dilutes the claims of that historical precedent.

Through political contestation, the subsequent impasse in which the Government had not been effective in its opposition or blocked the measure in the EU legislative process, and having further lost their legal challenge, the fragile political situation only amplified the fracturing of Commons' and executive relations. The fragility between the executive and legislature drove the policy into the deeply contentious political debate including the UK Government's then proposed EU referendum and the Prime Minister's high-level renegotiation with other member states—providing for Bogdanor's partial separation of powers. The European Parliament's specific competition at the recognised helm directly distorts the representative capacity of the Commons' in the eyes of some pressure groups. Campaigners and some voters had looked to the European parliamentary and court system for giving them the tax they desired. Furthermore, the growth of administrative powers threatens to unbalance the legislative as against heightened executive, tax-collecting powers, as the basis of mixed government. In particular, EU-sanctioned bodies realise their potential through a newly developed, original, and not Westminster-delegated authority. The historical constitutional form of Burke—that the sovereignty of Parliament is located in a balanced constitution configured around a trust between the Crown and Parliament (Craig 2012; Bourke 1999)—now incorporates the EU as a new steering hand into the recognised helm.

The subsequent chapter (Chapter 5) will argue that the Westminster Parliament has become unsettled because the UK's recognised helm has had European Parliament-level parliamentary representation competing with it. The case study of the Working Time Directive presents a UK recognised helm which has had European Parliament-level parliamentary representation competing in its capacity to collectively represent its electors. That inter-parliamentary competition produces an unsettling of the historically precedented capacity to collectively represent, as strongly embedded within previous historical constitutional forms, thereby diluting the strength of parliamentary sovereignty.

Bibliography

Bache, I. (2012). Multi-level Governance in the European Union. In D. Levi-Faur (Ed.), *The Oxford Handbook of Governance*. Oxford: Oxford University Press.

Bache, I., & Flinders, M. (2004). Multi-level Governance and the Study of the British State. *Public Policy and Administration, 19*(1), 31–51.

Barbière, C. (2017, March 6). FTT Blockage Illustrates Pitfalls of Multi-speed Europe. *Euractiv* [Online]. Available at https://www.euractiv.com/section/economy-jobs/news/ftt-blockage-illustrates-pitfalls-of-multi-speed-europe/. Accessed 25 June 2017.

Barker, A. (2013, September 10). EU Legal Opinion Against the FTT—Full Text. *Financial Times* [Blog]. Available at http://blogs.ft.com/brussels-blog/2013/09/10/eu-legal-opinion-against-the-ftt-full-text/. Accessed 16 September 2014.

Barker, A. (2014a, November 20). Osborne Gives Up on Challenge to Bank Bonus Cap. *Financial Times* [Online]. Available at https://www.ft.com/content/12d1ba3a-7094-11e4-9129-00144feabdc0. Accessed 21 November 2014.

Barker, A. (2014b, January 22). European Court Rejects UK Challenge Against EU Short-Selling Ban. *Financial Times* [Online]. Available at https://www.ft.com/content/68cbcb64-834c-11e3-aa65-00144feab7de. Accessed 25 January 2014.

Barker, A. (2014c, April 30). UK Loses Legal Challenge to EU Financial Transaction Tax. *Financial Times* [Online]. Available at https://www.ft.com/content/d846671a-d040-11e3-af2b-00144feabdc0. Accessed 5 May 2014.

BBC News. (2014, January 22). EU Court Rebuffs UK Legal Challenge to Short-Selling Law. *BBC News* [Online]. Available at http://www.bbc.co.uk/news/business-25845291. Accessed 25 January 2014.

Bellamy, R. (1996). The Political Form of the Constitution: The Separation of Powers, Rights and Representative Democracy. *Political Studies, 44*(3), 436–456.

Bellamy, R. (2007). *Political Constitutionalism: A Republican Defence of The Constitutionality of Democracy*. Cambridge: Cambridge University Press.

Bellamy, R. (2008). *Citizenship: A Very Short Introduction*. Oxford: Oxford University Press.

Blackstone, W. (1765). *Commentaries on the Laws of England (1765–1769)*. Chicago, IL: University of Chicago Press (this edition 1979).

Blauberger, M., & Schmidt, S. K. (2017). The European Court of Justice and Its Political Impact. *West European Politics, 40*(4), 907–918.

Bogdanor, V. (2009). *The New British Constitution*. Oxford: Hart Publishing.

Bogdanor, V. (2019). *Beyond Brexit: Towards a British Constitution*. London: I.B. Tauris.

Bourke, R. (1999). Sovereignty, Opinion and Revolution in Edmund Burke. *History of European Ideas, 25*(3), 99–120.

Bradley, A. (2011). The Sovereignty of Parliament—Form or Substance? In J. Jowell & D. Oliver (Eds.), *The Changing Constitution* (7th ed.). Oxford: Oxford University Press.

Bradley, A. W., & Ewing, K. D. (2010). *Constitutional and Administrative Law* (15th ed.). Harlow: Longman.

Burke, E. (1774). Speech to the Electors of Bristol. In E. J. Payne (Ed.). (1999), *Select Works of Edmund Burke* (Vol. 4). Indianapolis, IN: Liberty Fund. Available at http://oll.libertyfund.org/titles/burke-select-works-of-edmund-burke-vol-4. Accessed 17 December 2013.

Chown, J. (2011, November 25). *Written Evidence to the House of Lords' EU Economic and Financial Affairs and International Trade Sub-Committee*. Financial Transaction Tax, Oral and Written Evidence [Online]. Available at http://www.parliament.uk/documents/lords-committees/eu-sub-com-a/financialtransactiontax/fttfinalweb.pdf. Accessed 3 March 2012.

Conway, G. (2011). Retrieving a Separation of Powers in the European Union. In *The Limits of Legal Reasoning and the European Court of Justice* (pp. 172–200). Cambridge: Cambridge University Press.

Council of the European Union. (2013). *Council Meeting Economic and Financial Affairs Brussels* [Online]. Available at http://www.consilium.europa.eu/uedocs/cms_data/docs/pressdata/en/ecofin/134960.pdf. Accessed 1 March 2013.

Craig, D. (2012). Burke and the Constitution. In D. Dwan & C. J. Insole (Eds.), *The Cambridge Companion to Edmund Burke* (pp. 104–116). Cambridge: Cambridge University Press.

de Montesquieu, C. (1748). *The Spirit of the Laws* (A. M. Cohler, Ed.). Cambridge: Cambridge University Press (this edition 1989).

de Waele, H. (2010). The Role of the European Court of Justice in the Integration Process: A Contemporary and Normative Assessment. *Hanse Law Review, 6*(1), 3–26.

Dicey, A. V. (1885/1964). *An Introduction to the Study of the Law of the Constitution*. London: Macmillan.

Easson, A. (1989). Legal Approaches to European Integration: The Role of Court and Legislator in the Completion of the European Common Market. *Journal of European Integration, 12*(2–3), 101–119.

Egeberg, M., & Trondal, J. (2011). EU-Level Agencies: New Executive Centre Formation or Vehicles for National Control? *Journal of European Public Policy, 18*(6), 868–887.

Egeberg, M., & Trondal, J. (2017). Researching European Union Agencies: What Have We Learnt (and Where Do We Go from Here)? *Journal of Common Market Studies, 55*(4), 675–690.

EU Committee. (2012, March 30). *Towards a Financial Transaction Tax?* (HL Paper 287) [Online]. Available at https://publications.parliament.uk/pa/ld201012/ldselect/ldeucom/287/28704.htm. Accessed 10 August 2015.

EU Committee. (2013, December 10). *Financial Transaction Tax: Alive and Deadly* (HL Paper 86) [Online]. Available at https://publications.parliament.uk/pa/ld201314/ldselect/ldeucom/86/86.pdf. Accessed 10 August 2015.

Euractiv. (2013, April 17). *Parliament Gives Green Light to Cap Bankers' Bonuses* [Online]. Available at http://www.euractiv.com/euro-finance/parliament-curbs-bankers-bonuses-news-519181. Accessed 25 September 2015.

Euractiv. (2018, December 3). *Germany and France to Outline EU Financial Transaction Tax Proposal* [Online]. Available at https://www.euractiv.com/section/economy-jobs/news/germany-and-france-to-outline-eu-financial-transaction-tax-proposal/. Accessed 12 February 2019.

EUR-Lex. (2017). *Enhanced Cooperation* [Online]. Available at http://eur-lex.europa.eu/legal-content/EN/TXT/?uri=URISERV%3Axy0015. Accessed 7 April 2017.

Eurobarometer. (2011, June 22). *Europeans and the Crisis.* EB Parlemeter [Online]. Available at http://www.europarl.europa.eu/pdf/eurobarometre/2011/juin/22062011/eb752_financial_crisis_analytical_synthesis_en.pdf. Accessed 25 September 2015.

European Committee B. (2013, February 7). *Financial Sector (Taxation)* (House of Commons, Division No. 1).

European Union. (2019). *About the EU* [Online]. Available at http://europa.eu/about-eu/index_en.htm. Accessed 2 August 2014.

Ford, G. (2012, February 3). *Financial Transaction Tax a Trump Card for Labour?* Blog for Labour Movement for Europe [Blog]. Available at http://labourmovement.eu/2012/02/financial-transaction-tax-a-trump-card-for-labour/. Accessed 4 March 2013.

Francis, M., & Morrow, J. (1994). *A History of Political Thought in the Nineteenth Century.* London: Duckworth.

Freshfields Bruckhaus Deringer LLP. (2013). *Briefing New EU Rules on Bankers' Pay (Including the Bonus Cap)* [Online]. Available at http://www.freshfields.com. Accessed 25 September 2015.

Galligan, D. (2006). *Law in Modern Society.* Oxford: Oxford University Press.

Gilardi, F. (2002). Policy Credibility and Delegation to Independent Regulatory Agencies: A Comparative Empirical Analysis. *Journal of European Public Policy, 9*(6), 873–893.

Goldsworthy, J. (1999). *The Sovereignty of Parliament: History and Philosophy*. Oxford: Clarendon Press.

Guardian. (2012, August 22). Bonfire of the Quangos: The Victims [Online]. Available at https://www.theguardian.com/politics/2012/aug/22/bonfire-quangos-victims-list. Accessed 24 August 2012.

Hart, H. L. A. (1997). *The Concept of Law* (2nd ed.). Oxford: Clarendon Press.

Hayes-Renshaw, F. (2012). The Council of Ministers. In J. Peterson & M. Shackleton (Eds.), *The Institutions of the European Union* (3rd ed., pp. 68–95). Oxford: Oxford University Press.

Hirschl, R. (2004). *Towards Juristocracy: The Origins and Consequences of the New Constitutionalism*. Cambridge: Harvard University Press.

Hooghe, J., & Kassim, H. (2012). The Commission's Services. In J. Peterson & M. Shackleton (Eds.), *The Institutions of the European Union* (3rd ed., pp. 173–198). Oxford: Oxford University Press.

House of Commons. (2011, April 27). *Hansard*, Column 323, Division No. 258 [Online]. Available at https://publications.parliament.uk/pa/cm201516/cmhansrd/cm160224/debtext/160224-0002.htm. Accessed 3 May 2011.

House of Commons. (2013, June 18). *Hansard*, Column 787 [Online]. Available at https://publications.parliament.uk/pa/cm201314/cmhansrd/cm130618/debtext/130618-0002.htm#13061895000002. Accessed 19 June 2013.

Jack, M., Hutton, M., Johnson, C., Millar, D., Patrick, S., & Sandall, A. (Eds.). (2011). *Erskine May: Parliamentary Practice* (24th ed.). London: LexisNexis Butterworths.

Jessop, B. (2004). Multi Level Governance and Multi-level Meta Governance. In I. Bache & M. Flinders (Eds.), *Multi-level Governance* (pp. 49–74). Oxford: Oxford University Press.

Kassim, H. (2016a). *The European Council—The Who, What, Where, How and Why*. The UK in a Changing Europe Initiative [Online]. Available at http://www.ukandeu.ac.uk/explainers/the-european-council-the-who-what-where-how-and-why/. Accessed 5 July 2017.

Kassim, H. (2016b). *The European Commission*. The UK in a Changing Europe Initiative [Online]. Available at http://www.ukandeu.ac.uk/explainers/the-european-commission/. Accessed 5 July 2017.

Kassim, H. (2016c). *The EU: Institutions Explained*. The UK in a Changing Europe Initiative [Online]. Available at http://www.ukandeu.ac.uk/explainers/the-european-union-the-institutional-system-explained/. Accessed 5 July 2017.

Kassim, H. (2016d). *The Council of the European Union*. The UK in a Changing Europe Initiative [Online]. Available at http://www.ukandeu.ac.uk/explainers/the-council-of-the-european-union/. Accessed 5 July 2017.

Kastner, L. (2017, May 22). *How the Financial Industry Mobilized Against the European Financial Transaction Tax.* Sheffield Political Economy Research Institute [Blog]. Available at http://speri.dept.shef.ac.uk/2017/05/22/how-the-financial-industry-mobilized-against-the-european-financial-transaction-tax/. Accessed 30 June 2017.

Kelemen, R. D. (2012). Eurolegalism and Democracy. *Journal of Common Market Studies, 50*(Suppl. 1), 55–71.

Kelemen, R. D., & Schmidt, S. K. (2012). Introduction—The European Court of Justice and Legal Integration: Perpetual Momentum? *Journal of European Public Policy, 19*(1), 1–7.

King, A. (2007). *The British Constitution.* Oxford: Oxford University Press.

Kohler, M. (2014). European Governance and the European Parliament: From Talking Shop to Legislative Powerhouse. *Journal of Common Market Studies, 52*(3), 600–615.

Labour Party. (2014). *European Manifesto.* London: The Labour Party [Online]. Available at https://www.policyforum.labour.org.uk/uploads/editor/files/LABOUR_PARTY_euro_manifesto.pdf. Accessed 1 April 2016.

Labour Party Manifesto. (2017). London: The Labour Party [Online]. Available at http://www.labour.org.uk/page/-/Images/manifesto-2017/Labour%20Manifesto%202017.pdf. Accessed 20 August 2017.

Lieberman, D. (2006). The Mixed Constitution and the Common Law. In M. Goldie & R. Wokler (Eds.), *The Cambridge History of Eighteenth-Century Political Thought* (pp. 317–346). Cambridge: Cambridge University Press.

Loughlin, M. (2010). *Foundations of Public Law.* Oxford: Oxford University Press.

Lubert, H. L. (2010). Sovereignty and Liberty in William Blackstone's Commentaries on the Laws of England. *The Review of Politics, 72*(2), 271–297.

Marks, G., & Hooghe, L. (2004). Contrasting Visions of Multi-level Governance. In I. Bache & M. Flinders (Eds.), *Multi-level Governance* (pp. 15–30). Oxford: Oxford University Press.

Masterman, R. (2011). *The Separation of Powers in the Contemporary Constitution: Judicial Competence and Independence in the United Kingdom.* Cambridge: Cambridge University Press.

Mezey, M. L. (1979). *Comparative Legislature.* Durham, NC: Duke University Press.

Moscovici, P. (2017). *Speech by Commissioner Pierre Moscovici at the Commission's Tax Fairness Conference* [Online]. Available at http://europa.eu/rapid/press-release_SPEECH-17-1828_en.htm. Accessed 3 July 2017.

Norton, P. (1984). Parliament and Policy in Britain: The House of Commons as a Policy Influencer. *Teaching Politics, 13*(2), 198–221.

Norton, P. (1994). The Legislative Powers of Parliament. In A. Flinterman, A. Heringa, & L. Waddington (Eds.), *The Evolving Role of Parliaments in Europe*. Antwerp: Maklu.

O'Brennan, J., & Raunio, T. (2007). *National Parliaments Within the Enlarged European Union: From 'Victims' of Integration to Competitive Actors?* London: Routledge.

O'Gorman, F. (2012, November 22). *British Politics in the Long Eighteenth Century: A Defense of Political History*. Institute of Historical Research [Podcast]. Available at http://www.history.ac.uk/podcasts/franco-british-history-external/british-politics-long-eighteenth-century-defense-political. Accessed 25 November 2012.

Parker, G., & Barker, A. (2015, September 9). UK Seeks EU Treaty Overhaul to Protect City. *Financial Times* [Online]. https://www.ft.com/content/c147ea8c-5700-11e5-a28b-50226830d644. Accessed 10 September 2015.

Paternoster, D. (2016). *General Tax Policy*. Brussels: European Parliament [Online]. Available at http://www.europarl.europa.eu/atyourservice/en/displayFtu.html?ftuId=FTU_5.11.1.html. Accessed 7 April 2016.

Peters, G., & Pierre, J. (2004). Multi-level Governance and Democracy: A Faustian Bargain? In I. Bache & M. Flinders (Eds.), *Multi-level Governance* (pp. 75–89). Oxford: Oxford University Press.

Peterson, J. (2012). The College of Commissioners. In J. Peterson & M. Shackleton (Eds.), *The Institutions of the European Union* (3rd ed., pp. 96–123). Oxford: Oxford University Press.

Prokhovnik, R. (2008). *Sovereignty: History and Theory*. Exeter: Imprint Academic.

Raunio, T. (2009). National Parliaments and European Integration: What We Know and Agenda for Future Research. *The Journal of Legislative Studies, 15*(4), 317–334.

Raunio, T. (2011). The Gatekeepers of European Integration? The Functions of National Parliaments in the EU Political System. *Journal of European Integration, 33*(3), 303–321.

Raunio, T., & Hix, S. (2000). Backbenchers Learn to Fight Back: European Integration and Parliamentary Government. *West European Politics, 23*(4), 142–168.

Rubin, E. L. (2005). *Beyond Camelot: Rethinking Politics and Law for the Modern State*. Princeton, NJ: Princeton University Press.

Schmidt, V. A. (1999). European "Federalism" and Its Encroachments on National Institutions. *Publius: The Journal of Federalism, 29*(1), 19–44.

Schmidt, V. A. (2005). Democracy in Europe: The Impact of European Integration. *Perspectives on Politics, 3*(4), 761–779.

Sciaraffa, S. (2011). The Ineliminability of Hartian Social Rules. *Oxford Journal of Legal Studies, 31*(3), 603–623.

Skelcher, C. (2005). Jurisdictional Integrity, Polycentrism, and the Design of Democratic Governance. *Governance, 18*(1), 89–110.

Sprungk, C. (2013). Legislative Transposition of Directives: Exploring the Other Role of National Parliaments in the European Union. *Journal of Common Market Studies, 51*(2), 298–315.

Tabarelli, M. (2013). The Influence of the EU and the ECHR on "Parliamentary Sovereignty Regimes": Assessing the Impact of European Integration on the British and Swedish Judiciaries. *European Law Journal, 19*(3), 340–363.

Thompson, G., & Harari, D. (2013, September 17). *The Economic Impact of EU Membership on the UK* (House of Commons Library Standard Note SN/EP/6730) [Online]. Available at http://researchbriefings.parliament.uk/ResearchBriefing/Summary/SN06730. Accessed 5 November 2014.

Tomkins, A. (2013). What's Left of the Political Constitution? *German Law Journal, 14*(12), 2275–2292 [Online]. Available at http://www.germanlaw-journal.com/index.php?pageID=11&artID=1604. Accessed 12 December 2013.

Turpin, C., & Tomkins, A. (2011). *British Government and the Constitution: Text and Materials*. Cambridge: Cambridge University Press.

UK v Council of the EU. [2014]. Case C–209/13. Available at http://eur-lex.europa.eu/legal-content/EN/ALL/?uri=CELEX%3A62013CJ0209. Accessed 8 February 2015.

Van Aken, W. (2012). *Voting in the Council of the European Union Contested Decision-Making in the EU Council of Ministers (1995–2010)*. Stockholm: Swedish Institute for European Policy Studies [Online]. Available at http://www.sieps.se/sites/default/files/2012_2rap_1.pdf. Accessed 3 December 2012.

Walker, N. (2014, July). Our Constitutional Unsettlement. *Public Law*, 529–548.

Weiler, J. H. H. (1991). The Transformation of Europe. *Yale Law Journal, 100*(8), 2403–2483.

Weiler, J. H. H. (1994). A Quiet Revolution: "The European Court of Justice and Its Interlocutors". *Comparative Political Studies, 26*(4), 510–534.

Wonka, A., & Rittberger, B. (2010). Credibility, Complexity and Uncertainty: Explaining the Institutional Independence of 29 EU Agencies. *West European Politics, 33*(4), 730–752.

CHAPTER 5

Parliamentary Sovereignty, Collective Representation and EU Membership

Parliamentary sovereignty rests on the historically precedented basis that the 'collective representation' of the UK electorate through the Westminster Parliament provides a deeper connect than the specialist interest group representation pursued by the European Parliament. Under EU membership, the UK Parliament has become unsettled because European Parliament-level parliamentary representation competes with it, not for individual electoral interests, but over its capacity to collectively represent its electors. The recognition that the UK Parliament has become unsettled due to the distorting of its capacity to collectively represent is consistent with the well-recorded observations that the European Parliament exemplifies a high level of specialist 'functional' representation. Functional representation provides "instruments of linkage" between citizens and the European Parliament through lobbying channels to organise interest groups and social movements in order to influence EU policy-making (Berkhout et al. 2017; Marsh and Norris 1997, p. 158, contra Wessels 1999). In Strasbourg, the proposed boundaries to representation are defined through neo-corporatist approaches. Accordingly, social dialogue between key institutions and social partners is ingrained (Smismans 2016; Wendler 2017)—it is not primarily defined around majority-supported manifesto(s) turned into elected government agendas. Yet, as a whole, the European Parliament holds virtually no equivalent connect with the domestic electorate in a similar fashion to the national parliaments. The Westminster parliament operates 'nearer the people'. The same contrast cannot be made of the

J. McConalogue, *The British Constitution Resettled*,
https://doi.org/10.1007/978-3-030-25290-8_5

devolved assemblies whose territorial location and means of representation is closer to their electorate, albeit only on policy areas agreed to by Westminster.

Conceptually, the 'collective representation' of the people defines a Westminster model of representation characterised by both a 'trustee' representative status (in contrast to a delegate status) of its elected MPs. It also refers to a collective status of a deliberate assembly by which Parliament acts in the common, national interest (Burke 1774). Past historical constitutional forms, as precedents, present an English constitution in which governing at the helm is presented as politically contingent upon parliament's capacity to collectively represent its electors. It is plausible to consider that the feature of collective representation is described in all the historical forms explaining parliamentary sovereignty, although not effectively achieved until the full electoral franchise was established in 1928 giving women electoral equality with men, and further to 18–20 year-olds in 1969 throughout the seventh constitutional form. However, in the form of representation identified in the sixth historical constitutional form, for Burke, there is a sense of recognition in defining a collectively representative Parliament through mixed government in the eighteenth century (Craig 2012; Bourke 1999), which is central.

The case study of the Working Time Directive demonstrates that the recognised helm has experienced European Parliament-level parliamentary representation competing with its capacity to collectively represent its electors. In the UK context, political decisions are usually taken by politicians as accountable representatives, not judges or by other bodies. This is simply because MPs are electable as representatives, they are removable at the ballot box and are accountable to Parliament throughout their tenure and ultimately to their electors (Griffith 1979). The inter-parliamentary competition with the European Parliament, however, produces an unsettling of Parliament's historically precedented capacity to collectively represent a national electorate. The role of representation in this tribal sense is strongly embedded within precedented political historical constitutional forms, thereby unsettling parliamentary sovereignty. The European Parliament is strongly reliant on the Council, the Commission in particular (Aldrin and Hubé 2018; Greenwood 2018; Lindgren and Persson 2018) and the European Economic and Social Committee's shared neo-corporatist emphasis because it seeks to represent the approach taken by the shared central institutions (Wendler 2017). In the example of the Working Time Directive, this chapter will also look at the general reliance on 'constitutionalisation', as an attempt to construct constitutional texts defining EU-level individual rights by the European Parliament, in order to strengthen its representative linkages. Yet, here, a clear place can also be found for political parties and management of political partisanship in explaining the outcome of the Directive. The feature of representation of the collective interest is primary in defining political representation and its impact on parliamentary sovereignty.

5.1 Parliamentary Sovereignty and Historical Collective Representation by Parliament

The collective representation of the people has an inherent place in the historical development of the British constitution. The UK public currently elects 650 Members of Parliament to *represent* their interests and concerns in the House of Commons (UK Parliament 2019a). By collectively representing the electorate, MPs consider and propose new laws, and can scrutinise government policies by asking ministers questions about current issues either in the Commons Chamber or in Committees (UK Parliament 2019a). The Government cannot make new laws or raise new taxes without Parliament's agreement. The political party that wins the most seats at a General Election takes charge of the Government for five years, until the next General Election. The Government are therefore the candidates from political parties that voters' have elected to represent them in order to run the country. The leader of the winning party is appointed as Prime Minister and chooses other party members to work in the Government with them—as Cabinet ministers and junior ministers. Parliament is there to represent voters' interests and make sure they are taken into account by the Government.

The features of representation are to an extent described in most of the previous historical constitutional forms explaining parliamentary sovereignty. However, the form of representation identified in the sixth historical constitutional form in which there is a recognition of 'What the Crown-*in*-mixed constitutional Parliament enacts is law' (1690–1790s) is central. The ultimate rule described above required balance against its political conditions, including collective representation, to support the rule. It is in that explanatory historical constitutional form that the political theory of Edmund Burke has been and remains useful in contemporary understandings of representation—albeit Burke is writing for a pre-democratic age, at least 150 years before Britain establishes the full extension of the franchise. Even with Burke writing in a pre-democratic age, in his view, the English, or Westminster model of representation is characterised by Members of Parliament being elected to the House of Commons with a 'trustee' representative status (as opposed to being directly delegated) by voters and a collective parliamentary status acting in the national interest in that it "is a deliberative assembly of one nation, with one interest, that of the whole" (Burke 1774). In his now infamous 'Speech to the Electors of Bristol' of 3 November 1774, Burke conveys his understanding of the trustee nature of a representative in which he opposed "authoritative instructions" or "mandates issued" by constituents of "...which the member is bound blindly and implicitly to obey..." as they run "...contrary to the clearest conviction of his judgement and conscience". Therefore, on the definition of the Parliament itself, he argues it "... is not a congress of ambassadors from different and hostile interests" but as "...a deliberative assembly of one nation, with one interest, that of the whole", in which "local purposes" and "local prejudices" are set aside as a guide, in favour of "...the general good, resulting from the general reason of the whole." He countered that when voters choose an MP, she is not, for example, a member of Bristol, but a member of Parliament (Burke 1774).

The speech conveys at once both that the representative occupies a 'trustee' status (as opposed to a delegate status) and that Parliament itself occupies an institutional status of a deliberative assembly, with a unity of interest, incorporating the whole electorate (Burke 1774). That depth of understanding between voter and representative is even more greatly pronounced in a Letter from Burke to Sir Hercules Langrishe in 1792, in which he describes a notion of "Virtual representation" (Burke 1792). It is described as a process conveying "a communion of interests" and a "sympathy in feelings and desires" between "those who act in the name of any description of people and the people in whose name they act ..." (Burke 1792). He maintains that such representation "corrects the irregularities in the literal representation", by reinforcing "common interest and common sentiment" (Burke 1792). Burke was again re-stating the primacy of common interest in the act of political representation.

In this context, Burke saw political parties as strongly mediating between executive authority and parliament, having defined a political party in his 'Thoughts on the Cause of the Present Discontents' of 1770 as:

> ... a body of men united on public principle, which could act as a constitutional link between king and parliament, providing consistency and strength in administration, or principled criticism in opposition. (Burke 1770, pp. 431–432)

But the ordering of precedents is visible: there is first an institution with Members who can represent its electors as trustees in as their collective interest, followed secondly, by the governing party in the House of Commons governing consistently with that interest. The governing party would then be held to account for having discharged that interest at a subsequent election.

5.2 Parliamentary Sovereignty and Contemporary Collective Representation by Parliament

It is necessary to question the contemporary relationship between parliamentary sovereignty and the parliamentary collective representation model. Some contrast needs to be found with the underlying features of the popular sovereignty approach (Bogdanor 2009a) or a traditional party government model (Dalton et al. 2011; Sartori 2005; Adams 2001; Schmitt and Thomassen 1999; Dahl 1998). Those approaches tend to partially distort that connection and never wholly explain parliamentary sovereignty and its relationship to collective representation, particularly as impacted upon by the development of a European Parliament. The direct 'popular sovereignty' representation model (Bogdanor 2009a) often misconstrues the relationship between electors and trustees while marginalising the role of parties in Parliament. The party representation model (e.g. Dalton et al. 2011; Adams 2001), above all, overlooks the prime precedent of MPs who represent as trustees in the collective interest and thereby misunderstands electors as simply being represented by party.

In employing the term political 'representation', Hanna Pitkin (1967) provides one of the most helpful and broadly accommodating definitions used throughout studies of political representation in the social and political sciences. For Pitkin, to represent is simply to "make present again" (Pitkin 1967, p. 8). On this basis, political representation is the activity of making citizens' voices, opinions, and perspectives "present" by political actors speaking, advocating, symbolizing, and acting on their behalf in the public policy making process (Pitkin 1967). As Rehfeld persuasively argues, "political representation is not had for its own sake" and is created through a set of institutions for a very particular function (Rehfeld 2005, p. 148). In the Westminster model, elected representatives as MPs, support messages strongly affiliated to a core party philosophy (in practice, the Party Whip), although there remains room for individual manoeuvrability on party-political issues (Pettit 2009). The governing party in power inside Parliament is able to provide a legislative program as a self-policing corporate body (Pettit 2009, p. 85). The Westminster model of political representation—which includes the processes of authorisation and accountability through institutions—conveys the manner in which elected representatives collectively stand for the represented in the corporate body of parliament, with an agenda defined by the party in power (Pettit 2009). Political representation is deeply institutionalised under the Westminster model because those elected party representatives who form the legislature do so in the national interest and then form the government (and its opposition) in pursuit of the broader, collective interest.

5.2.1 The Challenge of Popular Sovereignty Approaches to Representation

From a 'popular sovereignty' perspective presented by Vernon Bogdanor (2009a, 2019), the modern theory of a popular constitutional state directly seeks to affirm the primacy of electors as delegating their representatives in the representation process at the expense of the doctrine of parliamentary sovereignty.

Firstly, for Bogdanor (2009a), on the British model, those who enjoy the right to make political decisions are empowered to do so by virtue of the representative mandate they have received from the electorate. Yet, this can rightly be contrasted, with the EU's highest constitutional principle whereby the separation of powers reflected between its central institutions (Council of the EU, the Commission, the Court of Justice and the European Parliament) and also in the division of power between the EU and the member states, marginalises that direct, unitary representative capacity (Bogdanor 2009a, 2019). While that argument is certainly valid, it is not clear on Bogdanor's argument what the reasons are for the distribution of EU level executive authority impacting upon the weakening of a legislature's right or ability to represent its electors. After all, many EU countries themselves have widely distributed constitutional separation of powers and executive machinery without that impacting upon the representative roles of their legislatures.

Second, for Bogdanor, the House of Commons is an executive-sustaining parliament, whereas the European Parliament, by contrast, operates by sustaining a dialogue with other Community institutions (Bogdanor 2009a, 2019, p. 44). However, it might also be considered that the central EU institutions are, to a degree, political actors, not least because of their overarching commitment to enhanced European integration, if not, federalism. That is to argue, and contrary to Bogdanor, the European Parliament as a neo-corporatist body can in practice help sustain both its Commission as well as supporting an inter-institutional dialogue. Throughout its history, the European Parliament, in particular, has sought parity with the Council particularly through co-legislating with the Council (Bux 2017; Hix and Høyland 2013, p. 172) and a greater fusion with the political powers of the central institutions. It is the European Parliament's approach to 'functional representation' through its being a collaborative chamber representing the mandates, political interaction and views of the other EU institutions (Jarman 2011) and through dialogue with social partners that characterises its key strength. Given its historical development as a collaborative, legitimising feature of an executive, administrative body, it cannot seek a national-style 'collective representation' of an EU-electorate.

Yet, at the same time, the European Parliament's position of functional representation (Marsh and Norris 1997, p. 158) has not only moved the British constitutional model away from its instincts in a collective representative model, previously shoring up parliamentary sovereignty, but even further removed it from a delegated model in which electors seek a direct connection with decision-making bodies. Bogdanor asserts a top-down parliamentary sovereignty system derived from the past as being inconsistent with the social and political pressures of modern politics, which promote a greater degree of popular power (Bogdanor 2009b); yet, Britain's experience of the EU's representative institutions suggests an even greater removal of electors from parliamentary decision-makers (let alone direct decision-making), not a design which incorporates them.

Third, for Bogdanor, the Commons is fundamentally a debating chamber dominated by the binary dialogue between government and opposition. EU legislation does not conform to that binary pattern of politics (see also Smith 2017, p. 77), and there is no party-supported government in the European Parliament seeking to promote its legislation and policies (Bogdanor 2009a, 2019, p. 45). However, Westminster's binary pattern of politics in which government and opposition battle over policy need not be considered as completely incompatible with the European Parliament-style of consensual political representation. Thomassen (1999) and several theorists have argued that the more formal introduction of a party government model for Strasbourg would help to politicise the relationship between the European Parliament and the Commission and create a pattern of government and opposition within Parliament (Thomassen 1999, p. 236). Voters would then reward or punish parties for supporting or opposing the Commission. However, for Bogdanor, in contrast to Westminster, the European Parliament as it currently exists is a consensual, working legislature. That assumption sits uneasily with the observation that politics inside the European Parliament is broadly dominated by political parties. In the European Parliament, political groups dominate the agenda (and selection of key positions and forming alliances), while imposing some degree of party discipline (Hix 2016), albeit European party umbrella groups could not be said to have mirrored national party discipline (Marsh and Norrris 1997, p. 155).

Fourth, for Bogdanor, the European Parliament is a multiparty parliament, operating through carefully constructed coalitions, a kind of "Coalitional politics of this kind" which "is largely unfamiliar to British politicians" (Bogdanor 2009a, 2019, p. 46). Of course, on this point, it might be observed that Britain has since adapted to recent coalition and confidence arrangements in which parties, by agreement, prop up others in government. That means that the supposed binary approach that characterises Westminster, however, is not strictly precise—the binary political scheme is resistant to the idea of an overarching primacy of collective representation of the electorate at Westminster. Political representation is presupposed by a prime national legislature able to practically represent as an institution (Rehfeld 2005, p. 36) and the legislature representing the common interest 'in respect to' its national electors (Rehfeld 2005, p. 149). There is no real justification to establishing a national representative legislature without reference to a broader "good of all, whatever the good of all may turn out to entail" (Rehfeld 2005, p. 149). The direct 'popular sovereignty' representation misconstrues the broader relationship between electors and trustees while marginalising the role of parties.

The drift toward a popular British constitutional state, toward popular sovereignty as contrasted with parliamentary sovereignty, and toward electors delegating 'mandated' representatives (as opposed to collectively entrusting them), does not materialise in any major form under EU membership. Parliament and political parties are increasingly relevant. The suggestions of a drift away from parliamentary sovereignty and towards a popular sovereignty model under EU membership seem unevidenced. The impact of the EU's separation of powers on domestic representation by itself need not have a substantial impact. The claim that Westminster is an executive-sustaining parliament while the European Parliament is a consensual one (Bogdanor 2019, p. 44), fails to recognise the part-federal objectives of the EU institutions, including the European Parliament, which sustains the Commission's policies. Westminster operates on a binary government-opposition style; but the European Parliament, though consensual, does also occupy some aspects of a binary politics, competing to some degree over the Westminster model of representation and sovereignty.

5.2.2 The Challenge of the Traditional Party Government Model

Since political parties are a feature of both Westminster and European Parliament representative systems, a brief consideration is necessary of the traditional party government model, emphasising the role of political parties in political representation (Sartori 2005; Dahl 1998). Dalton et al. (2011) have described the assumptions by which British and European political representation is dominated by parties in a political system where representatives acted as trustees, strongly mediated by political parties (Dalton et al. 2011, pp. 22–23). It is an approach to political representation relevant to a parliamentary system with strong political parties. Parties rather than candidates are viewed as the main political actors. It is political parties, not individual legislators that are the primary vehicles that articulate citizens' policy beliefs and convert them into public policies (Adams 2001, p. 3). The party government model therefore examines the congruence, or not, between voters and their selected party. The voters are assumed to be those who support the parties in a nation. Voters' choices of parties then provide them with a method of exercising control over the actions of individual legislators and through these over the affairs of government (Adams 2001, p. 4). The parties consist of their representatives acting as a collective.

It is assumed party members act in unison and that they vote as a bloc in Parliament. It is parties that exercise control over the government agenda and policy-making process in Parliament. When voters choose parties they are given indirect control over the actions of legislators and affairs of government. The model strongly suggests that to the extent that competing parties present divergent, stable policies and citizens use these policies as the basis for their voting decisions, parties provide effective vehicles for representing the electorate's political beliefs (Adams 2001, p. 5). In empirical studies, broad congruence is found between the Left-Right socio-economic position of the median voters and the Left-Right position of the governing parties (Dalton et al. 2011, p. 23).

'Party' occupies an essential and powerful mediating role in the development of the Westminster system, but as with Bogdanor's delegating-voter, it need only be considered secondary to the exercise of powers in the British constitution. The traditional party government representation model, above all, overlooks the prime precedent of Members who represent as trustees in the collective interest and therefore electors as not simply being represented by party. Nonetheless, the centrality of party is demonstrated by the House of Commons' own guide to all members of the public entitled, 'You and Your MP' (UK Parliament 2019b). The guide specifies to the general public—that is, to voters of all political parties and none—that:

> At times a constituent's demands may conflict with party policy and your MP will have to decide where their first loyalty should lie. The MP may decide that a majority of constituents would support the party policy – after all that is likely to be one of the reasons why they elected him or her. (UK Parliament 2019b, p. 2)

The collective representation of the electorate, reinforced by the process of election and through an institution which has primacy among the others, provides the framework of political parties. It returns political parties to the central nature of political representation, which is presupposed by a prime national legislature able to practically represent as an institution (Rehfeld 2005, p. 36) and the legislature representing the common interest in respect of national electors (Rehfeld 2005, p. 149).

The British constitution (in Burke's eyes) primarily incorporates party to enmesh the link between executive power and the legislature. The party government model is therefore mostly feasible for the powerful emphasis it places on a political party representative as trustee in the policy—and law-making process, of articulating voters' political beliefs and their conversion into official public policy or legislation. Mair and Thomassen (2010) acknowledge the absence of party in explaining collective representation in the context of the EU when they argue:

> In effect, Parliament within this model of party government loses the capacity to function in the way that Edmund Burke once favoured: 'The virtue, spirit and essence of a House of Commons consists in its being the express image of the feelings of the nation.' (Mair and Thomassen 2010, p. 31)

The political analysis offered by Burke of a collective-style, virtual representation has often been overlooked when interpreting the European Parliament.

To some degree, however, it is far more complicated to analyse the system of representation employed by the EU using the party government model (Schmitt and Thomassen 1999, p. 16; Katz and Wessels 1999, p. 243). The model is said to be "highly problematic when applied to the context of the European Union" (Marsh and Norris 1997). The European Parliament has no experience of collective representation of a European-wide electorate but it has a weak form of electoral representation and a strong form of functional representation through EU-level, neo-corporatist partnerships. European level parliamentary representation has meant that UK citizens, as EU citizens, are able to vote directly—under a proportional representation system—for MEPs (73, in the UK's case) as their regionally elected representatives in the EU. Marsh and Norris (1997) argue that 'functional representation' creates alternative linkages between citizens and the European Parliament. This form of representation enables lobbying channels to organise interest groups and social movements for them to influence EU policy-making (Berkhout et al. 2017; Marsh and Norris 1997, p. 158). The different forms of political representation such as functional representation are "insufficiently, strongly developed" in the European Parliament (Marsh and Norris 1997), yet it is central to identify that those alternative instruments of linkage exist and that they underpin representation. The role of major groups, particularly economic groupings, is formally recognised and particularly through the European Economic and Social Committee. Elected MEPs can often see their role as spokespersons for trade union groups, farming and small business groups. Pluralist theories have emphasised that interest groups therefore provide another linkage between citizens and the EU, by being represented through this functional method. In Strasbourg, the proposed boundaries to representation are defined through a neo-corporatist strategy (Pérez Durán 2018; Smismans 2016) in which social dialogue between key institutions and social partners is seen as essential (Wendler 2017). Its purposes are less defined through election, because it is not structured around majority-supported manifesto(s) turned into elected government agendas.

The electorate can influence the Union both indirectly through the choice of parties in national elections and directly through elections to the European Parliament (Marsh and Norris 1997, p. 154). European elections tend to be fought by national political parties often mainly on national issues and voters make their choice on the basis of their opinions on national issues (Weiler 1999, p. 266)—or to reward or punish the governing party (Hix and Marsh 2007). Consequently, it might be argued, EU elections fail as an instrument of democracy at the European level—they fail to link policy preferences of "the European people" to the decision-making process in the European Parliament (Costello et al. 2012, p. 1229). European elections are often viewed as second-order national elections (Nugent 2010, p. 192). In theory, the party government model might claim to work effectively in the European Parliament on the basis that:

i. cohesive and unified parties within the European Parliament need to offer alternative policy programmes;
ii. the electorate needs to choose parties based on performance;
iii. the outcome of elections link voters' preferences with a policy making process in the European Parliament.

But, those conditions are often faced with a confusing reality in which European party groups are loosely co-ordinated umbrella organisations with lesser party discipline than nationally (Marsh and Norris 1997, p. 155). In the European Parliament, for example, three dimensions are found necessary to describe the policy attitudes of voters and candidates: an economic left/right dimension, a cultural dimension capturing attitudes towards a broad range of social issues, and a dimension capturing attitudes towards the EU (Costello et al. 2012, p. 1245). Importantly, both parties and MEPs within Parliament "… do seem to serve an effective representative role, with the congruence between the European electorate and Parliament being much more pronounced than is generally credited" (Mair and Thomassen 2010, p. 33). Voting on left-right lines has been increasingly common in the European Parliament, with ideological grounds being central to votes through 'grand coalition' alliances (Nugent 2010, p. 198; Hix et al. 2007). It is, at best, a partial model of European Parliament representation but which explains only one facet of distinct representation pursued by the European Parliament; in Westminster, the party government model might be seen as much more central to its almost singular mode of electoral representation. The case study of the Working Time Directive can better illustrate the source of inter-parliamentary competition.

5.3 Parliamentary Sovereignty, Collective Representation and EU Membership: The Case of the Working Time Directive

The Working Time Directive provides an illustration that the recognised helm has had European Parliament-level functional representation joined with it, distorting Parliament's capacity to collectively represent its electorate. That competition produces an unsettling of the historically precedented capacity of Parliament to collectively represent its electors as strongly embedded within domestic political conventions, thereby signifying a shift in the meaning of parliamentary sovereignty.

The Working Time Directive has been designed to protect workers' health and safety and ensure that working hours must meet minimum standards applicable throughout the EU, including the UK. The EU's latest Working Time Directive (2003/88/EC) requires EU countries to guarantee rights for all workers, including among other features: a limit to weekly working hours, which must not exceed 48 hours on average, including any overtime; a minimum daily rest period of 11 consecutive hours in every 24 and a rest break during working hours if the worker is on duty for longer than 6 hours; and a minimum weekly rest period of 24 uninterrupted hours for each 7-day period, in addition to the 11 hours' daily rest (European Commission 2015). There is an individual 'opt out' in which individuals can opt out of the 48-hour week under specified conditions. The Working Time Regulations (1998) implement the European Working Time Directive in UK law. Before that point, rights on hours of work and the right to time off were agreed in individual job contracts (Adnett and Hardy 2001, p. 119).

5.3.1 *Impacting on the UK's Social and Employment Law and the UK Constitution*

The actions and decisions of the European Parliament put it at the centre of drafting the Working Time Directive as it currently exists. The creation of the Working Time Directive rested on the European Parliament's Committee on Women's Rights motion for Resolution in March 1989 (European Parliament 1989a), key events in November 1989, its passing a number of Resolutions relating to the draft Community Charter of Fundamental Social Rights (Hantrais 2017; European Parliament 1989b, c, d), its introducing the requirement of four weeks' annual leave in its first reading in February 1991 (European Parliament 1991) and the development of a common position on the Directive, approved by the European Parliament in October 1993 (European Parliament 1993). That presentation of where power sat in relation to representatives came at considerable expense to the severely weakened approaches of UK ministers attending the Council and the authority of MPs in Westminster itself.

On a practical level, the Working Time Directive provided legislation for the organisation and reduction in working time in the UK and all EU member states. Before that point, the Conservative Government had historically resisted what it viewed as inflexible and burdensome labour and social laws being imposed on business (Lourie 1996). Legislation designed to protect young people's, children's and, women's hours began to be introduced at the beginning of the nineteenth century in response to hugely concerning conditions prevailing in factories and mines on top of the extremely long hours worked in factories, mines and shops (Lourie 1996, Annex 2).

It is notable however both that there have been very few UK legislative restrictions on the hours of work of adult males (Adnett and Hardy 2001) and that many of those historical legal restrictions, except those affecting children under school leaving age and those on drivers' and pilots' hours, had then been repealed (Rogowski 2015; Lourie 1996). On employment law, it is worth bearing in mind the partisanship of the dominant governing party-in-Parliament remained a determining factor in the incorporation of the Directive. Throughout the 1980s, the mainstream Conservative Party argued that such legal working time controls were outdated or reduced the flexibility and competitiveness of UK business (Rogowski 2015, p. 236). Alternatively, the then mainstream

Labour Party (in opposition) asserted the protection of the worker's 'working time' workplace rights as essential to safeguard their labour and interests against big business and vested interests.

5.3.2 *Westminster's Collective Representation Versus Neo-Corporatist, Functional Representation*

The European Parliament itself, while providing some democratic legitimation for making laws and policies under its own remit, cannot claim to 'collectively represent' its own domestic electorate as it does not classically compete as a formal Parliament with Westminster in that sense. There is no direct conflict in European Parliament-Westminster 'collective representation' of electors—because the European Parliament does not operate with that form of representation. Nonetheless, the European Parliament pursued a form of functional representation (Marsh and Norris 1997, p. 158) which impacted upon Westminster's concept of collective representation.

An exemplary resolution following a report by the European Parliament's Committee on Social Affairs and Employment in November 1983 on a Commission proposal for a recommendation on the reduction of working time conveys that its neo-corporatist approach relied upon the European Parliament, Council, Commission and the European Economic and Social Committee's shared emphasis on a proposal (European Parliament 1983). The neo-corporatist emphasis in the early resolution is clear from its uncomfortable statement of "having regard to the clashes between the social partners as to the effect of a reduction in working time on employment and the costs of a reduction of working time" (European Parliament 1983). The European Parliament's fundamental commitment to partnership at Community level action is such that it "... stresses that the lack of agreement between the social partners at European level ..." should not lead to "...collective-agreement initiatives in the member states which are geared to Community aims being delayed or blocked" (European Parliament 1983). There was, however, a stalling process because the Council had been forced to acknowledge in 1984 that it was unable to reach unanimous agreement with the UK on the proposal. The ministers acting for the Government had vetoed the measure as being unconducive to improving employment (Rogowski 2015; Stothers and Porter 2011).

Again, however, the European Parliament demonstrated its cooperative, neo-corporatist approach and determination, for example, in September 1984, when the Socialist Group's European Parliament Resolution called on the Council to "make a prompt and positive response" to all the European Parliament resolutions passed urging a reduction in working time (European Parliament 1984). By emphasising social partnership, it called on the Commission to support all trade union and management initiatives likely to provide industries and regions with approaches to the reduction of working time (European Parliament 1984). The resolution requested that the nine governments who had previously expressed their support in the council for "working time" proposals of the Commission and European Parliament "should implement these proposals" e.g. irrespective of the UK. The resolution itself was sent to the Council, the Commission, the member state governments, the Union Industries of the European Community (UNICE) and the European Trade Union Confederation (ETUC).

So, in 1988, given the UK's ongoing resistance, an alternative path had to be found by the European Parliament (namely, the Committee on Social Affairs and Employment) and other institutions and pro-Working Time Directive member states to proceed as they agreed and thereby circumvent the UK veto. In the meantime, the European Economic and Social Committee, the Commission and Parliament, by partnership and collaboration, between 1988 and 1989, produced and passed a draft Community Charter of Fundamental Social Rights (Hantrais 2017; Lourie 1996; European Parliament 1989a, b, c). The European Parliament notably sought to strengthen it and remove national controls over the draft. In November 1989, it was passed as a "solemn declaration" by the member states with the exception of the UK (Lourie 1996; European Parliament 1989b). Fundamentally, the Commission produced an action programme to implement the Directive and the European Parliament urged for the legislation to be created by the end of 1990. The European Economic and Social Committee and Parliament partnership, again, strengthened the proposals, for example, to ensure 4 weeks annual leave (European Parliament 1989a, b, c, d). The Directive was delayed in the Council for some time and the European Parliament passed an amended and strengthened version in October 1993 (European Parliament 1993). It was adopted in the Council on 23 November 1993 (as Council Directive 93/104/EC), where the UK controversially abstained in the vote.

In urging proposals for working time in its 1983 Resolution (European Parliament 1983), the European Parliament (through the Committee on Social Affairs and Employment) is evidently reliant on the Council, Commission and the European Economic and Social Committee's shared neo-corporatist emphasis because it seeks to represent the approach taken by the shared central institutions. It is also concerned only with binding, supranational commitment, not watered-down national promises, on working time. The entire rationale for it having grown so frustrated at the dialogue and agreement having broken down between collaborative social partners, as described in the 1983 Resolution (European Parliament 1983) is because of the European Parliament's reliance on neo-corporatism and mode of functional representation which occurs through social dialogue and inter-institutional agreement, rather than direct representation of electors. The attempts to bolster its alternative linkages of representation beyond the citizen-representative link were being frustrated.

The characterisation of the European Parliament's interactions through neo-corporatism and social dialogue opens up the possibility to competitively steering, with a hand at the helm. In multi-level governance approaches, Jessop (2004) views 'meta-steering' as central to many of the disputes over EU integration and state changes, as part of the EU agenda itself, especially regarding the different steps in integration (Jessop 2004, p. 62). In particular, Jessop (2004) approaches the tendency towards 'meta-steering' as reflected in the increasing resort to partnerships, comitology, social dialogue, in guiding European integration and to steer EU policy making and implementation.

The character of the contemporary European Parliament reflects those neo-corporatist and collaborative practices. It is the only institution which is directly elected, with MEPs selected by UK voters and from all EU states voters every five years. The institution seats 751 MEPs—including 73 from the UK—and has gained broad powers through the Treaties (Shackleton 2012). It is one of the EU's main law-making institutions, along with the Council of the EU. In legislative terms, today's European Parliament takes part in the three-stage ordinary legislative procedure with the Council of the EU on an equal status with it, as "co-legislature", in order to legislate (Bux 2017; European Union 2019; Hix and Høyland 2013, p. 172; European Scrutiny Committee 2013; Shackleton 2012, p. 137; see Bradley and Ewing 2010, p. 122). The field of policies covered by the ordinary legislative procedure has since increased under the Lisbon Treaty, providing the European Parliament with further powers to influence the content of certain laws. UK voters elect MEPs to an institution only on the basis that is recognised as an institution in the recognised helm having the main role of debating and passing European laws, with the Council, as well as scrutinising other EU institutions, particularly the Commission, to make sure they are working democratically (European Union 2019). In terms of legislation passed by the EU impacting upon the UK, the EU determines more than 50% of its legislation (on that proportion, see Geddes 2013, p. 7; Miller 2010; Triesman 2006), through non-UK, EU representative/legislative bodies of the European Parliament with its own directly elected representatives in addition to other EU institutions. Nonetheless, it is still national parliaments, rather than the European Parliament directly that guarantees democratic principles are respected and that the importance of national parliaments playing "a central role in the European institutional system is thus the *condition sine qua non* of democracy" in Europe (Neyer 2014, p. 125). Irrespective of the European Parliament's direct election under a system of proportional representation, it is reported to suffer generally from a 'democratic deficit'.

Following the early UK veto over working time proposals, the hardened 1984 Socialist Group's European Parliament motion for a Resolution sought even greater representation through social dialogue between the Commission and trade union and management initiatives (European Parliament 1984). It urged that degree of inter-institutional agreement to the extent that the other nine pro-working time member states should proceed without the UK. The Resolution requested that the European Parliament view be sent to the major European trade union bodies. The allied work with the European Economic and Social Committee in strengthening the proposals in the early 1990s and the urging for the Commission to deepen relations with social partners to produce working time law in the 1989 European Parliament Resolution is further evidence of representation through social dialogue with partners plus inter-institutional agreements. The European Economic and Social Committee is part of the neo-corporate institutional means of representation in the sense that it is a "consultative body" that closely cooperates with the European Parliament (as well as the Council and the European Commission). The Committee promotes the representation of the views of Europe's major socio-occupational interest, workers and employers groups and others (European Economic and Social Committee 2016).

The deeply ingrained nature of representation through social dialogue (Wendler 2017) is reflected neatly in one of the European Parliament's proposed amendments to the Working Time Directive in February 1991, on first reading. The amendment demanded that the member states themselves adopt measures to ensure agreements on working time between social partners would be legally binding (European Parliament 1991). When considering social partners, the EU comfortably absorbs national social partnerships with employer and workers organisations into its own social dialogue in a way that Westminster partly rejected. This difference produces a competitive distortion of the domestic legislature as a primary political actor able to collectively represent its constituents on social and employment interests.

The Conservative governing party-in-Parliament as the representative self-policing 'corporate body'—collectively standing for the represented in that corporate body of parliament through an agenda defined by party (Pettit 2009, p. 85)—had previously been the space for resolving contested labour laws. In that political space, the acceptance and irreversibility of the imposed EU policy, then law, demonstrated the unaccountability of ministers at Westminster in making laws and policies in the national interest. It shifted the space for resolving deeply contested labour laws into a wider domestic situation taking place in the UK by the mid-1990s: a strong desire to change the UK's governing party-in-Parliament. Given the impasse at the European level, the UK's governing New Labour Party in 1997 signed up to the Social Chapter and subsequent legislation such as the Working Time Directive (Hantrais 2017; Lourie 1998), which it had pledged in the General Election. It did not address the impasse as such, but through its acceptance of the Directive brought a small degree of political settlement and EU-UK policy consistency, despite the ongoing practical failures in implementing the legislation since that date.

European Parliament representation on the other hand is exemplified by a second-order collaborative legislature set up as a politically representative institution (while unable to represent a unified European interest). It represents, as a neo-corporatist body, the approaches of other central institutions and its social partners (Smismans 2016) while only weakly representing its electors. The existence of multi-representation government as described in practices, and part-federal representative government as described in the Treaties, however, make the party government model both useful and relevant. Elective and professional interest 'functional' representation in the European Parliament works by creating 'instruments of linkage' (Marsh and Norris 1997, p. 158) as opposed to operating through Westminster's 'collective representation'. Collective representation by MPs of their electors is defined strongly by their political parties, when in Government, remaining accountable to parliament and through regular elections to the electorate, who retain ultimate decision-making capacities. It is sovereignty-affecting at Westminster because collective representation allows the governing party to be a self-policing 'corporate body', collectively standing for the represented in that corporate body through an agenda defined by party (Pettit 2009, p. 85). Collective representation is distorted at Westminster when representatives of the governing domestic political parties become less accountable to parliament because their party policies are bypassed by the policymaking of the European Parliament. Under EU membership, the UK Parliament has become constitutionally unsettled because the UK's recognised helm has had European Parliament-level parliamentary representation competing with it—not as a competing delegation of representatives—but in relation to its 'trustee' capacity to collectively represent its electors through the governing political party.

5.3.3 Supranationalist Representation

The ongoing and repetitive statements by the European Parliament in its Resolutions to ensuring a supranational commitment to working time reduction, as distinct from weaker, non-binding national pledges, served to remind the Commission to strengthen its binding requirements at the supranational level. It is also a reminder that the Commission and European Parliament are vital supranational elements—the Commission as government, the European Parliament as representative parliament—within a multi-representational, federal architecture. The 1983 Resolution is heavily critical of the Commission's proposal at this stage for not sufficiently ingraining the law at the Community level. It positively warns off collective agreement initiatives in member states (European Parliament 1983). The Socialist Group's 1984 motion for a Resolution pressing for the nine member states to take up the working time proposals of the Commission and European Parliament (European Parliament 1984), irrespective of the UK, is again supranational in its objective. The subsequent manoeuvre in the late 1980s in utilising the draft Community Charter is an attempt to create one of a number of constitutional documents for government at the European level. The step of adopting the Working Time Directive under Article 118a (Lourie 1996), thereby relying on a qualified majority rather than unanimity in the Council (Rogowski 2015, p. 236), affirms the supranational decision-making procedure as essential to making genuine 'European decisions'. It is that exercise of supranational decision-making by a supranational institution seeking to bring about a request in law at a supranational level, as well as its interpretation of the Treaties (under Article 118a) which achieved a sidestepping of the consent of the UK through qualified majority voting (Martinsen and Wessel 2014, p. 14). The process marginalised and bypassed the understanding of Westminster politics defined by a representative legislature able to govern consistently with Burke's common interest, or Rehfeld's "good of all" (Rehfeld 2005, p. 149). The essence of supranational decision-making in this way is that the EU, with procedural approval from its parliamentary institution, competitively distorts the domestic legislature's ability to make decisions, consistent with collective representation in the electorate's interest.

5.3.4 Representation Through Constitutionalisation

Representation can also occur at the EU-level by reference to 'constitutionalisation' as a means to strengthen its representative linkages. It is of relevance in the broader 'constitutionalisation' process that in late 1989, the European Parliament (through the Committee on Social Affairs and Employment and Committee on Women's Rights) had pushed for the Community Charter of the Fundamental Social Rights of Workers alongside measures for the reorganization of working time (Hantrais 2017; Adnett and Hardy 2001, p. 115; European Parliament 1989b, c). During that process, in November 1989, the European Parliament adopted the text of one resolution on the Community Charter of Fundamental Social Rights, convinced that the adoption by the Council of that Charter "constitutes a first step towards the establishment of fundamental social rights in the European Community ..." (European Parliament 1989b). Nevertheless, it criticised the draft as a "watering down", as "inadequate" and "imprecise" not least because of "the repeated references to 'national legislation' and 'national practices... which must on no account be allowed to weaken the fundamental nature of the rights set out in the Charter" (European Parliament 1989b). The resolution expressed references to the opinion of the

European Economic and Social Committee on fundamental Community social rights and the Declaration on Fundamental Rights and Freedoms adopted earlier that year. The resolution is supportive of the International Labour Organization conventions in making those claims. Another separate European Parliament resolution, again, passed in the same period on the attainment of economic and social cohesion lays bare the European Parliament's frustration at the Council's inability to provide worker's rights through a constitutional source—they were "not satisfied merely with a solemn declaration by the Council on the basic social rights of workers" (European Parliament 1989d). That Charter was signed by all Heads of Government of the member states of the European Community except the UK at Strasbourg in December 1989 (Adnett and Hardy 2001, p. 115; Lourie 1996).

The European Parliament commitment to a form of representation through social partnership and constitutionalisation, in spite of UK resistance to the measure, was further demonstrated in the European Parliament (through the Committee on Social Affairs and Employment) resolution of September 1990. The resolution related to the Commission's impending action programme on the implementation of the Charter for 1991–1992 and working time (European Parliament 1990). The Commission itself had submitted its proposal for a Draft Directive concerning certain aspects of the Organisation of Working Time to the Council of the EU in September 1990 (Lourie 1996). The European Parliament resolution pushed the Commission to submit to the Council by 31 December 1991 its proposals in a legislative programme, along with tighter changes made by the European Parliament with a view to adoption of the legislation by 1 January 1993 (European Parliament 1990). The UK Conservative government objected to that Directive from the beginning (Rogowski 2015), arguing that it would impose burdens on employers, interfere in the relations between employers and employees, while reducing competitiveness and flexibility (Rogowski 2015, p. 236; see Bolick 1995). It was not seen as necessary on the grounds of health and safety (Lourie 1998, p. 19; Lourie 1996). It was only when the proposal for a Council Working Time Directive came before the European Parliament in February 1991 for first reading that it was approved with 39 amendments (European Parliament 1991). One amendment (no. 2) called upon the Community to at least respect certain Conventions of the International Labour Organization (ILO) in seeking working time reduction. The European Parliament approved the

Commission proposal subject to Parliament's amendments at that first reading.

The most unexpected facet of representation at the European level in the example of the Working Time Directive is its general reliance on 'constitutionalisation' as a means to strengthen its representative linkages. The constitutional sources of the EU Treaties–notably through the Single European Act, the draft Community Charter (which strongly impacted the Social Chapter), the International Labour Organization (ILO) Conventions (e.g. Adnett and Hardy 2001, p. 120), the Declaration of Fundamental Rights and Freedoms, the November 1996 ECJ judgement against the UK and ECJ case law—had provided consolidated and clarified, written expressions of rights which supported the overall objective of reducing working time. That political turned constitutional project is at odds with the Westminster system, with its partly written but wholly uncodified constitution. In both a 1989 Resolution and on the above first reading of the Directive in 1991, the European Parliament is reliant on the ILO Conventions—setting out the principles of international labour law—in seeking a reduction of working time, which as well as helping to consolidate the European Community standard is, by its nature, a strong international (not merely European Community) standard. It is already well documented that the European Economic and Social Committee and European Parliament have repeatedly called on the Commission to draw on ILO standards in formulating social policy (Rönnmar 2011, p. 41; see Adnett and Hardy 2001, p. 120). The Westminster system has historically rejected extensive, written rights-based documents—including many ILO Conventions—as a source of governing law and political schemes.

The UK Government, after all, rejected the Community Charter, did not participate in several historical ILO Conventions and took the Commission to the ECJ over the Working Time Directive law (Adnett and Hardy 2001). It is notable after the 1988 period the Charter and other 'fundamental rights' expressions provided significant weight in relation to the European Parliament's representative authority when supporting legislation for the reorganisation of working time (see Hantrais 2017). At that early point, the European Parliament had little reputation or recognition as a legitimate legislature able to represent the views or sentiments of its electors, even though it perhaps did not necessarily require it. When it came to constitutionalisation as a tool of representation, the EU promotes citizens texts and documents with material, claimable rights as authoritative guidance. This creates a competitive distortion of the domestic legislature as a primary political actor able to collectively represent the collective interest in the absence of constraining, inflexible, written, rights-based, authoritative guidance.

5.3.5 *Competitive Partisanship and Party Government*

Westminster's capacity to collectively represent an electorate is competitively distorted in the face of EU-level multi-representational government. The competitive, partisanship demonstrated at both the Westminster and Strasbourg levels is meaningful to the outcome and implementation of the Working Time Directive. Within the political cultures generally, just as the socialist approach to a social Europe in the vision of Jacques Delors hardened the UK Conservative government's stance on social and labour law, so too did Thatcher's free market stance harden the European Parliament's political resolve to create a Community-wide labour code (Dimitrakopoulos 2013). The partisanship created a fluidity of political culture which in Strasbourg was generally supportive of the Working Time Directive and labour market regulation, irrespective of domestic support or opposition in member states.

This observation on bi-party partisanship in political culture is an important point of evaluation because in attempting to characterise EU and Westminster representation in the context of the Working Time Directive, it is central that in Westminster, a national Conservative administration had been elected for the duration of the 1979–1997 period. It viewed itself as 'deregulatory' and seeking reductions in the burdens of inflexible social and employment legislation imposed on business (Adnett and Hardy 2001; Bolick 1995). It rejected the notion of 'social Europe'—and by extension the legislative binds of working time legislation, which during the 1980s Margaret Thatcher strongly resisted. The Conservative government notably maintained an opt-out on the Social Chapter on the Maastricht Treaty (Gowland et al. 2010, p. 103). The domestic Labour Party, while weakened, Eurosceptic and in opposition, opposed the Conservatives on all those policies. On the other hand, the European Parliament as a whole, contained a much greater number of pro-working time socialist MEPs in its political grouping throughout the European Parliament elections of 1984, 1989 and 1994. The British Labour Party and the political left in Europe, along with its strong sub-national relationship with the trade union movement on the whole favoured and mostly campaigned for strengthening social and employment law, a more comprehensive vision of a social Europe and along with it, the Working Time Directive. In Strasbourg, the Socialists were therefore the largest majority groupings in the first four elected European Parliament's (1979–1999) and the centre left has held the majority for the duration of this period (Hix et al. 2003, p. 315). This is important to bear in mind even where there is cooperation with the European Parliament. Where there are low levels of support for the European Parliament in a national parliament, a competitive logic develops that involves zero sum institutional competition. The empowerment of the European Parliament, as a supranational competitor, generates pressure on national parliaments to take measures to protect their authority (Winzen 2015, p. 79).

The entire period responsible for the creation of the Working Time Directive contrasts with a domestic, deregulatory Conservative administration from 1979 to 1990 under the premiership of Margaret Thatcher, then from 1990 to 1997 under John Major. It was following events under the Major government that the UK took the Commission to the ECJ, and subsequently lost, that it was required to implement the Directive (*UK v Council of the European Union* [1996]; Lourie 1998). It followed in Tony Blair's, post-1997 newly elected Labour administration that the UK then opted into EU social legislation and introduced the regulations in 1998 (Rogowski 2015; Barysch 2013). This partisanship impacting upon the respective legislatures, demonstrates a recognition of their representative strength. While the EP and national parliaments co-exist in the same political environment, not only by sharing in common democratic representation in the EU's 'multilevel parliamentary field' but in part vis-a-vis the same electorate, this can lead to institutional competition (Winzen 2015, p. 76). In particular, the significant and hardened role played by the socialist grouping in the European Parliament—pursued through the Progressive Alliance of Socialists and Democrats (S&D) combined with the European People's Party (EPP) in helping to produce the EU working time legislation—can be contrasted with the resistance exerted by a national, majority Conservative administration in Westminster.

The bi-partisanship was again more widely illustrated to the public at large in the ongoing battles between the UK Prime Minister Margaret Thatcher, a Conservative free-marketeer, and the then EU Commission

President, a socialist, Jacques Delors over that Charter. Support for the EP among national parties tells us whether their parliament tends to regard the EP as a competitor or ally (Winzen 2015). When, in 1989, Delors presented a Charter of Fundamental Social Rights, the reason it was adopted by all member states except the UK had been that Thatcher opposed it on the grounds that it would restrict free enterprise (Raileanu-Szeles 2013, p. 34; Adnett and Hardy 2001, p. 115). Even when the Charter-influenced Social Chapter (Lourie 1997, p. 10) was finally attached to the Maastricht Treaty in 1992, Britain deployed its opt-out under John Major's government to prevent it becoming part of UK law at that stage (Lourie 1997).

The UK Government under John Major claimed an opt-out from the Directive. For the UK's purposes, it made an application for the annulment of the Directive to the ECJ in March 1994 (Lourie 1996). The ECJ had rejected the UK Government's challenge to the Directive (Lourie 1998; *UK v Council of the European Union* [1996]). In sum, the UK had "no option but to obey the law", as the Government minister was forced to concede (Adnett and Hardy 2001, p. 120). Directives, as legislative acts, set out the objective that all EU countries must achieve but in which it is up to the individual countries to decide how, by implementing legislation (European Union 2019). Despite losing its case before the ECJ in 1996, the Conservative Government did not implement the Directive until the adoption of the enforcing Working Time Regulations 1998, which entered into force on 1 October 1998 (Lourie 1998). This adoption process took place under the later New Labour government in 1997, who accepted the Social Protocol to the Maastricht Treaty and also accepted an updated Working Time Directive, which was adopted in November 2003 and brought it into effect (Hantrais 2017; Dimitrakopoulos 2013). The European Parliament has continued to be at the forefront of unsuccessful and ongoing attempts to end Britain's individual opt-out from the Working Time Directive and the UK finally being forced to limit the working week to 48 hours for all employees.

The management of partisanship in legislating for the Working Time Directive demonstrated at a deeper institutional level how the federal structures of the European Parliament, through electoral and functional representation, however weak, were functioning at the European level. On first interpretation, Bogdanor (2009a) is accurate to hold that the European Parliament is not an executive-sustaining parliament where members of the executive are drawn from the voter-elected legislature in similarity to the Westminster model. Yet the European Parliament is an executive-approving parliament—with consultative and advisory powers preceding the Maastricht Treaty—whose opinions and votes issued to members of the governing Commission and Council are driven to conform or amend their behaviour in governing.

Since the European Parliament exists in a complex system of multi-tiered government, its representative capacity exists in a complex multi-representation, part-federal government. Traditional lines of accountability and authority under the Westminster model are diffused under the European Parliament model, but nonetheless political party remains relevant to its representative ability. Schmitt and Thomassen (1999, p. 17) argue that the EU is a multi-tiered system of government. It has several layers of European government, each with its own system of political representation. Of course, European government is different from state government based upon a responsibility to a significant majority in parliament. Nor is there a European people whose sovereignty is embodied in the European Parliament. However, as Schmitt and Thomassen (1999) argue, the Treaties (Article 138a TEU) on which the European political institutions are based provide for a system of political representation as expressed in the responsible party model. The Treaties provide the goal to which the Union should aspire, albeit an objective for a federal Europe. That interpretation of the Treaties makes the party government model relevant. As Costello et al. (2012) have argued, while European political parties do not compete for the votes of a European electorate (Costello et al. 2012, p. 1229) and while there is no true European system of political representation, that does not mean European elections cannot provide an "'instrument of linkage". In the European Parliament, parties are instruments of linkage with less power of direction at the recognised helm; in Westminster, parties are both well-established instruments of linkage as well as instruments of direction at the helm.

Claims to Parliament's sovereignty rest on a binary politics conducted through the Westminster system. The performance of EU politics which creates linkages into that binary party politics in a European Parliament therefore undermines the claims to parliamentary sovereignty. The serious difficulty many theorists have in accepting that binary party-based government-opposition politics has some level of explanation within European Parliament-level representation is because of its reliance on a theory which suggests that European Parliament-level is, at least in part, a parliament incorporated into a European federation. To accept federation is to accept a specific distributed state structure at the European level, which alters the claims to sovereignty in the member states and is not always accepted in the existing research (Moravcsik 2008; Blankart 2007; Majone 2006). Yet, in following Thomassen's reasoning of multi-tiered government and the federal interpretation of the EU by Annett (2010), it should also be understood that European multi-tiered government is indeed part-confederation and part-federation (McCormick 2015, p. 38; Burgess 2006), just as those arrangements are part-supranational and part-intergovernmental. When representation is pursued at the European Parliament-level, it can divert to a federal, representation mechanism through political parties, which includes the majority socialist support behind the Working Time Directive. One reason why political groupings first formed in the European Parliament had been the conscious effort to establish a federal form of political organisation in the EU-level institutions (Hix et al. 2003, p. 313). Given that the European Parliament exists in a part-federal structure and where its representation is only poorly and part-elective, it is only true for one part of European Parliament representation. Yet, however minimal and unusual, it is essential in reflecting the role of a partisan political party belief system in a proto-bicameral, non-majoritarian, consensus-seeking, Strasbourg-setting.

The collective representation of the electorate at Westminster over substantive areas of government policy works effectively when it is elevated beyond the partly elective and strongly functional representation pursued by the European Parliament. There have been some theoretical omissions in recognising the contemporary relationship between parliamentary sovereignty and the parliamentary collective representation model. Both the popular sovereignty representation approach (Bogdanor 2009a) and the party government approach distort that connection, which has understated the impact of European parliamentary representation. Delegate—and party-representation models have importance and utility in relation to parliamentary sovereignty but only in so far as they are presupposed by the primacy of a national legislature (consistent with Rehfeld 2005, p. 36) able to practically and collectively represent its electorate. That process of representing is driven toward a collective interest, brought to bear in the Government's majority party inside the House of Commons, with its manifesto-turned-agenda, governing consistently with that interest. The European Parliament can undermine that representation process.

While European Parliament binary politics is not strictly organised through government-opposition parties as in Westminster, the parties are importantly organised into party-based, political-affiliation blocs. Through blocs, where the majority socialist groupings held ideological power over those not in that grouping throughout the 1980s and 1990s and provided their approval or amendment to Commission and Council decisions. The dominance of the Progressive Alliance of Socialists and Democrats (S&D) in relation to the European People's Party (EPP) in Strasbourg and the relevance of working time to the political culture and vision of the political left on the Left-right dimension strongly aided the European Parliament's representative capacity. That symbolises a challenge to the view in which European Parliament representation is identified as distinct from Westminster or rejects any notion of attempted EU federation party-politics as defining representation at the European level. Stable and cohesive political parties in the S&D and EPP groupings do have relevance and binary politics is feasible (consistent with Hix 2016; Hix et al. 2007) within a part-federal system, in line with the party government model, despite the strength of other forms of representation. The lineage in which parliamentary sovereignty depends on political representation that, in turn, relies on binary party competition is undermined.

Consistent with Mair and Thomassen (2013), competing parties can operate with at least a partially effective representative role in the European Parliament. The acceptance of party and of party-approving parliament is valuable however but only in so far as it is a second-order, collaborative legislature unable to represent a unified European interest in respect of a European electorate. On the other hand, Westminster's capacity to collectively represent had been dis-empowered when the governing Conservative Party became less accountable to Parliament. Given its pledges to veto and prevent the Directive from coming into action in the UK, the party's policy was bypassed by the policy-making of the European Parliament. The bypassing of Parliament in this manner strongly indicates the reverse of Bogdanor's (2009a) assumption in which EU representation affirms the popular power of British voters for they and their direct and indirect pathways to political representation are minimised. The exception to the rule in the creation of the Working Time Directive might be domestic, minority opposition groups and broad trade union movement on the political left. In resisting Thatcher's policies domestically, they viewed working time legislation as a universal,

European-wide solution to their campaign to improve national working conditions. The European Parliament representation process competitively distorts the domestic legislature in its ability to collectively represent its constituents. The governing party in the House of Commons, which is charged with producing laws and policies, is radically bypassed by Strasbourg policy-making.

5.4 Conclusion

The Working Time Directive provides a very useful illustration, and often for unexpected reasons, that the UK's recognised helm has experienced European Parliament-level functional representation competing with its capacity to collectively represent its electors. That competition produces an unsettling of the historically precedented capacity for collective representation as strongly embedded within historical constitutional forms, thereby diluting the strength of parliamentary sovereignty. Whereas the UK's (Conservative) governing party-in-Parliament as the representative self-policing corporate body (Pettit 2009) had previously been the space for resolving contested labour laws, the acceptance and the irreversibility, of the imposed EU policy, then law, demonstrated the unaccountability of ministers at Westminster in making laws and policies in the collective interest. In urging proposals for working time, it is notable that the European Parliament was strongly reliant on the Council, Commission and the European Economic and Social Committee's shared neo-corporatist emphasis because it seeks to represent the approach taken by the shared central institutions (Smismans 2016; Wendler 2017). The European Parliament had been eager to ensure a supranational commitment to working time reduction, as distinct from weaker, non-binding national pledges. The supranational commitment served to remind the Commission to strengthen its binding requirements at the supranational level. It had also been a reminder that the Commission and European Parliament are vital supranational elements—the Commission as government, the European Parliament as representative parliament—within the multi-representational architecture. The most unexpected facet of representation at the European level in the example of the Working Time Directive is its general reliance on 'constitutionalisation' as a means to strengthen its representative linkages. Yet, here, a clear place can be found for party and management of political partisanship in explaining the outcome of the Directive. Westminster's capacity to collectively represent had been disempowered when the governing Conservative Party became less accountable to Parliament, given its pledges to veto and prevent the Directive from coming into action in the UK. The party's policy was bypassed by the policy-making of the European Parliament. The bypassing of Parliament in this manner puts EU-level representation at odds with both parliamentary and popular sovereignty models, for voters' direct and indirect pathways to political representation are minimised.

The subsequent chapter (Chapter 6) explains that Parliament's sovereignty has been effectively unsettled because the recognised helm has incorporated EU-level fundamental rights schemes. In that process, EU fundamental rights schemes protected by the courts become constitutionally strengthened, entrenched in codes of written and legal form. That can be contrasted with the medieval precedents (in the first historical constitutional form) presenting an English constitution in which governing at the helm is presented as legally distinct but politically contingent upon its capacity to determine and respect fundamental rights. Contemporary EU rights are alternatively expressed as unchallengeable legal instruments beyond ordinary politics, in contrast to the precedented and minimalist protection afforded by Parliament. The case study of the EU free movement right makes evident that the recognised helm has had EU rights incorporated into its constitution, enabling a dependency upon EU-level rights. The submission of the domestic legislature to the courts, along with a final binding effect upon the executive, unsettles parliamentary sovereignty.

Bibliography

Adams, J. F. (2001). *Party Competition and Responsible Party Government: A Theory of Spatial Competition Based Upon Insights from Behavioral Voting Research*. Ann Arbor: University of Michigan Press.

Adnett, N., & Hardy, S. (2001). Reviewing the Working Time Directive: Rationale, Implementation and Case Law. *Industrial Relations Journal, 32*(1), 114–125.

Aldrin, P., & Hubé, N. (2018). From Democracy by Proxy to Stakeholder Democracy: The Changing Faces of an EU Founding Value. In F. Foret & O. Calligaro (Eds.), *European Values: Challenges and Opportunities for EU Governance*. London: Routledge.

Annett, I. (2010). The Case of the EU: Implications for Federalism. *Regional & Federal Studies, 20*(1), 107–126.

Barysch, K. (2013). *The Working Time Directive What's the Fuss About?* [Online]. Available at http://www.cer.eu/sites/default/files/publications/attachments/pdf/2013/pb_workingtimedir_kb_26april13_bl-7268.pdf. Accessed 14 May 2013.

Berkhout, J., Hanegraaff, M., & Braun, C. (2017). Is the EU different? Comparing the Diversity of National and EU-Level Systems of Interest Organisations. *West European Politics, 40*(5), 1109–1131.

Blankart, C. (2007). The European Union: Confederation, Federation or Association of Compound States? *Constitutional Political Economy, 18*(2), 99–106.

Bogdanor, V. (2009a). *The New British Constitution*. Oxford: Hart Publishing.

Bogdanor, V. (2009b). *The New British Constitution*. London: Gresham College [Online]. Available at https://www.gresham.ac.uk/lectures-and-events/the-new-british-constitution. Accessed 20 June 2014.

Bogdanor, V. (2019). *Beyond Brexit: Towards a British Constitution*. London: I.B. Tauris.

Bolick, C. (1995). Thatcher's Revolution: Deregulation and Political Transformation. *The Yale Journal on Regulation, 12*(2), 527–548.

Bourke, R. (1999). Sovereignty, Opinion and Revolution in Edmund Burke. *History of European Ideas, 25*(3), 99–120.

Bradley, A. W., & Ewing, K. D. (2010). *Constitutional and Administrative Law* (15th ed.). Harlow: Longman.

Burgess, M. (2006). *Comparative Federalism: Theory and Practice*. London: Routledge.

Burke, E. (1770). Thoughts on the Cause of the Present Discontents. In E. J. Payne (Ed.). (1999), *Select Works of Edmund Burke* (Vol. 1). Indianapolis, IN: Liberty Fund. Available at http://oll.libertyfund.org/titles/burke-select-works-of-edmund-burke-vol-1–5. Accessed 3 December 2013.

Burke, E. (1774). Speech to the Electors of Bristol. In E. J. Payne (Ed.). (1999), *Select Works of Edmund Burke* (Vol. 4). Indianapolis, IN: Liberty Fund. Available at http://oll.libertyfund.org/titles/burke-select-works-of-edmund-burke-vol-4. Accessed 17 December 2013.

Burke, E. (1792). A Letter to Sir Hercules Langrishe on the Catholics of Ireland. In E. J. Payne (Ed.). (1999), *Select Works of Edmund Burke* (Vol. 4). Indianapolis, IN: Liberty Fund. Available at http://www.econlib.org/library/LFBooks/Burke/brkSWv4c6.html. Accessed 16 January 2014.

Bux, U. (2017). *The European Parliament: Historical Background* [Online]. Available at http://www.europarl.europa.eu/ftu/pdf/en/FTU_1.3.1.pdf Accessed 12 March 2017.

Costello, R., Thomassen, J., & Rosema, M. (2012). European Parliament Elections and Political Representation: Policy Congruence Between Voters and Parties. *West European Politics, 35*(6), 1226–1248.

Council Directive 93/104/EC. (1993, November 23). *Concerning Certain Aspects of the Organization of Working Time* [Online]. Available at http://data.europa.eu/eli/dir/1993/104/oj. Accessed 1 May 2017.

Craig, D. (2012). Burke and the Constitution. In D. Dwan & C. J. Insole (Eds.), *The Cambridge Companion to Edmund Burke* (pp. 104–116). Cambridge: Cambridge University Press.

Dahl, R. (1998). Justifying Democracy. *Society, 35*(2), 386–392.

Dalton, R. J., Farrell, D., & McAllister, I. (2011). *Political Parties and Democratic Linkage: How Parties Organize Democracy.* Oxford: Oxford University Press.

Dicey, A. V. (1885/1964). *An Introduction to the Study of the Law of the Constitution.* London: Macmillan.

Dimitrakopoulos, D. G. (2013, April 24). *Debates over the EU's Working Time Directive Epitomise the Conflict Between Neo-Liberal and Centre-Left Visions of Europe.* London School of Economics Blog on European Politics and Policy [Blog]. Available at http://blogs.lse.ac.uk/europpblog/2013/04/24/debates-over-the-eus-working-time-directive-epitomise-the-conflict-between-neo-liberal-and-centre-left-visions-of-europe/. Accessed 10 April 2017.

European Commission. (2015). *Working Conditions—Working Time Directive* [Online]. Available at http://ec.europa.eu/social/main.jsp?-catId=706&langId=en&intPageId=205 Accessed 12 August 2015.

European Economic and Social Committee. (2016). *Overview* [Online]. Available at https://europa.eu/european-union/about-eu/institutions-bodies/european-economic-social-committee_en. Accessed 2 February 2016.

European Parliament. (1983, December 19). Resolution Closing the Procedure for Consultation of the European Parliament on the Proposal from the Commission of the European Communities to the Council for a Recommendation on the Reduction and Reorganization of Working Time. *Official Journal of the European Communities, C 342, 26*, 147.

European Parliament. (1984, October 15). Resolution on the Reorganization of Working Time. *Official Journal of the European Communities, C 274, 27*, 40.

European Parliament. (1989a, April 17). Resolution on the Commission's Work Programme for 1989. *Official Journal of the European Communities, C 96, 32*, 56–57.

European Parliament. (1989b, December 27). Resolution on the Community Charter of Fundamental Social Rights. *Official Journal of the European Communities, C 323, 32*, 44.

European Parliament. (1989c, December 27). Texts Adopted by the European Parliament on 1: Community Charter of Fundamental Social Rights—Social and Economic Cohesion (b) Doc. B3-510/89 Resolution on Economic and Social Cohesion. *Official Journal of the European Communities, C 323, 32*, 48.

European Parliament. (1989d, December 27). Texts Adopted by the European Parliament on 1: Community Charter of Fundamental Social Rights—(c)

Doc. B3-511/89 Resolution on the Attainment of Economic and Social Cohesion. *Official Journal of the European Communities, C 323, 32*, 44–48.

European Parliament. (1990, October 15). Resolution on the Commission's Action Programme Relating to the Implementation of the Community Charter of Fundamental Social Rights for Workers-Priorities for 1991–1992. *Official Journal of the European Communities, C 260, 33*, 167.

European Parliament. (1991, March 18). Legislative Resolution (Cooperation Procedure: First Reading) Embodying the Opinion of the European Parliament on the Commission Proposal for a Council Directive Concerning Certain Aspects of the Organization of Working Time. *Official Journal of the European Communities, C 72, 34*, 95.

European Parliament. (1993, November 22). Decision on the Common Position Established by the Council with a View to the Adoption of a Directive Concerning Certain Aspects of the Organization of Working Time [C3-0241/93 - SYN 295]. *Official Journal of the European Communities, C 315*, 125–129.

European Scrutiny Committee. (2013, November 28). *Reforming the European Scrutiny System in the House of Commons* (HC 109-I) [Report]. Available at https://publications.parliament.uk/pa/cm201314/cmselect/cmeuleg/109/109.pdf Accessed 12 December 2013.

European Union. (2019). *About the EU* [Online]. Available at http://europa.eu/about-eu/index_en.htm Accessed 2 August 2014.

Geddes, A. (2013). *Britain and the European Union*. London: Palgrave Macmillan.

Gowland, D., Turner, A., & Wright, A. (2010). *Britain and European Integration Since 1945: On the Sidelines*. London: Routledge.

Greenwood, J. (2018). NGOs in the European Union. In A. Kellow & H. Murphy-Gregory (Eds.), *Handbook of Research on NGOs*. Cheltenham: Edward Elgar.

Griffith, J. A. G. (1979). The Political Constitution. *Modern Law Review, 42*(1), 1–21.

Hantrais, L. (2017). *The Social Dimension in EU and UK Policy Development: Shaping the Post-Brexit Legacy* (Working Paper, CIS/2017/04). London: Centre for International Studies, London School of Economics. Available at http://www.lse.ac.uk/internationalRelations/centresandunits/CIS/documents/The%20Social%20Dimensions%20in%20EU.pdf. Accessed 15 June 2017.

Hart, H. L. A. (1997). *The Concept of Law* (2nd ed.). Oxford: Clarendon Press.

Hix, S. (2016). *The European Parliament* [Online]. Available at http://ukandeu.ac.uk/explainers/the-european-parliament/. Accessed 5 July 2017.

Hix, S., & Høyland, B. (2013). Empowerment of the European Parliament. *Annual Review of Political Science, 16*, 171–189.

Hix, S., Kreppel, A., & Noury, A. (2003). The Party System in the European Parliament: Collusive or Competitive? *The Journal of Common Market Studies, 41*(2), 309–331.

Hix, S., & Marsh, M. (2007). Punishment or Protest? Understanding European Parliament Elections. *Journal of Politics, 69*(2), 495–510.

Hix, S., Noury, A., & Roland, G. (2007). *Democratic Politics in the European Parliament*. Cambridge: Cambridge University Press.

Jarman, H. (2011). Collaboration and Consultation: Functional Representation in EU Stakeholder Dialogues. *Journal of European Integration, 33*(4), 385–399.

Jessop, B. (2004). Multi-level Governance and Multi-level Meta Governance. In I. Bache & M. Flinders (Eds.), *Multi-level Governance* (pp. 49–74). Oxford: Oxford University Press.

Katz, R., & Wessels, B. (1999). Parliaments and Democracy in Europe in the Era of the Euro. In R. Katz & B. Wessels (Eds.), *The European Parliament, National Parliaments, and European Integration* (Chapter 6). Oxford: Oxford University Press.

Lindgren, K. O., & Persson, T. (2018). Participatory Governance in the European Union. In H. Heinelt (Ed.), *Handbook on Participatory Governance*. Cheltenham: Edward Elgar.

Lourie, J. (1996, November 19). *The Working Time Directive* (House of Commons Library Research Paper 96/106) [Online]. Available at http://researchbriefings.files.parliament.uk/documents/RP96-106/RP96-106.pdf. Accessed 11 April 2017.

Lourie, J. (1997, September 2). *The Social Chapter* (House of Commons Research Paper 97/102) [Online]. Available at http://researchbriefings.files.parliament.uk/documents/RP97-102/RP97-102.pdf. Accessed 12 November 2013.

Lourie, J. (1998, August10). *Working Time Regulations SI 1998 No 1833* (House of Commons Library Research Paper 98/82) [Online]. Available at http://researchbriefings.files.parliament.uk/documents/RP98-82/RP98-82.pdf. Accessed 11 April 2017.

Mair, P., & Thomassen, J. (2010). Political Representation and Government in the European Union. *Journal of European Public Policy, 17*(1), 20–35.

Mair, P., & Thomassen, J. (2013). *Political Representation and European Union Governance*. London: Routledge.

Majone, G. (2006). The Common Sense of European Integration. *Journal of European Public Policy, 13*(5), 607–626.

Marsh, M., & Norris, P. (1997). Political Representation in the European Parliament. *European Journal of Political Research, 32*(2), 153–164.

Martinsen, D. S., & Wessel, A. U. (2014). On the Path to Differentiation: Upward Transfer, Logic of Variation and Sub-optimality in EU Social Policy. *Journal of European Public Policy, 21*(9), 1255–1272.

McCormick, J. (2015). *European Union Politics* (2nd ed.). London: Palgrave Macmillan.

Miller, V. (2010, October 13). *How Much Legislation Comes from Europe?* (House of Commons Library Research Paper 10/62) [Online]. Available at http://researchbriefings.parliament.uk/ResearchBriefing/Summary/RP10-62. Accessed 10 November 2014.

Moravcsik, A. (2008). The European Constitutional Settlement. *World Economy, 31*(1), 158–183.

Neyer, J. (2014). Justified Multi-level Parliamentarism: Situating National Parliaments in the European Polity. *The Journal of Legislative Studies, 20*(1), 125–138.

Nugent, N. (2010). *The Government and Politics of the European Union* (7th ed.). London: Palgrave.

Pérez Durán, I. (2018). Interest Group Representation in the Formal Design of European Union Agencies. *Regulation & Governance, 12*, 238–262.

Pettit, P. (2009). Varieties of Public Representation. In I. Shapiro, S. C. Stokes, E. J. Wood, & A. S. Kirshner (Eds.), *Political Representation* (pp. 61–89). Cambridge: Cambridge University Press.

Pitkin, H. F. (1967). *The Concept of Representation*. Berkeley: University of California Press.

Raileanu-Szeles, M. (2013). *Re-examining EU Policies from a Global Perspective: Scenarios for Future Developments*. London: Palgrave Macmillan.

Rehfeld, A. (2005). *The Concept of Constituency: Political Representation, Democratic Legitimacy, and Institutional Design*. New York, NY: Cambridge University Press.

Rogowski, R. (2015). Implementation of the EU Working Time Directive in the United Kingdom. In J.-C. Barbier, R. Rogowski, & F. Columb (Eds.), *The Sustainability of the European Social Model: EU Governance, Social Protection and Employment Policies in Europe* (pp. 231–252). Cheltenham: Edward Elgar.

Rönnmar, M. (2011). *Labour Law, Fundamental Rights and Social Europe*. London: Bloomsbury.

Sartori, G. (2005). Party Types, Organisation and Function. *West European Politics, 28*(1), 5–32.

Schmitt, H., & Thomassen, J. (1999). *Political Representation and Legitimacy in the European Union*. Oxford: Oxford University Press.

Shackleton, M. (2012). The European Parliament. In J. Peterson & M. Shackleton (Eds.), *The Institutions of the European Union* (3rd ed., pp. 124–147). Oxford: Oxford University Press.

Smismans, S. (2016). Regulatory Procedure and Participation in the European Union. In F. Bignami & D. Zaring (Eds.), *Comparative Law and Regulation*. Cheltenham, UK: Edward Elgar.

Smith, J. (2017). National Parliaments and the European Union—A View from Westminster. In D. Jancic (Ed.), *National Parliaments After the Lisbon Treaty and the Euro Crisis: Resilience or Resignation?* Oxford: Oxford University Press.

Stothers, C., & Porter, A. (2011). *Paid Annual Leave in the United Kingdom: The Problem of Holiday Pay* [Online]. Available at http://www.thomasmore.co.uk/imagelibrary/holiday%20pay%20article.pdf. Accessed 11 July 2017.

Thomassen, H. S. J. (1999). *Political Representation and Legitimacy in the European Union*. Oxford: Oxford University Press.

Triesman, Lord. (2006, February 28). HL Deb, c130.

UK Parliament. (2019a). *Information* [Online]. Available at www.parliament.uk. Accessed 3 January 2014.

UK Parliament. (2019b). *You and Your MP* [Online]. Available at http://www.parliament.uk/documents/commons-information-office/Brief-Guides/You-and-Your-MP.pdf. Accessed 8 September 2013.

UK v Council of the European Union. [1996]. Council Directive 93/104/EC Concerning Certain Aspects of the Organization of Working Time—Action for Annulment (Case C-84/94). Available at http://curia.europa.eu/juris/liste.jsf?language=en&jur=C,T,F&num=C-84/94&td=ALL. Accessed 11 April 2017.

Weiler, J. (1999). *The Constitution of Europe: "Do the New Clothes Have an Emperor?" And Other Essays on European Integration*. Cambridge: Cambridge University Press.

Wendler, F. (2017). The Cooperation of the European Union with Employer and Labor Associations. In R. Biermann & J. A. Koops (Eds.), *Palgrave Handbook of Inter-organizational Relations in World Politics* (pp. 611–626). London: Palgrave Macmillan.

Wessels, B. (1999). European Parliament and Interest Groups. In R. Katz & B. Wessels (Eds.), *The European Parliament, National Parliaments, and European Integration* (Chapter 6). Oxford: Oxford University Press.

Winzen, T., Roederer-Rynning, C., & Schimmelfennig, F. (2015). Parliamentary Co-evolution: National Parliamentary Reactions to the Empowerment of the European Parliament. *Journal of European Public Policy, 22*(1), 75–93.

Working Time Directive 2003/88/EC of the European Parliament and of the Council. (2003, November 4). *Concerning Certain Aspects of the Organisation of Working Time* [Online]. Available at http://data.europa.eu/eli/dir/2003/88/oj. Accessed 10 February 2013.

CHAPTER 6

Parliamentary Sovereignty, the EU Free Movement of Persons and the Precedent of Fundamental Rights Provision

Parliament derives a fundamental aspect of its sovereignty from a historically precedented foundation in which the provision of fundamental rights is made through recourse to political, parliamentary mechanisms (Dicey 1964) rather than the subordinate provision offered by the courts (Tabarelli 2013, p. 344). Under EU membership, the UK Parliament has however grown more unsettled because the recognised helm has incorporated EU-level fundamental rights schemes. In that process, EU fundamental rights schemes protected by the courts become constitutionally elevated and entrenched in codes of written and legal form. As such, rights are expressed as unchallengeable instruments above ordinary, representative politics—complete with EU legal supremacy, direct effect and ECJ jurisdiction—and in distinction to the historically precedented and minimalist provision afforded by Parliament. The submission of the domestic legislature in that key respect to the courts, along with a final binding effect upon the executive, impacts upon and dilutes the strength of parliamentary sovereignty.

Within the expanding scope of human rights, 'fundamental rights' describes rights which are claimed to be of greater or particular significance which cannot be derogated from. The term "human rights" is used in international law arenas; whereas rights guaranteed by constitutions at the national level are most often referred to as "fundamental rights". In some interpretations, both can often be referring to the same substance. Contemporary rights are categorised as fundamental when they guarantee that no one living in a free democratic society such as

J. McConalogue, *The British Constitution Resettled*,
https://doi.org/10.1007/978-3-030-25290-8_6

the UK should be free to forego (Bingham 2010). Those rights have included: the right to life; the right that no one shall be subject to torture or to inhuman or degrading treatment or punishment; the right that no one shall be held in slavery or perform forced labour; and the right to a fair trial. It is held that those rights must be secured without discrimination on grounds of sex, religion, race, colour, language, political opinion, national or social origin (Bingham 2010, pp. 10–36). Domestically, systems for the provision of fundamental rights present a challenge and constraint upon the authority of decision-makers. It therefore becomes the function of the system as a whole to ensure that decisions made on behalf of the general interest do not neglect or deny individual rights (Muir 2014, p. 29). There is however no universal consensus on fundamental rights, even among developed countries (Bingham 2010, p. 68).

The first historical constitutional form presents an English constitution in which governing at the helm is presented as legally distinct but politically contingent upon its capacity to determine and respect fundamental rights. The law and the law-making sovereign were "mutually conditioned", contingent, reciprocal and interdependent at the helm, even though the sovereign retained the power to govern the realm (Kantorowicz 1957, pp. 153, 155). In contrast, this chapter considers how the modern neo-Diceyan view of the British constitution *disregards* that contingency (Dicey 1964); the radical common law constitutionalism school (Allan 2013) *overstates* it and; the constitutional state perspective (Bogdanor 2009) *overlooks* that contingent relationship. Those interpretations of the British constitution have misplaced EU fundamental rights in a political and constitutional context, if not underestimated their supremacy to European Convention- and international-rights. This chapter addresses those oversights through appealing to the 'political constitutionalism' of Jeremy Waldron (1999), Richard Bellamy (2007), and Adam Tomkins (2013). Such an account attends to the primacy of political legitimacy over constitutional entrenchment and challenges the contemporary narrow determination of rights by courts in favour of a shared responsibility by the executive, the legislature and judiciary. It reassesses the approach of supranational legalism in determining EU rights through the prism of democratic parliamentary majorities.

The case study of the EU free movement right demonstrates that the UK recognised helm has incorporated EU rights into its constitutional structure through a dependency upon EU-level rights by individuals in the UK, as EU citizens, in order to protect their interests to move freely.

This contemporary right has led to the strengthening of the UK judiciary as a rights-adjudicating court system as it fuses ever-closer into the Luxembourg court system. The judicial strengthening has come at the expense of the dilution of the UK Parliament as a rights-providing institution. The deep political claims made to the constitutional and institutional entrenchment of the rights themselves, irrespective of political legitimacy, combined with the disappearing consensus between the arms of state and community in protecting rights, has progressed this continued legislative decline and judicial advance in the UK, impacting indirectly upon the unsettling of parliamentary sovereignty.

6.1 Parliamentary Sovereignty and Historical Fundamental Rights Provision

Fundamental rights have a unique but reflexive role in the historical development of the British constitution. The development of modern British-EU citizens as rights-bearing individuals evolved from Royal subjects with very basic rights granted by royal privilege through to British subjects of Empire with limited, implicit privilege-determined rights, then UK citizens with limited statutory rights determined by the state, to UK citizens enjoying a greater, wide bundle of rights as EU citizens. Although Dicey in his seminal 1885 work, 'An Introduction to the Study of Law of the Constitution', accepted such key principles and rules as "the conventions of the Constitution" which regulate relationships, he accepted them as non-legal additions to the constitution. Dicey's work embodied the subordination of court-based fundamental rights provision in Parliament's role (Tabarelli 2013, p. 344) in the sense that no higher, fundamental right framework was required where freedom was protected by common law custom and Parliament checked the unwieldiness of the executive (Bradley and Ewing 2010, p. 397; Francis and Morrow 1994, p. 23). The relevance of that view has been lost in contemporary Britain. At that time, national citizens equipped with material rights which they could read from a constitution or charter was simply not precedented. As Royal subjects, their British nationality developed from an allegiance to the Crown owed by them in return for which the Crown had no power to expel them from the realm (Bradley and Ewing 2010, p. 418). People born within the Crown's dominions became a subject. The major common law division was between British subjects and aliens (foreigners). It was only in the later part of the twentieth century in post-imperial

Britain that Parliament wrote national subjecthood and immigration into parliamentary law—the Immigration Act 1971 and the British Nationality Act of 1981—with the former drawing on the deep division between European Community and non-European Community freedom of movement rights (Bradley and Ewing 2010). EU citizenship then adopted a formal legal status in the Maastricht Treaty of 1993.

The Maastricht Treaty (Treaty on European Union) itself then explicitly included the right to move and reside freely in member states (subject to limitations and conditions) under the concept of EU citizenship, along with a number of associated rights. So, the principle of free movement was significantly incorporated through the Maastricht Treaty as a core part of the concept of 'EU citizenship' (Marzocchi 2017; Ruhs and Palme 2018, p. 1483; Schmidt et al. 2018, pp. 1391–1394). The European Commission says it is the right most closely associated with EU citizenship (Peter 2014). The Treaty formally created the European Union and formalised the recognition of the status of EU citizens with their associated rights, as claimable for every national of a member state. EU citizenship offers significant potential for the provision of fundamental rights (van den Brink 2012). The principle has itself evolved as a definition over time from the right to free movement for workers, or those economically active in the EU labour market, to then apply also to job-seekers, the self-employed, students and the self-sufficient e.g. retired persons. Under the Treaties, the free movement of persons is an area of 'shared competence' so that where the EU has enacted legislation, the UK does not have competence to act other than in accordance with that legislation.

The subsequent EU treaties including Amsterdam (1997), Nice (2001), and Lisbon (2007) have entrenched EU citizenship as a bundle of rights built around 'free movement' and 'non-discrimination' between and across EU member states (Isin and Saward 2013, p. 1). The development of modern British-EU citizens as rights-bearing individuals developed from Royal subjects with very basic rights granted by royal privilege (medieval), to British subjects during Empire with limited, implicit privilege-determined rights, to UK citizens with limited statutory rights determined by the state, to UK citizens enjoying a greater, wide bundle of rights as EU citizens which have been determined by the EU as assented to by UK and 27 other European governments.

The character of parliamentary sovereignty has been historically dependent upon Parliament respecting the customs of fundamental law. It is notable that the historical development of the sovereignty invested in governing through Parliament is legally separate but politically contingent upon the development of fundamental law and rights provision. It is that first episodic historical constitutional form within a historically evolving approach of eight potential historical forms which demonstrated that the development of parliamentary sovereignty was dependent upon respecting the customs of fundamental law. That interpretation of Bracton leads to the understanding of sovereignty as government through the helm, which can be understood from the vantage point of the period of medieval kingship in the centuries preceding the Reformation in the thirteenth and fourteenth centuries. The important relationship is that baronial counsel reinforced the moral—albeit, not legal—duty of fundamental law that the Crown was now subject to and must respect. That historical form responds to an interpretation of Bracton's medieval constitutionalism in which law and the legislative sovereign at the 'helm' of the medieval state, were defined by a political relationship even though the sovereign retained the power to govern the realm (Kantorowicz 1957, p. 153). The governing at the helm of the state is then, both legally separate but politically contingent upon the capacity to respect fundamental law and rights.

6.2 Parliamentary Sovereignty and Contemporary Fundamental Rights Provision

In understanding the contemporary relationship between UK parliamentary sovereignty and fundamental rights, there are ample contrasts to be made to the underlying features of the neo-Diceyan view, a radical common law constitutionalism or a constitutional state perspective—which undermine that connection and never wholly explain parliamentary sovereignty and its relationship to fundamental rights, as unsettled by EU membership. In a modern, neo-Diceyan political landscape, contemporary Britain has shifted gradually toward a fundamental rights framework of some sort—which Dicey himself saw as unnecessary (Francis and Morrow 1994, p. 23). One of the major developments which has led to a framework being incorporated into the UK is through the rights introduced to UK citizens, as EU citizens. The historical precedents of Bracton present a constitution in which governing at the helm is presented as legally distinct but politically contingent upon its capacity to determine and respect fundamental rights. This chapter appeals to the 'political constitutionalism', as the politics of rights, giving weight to an account of the primacy of politics over institutional rights-entrenchment in relation to parliamentary sovereignty.

Most notably, the introduction of 'EU citizenship' through the EU Treaties means that UK citizens as EU citizens are able to appeal to directly enforceable modern EU fundamental rights (Nugent 2010, p. 225), as against rights previously determined through a national constitutional structure. They are material rights, not ancient privileges. Citizens generally have to appeal to courts, not Parliament in claiming those rights. Neither can Parliament redefine those rights or in any way abridge them. The process to realise a claimable EU or national right is through a legal and judicial process, not a political or parliamentary process, and the process of determining, maintaining and protecting rights had gradually become a matter for the courts (Bogdanor 2019, p. x), not Parliament. They are claimable as entrenched tools of entitlement but they are not tools strictly subject to political or parliamentary decision-making as consented to by the political community. That argument identifies with the political constitutionalism of Jeremy Waldron (1999), Richard Bellamy (2007), and Adam Tomkins (2013), who have each convincingly addressed how judgements about decisions, including rights, cannot be legitimately entrenched or handled by judicial or technical bodies that are isolated from accountable and democratic processes.

The proposition that EU fundamental rights have unsettled UK parliamentary sovereignty only partially rests upon the changing nature of the individual as a Crown's subject which has been altered. This occurred partly through the UK's own national legislation in the 1970s and 1980s, including the Immigration Act 1971 and the British Nationality Act 1981 (Bradley and Ewing 2010). What was more notable, however, after the Maastricht Treaty was the morphing of UK subjecthood into that of EU citizen. This is a fundamental feature, but by itself, has only a limited explanatory power. The move to EU citizenship explains the shift in the individual's access to a system of rights which were almost exclusively an expression of parliamentary-determined privileges towards access to a system of immediately codified, court-determined entitlements. It partially explains the displacement of an individual's allegiance to Crown-determined-rights to a citizen's legal obligations within a broad, contractual set of rights, or material/text-based constitution. It also in part explains the shift from obligation to 'a nation' as a political entity toward the rights of a citizen in relation to their state. But it is absent in explaining how a political community provides the legitimacy for any potential constitutional entrenchment of certain rights—EU, international or otherwise—and how the consensus between officials in the arms of the state determines the impact of EU fundamental rights upon parliamentary sovereignty.

6.2.1 Constitutional State Theory and the Entrenchment of Codified Rights

In the existing research, the 'constitutional statist' perspective is incompatible with recognising the contemporary connection between parliamentary sovereignty and fundamental rights. Part of the incompatibility arises from *overlooking* the historical precedent describing parliamentary sovereignty as enabling Parliament to politically determine fundamental law and rights. The constitutional state perspective assumes instead that the *entrenchment* of written, codified, fundamental rights trumps their parliamentary legitimacy and sovereignty. Vernon Bogdanor (2009, p. 57) in his central argument in *The New British Constitution*, argues that the post-2007 era of constitutional reform, together with Britain's entry in 1973 into the European Communities, has had the effect of replacing one constitution—that is the UK's Diceyan doctrine of parliamentary sovereignty and its comparatively weaker provision of fundamental rights among European Community members—with a new constitution. The main elements of the new constitution include stronger provisions afforded to fundamental rights in the UK and a part of which is already due to separate European Convention (non-EU) rights under the Human Rights Act as well as EU-derived rights enabled under the European Communities Act.

The Human Rights Act itself is supposedly the cornerstone of the new constitution. He suggests those reforms strengthened the idea of Britain adopting a written or codified constitution (Bogdanor 2019) and the potentiality for a popular constitutional state (Bogdanor 2009, pp. i–xiii). It is further claimed that judges fear and act on the basis that Parliament and government cannot be trusted in several circumstances to refrain from passing legislation inconsistent with fundamental rights (Bogdanor 2012). It is not verifiable however that the emergence of a popular constitutional state, based on those multiplicity of features, including the development of EU-level and European Convention on Human Rights-level fundamental rights, is evident now or even potentially in the future. The old constitution, he theorises, was based on the sovereignty of Parliament; the new constitution is based on a constitutional state with a stronger provision of human rights (Bogdanor 2009, pp. i–xiii, 87). That proposition does not sit well with the observation that despite the Human Rights Act, there remains a well-evidenced lack of human rights culture in the UK (Ziegler et al. 2015).

In later research, Bogdanor overlooks the relevance of fundamental rights in the historical shaping of parliamentary sovereignty by almost singularly describing parliamentary sovereignty as being limited by the European Communities Act 1972 (Bogdanor 2012). He claims the Act altered the rule of recognition—meaning that Parliament cannot derogate from European Community law. Since national courts have to apply European Community law where inconsistent with national law (Craig 2011, p. 116), it is claimed the European Communities Act limits Parliament's substantive power (Bogdanor 2019, p. 72, Bogdanor 2012, pp. 184–186, contra Goldsworthy 2012; Bogdanor 2009). On those terms, the rule of law embodied by fundamental rights is superseding the rule of recognition (Bogdanor 2009, p. 74). In describing that bolstering of rights under the rule of law, constitutional state theory recognises but worryingly consigns Hart's rule of recognition to the past, and as being superseded by the rule of law. On those terms, after all, the past is a foreign country (Bogdanor 2019, p. 1). Furthermore, it has frequently not been the case of accepting either the sovereignty of Parliament or of fundamental rights provision as Bogdanor appears to assume: the UK has simultaneously experienced both parliamentary sovereignty and a politically, subordinated fundamental rights provision scheme. Part of the assumed segregation arises from overlooking the historical and political medieval precedent of how parliamentary sovereignty, though legally distinct, was made politically contingent upon fundamental law and rights. Bogdanor's theory constructs a deepened tension between parliamentary sovereignty and fundamental rights.

Finally, if one were to accept that there is a development of a UK constitutional state, it seems logical that post-European Communities Act arrangements with EU legal supremacy and ECJ jurisdiction over the UK in the past forty years would have a vastly greater and binding impact on the stronger provisions afforded to fundamental rights through the courts and an undermining of the doctrine of parliamentary sovereignty than those provisions afforded through the Human Rights Act. Bogdanor instead relies on non-EU, European Convention-based rights and obligations under the Human Rights Act as being the cornerstone of the new constitution, when there is no such supremacy afforded by that Act. Parliament's sovereignty is said to be explicitly preserved and the courts are merely obliged to issue a 'declaration of incompatibility' (see Bradley 2011, p. 64). The reasoning which overstates European Convention rights relative to the impact of EU rights tends to overlook the distinction in constraints between Charter-, Convention- and international-rights. It thereby overlooks the serious constraints imposed on parliamentary sovereignty by EU-level rights.

6.2.2 From Treaty- to Convention- to EU-Rights: Claimable Legal Rights Preceding Parliamentary Sovereignty

The UK's historical system of rights ultimately provided by Parliament can be viewed as contrary to the court-provided, legally-claimable rights in the EU political system. One observable contrast is the way in which UK parliamentary sovereignty has been severely diluted by entrenched EU-level rights accorded to EU citizens through the implementation of the EU Charter of Fundamental Rights. This stands in contrast to a comparatively weaker dilution of sovereignty by partially entrenched European Convention-rights and an understanding of sovereignty relatively unaffected by international Treaty obligations. Under the Charter, the UK's recognised helm has recently had a written single document defining the fundamental rights protected in the EU incorporated into its constitutional structure.

In the past, fundamental rights had been considered a 'peripheral' element of the EU construction (Hrestic 2014). By incorporating the Charter, a high-level provision provided by the courts is entrenched in codes of written and legal form in contrast to the historical provisions afforded by Parliament. The Charter is primary EU law, bringing together fundamental rights protected in the EU under a single document (European Commission 2017). As Koen Lenaerts has observed, "By rendering fundamental rights visible and by merging and systematising in a single document the sources of inspiration scattered in various national and international legal instruments, the Charter marks a new stage in the process of European integration" (Lenaerts 2012, p. 375). It is enforced by the Court of Justice. At every step, from the EU legislative process to the application of EU law at the national level, the rights and principles of the Charter are taken into account. The right of the free movement of persons, for example, is incorporated into the Charter itself under Article 45(1) which specifies "Every citizen of the Union has the right to move and reside freely within the territory of the member states" (European Commission 2017). Since 1 December 2009, when the Treaty of Lisbon entered into force, the EU Charter of Fundamental Rights stands on an equal footing with the EU Treaties (European Commission 2017).

The UK's historical system of Parliament-provided rights is minimalist compared to the partially protected Convention-rights and fully supreme EU-rights. It has been concluded that the Charter is directly effective in the UK with supremacy over inconsistent national law, albeit it does not apply to all areas of national law (European Scrutiny Committee 2014; European Commission 2017). It only applies to those areas that fall within the scope of EU law. Whilst existing human rights litigation in the UK most often comes within the framework of the European Convention on Human Rights, the important focus must be on the way in which EU law in 2009 "codified a wide number of human rights, which it calls fundamental rights, in the form of the Charter" (European Scrutiny Committee 2014). The UK's historical system of Parliament-derived rights is almost completely contrary to the centralised, legally-claimable rights in the EU system. The Charter not only provides an additional source of human rights law, but includes rights not specifically mentioned in the European Convention. This can go beyond the provision afforded by the European Convention and it is set to become a more contemporary and relevant catalogue of rights than the now aged, mid-twentieth century European Convention on Human Rights (Douglas-Scott 2015, p. 259).

The EU legal framework distinguishes it strongly from other international organisations. By specifically focusing on the constraints imposed on parliamentary sovereignty by EU-level fundamental rights, it ought to be recognised that whereas the courts cannot strike down Acts of Parliament under the Human Rights Act (incorporating the European Convention on Human Rights), EU legislation and fundamental rights have direct legal "unconditional supremacy" for UK/EU citizens (Lebeck 2007, p. 199). That legal framework is what distinguishes the EU from other international organisations (Nugent 2010, p. 225). EU rights override inconsistent national legislation and European institutions can politically act in accordance with that legal power. It can be acknowledged, as Bogdanor (2009) does, the balance between parliamentary sovereignty and European-wide fundamental rights provision, or more generally the rule of law, has become more pertinent, if not controversial, since the Human Rights Act 1998 was passed, incorporating the European Convention on Human Rights (Bogdanor 2009, pp. i–xiii, 87).

The European Convention did give individuals the right to complain of breaches of their Convention rights. The Human Rights Act in 1998 then meant it was possible to enforce 'foreign' Convention-rights in the domestic courts, not only in Strasbourg (Bradley and Ewing 2010, pp. 401–407). In content, there are many similarities between the EU Charter of Fundamental Rights and the European Convention on Human Rights. Prospective EU members are asked to sign up to the European Convention although there is no explicit request or obligation for current EU members (McHarsky-Todoroff 2015; Miller 2014). The Act allowed that subordinate legislation in the UK not compatible with the Convention's fundamental rights could be quashed or disapplied. Primary legislation such as Acts of Parliament which were not compatible with Convention rights remained in force but the High Court would only issue a 'declaration of incompatibility' where ministers would be expected to remedy or make amendments to remedy the Act in order to remove the incompatibility (Bradley 2011, p. 64). That can be contrasted to a position in which EU law—directly supreme over UK law—developed into an individual rights-based system. Mechanisms such as the "direct effect" of EU law allows individuals to themselves claim EU rights against the member states in an increasingly large number of settings (Muir 2014, p. 28). Legal supremacy, direct effect and preliminary rulings referring matters to the ECJ all mean judges are obliged as a "powerful check" to give effect to the interpretation of EU law and fundamental rights adopted by the ECJ irrespective of whether a domestic higher court might disagree with this (Muir 2014, p. 36). The court aims to ensure that the law is observed in the interpretation and application of the Treaties across the EU (Article 19 TEU; Bradley and Ewing 2010, p. 122).

Many of the doctrines of EU law that have posed the greatest challenge for the UK's parliamentary sovereignty are often not to be found in the articles of the Treaties, nor even in European law specifically, but in the case law of the ECJ (Tomkins 2010, para. 34). The doctrine of 'direct effect' means that individuals in the UK can bring actions in national courts in order to vindicate rights secured to them under the Treaty or EU legislation (Craig 2011, p. 122), as against purely domestic rights in the domestic courts. It has the effect of making EU law 'the law of the land' and dramatically increased the number of cases brought by individuals to national courts to defend rights accorded to them under EU law (Hix and Høyland 2011, p. 84; Weiler 1991). A treaty provision can have direct effect where a private party can rely upon it against another ('horizontal direct effect') and by a private party against the state ('vertical direct effect') (Hix and Høyland 2011, p. 84; Bradley and Ewing 2010, p. 129). The doctrine of EU legal supremacy (*Costa v ENEL* [1964]), of individuals invoking direct effect in their national courts (*Van Gend en Loos* [1963]), of indirect effect (*Marleasing* [1990]) or of state liability (*Francovich* [1991] and *Factortame* [1990]) or the law relating to the Charter of Fundamental Rights (e.g. the Opinion of the Advocate General in *Zambrano* [2011]) are all examples of those challenges. The Charter entrenches those rights found in the case law of the ECJ (European Commission 2017).

However, compare that incorporation of entrenched, directly effective EU fundamental rights and part-entrenched Convention rights into the UK's national constitutional structure with that of other internationally binding rights and obligations. The post-war international law environment required an introduction of a rights regime with new obligations to be imposed on the UK. Yet, international Treaty law has not posed an equivalent challenge or represented a direct constraining effect as supranational EU fundamental rights have on UK parliamentary sovereignty. Lebeck (2007) examines the strict differentiation between public international treaties emphasising relations between governments, rather than relations between individual rights in domestic public law. International human rights are established directly by treaties, whereas EU fundamental rights have been recognised over time through the case law of the EU. Parliament should in theory take into account the UK's obligations in relation to international law when it legislates, but in practice the courts would not hold an Act void on the basis that it conflicts with principles of international law (Bradley and Ewing 2010, p. 57). Rights agreed to by international Treaties must nevertheless strictly be approved by Parliament if there is to be a change in national law. Although European Community-law emerged from such treaty-law which is treated as a part of public international law (Lebeck 2007, p. 198), it marked a departure from those previous constraints.

Where the EU claims directly effective domestic powers, most international legal orders can only claim decision-making powers that aim to influence decisions in domestic legal orders—but which are not usually "directly effective" (Lebeck 2007, p. 199). The rights of both the European Convention on Human Rights as well as European Community-law cannot be understood as merely treaties under public international law. They both have claimed to have acquired certain constitutional characteristics that distinguish them from other forms of international cooperation and also provided them with a constitutional authority (Lebeck 2007, p. 201). The European Convention on Human Rights is a constitutional document—but the constitutionalisation of the European Community started with the creation of the ECJ and its statement in case law (particularly, beginning with the case *Costa v ENEL* [1964]). Those international-level constraints are distinguishable from the Charter and Convention constraints.

6.2.3 Common Law Constitutionalism and the Entrenchment of Rights

Similar to Bogdanor's (2009) approach in the existing research, a uniquely distinct common law perspective in the radical theory of national common law constitutionalism (Allan 2011, 2013) might be viewed as equally problematic. That perspective directly seeks to overstate the primacy of a national common law, court-decided, entrenched fundamental rights architecture at the expense of the doctrine of parliamentary sovereignty (Allan 2013). The historical constitutional form that the provision of fundamental rights by the courts is subordinate to the political provisions provided by Parliament is incompatible with today's rights-based, court-primacy theories of domestic, radical common law judges and constitutional theorists. The common law argument accepts the supremacy of the judges through EU level fundamental rights and the resulting dilution of UK-level parliamentary sovereignty. The radical theory of common law constitutionalism seeks to affirm the primacy and sovereignty of a national common law, court-decided, entrenched fundamental rights architecture and a displacement, if not rejection, of the doctrine of parliamentary sovereignty (Gordon 2015, pp. 126–131, contra Lakin 2018). Parliamentary sovereignty is expendable for Allan (2011) because judicial loyalty to EU principles can justify the disapplication of Acts of Parliament inconsistent with EU law. If parliamentary sovereignty is said to be derived as a principle of the common law, domestic courts might conceivably seek to modify the doctrine in the same way that they can change other common law principles (Young and Gee 2016). The theory supposes the judiciary would pursue that practice even if that were to qualify the exercise of parliamentary sovereignty (Allan 2011, p. 162). It offers a theory that parliamentary sovereignty can be diluted by EU fundamental rights. The challenge of common law constitutionalism to parliament as a provider of fundamental rights is best answered by the political constitutionalist model. The reason for this response lays with the very mechanisms through which the people authorise their political and legal representatives and hold them to account which comprise the fundamental rules of the UK constitution and its rights. Such a parliamentary model can still withstand rights review and a 'weak' form of Convention rights-based judicial review, in which a declaration of incompatibility by the appropriate court is possible (Bradley 2011, p. 64), providing it is advisory or can be overridden or put to one side by the legislature (Bellamy 2014).

It is an overstatement to suggest EU fundamental rights are altogether entrenched in relation to rights derived from Parliament. Yet, the EU implication of radical common law constitutionalism has been that the UK constitution has specially "entrenched" EU-level fundamental rights incorporated into it. As Allan (2010) maintains, the 1972 Act meant EU law with its rights "has been entrenched" (Allan 2010). As entrenched rights, they act as a substantive limitation upon legislative supremacy, which opens the way to the broader idea that the voluntary European Communities Act substantively and legally limited Parliament (see Bogdanor 2019, p. 72; Bogdanor 2012, pp. 184–186, contra Goldsworthy 2012). While Allan does mostly allow that the European Communities Act can be expressly repealed if necessary, the Act is said to be subject to a "qualified immunity" to that enjoyed by national, common law fundamental rights, including the Magna Carta and the Bill of Rights 1689. Allan also therefore refers to a "special entrenchment" of European Community law (Allan 2013, p. 148). Despite those claims to entrenchment of EU rights, there is little to no evidence to suggest that there has been a contemporary change in the rule of recognition itself or the underlying consensual understanding of British state officials that judges still do not have the authority to declare a statute invalid (see Bingham 2010; Goldsworthy 1999, p. 253).

6.2.4 *Political Constitutionalism: A Response to Constitutional State Theory and Common Law Constitutionalism*

The argument that EU fundamental rights have weakened UK parliamentary sovereignty rests on the constitutional entrenchment of the rights themselves—but that subsidiary concern itself rests on settling the broader question of their political legitimacy. In order of intensity, the UK system has veered between:

- Centuries of non-entrenched parliament-provided rights.
- Then, over nineteen years of statutorily entrenched European Convention-rights (under the Human Rights Act) but which are enforced by only weak judicial review.
- Then, forty-four years of entrenched directly effective ECJ rights brought in under the European Communities Act and founded on the Luxembourg court's case law, through to;
- Directly effective entrenched EU rights founded on a constitutional EU Charter of Fundamental Rights since the Lisbon Treaty of 2009 gave full effect to that Charter (Howe 2013).

The latter marks the height of EU fundamental rights as being constitutionally entrenched. It explains the shift from a UK individual's access to Parliament-provided rights toward their access to claimable, directly effective rights due to them in a national court. The entrenchment reinforces the supremacy of EU rights—it creates and is an effect of a system which stabilises the supremacy of EU law. It explains how rights have been displaced from a stage in which rights are parliament-provided to one in which they are partially provided by courts. That also means it helps to explain the move from a consensual system in which rights cause acts to be reviewed by Parliament to an internally antagonistic constitutional system in which rights enable acts to be reviewed in courts. But statements of the 'entrenchment' of rights fail to address the ultimate and broader question of political legitimacy of those rights—and the role Parliament plays in providing that legitimacy. Parliament-provided rights cannot become entrenched in this manner because rights are deferred to a forum of contested politics in which they are pursued as amendable—that means, subject to politics—and enacted only when there is the necessity to convince a parliamentary majority. So, in member states such as the UK with a specific type of basic social security model, potentially more greatly predisposed to demand restrictions on the social rights of mobile EU workers (Ruhs and Palme 2018), it demands that those EU-level rights must be held as amendable and subject to politics.

In the existing literature, such recognised problems of overlooking historical precedent carries with it the consequence of the blurring of EU fundamental rights as arising simply from international obligations, or as equivalent to Convention-rights, or of supposing that European Communities Act rights alters the rule of recognition. This has led to a broader emphasis on an entrenched, court-decided rights architecture which has created a bias toward mainstream common law constitutionalist interpretation. The role of institutional politics is considered irrelevant. Fundamental rights are seen as irremovable or entrenched features, above politics. Jeremy Waldron and other political constitutionalists have consistently argued against this weight of scholarship assuming that the rules governing the legal system and the political system should be constitutionally entrenched (Waldron 1999). The strong degree of EU fundamental right entrenchment does not depend on EU or UK legality, as is often assumed, but on the political legitimacy of rights within the political system. The fast-developing system of rights is progressively framed by ECJ case law (Blauberger and Schmidt 2017), and not Parliament.

The EU Charter of Fundamental Rights has directly led to a significant expansion of the scope of matters (not just on fundamental rights) subject to EU law (Howe 2013). The broadened expansion scope of issues falling under the Charter has led to a diminution of the UK Parliament's role, and a judicialisation of rights which should otherwise be the subject of decision by democratically elected and accountable politicians (Howe 2013). The danger is that rights are increasingly made in the context of practices with poorly developed political legitimacy i.e. by less accountable European courts, European commissioners and appointed ministers at the Council of the European Union, which bypass elected representatives in legislatures and direct accountability to the political community.

The difficulties of legitimacy in those decisions can be addressed through an appeal to political constitutionalism—although that does not mean to reject all the rules of legal constitutionalism (see Gee and Webber 2010, p. 273; Loughlin 2003). For example, it does not warrant the assumption that Hart's rule of recognition no longer exists, as Bogdanor (2009) theorises. As Goldoni (2013) summarises, a political constitutionalist model proposes that: (i) decisions about rights are better left to the political and parliamentary process, while (ii) judicial reasoning must accept a subordinate role in that respect as well as keeping the government in check and protecting the political process itself (Goldoni 2013). Some emphasis must be placed on the analysis of institutions. Parliaments, as political institutions, are capable and better at reasoning and deciding about the content of rights than courts. For that reason, it can be more accurate, as Wilkinson (2013) has already argued, to refer to 'parliamentary' constitutionalism as opposed to 'judicial' constitutionalism.

Politics matters. Fundamental rights, or constitutional rights, should not be considered to be pre-political or above politics, but, instead, ought to be deeply embedded in the political process. It is consistent with Waldron's (1999) political constitutionalism that such fundamental rights are subject to the 'circumstances of politics'. That process involves both the recognition of a plurality of perspectives on common problems which leads to pervasive disagreement. A legitimate process also requires the recognition of the need to make decisions that address the fact that there is a plurality (Waldron 1999; Goldoni 2012, p. 929). Rights are protected but on the basis that they have a constitutive collective dimension, defended as common goods of a political community, rather than individual entitlements. The openness to politics entails the rejection of constitutional entrenchment, as recognised by Bogdanor (2009) and Allan (2013). The arguments for protecting fundamental rights by legal entrenchment pre-empts future political action of the community and other arms of government without providing a solid justification. By removing rights from politics, it attaches only legal significance and views them as politically non-negotiable, irreversible, unamendable and non-reviewable. Constitutional entrenchment alienates rights from their political context and, alongside a strong form of judicial review, fosters a detrimental judicial culture of rights.

Political constitutionalism is largely justifiable since the UK reasonably disagrees about the rights (e.g. underpinning the extension of benefits in the welfare state, to social housing, to fertility treatment) because they disagree on the substantive outcomes, or common good, that a society committed to democratic ideals should achieve. The democratic process is more legitimate than the judicial process at resolving these disagreements, and it offers an effective mechanism for upholding the key constitutional goods of individual rights and the rule of law

(Bellamy 2007; Waldron 1999). On a practical level, Bellamy and Weale (2015) concede liberal democracies combine different degrees of legal and political constitutionalism. The UK constitution is a reflection of that mix. One defining juxtaposition in which legal constitutionalism meets political constitutionalism derives from the contrast of constitutional entrenchment of rights with their political legitimacy. After all, legal entrenchment does not by itself fully explain why the breakdown in inter-institutional comity and political consensus between officials in the arms of state enables EU fundamental rights to dilute parliamentary sovereignty. The shift away from politics can be explained as the displacement of a political consensus between the executive, the legislature and the judiciary as being responsible for fundamental rights provision. In its place, a strengthened judicial power is elevated in contrast to the executive and legislature and becomes more narrowly responsible for fundamental rights provision.

6.2.5 *The Shared Deferral Approach to Fundamental Rights*

EU membership has unsettled parliamentary sovereignty by delegitimising Britain's fundamental rights provision. The creation of rights-provision previously rested on the historically precedented basis that the executive, the legislature and the judiciary enjoyed an official consensus in which they all shared responsibility for that rights provision. Under the traditional Westminster model, a form of official consensus exists between the branches of the state including Parliament in exercising a shared responsibility for that provision. Radical common law constitutionalists and constitutional statists have therefore narrowly and wrongly overemphasised an advance in judicial power as leading and finalising what constitutes rights, which disregards the role of intra-state consensus.

Hunt et al. (2012) criticise the false choice between the legislature and the judiciary in protecting rights. The choice between either one acting as the guardian of fundamental rights is being misplaced and increasingly rejected. In place of that old dichotomy, they argue there is now a consensus that all branches of the state—including the executive, the legislature and the judiciary—have a shared responsibility for the provision and realisation of fundamental rights. This shared deferral might be reframed to explain that such a consensus is not a new one—it is a neat historical accompaniment to the rule of the recognised helm.

Furthermore, while there has long been a consensus behind officials in maintaining the ultimate rule (Goldsworthy 1999, 2010; Hart 1997), it might be considered there has also been a similar, secondary-level consensus between state and legal officials in which the provision of fundamental rights by the executive, the legislature and the judiciary are to be protected albeit in a subordinate position in relation to the ultimate rule. By acknowledging the role of politics, there is a broader assumption that the law of the legislature (statute) should not be seen as a unitary person with a single will but shared consensus emerging out of a broad plurality of proposals (Waldron 1999), not to be navigated around.

While theories of the British constitution must understand parliamentary sovereignty relative to the whole constitution, as Allan (2013, p. 23) argues, that does not mean the British constitution must now tend towards the judicial power of the common law courts as characterising what constitutes rights. This has been pursued to the extent that the latter approaches view rights as above politics. Consensus, inter-relationships and comity between the branches of government and the political community are given insufficient attention. Bogdanor attributes an enhanced dialogue between the judiciary, Parliament and government as arising from the provision of rights through the Human Rights Act (Bogdanor 2009, p. 68), but the shared deferral and consensus well predated that 1998 Act. In so doing, Bogdanor (2009) has tended to disregard the historical role of that 'shared responsibility' or even 'consensus'. Furthermore, many would argue that the enhanced dialogue for the provision of rights in fact broke down further (and was therefore not enhanced) after the Human Rights Act and other associated legislation. Arguably, any dialogue has been in constant decline since the UK's incorporation into the then European Communities. Neo-Diceyan thinking pervading mainstream legal constitutionalism also gives the confusing impression that parliamentary sovereignty is on par with the 'rule of law' and in which a statement of the relationship with fundamental rights provision is not specified.

The transfer of fundamental rights provision as historically subject to 'shared deferral' moves over to a tightly, legally-defined power under EU membership. The shared deferral is absent and there is a greater singular deferral to the courts. That pivotal point reflects the change in the meaning and strength of fundamental rights. The Europeanisation process suggests again the reverse of Bogdanor's popular constitutional statism in contemporary Britain: a more narrowly defined (less distributed) power centred on the court-provided rights in which the politics of popular, elected representatives in Parliament is increasingly disassociated from the content of rights. The courts trump Parliament. In that process, following EU membership, a greater, shared deferral of rights-making power (which, for Bogdanor, might be expected under a written constitutional order) is being replaced, or at least weakened with a narrowly-defined rights-making power.

6.2.6 Democratic Parliamentary Majorities as Guarantors of Fundamental Rights and Parliamentary Sovereignty

In the existing research, political constitutionalism also remedies the omission of the role of parliamentary majorities in making parliamentary sovereignty contingent upon rights. EU fundamental rights have diluted Parliament's sovereignty because the subordinate provision of fundamental rights by the courts—which previously posed only minor limits on the will of the Government's parliamentary majority in constituting sovereignty—now defies its subordination to the will of that majority. In theory, Parliament is sovereign because it rests on the basis that the provision of fundamental rights by self-restrained judges is subordinate (Tabarelli 2013, pp. 344–345) and poses very few limits on the political will of the Government's parliamentary majority. It is often identified in the literature that fundamental rights expressed as pre-political features, have the effect of constraining public reasoning and parliamentary settlement and enable a limit on parliamentary majority rule (see Goldoni 2013). EU fundamental rights provision calls into question, to an "unprecedented extent", sensitive governmental policy areas through a rights-based process of Europeanization (Muir 2014). The proposition that the provision of fundamental rights constitutes a primary function of the state, to be exercised within the framework of the constitution, through the action of its democratically elected Parliament presents an insurmountable problem for common-law and constitutionalist statist theories in general.

It is to be expected that EU fundamental rights have diluted parliamentary sovereignty previously resting on the assumption that legitimate fundamental rights provision is derived from national parliamentary majoritarianism—because parliamentary sovereignty now rests on a weaker assumption in which rights are provided and protected by a non-elected, less accountable supranational legalist architecture. Westminster majoritarianism provides a representative and democratically accountable foundation (Lijphart 1999)—legalism does not. Supranational legalism provides a legal, technical and judicial competence for decisions which reinforce an EU-wide legal system—parliamentary majoritarianism does not. As EU rights are enforced by individuals often against the actions of their own state, including Acts of Parliament, a democratic question naturally emerges. The laws enacted by Government majorities in national parliaments have become subject to rights interpreted by a supranational court, even where those laws are inconsistent with the constitutional interpretation of parallel rights (see Pérez 2009, p. 15). A supranational court by its very nature makes legal decisions on a judicial, non-majoritarian basis. The ECJ is therefore a directly non-accountable institution and it belongs to a supranational system of governance in which the introduction of a fundamental rights system at the supranational level has been viewed as one of its greatest achievements (on the latter point, see Fabbrini 2014, p. 9). Protecting human rights specifically performs a function in the development of a political union at the EU-level and highlights the major role played by the ECJ along with national courts as guarantor of individuals' rights (Egger 2006, p. 551; Mayoral 2017).

There is one underlying theme which underpins the role of democratic parliamentary majorities in constituting rights. The exercise of EU fundamental rights represents a shift from majority-backed rights to a position of majority-limited rights. Rights have been displaced from a stage in which rights reflect majoritarian decision-making as determined in parliamentary elections to one in which they are decided by non-elected, judicial or technical bodies, courts or tribunals. The shift from Parliament to legalism in the provision of rights is coupled with the shift from majority-backed rights to the position of majority-limited rights. Pérez (2009) persuasively addresses how the judicial review of legislation by the ECJ poses a counter-majoritarian difficulty since the decisions of the body representing the people are struck down by judges lacking public accountability.

Domestically, in the executive, the role of ministers leading Department advisers is then diluted in the recognised helm. Their carefully-devised policies and Government Bills are drafted in accordance with the provision of EU fundamental rights. Yet those rights were already decided in the ECJ in the absence of consent of a majority in the House of Commons. Through the ECJ pursuing a process of filling in the case law gaps (Blauberger and Schmidt 2017; Ferraro and Carmona

2015), the court deprives the UK's ultimate rule of the parliamentary will of the Government-in-Commons majority in significant policy areas. In that process, the provision of fundamental rights by judges is superior to any potential provision offered by the elected majority in the House of Commons.

In contrast to the view that governing at the helm is presented as legally distinct but politically contingent upon its capacity to determine and respect fundamental rights:

- the modern neo-Diceyan (1964) tradition *disregards* that contingency;
- the tradition of the common law constitutionalism school (Allan 2013) *overstates* the relationship and;
- the constitutional state perspective (Bogdanor 2009) *overlooks* that contingent relationship through its appeal to popular sovereignty and the enhanced role of the courts.

Those interpretations of the British constitution have tended to misplace EU fundamental rights in a political and constitutional context, if not underestimated their legal supremacy and weight of political authority in relation to Convention- and international-rights.

6.3 Parliamentary Sovereignty and Rights Provision Under EU Membership: The Free Movement of Persons

The EU fundamental right of free movement of persons unsettles the UK's own historically subordinate fundamental rights scheme, further diluting the strength of parliamentary sovereignty. The European Economic Community (EEC) established a common market in which the citizens of member states enjoyed freedom of movement for economic purposes. This is now understood as a freedom of movement and residence guaranteed as an aspect of EU citizenship, extended to family members without regard to nationality (Bradley and Ewing 2010, p. 418). The free movement of persons is understood as a fundamental right at the EU-level (Schmidt et al. 2018, p. 1391).

EU nationals have the right to free movement under the EU Treaties, including the right to live and work in any of the other member states of the union. Prior to Brexit, EU citizens have a right of entry and residence to the UK and other states as long as they are coming to the country in the exercise of a Treaty right e.g. the right to take up employment or to set up business (HM Passport Office 2014). Student and self-sufficient persons (e.g. retired persons) also have right to entry and residence in a non-economic capacity. (Individuals in Iceland, Liechtenstein and Norway as part of the European Economic Area, enjoy freedom of movement within that area which includes the EU.) A US citizen in contrast must apply, for example, for a Standard Visitor visa if they want to visit the UK for leisure, business, or to receive private medical treatment but that is for six months only. For shorter 90 day visits, the need for a visa is waived. Citizens from all other parts of the world also follow a complex system of visa arrangements. Their right to freely move across borders does not exist as it does within the EU and not without extensive conditions and significant bureaucratic obstacles.

The right of the free movement of persons for EU citizens is one of the four 'fundamental freedoms' that comprise what is known as the EU's single market—which is based on the idea of ensuring the free movement of persons, goods, services and capital. The single market is central to the original Treaty of Rome, for the original six members of the then EEC. It was not however until the Single European Act 1987, amending the Treaty of Rome, that created a single internal market, which had otherwise proved difficult under the existing EU Treaties. Article 2 of the Treaty of Rome in 1957 had set out the objectives of the then EEC to establish a common market and Article 3(1)(c) EEC provided that the Community aspired to 'the abolition, as between member states, of obstacles to freedom of movement for[...]persons'. The free movement rights set out in this Treaty were confined to persons who exercised economic activity and were a national of a member state.

The principle of free movement is qualified at the EU level because since the formation of the EU, specific rules have been written to provide for the movement of only certain groups of EU 'workers' within its territory. These are distinguishable from the rules applicable to nationals from outside the EU ('third country nationals') which will not be discussed in this chapter. It therefore included key supporting provisions to ensure rules within individual national social security systems would not act as a barrier/disincentive for workers and their families to move between member states. Other associated Treaty provisions permitted the general principle of non-discrimination on the grounds of nationality; for example, a German worker in the UK must enjoy the same treatment as a British worker working outside the UK but within the EU.

The free movement principle also only applies when there is movement between member states and is not to be applied to internal domestic situations. Fundamental 'freedoms' tend to be legally and materially categorised as fundamental 'rights'. Specifically, fundamental rights were in fact not directly acknowledged in the original Treaty of Rome and the EU still lacks a comprehensive fundamental rights competence (Douglas-Scott 2015, p. 273). The Union is said to have a limited capability as a human rights organisation. Originally, fundamental rights were considered as 'peripheral' to the objectives of the EU construction (Hrestic 2014).

6.3.1 *The Right to Freedom of Movement of Persons—The Qualifications*

From early on, two significant measures implemented the rights of free movement for workers in the 1960s—Council Directive (68/360) on free movement for workers within the then European Community and EEC Regulation (1612/68) on the abolition of restrictions on movement and residence within the EC for workers of member states and their families. The UK has historically contested specific aspects of border control policy relating to the conditionality of free movement. The UK and Ireland did not participate in the Schengen Agreement—designed, in 1985, to abolish immigration controls between EU states (Bradley and Ewing 2010, p. 440). The Amsterdam Treaty in 1997 confirmed that the UK and Ireland would not be bound by the Schengen acquis but later participated in some measures—for example, police forces sharing law enforcement data through the Schengen Information System—to the extent that EU politics and law still exercises a dominant influence on UK immigration policy (Sobolewska and Ford 2016).

This further developed in the 1990s, when the EC adopted three Directives which conferred a general right of movement and residence on the retired, students and those with independent means, on the basis that they had sufficient resources and medical insurance. As one Coalition Government policy document on the free movement of persons in the single market observed of those pre-Maastricht changes in the 1990s, "This reflected the gradual change which had been taking place in relation to the link between economic activity and free movement – moving towards the idea of migrants as individuals with rights in their host member state" (Home Office 2014). EU powers were enlarged to include matters that affected individuals as human beings and not just as economic actors (Pérez 2009, p. 14). In the contemporary EU, more than 3.2 million EU citizens live in the UK (Hawkins 2017) and 1.2 million UK citizens live abroad within the EU (McGuinness 2017).

The right to free movement of persons was further clarified in legislation in 2004 by the 'Free Movement Directive' (Directive 2004/38/EC) and the 'Free Movement of Workers Regulation' (Regulation 1612/68 by Regulation 492/2011) (Marzocchi 2017). Following the adoption of this Directive, the ECJ sought to expand free movement rights through a series of rulings. Specific ECJ rulings have notably "created significant adjustment pressures" for member states' social policies (Schmidt et al. 2018, p. 1392). The rules have been significantly expanded in scope to cover the family members of workers who choose to exercise their free movement rights. However, EU Treaty provisions from the beginning have allowed for the 'export' of particular benefits. If a British person remains eligible for a benefit in the UK, they can still receive it in another, and likewise EU persons in the UK. The ongoing seminal ECJ cases of *Baumbast* confirmed the contemporary severing of the relationship between migration and the need to be economically active (*Baumbast and R v Secretary of State for the Home Department* [1999]), the *Metock* [2008] judgement extended the free movement rights even further for family members, and *Zambrano* [2011] on deciding the criteria for the 'right to reside' for EU citizens. There is also some evidence of a "restrictive turn" in the ECJ, subsequently halting the expansion of rights since late 2014, for those who are not economically active (Blauberger et al. 2018; Schmidt et al. 2018, pp. 1395–1396). Nonetheless, the right of the free movement of persons has focused on its understanding as a fundamental right at the EU-level.

In this context, it is notable that several recent UK-specific EU interventions between 2013 and 2016 sought to alter or change the character of the EU right to free movement. Those claims and (re)negotiations took place during the British debate ahead of the UK Referendum on EU membership—and subsequently played a significant part in the majority decision of the British people to leave the EU in June 2016 (Curtice 2017; see also Heindlmaier and Blauberger 2017; Sobolewska and Ford 2016; Hobolt 2016; Ford 2019). In practice, the UK has been the only country at this stage that suggested restrictions on free labour mobility itself (Ruhs and Palme 2018, p. 1486). Before inviting the voters in the 2016 referendum to make their choice, and whilst legislating for the referendum itself, David Cameron, as Prime Minister, had been seeking to renegotiate the terms of the UK's EU membership—with voters essentially being asked to decide whether the UK should remain a member of the EU under his newly renegotiated arrangements or to leave the EU altogether. Ahead of those renegotiations, one of David Cameron's early statements in the *Financial Times* entitled 'Free movement within Europe needs to be less free', stated that "It is time for a new settlement which recognises that free movement is a central principle of the EU, but it cannot be a completely unqualified one" (Cameron 2013; Ruhs and Palme 2018, p. 1481). During the Coalition Government period (2010–2015), the Prime Minster had already faced considerable pressure on the issue of EU immigration (Sobolewska and Ford 2016) from within his own party and Government's then coalition-shared parliamentary majority. Following the 2016 referendum, Theresa May's Conservative party and government are committed (so far) to ending the free movement of people throughout withdrawal negotiations, as is the Labour Party in its 2017 general election manifesto.

6.3.2 *The Impact of the EU Right to Free Movement Upon the UK's Historical Fundamental Rights Scheme*

The example of the EU free movement right demonstrates that the recognised helm has had EU rights incorporated into its constitution. This is achieved through a dependency upon EU-level rights by individuals in the UK, as EU citizens. It elevates the UK judiciary as a rights-adjudicating court system as it fuses ever-closer into the Luxembourg court system. This dilutes the domestic legislature as a rights-providing institution. Deep political claims are made as to the constitutional and institutional entrenchment of those 'non-negotiable' rights themselves, irrespective of their political legitimacy. The process of subverting rights legitimacy has progressed this continued legislative decline and judicial advance in the UK, impacting indirectly upon the unsettling of parliamentary sovereignty.

With the introduction of EU free movement rights, several national executive powers come into play that others might argue have enhanced UK parliamentary sovereignty. The existing, centuries-old entrenched English common law approach that British subjects were free to do as they pleased unless expressly prohibited by law (Bradley and Ewing 2010, p. 418) smoothed the way for free movement. The UK Government has been not merely a willing participant in promoting free movement rights, whether as provisions through national, EU or international mechanisms, but has been an active agent in promoting that right. But the reason why EU free movement has not reconfigured the executive to enhance parliamentary sovereignty is that the character and strength of that fundamental right is judicially-determined and presented as insurmountable by the legislature from the viewpoint of the unwieldiness of the executive. For the executive, it is torn when the free movement principle and policy is exercised, administered and protected as it dutifully permits free movement for UK and EU citizens in airports and ferry ports while at the same time, sharing its decision-making capacity over the policy. They must heed the judges who apply broad, conditions over the free movement principle—for example, the provision of welfare to those freely moving to the UK—which helps to explain why disputes over that right are politically contentious. In that political environment, there has been an uneasy coupling of free movement and social solidarity revolving around national welfare states (Geddes and Hadj-Abdou 2016, p. 222).

6.3.3 *The Judicialisation of the Freedom of Movement of Persons*

Judicial rights-adjudicating and executive rights-respecting powers are distinct at the recognised helm but judicial decision-making has nonetheless moved into the scope and political space previously defined by parliamentary decision-making. As observed in Chapter 4, a substantial body of literature explains how European integration tends to encourage an enhanced judicialisation of politics (Weiler 1991, 1994), or 'Eurolegalism' (Kelemen 2012, p. 55). This assumes that judicial institutions can answer deeply political questions on what constitutes a fundamental right within the political community. 'Direct effect' has meant that judicial EU institutions are incorporated into the UK constitution with a direct, claimable relationship by UK-EU citizens of EU individual rights in their own national courts. This marks a direct competitive overreach of judicial- over parliamentary-rights determination which impacts beyond the weakening of legislative powers in the Commons to have its way vis-a-vis court-adjudicated EU-level rights and the unsettling of parliamentary sovereignty.

The incorporation of the free movement of persons into law as historical 'fundamental right', despite those rights being peripheral to the original EU construction (Hrestic 2014), presents the right as pre-political, politically inarguable, unquestionable, or non-contestable concrete law. EU membership brought about a significant expansion of judicial power, not least because of the supremacy of EU law (Blauberger and Schmidt 2017; Tabarelli 2013, p. 346). Such a bypassing of political contestation occurs as national judiciaries become independent of the executive and parliament functions as a consequence of their EU-related roles (Schmidt 2005). Yet that process lacks both parliamentary legitimacy (consistent with Bellamy 2007) and ministerial accountability (consistent with Tomkins [2013]) when the ECJ's principles of divorcing free movement from economic migration (*Baumbast* [1999]) and the extension of the right to family members (*Metock* [2008]) and the 'right to reside' (*Zambrano* [2011]) are not subject to the consent of Parliament or a consensus among other state institutions. Schmidt et al. (2018) acknowledge such a "high degree of judicialisation of decision-making" relating to free movement and welfare equal treatment policies (Schmidt et al. 2018, p. 1392).

The scope of judicial rights-provision widens into the sphere of legislative and executive political decision-making at the recognised helm when the ECJ interacting with EU level-rights decides on the operation of the free movement right. The Court has "repeatedly expanded rights, which member states were eager to restrict for EU workers" (Schmidt et al. 2018, p. 1393). It has 'fenced off' the pervasive disagreement over immigration and recognition of the plurality within a community which for Waldron (1999) is fundamental for the recognition of rights. The fundamental right in the political sphere is contested and the open-ended politics over the freedom of movement in relation to UK as EU citizens remains contested. A judicial power with the previous obligation to give effect to the statutes of Parliament under the traditional Westminster model now overlaps at the recognised helm with the provision of rights usually reserved for the executive-supporting majority-in-Parliament. The judiciary therefore further overreaches into the dominant, partisan, Government majority in the House of Commons who might otherwise expect a consensual, intra-state responsibility in the determination of rights.

Prior to the EU referendum, it is precisely because of EU leaders (notably, Chancellor Merkel) informing the then Prime Minister, David Cameron, of its status that he finally accepted the free movement right as non-negotiable (Mason and Oltermann 2014; Tisdall 2014). It affirmed that the entrenchment of the written, codified EU right to free movement trumped their political contestation through the European Council and in Westminster. The assumption that Parliament retains its sovereignty rests on the precedential basis that the subordinate provision of fundamental rights in the courts is less entrenched than Parliament (Tabarelli 2013, p. 344). But that proposition no longer resonates with the political operation of the free movement principle.

In practice, the EU scheme of fundamental rights, such as broad free movement rights have been decided upon without sufficient political legitimacy and consent of the political community. This is why Parliament, being more accountable, makes better work of rights provision. It can provide, negotiate, remedy and balance in line with the consent of the governed. Yet the provision of EU free movement rights has proceeded under a special legal and political entrenchment, if not only because of supremacy of EU law over UK law, the jurisdiction of the ECJ in settling fundamental rights disputes, the placement of free movement in the Charter incorporated into the Lisbon Treaty and through the progressive framing of that right in ECJ case law. In turn, ECJ interpretation becomes Treaty and impacts all subsequent legislation (Schmidt et al. 2018, p. 1394). In terms of jurisdiction, the ECJ has gained a fuller jurisdiction on legal questions following the Lisbon treaty, to decide on Union-member states exclusive or shared competences and provision of fundamental rights (Ferraro and Carmona 2015). Parliament is practically unsettled—and so too are the people—given that the ultimate rule of parliamentary sovereignty no longer operates on its precedented foundation. Through EU interaction, the provision of the fundamental right to free movement is presented as a politically immovable, non-negotiable, fully court-resolved, legally entrenched instrument with finality.

6.3.4 The Non-negotiable Right and the 'Fencing Off' of Politics

At the very most, as the House of Commons' European Scrutiny Committee Legal adviser suggested, David Cameron's pre-referendum renegotiated package (Miller 2016) contained a draft declaration by the European Commission on issues related to the abuse of the right of free movement of persons. It contained only a promise to adopt a proposal to "complement" the 2004 Directive relating to free movement rights of third country nationals. It promised to clarify the scope for member states to deport undesirable EU citizens in guidelines and examine future amendment in the 2004 Directive (Ridout 2016). Attempts to modify the right had been approached as politically insurmountable by the executive in the European Council or the process of resolving contested issues in the national Parliament. The basic right to free movement, even since the Maastricht Treaty and the 2004 Directive, is itself firmly entrenched. However, the degree of entrenchment of free movement depends not on legality as is often assumed but on political legitimacy and the consent of the governed. Since there is jointly domestic pervasive disagreement over immigration in UK politics and EU integration favours the courts, questions over political legitimacy and the disagreement are marginalised by EU legal integration. While the UK accepted as legitimate since the European Communities Act 1972 and its 1975 referendum the principle and right to EC free movement, the gradually developing conditionality of decisions, progressively framed by ECJ case law (described by Blauberger and Schmidt 2017; Ferraro and Carmona 2015), were made in the context of weaker political legitimacy. Decisions by courts and ministers at the European Council effectively bypasses elected representatives in legislatures. In so far as that process proceeds, it bypasses the consent of the electorate. After all, judges in all contexts help to shape law but this is "especially true" in the EU where gaps must be filled in its legal framework and courts "… have much more manoeuvrability available to them than is customary within states" (Nugent 2010, p. 225). In short, the Prime Minister could not renegotiate the associated, entrenched rights during the 2015–2016 period—it was mostly not allowed on the renegotiation menu (Fleming 2013). Parliamentary sovereignty no longer operates on the precedented basis in which rights are subject to politics and negotiation. In this instance, the provision of free movement is at the very least part-entrenched and deemed politically non-negotiable in relation to the ultimate rule.

6.3.5 *Parliamentary Sovereignty and the Shared Responsibility for Rights Provision*

The EU right to free movement has further unsettled parliamentary sovereignty previously resting on the historically precedented basis that the executive, the legislature and the judiciary enjoyed an official consensus in which they all have a shared responsibility for rights provision. Domestically, this has been further mediated by recent constitutional changes which have removed the official consensus between the arms of government, notably by the removal of the old Lord Chancellor's under the Constitutional Reform Act 2005, previously acting as a driver to cement that consensus (Gee et al. 2015). The ECJ rulings of *Baumbast* [1999] and *Metock* [2008] and *Zambrano* [2011] are court rulings, not parliamentary votes. They create claimable rights through ECJ case law, not through political debate. That is not a shared responsibility. The principle of 'direct effect' more generally, as enshrined by the ECJ, enables individuals to immediately invoke an EU provision before a national court or ECJ in relation to certain European acts, independent of whether a national law test exists. An ECJ judgement is legally binding on the national court. The national court is the only one to resolve a dispute but it must apply the law provided by Luxembourg (Mayoral 2017). The primacy of the executive, as mentioned above is torn. On the one hand, it is elevated through the enforcer role of protecting free movement through passport controls and in acting against any barriers. On the other hand, judges marginalise the authority of government-in-Parliament by acting above politics when those contested rights and limits are provided in the absence of intra-state consensus and the consent of the governed. That could not be described as rights provision by consensus.

The deference to the courts displaces what Hunt et al. (2012) refer to as the consensus and shared responsibility between the branches of government for rights provision. Free movement rights and their limits (in my view) are deferred almost singularly to, the courts. Parliament is practically less sovereign when the incorporation of free movement rights unsettles that precedented foundation. The provision of the right to free movement is deferred on a skewed basis to the EU and national judiciary first, the torn position of the national executive second and only if irresolvable by law, to the ultimate loser in European integration, Parliament itself. The UK has of course voluntarily agreed to the power of the ECJ under the EU Treaties. The Court of Justice of the EU (CJEU) in Luxembourg—consisting of both the ECJ and the General Court—is the EU's judicial institution and therefore for the UK.

The right to free movement and its constraints have been, like other EU fundamental rights, historically framed progressively by the ECJ, then laid down as principle in the Lisbon Treaty and the associated

Charter. This process has turned deeply political questions of providing for the rights of free movement by shared consensus into legalistic, judicial and procedural matters. As such, they are to be decided almost solely and divisively by judges in courts or lawyers serving the executive, not to elected politicians in Parliament.

The resulting marginalisation of politics from the shared consensus is also proven by David Cameron's attempt to renegotiate the fundamental rights of free movement at the European Council. This provides evidence of the marginalisation of politics in determining rights. It demonstrates that the Prime Minister-led political process of renegotiation at the European Council is subverted to the legal process of providing judicial rights under EU membership. The very nature of EU rules provides for the constitutional strengthening of the Prime Ministerial-executive through its fusion with EU governmental machinery being made dependent upon the Prime Minister, with other Heads of State and respective Presidents of the European Council and Commission interacting to make decisions at the highest political level in the European Council (Kassim 2016a). The legislature clearly has no such comparable connection or scrutiny to that of Prime Ministerial power within European Council-level institutional decision-making. The system of court-deferred rights ends up taking precedence over politically (re) negotiated rights. The transfer of the fundamental rights of free movement being subject to 'shared deferral' across the different constitutional actors is subject increasingly to the more singular deferral to the courts after the Maastricht Treaty and the subsequent 2004 Directive. The shift is pivotal, reflecting the change in meaning of fundamental rights. In that process, EU citizenship provided fertile breeding ground for directly effective claimable rights to be brought into operation.

It would be an exaggeration of this claim to suggest that such transformation underpinned a path to a popular constitutional state in which fundamental rights were elevated and the rule of recognition diminished, as Bogdanor (2009) argues. The change from a 'shared deferral' system of fundamental rights to a singular deferral under EU membership, suggests the reverse of popular constitutional statism: a more narrowly defined power centred on the judiciary-deferred rights in which the relationship with popular, elected representatives in Parliament is disassociated from the content of rights. Furthermore, the shift suggests a more shared deferral of rights-making power (which might be expected under a written constitutional order) is being replaced, or at least diluted. If there is anything suggesting a 'constitutionalisation' of EU fundamental rights, it is more akin to Loughlin's (2010) interpretation of *Marbury v Madison* [1803] in US constitutional history (see Loughlin 2010, p. 296). One might argue a blurred relationship develops between UK statute and the fundamental law of the European Communities Act 1972. That has meant, instead of a consensus between the arms of government, a formal hierarchy begins to develop between the judiciary and the other branches of government for deferring constitutional interpretation of political problems where fundamental rights are relevant.

6.3.6 Parliamentary Sovereignty, the Free Movement of Persons and the House of Commons Majority

It was first argued that EU free movement unsettled Parliament's sovereignty because the subordinate provision of fundamental rights by the courts—which previously posed only minor limits on the will of the Government's parliamentary majority and constituting sovereignty—now imposes more substantive limits on the will of that majority. In the case of free movement rights, a backbench business debate on stopping mass immigration from Romania and Bulgaria in April 2013 and the two Conservative rebellions—one on extending restrictions for Romanian and Bulgarian migration, another on the deporting of foreign criminals—created systematic political pressure upon the Prime Minister by his own colleagues (BBC News 2014; Backbench Business Committee 2013). Numbers in welfare migration and welfare abuses can, after all, carry an immense risk of politicisation (Schmidt et al. 2018, p. 1392). While this acted as political pressure, it was not sufficient enough to form a parliamentary majority (in all cases). While there was substantial friction created, David Cameron in supporting free movement rights did not transgress the will of the parliamentary majority. The rebellion of his colleagues did impact upon the will of the parliamentary party, which indirectly affects that majority. The Government's support for the EU fundamental right to free movement did not strictly transgress the Government's parliamentary majority but it did unsettle that majority as it interacted with his own party's messaging and policy. It is likely that effect which led David Cameron to incorporate such a message and a referendum into his General Election manifesto of 2015 (Conservative Party Manifesto 2015) and his earlier post-2013 EU renegotiation demands.

The theory that Parliament is sovereign on the basis that the provision of fundamental rights by judges is subordinate and poses no major limits on the will of the Government's parliamentary party majority fails to reconcile itself with the implementation of EU-level fundamental rights schemes. In that context, the Government's parliamentary party majority has a marginalised place in determining or finalising or setting out the operational criteria for such measures. Where the meaning and limitations upon free movement rights are subject to pervasive disagreement, there is no forum at the democratic level to resolve the disagreement because the Government's party majority has been marginalised in making decisions in relation to the right. It could ultimately legislate against an EU fundamental right measure but not without serious political consequences such as infringement proceedings. When considering free movement, predominantly Conservative government backbench MPs in the above cases were warned by the then Home Office ministers that their policies and objectives were 'illegal' (Mallett 2014). Those statements reinforce the point that fundamental rights are claimed to be entrenched and that the politics and legitimacy of rights is to be marginalised at all costs. The limitations on free movement through immigration policy, previously the subject of parliamentary debate and vote, bypass the parliamentary institution and are presented as inarguable legal facts. Yet rights should only be taken seriously in a political system on the grounds that the system allows majority voting to settle disagreements as to what constitutes rights (Waldron 1999, p. 307). Currently, under EU membership, national legislatures have lost traditional legislative powers of initiative and approval (Schmidt 2005). The sheer magnitude of the impact of the Treaty of Rome, the 1960s and 1990s developments in EU legislation, the Maastricht Treaty and the 2004 Directive and Regulations have been voluntarily accepted by the executive-in-European Council to embrace the free movement of persons principles but with a voluntarily accepted cost to Parliament. What is clear is first the more obvious governmental recognition of the legislation and Treaty provisions supporting free movement rights. Recognition occurs because the ministerial executive acquires an aspect of its political legitimacy through the Council of the EU and European Council and Intergovernmental Conferences, respectively—including the signing of the Lisbon Treaty along with Article 45(1) of the Charter associated with it. Yet less obvious has been the progressive framing of case law in the ECJ such as *Baumbast* [1999] and *Metock* [2008] and *Zambrano* [2011], through a process of filling in the gaps (e.g. Blauberger and Schmidt 2017; Ferraro and Carmona 2015). That EU-level judicial process deprives the ultimate rule of the will of the Government's parliamentary majority in significant policy areas in which the provision of fundamental rights by judges is superior to the potential provisions afforded by the elected majority in the House of Commons.

6.4 Conclusion

Under EU membership, the UK Parliament has become constitutionally unsettled because the recognised helm has had EU-level fundamental rights schemes incorporated into it, including that of the EU free movement of persons. In that process, EU fundamental rights schemes protected by the courts become constitutionally strengthened, often expressed as unchallengeable instruments and above ordinary politics. EU rights are held to stand beyond the precedented form of negotiable and minimalist rights-provision afforded by Parliament. The historical precedents of the British constitution in which governing at the helm is presented as legally distinct but politically contingent upon its capacity to determine and respect fundamental rights has been severely diluted in the modern governing process.

The EU free movement right demonstrates that the recognised helm has had EU rights incorporated into its constitutional network, ultimately leading to the dilution of the domestic legislature as a rights-protecting institution. What is seen by mainstream legalist interpretation and constitutional state perspectives as EU rights experiencing an enhanced depth of constitutional entrenchment of the rights themselves has isolated itself from questions of political legitimacy and parliamentary majorities. Its further tendency to disregard the disappearing consensus between the arms of state and community in protecting rights has neglected this important dimension. The consequence of that EU interaction has contributed towards the continued legislative decline and judicial advance in the UK, impacting upon and unsettling parliamentary sovereignty.

The subsequent chapter (Chapter 7) will argue that where the UK Parliament has become unsettled under EU membership due to the incremental removal of parliamentary power over policy and law, such a separation leaves open an executive-legislature accountability gap. The EU Referendum of June 2016 and Parliament's subsequent and ultimate power to decide on the substantive issues relating to the Withdrawal Agreement permits (or not) the executive to pursue a constitutional resettlement, if it so chooses, to address the historical dilution of parliamentary powers. It signifies the resettlement of Parliament with a historically precedented basis—namely, of government pursued through the consent of the electorate—in which the operation of Parliament's ultimate decision-making power over political decisions is protected by the Government-in-Parliament on behalf of a consenting electorate. Subsequent developments in determining the UK Government's 'Brexit' policy, including the settling of the withdrawal agreement, have suggested a major, if not enhanced role for politics in determining the character of Parliament's sovereignty. The foremost implication is that the referendum and subsequent parliamentary episodes relating to EU withdrawal have enhanced, not eroded, the principle of representative government and parliamentary sovereignty.

Bibliography

Allan, T. R. S. (2010, December 7). *'Evidence (26)' in House of Commons' European Scrutiny Committee* (The EU Bill and Parliamentary Sovereignty, HC 633-I) [Online]. Available at https://www.publications.parliament.uk/pa/cm201011/cmselect/cmeuleg/633/633i.pdf. Accessed 12 December 2013.

Allan, T. R. S. (2011). Questions of Legality and Legitimacy: Form and Substance in British Constitutionalism. *International Journal of Constitutional Law, 9*(1), 155–162.

Allan, T. R. S. (2013). *The Sovereignty of Law: Freedom, Constitution and Common Law*. Oxford: Oxford University Press.

Amsterdam Treaty. (1997). *The Treaty of Amsterdam Amending the Treaty on European Union, the Treaties Establishing the European Communities and Certain Related Acts.* Available at http://www.europarl.europa.eu/topics/treaty/pdf/amst-en.pdf. Accessed 1 February 2019.

Backbench Business Committee. (2013, April 22). *Debate on Bulgarian and Romanian Immigration E-petition.* UK Parliament [Online]. Available at http://www.parliament.uk/business/committees/committees-a-z/commons-select/backbench-business-committee/news/debate-on-e-petition-on-bulgarian-and-romanian-immigration-/. Accessed 25 April 2013.

Baumbast and R v Secretary of State for the Home Department. [1999]. Case C-413/99. Available at http://eur-lex.europa.eu/legal-content/EN/TXT/?uri=CELEX%3A61999CJ0413. Accessed 26 January 2014.

BBC News. (2014, January 1). Romania and Bulgaria EU Migration Restrictions Lifted. *BBC News* [Online]. Available at http://www.bbc.co.uk/news/world-europe-25565302. Accessed 10 January 2014.

Bellamy, R. (2007). *Political Constitutionalism: A Republican Defence of the Constitutionality of Democracy*. Cambridge: Cambridge University Press.

Bellamy, R. (2014). The Democratic Legitimacy of International Human Rights Conventions: Political Constitutionalism and the European Convention on Human Rights. *European Journal of International Law, 25*(4), 1019–1042.

Bellamy, R., & Weale, A. (2015). Political Legitimacy and European Monetary Union: Contracts, Constitutionalism and the Normative Logic of Two-Level Games. *Journal of European Public Policy, 22*(2), 1–18.

Bingham, T. (2010). *The Rule of Law*. London: Penguin.

Blauberger, M., & Schmidt, S. K. (2017). The European Court of Justice and Its Political Impact. *West European Politics, 40*(4), 907–918.

Blauberger, M., Heindlmaier, A., Kramer, D., Martinsen, D. S., Thierry, J. S., Schenk, A., & Werner, B. (2018). ECJ Judges Read the Morning Papers. Explaining the Turnaround of European Citizenship Jurisprudence. *Journal of European Public Policy, 25*(10), 1422–1441.

Bogdanor, V. (2009). *The New British Constitution*. Oxford: Hart Publishing.

Bogdanor, V. (2012). Imprisoned by a Doctrine: The Modern Defence of Parliamentary Sovereignty. *Oxford Journal of Legal Studies, 3*(1), 179–195.

Bogdanor, V. (2019). *Beyond Brexit: Towards a British Constitution*. London: I.B. Tauris.

Bradley, A. (2011). The Sovereignty of Parliament—Form or Substance? In J. Jowell & D. Oliver (Eds.), *The Changing Constitution* (7th ed.). Oxford: Oxford University Press.

Bradley, A. W., & Ewing, K. D. (2010). *Constitutional and Administrative Law* (15th ed.). Harlow: Longman.

Cameron, D. (2013, November 26). Free Movement Within Europe Needs to Be Less Free. *Financial Times* [Online]. Available at https://www.ft.com/content/add36222-56be-11e3-ab12-00144feabdc0. Accessed 25 January 2014.

Conservative Party. (2015). *Conservative Party Manifesto*. London: The Conservative Party. Available at https://s3-eu-west-1.amazonaws.com/manifesto2015/ConservativeManifesto2015.pdf. Accessed 20 July 2015.

Costa v E.N.E.L. [1964]. Judgment of the Court Reference for a Preliminary Ruling: Giudice Conciliatore di Milano—Italy. Case 6-64. Available at http://eur-lex.europa.eu/legal-content/EN/TXT/?uri=CELEX%3A61964CJ0006. Accessed 1 February 2017.

Council Directive 68/360/EEC of 15 October 1968 on the Abolition of Restrictions on Movement and Residence Within the Community for Workers of Member States and Their Families.

Craig, P. (2011). Britain in the European Union. In J. Jowell & D. Oliver (Eds.), *The Changing Constitution* (7th ed., pp. 104–133). Oxford: Oxford University Press.

Curtice, J. (2017). Why Leave Won the UK's EU Referendum. *Journal of Common Market Studies, 55*(Suppl. 1), 19–37.

de Bracton, H. (1235). *De legibus et consuetudinibus Angliae* [On the Laws and Customs of England] [Online]. Available at http://bracton.law.harvard.edu. Accessed 17 January 2013.

Dicey, A. V. (1885/1964). *An Introduction to the Study of the Law of the Constitution*. London: Macmillan.

Douglas-Scott, S. (2015). The Relationship between the EU and the ECHR Five Years on from the Treaty of Lisbon. In S. de Vries, U. Bernitz, & S. Weatherill (Eds.), *The EU Charter of Fundamental Rights as a Binding Instrument: Five Years Old and Growing* (pp. 21–46). Oxford: Hart Publishing.

EEC Regulation No. 1612/68 of the Council of 15 October 1968 on Freedom of Movement for Workers Within the Community.

Egger, A. (2006). EU-Fundamental Rights in the National Legal Order: The Obligations of Member States Revisited. *Yearbook of European Law, 25*(1), 515–553.

European Commission. (2017). *The Charter of Fundamental Rights of the EU* [Online]. Available at http://ec.europa.eu/justice/fundamental-rights/charter/index_en.htm. Accessed 8 July 2017.

European Scrutiny Committee. (2014, April 2). *The Application of the EU Charter of Fundamental Rights in the UK: A State of Confusion* (HC 979) [Online]. Available at https://publications.parliament.uk/pa/cm201314/cmselect/cmeuleg/979/979.pdf. Accessed 8 August 2015.

European Union. (2014). *About the EU* [Online]. Available at http://europa.eu/about-eu/index_en.htm. Accessed 2 August 2014.

Fabbrini, F. (2014). *Fundamental Rights in Europe*. Oxford: Oxford University Press.

Factortame: *The Queen v Secretary of State for Transport, ex parte: Factortame Ltd and Others*. [1990]. Judgment of the Court of 19 June 1990. Reference for a Preliminary Ruling: House of Lords—United Kingdom. Case C-213/89. Available at http://eur-lex.europa.eu/legal-content/EN/TXT/?uri=CELEX%3A61989CJ0213. Accessed 21 June 2014.

Ferraro, F., & Carmona, J. (2015). *Fundamental Rights in the European Union—The Role of the Charter After the Lisbon Treaty*. Brussels: European Parliamentary Research Service. Available at http://www.europarl.europa.eu/RegData/etudes/IDAN/2015/554168/EPRS_IDA(2015)554168_EN.pdf. Accessed 15 May 2016.

Fleming, J. (2013, November 28). Brussels Hits Back at UK's 'Nasty' Proposal Against Free Movement. *Euractiv* [Online]. Available at http://www.euractiv.com/section/justice-home-affairs/news/brussels-hits-back-at-uk-s-nasty-proposal-against-free-movement/. Accessed 30 November 2013.

Ford, R. (2019, January 22). Immigration: Is Public Opinion Changing? In The UK in a Changing Europe, *Brexit and Public Opinion 2019* [Online]. Available at https://ukandeu.ac.uk/wp-content/uploads/2019/01/Public-opinion-2019.pdf. Accessed 5 February 2019.

Francis, M., & Morrow, J. (1994). *A History of Political Thought in the Nineteenth Century*. London: Duckworth.

Francovich v Italian Republic. [1991]. Cases C-6/90 and C-9/90.

Geddes, A., & Hadj-Abdou, L. (2016). An Unstable Equilibrium: Freedom of Movement and the Welfare State in the European Union. In G. Freeman & N. Mirilovic (Eds.), *Handbook of Migration and Social Policy*. Cheltenham: Edward Elgar.

Gee, G., Hazell, R., Malleson, K., & O'Brien, P. (2015). *The Politics of Judicial Independence in the UK's Changing Constitution*. Cambridge: Cambridge University Press.

Gee, G., & Webber, G. C. N. (2010). What Is a Political Constitution? *Oxford Journal of Legal Studies, 30*(2), 273–299.

Goldoni, M. (2012). Two Internal Critiques of Political Constitutionalism. *International Journal of Constitutional Law, 10*(4), 926–949.

Goldoni, M. (2013). Constitutional Reasoning According to Political Constitutionalism: Comment on Richard Bellamy. *German Law Journal, 14*(8), 1053–1076.

Goldsworthy, J. (1999). *The Sovereignty of Parliament: History and Philosophy*. Oxford: Clarendon Press.

Goldsworthy, J. (2010). *Parliamentary Sovereignty: Contemporary Debates*. Cambridge: Cambridge University Press.

Gordon, M. (2015). *Parliamentary Sovereignty in the UK Constitution*. London: Hart Publishing.

Hart, H. L. A. (1997). *The Concept of Law* (2nd ed.). Oxford: Clarendon Press.

Hawkins, O. (2017, June 29). *Migration Statistics* (House of Commons Briefing Paper SN06077) [Online]. Available at http://researchbriefings.parliament.uk/ResearchBriefing/Summary/SN06077. Accessed 10 July 2017.

Heindlmaier, A., & Blauberger, M. (2017). Enter at Your Own Risk: Free Movement of EU Citizens in Practice. *West European Politics, 40*(6), 1198–1217.

Hix, S., & Høyland, B. (2011). *The Political System of the European Union*. London: Palgrave Macmillan.

HM Passport Office. (2014). *Guidance on Dealing with Applications from Children Born in UK to European Union Nationals* [Online]. Available at https://www.gov.uk/government/uploads/system/uploads/attachment_data/file/374616/TreatyRightsPolicy.pdf. Accessed 3 December 2014.

Hobolt, S. B. (2016). The Brexit Vote: A Divided Nation, A Divided Continent. *Journal of European Public Policy, 23*(9), 1259–1277.

Home Office. (2014). *Review of the Balance of Competences Between the United Kingdom and the European Union: Single Market—The Free Movement of Persons* [Online]. Available at https://www.gov.uk/government/uploads/system/uploads/attachment_data/file/227069/2901084_SingleMarket_acc.pdf. Accessed 10 November 2014.

Howe, M. (2013, January). *Written Evidence from Martin Howe QC.* Submission to the European Scrutiny Committee Inquiry on the Application of EU Charter of Fundamental Rights in UK [Online]. Available at http://data.parliament.uk/writtenevidence/committeeevidence.svc/evidencedocument/european-scrutiny-committee/the-application-of-the-eu-charter-of-fundamental-rights-in-the-uk/written/5178.pdf. Accessed 14 February 2014.

Hrestic, M.-L. (2014, September). The Consequences of the "Constitutionalization" of the Charter of Fundamental Rights of the European Union. *Procedia—Social and Behavioral Sciences, 149*, 404–408.

Hunt, M., Hooper, H., & Yowell, P. (2012). *Parliaments and Human Rights Redressing the Democratic Deficit.* London: Arts & Humanities Research Council.

Isin, E. F., & Saward, M. (2013). *Enacting European Citizenship.* Cambridge: Cambridge University Press.

Kantorowicz, E. H. (1957). *The King's Two Bodies: A Study in Medieval Political Theology.* Princeton, NJ: Princeton University Press.

Kassim, H. (2016a). *The European Council—The Who, What, Where, How and Why.* The UK in a Changing Europe Initiative [Online]. Available at http://www.ukandeu.ac.uk/explainers/the-european-council-the-who-what-where-how-and-why/. Accessed 5 July 2017.

Kelemen, R. D. (2012). Eurolegalism and Democracy. *Journal of Common Market Studies, 50*(Suppl. 1), 55–71.

Lakin, S. (2018). The Manner and Form Theory of Parliamentary Sovereignty: A Nelson's Eye View of the UK Constitution? *Oxford Journal of Legal Studies, 38*(1), 168–189.

Lebeck, C. (2007). National Constitutional Control and the Limits of European Integration—The European Arrest Warrant in the German Federal Constitutional Court. *Public Law, 1*, 23–32.

Lenaerts, K. (2012). Exploring the Limits of the EU Charter of Fundamental Rights. *European Constitutional Law Review, 8*(3), 375–403.

Lijphart, A. (1999). *Patterns of Democracy: Government Forms and Performance in Thirty-Six Countries.* New Haven: Yale University Press.

Lisbon Treaty. (2007, December 17). Amending the Treaty on European Union and the Treaty Establishing the European Community. *Official Journal of the European Communities, C 306, 50*, 1.

Loughlin, M. (2003). *The Idea of Public Law*. Oxford: Oxford University Press.

Loughlin, M. (2010). *Foundations of Public Law*. Oxford: Oxford University Press.

Mallett, C. (2014, January 31). Rebel Tory Amber Valley MP Nigel Mills Lashes Government over Immigration Vote Tactics. *Derby Telegraph* [Online]. Available at http://www.derbytelegraph.co.uk/rebel-tory-amber-valley-mp-nigel-mills-lashes/story-20531017-detail/story.html. Accessed 2 February 2014.

Marbury v Madison. [1803]. 5 US Supreme Court. 137.

Marleasing SA mot Comercial Internacional de Alimentacion SA. [1990]. Mål C-106/89. Available at http://eur-lex.europa.eu/legal-content/SV/ALL/?uri=CELEX:61989CJ0106. Accessed 7 June 2013.

Marzocchi, O. (2017). *Free Movement of Persons*. Brussels: European Parliament [Online]. Available at http://www.europarl.europa.eu/atyourservice/en/displayFtu.html?ftuId=FTU_2.1.3.html. Accessed 1 April 2017.

Mason, R., & Oltermann, P. (2014, November 3). EU Freedom of Movement Non-negotiable, Says Germany. *Guardian* [Online]. Available at https://www.theguardian.com/world/2014/nov/03/eu-freedom-of-movement-non-negotiable-germany. Accessed 4 November 2014.

Mayoral, J. A. (2017). In the CJEU Judges Trust: A New Approach in the Judicial Construction of Europe. *Journal of Common Market Studies, 55*(3), 551–568.

McGuinness, T. (2017). *Brexit: What Impact on Those Currently Exercising Free Movement Rights?* (House of Commons Library Briefing Paper No. 7871) [Online]. Available at http://researchbriefings.files.parliament.uk/documents/CBP-7871/CBP-7871.pdf. Accessed 11 April 2017.

McHarsky-Todorof, E. T. (2015, February 16). *Would the UK Be Forced to Exit the EU If It Exits the ECHR?* King's EU Law Blog [Blog]. Available at https://blogs.kcl.ac.uk/kslreuropeanlawblog/?p=860#more-860. Accessed 3 December 2015.

Metock (Blaise Baheten) and Others v Minister for Justice, Equality and Law Reform. [2008]. Reference for a Preliminary Ruling: High Court—Ireland. Judgment of the Court (Grand Chamber) of 25 July 2008. Case C-127/08. Available at http://curia.europa.eu/juris/liste.jsf?language=en&num=C-127/08. Accessed 1 June 2014.

Miller, V. (2014, March 26). *Is Adherence to the European Convention on Human Rights a Condition of European Union Membership?* (House of Commons Briefing Paper SN06577) [Online]. Available at http://researchbriefings.parliament.uk/ResearchBriefing/Summary/SN06577. Accessed 26 April 2014.

Miller, V. (2016). *UK's EU Reform Negotiations: The Tusk Package* (House of Commons Library Briefing Paper No. 7497) [Online]. Available at http://researchbriefings.files.parliament.uk/documents/CBP-7497/CBP-7497.pdf. Accessed 11 April 2017.

Muir, E. (2014). Fundamental Rights: An Unsettling EU Competence. *Human Rights Review, 15*(1), 25–37.

Nice Treaty. (2001). *Treaty of Nice Amending the Treaty on European Union, the Treaties Establishing the European Communities and Certain Related Acts.* Available at https://eur-lex.europa.eu/legal-content/EN/TXT/PDF/?uri=CELEX:12001C/TXT&from=EN. Accessed 20 January 2019.

Nugent, N. (2010). *The Government and Politics of the European Union* (7th ed.). London: Palgrave.

Pérez, A. T. (2009). *Fundamental Rights Conflicts in the European Union.* Oxford: Oxford University Press.

Peter, L. (2014, November 28). Q&A: EU Freedom of Movement. *BBC News* [Online]. Available at http://www.bbc.co.uk/news/world-europe-25237742. Accessed 3 December 2014.

Ridout, A. (2016). *The Inquiry into the UK Government's Renegotiation of EU Membership: Parliamentary Sovereignty and Scrutiny: Preliminary Note on the Outcome of Negotiations* [Online]. Available at https://www.parliament.uk/documents/commons-committees/european-scrutiny/Committee%20Legal%20Opinions%20240216.pdf. Accessed 7 June 2016.

Ruhs, M., & Palme, J. (2018). Institutional Contexts of Political Conflicts Around Free Movement in the European Union: A Theoretical Analysis. *Journal of European Public Policy, 25*(10), 1481–1500.

Schmidt, V. A. (2005). Democracy in Europe: The Impact of European Integration. *Perspectives on Politics, 3*(4), 761–779.

Schmidt, S. K., Blauberger, M., & Martinsen, D. S. (2018). Free movement and equal treatment in an unequal union. *Journal of European Public Policy, 25*(10), 1391–1402.

Sobolewska, M., & Ford, R. (2016). The Politics of Immigration: Old and New. In R. Heffernan, C. Hay, M. Russell, & P. Cowley (Eds.), *Developments in British Politics 10* (10th ed., pp. 221–243). London: Palgrave.

Tabarelli, M. (2013). The Influence of the EU and the ECHR on "Parliamentary Sovereignty Regimes": Assessing the Impact of European Integration on the British and Swedish Judiciaries. *European Law Journal, 19*(3), 340–363.

Tisdall, S. (2014, November 7). Cameron Plan to Curb EU Freedom of Movement Falls on Closed Ears. *Guardian* [Online]. Available at https://www.theguardian.com/world/2014/nov/07/cameron-eu-freedom-of-movement-helsinki. Accessed 7 November 2014.

Tomkins, A. (2010). *Written Evidence to the European Scrutiny Committee, Clause 18 of the Bill: Parliamentary Sovereignty and EU Law*. The EU Bill and Parliamentary Sovereignty. Available at https://publications.parliament.uk/pa/cm201011/cmselect/cmeuleg/633ii/633we02.htm. Accessed 5 December 2010.

Tomkins, A. (2013). What's Left of the Political Constitution? *German Law Journal, 14*(12), 2275–2292 [Online]. Available at http://www.germanlaw-journal.com/index.php?pageID=11&artID=1604. Accessed 12 December 2013.

Van den Brink, M. J. (2012). EU citizenship and EU Fundamental Rights: Taking EU Citizenship Rights Seriously? *Legal Issues of Economic Integration, 39*(2), 273–290.

Van Gend & Loos v Netherlands Inland Revenue Administration [1963, 5 February]. Judgment of the European Court of Justice. Case 26-62 [Online]. Available at http://eur-lex.europa.eu/legal-content/EN/TXT/?uri=CELEX%3A61962CJ0026. Accessed 30 May 2014.

Waldron, J. (1999). *Law and Disagreement.* Oxford: Oxford University Press.

Weiler, J. H. H. (1991). The Transformation of Europe. *Yale Law Journal, 100*(8), 2403–2483.

Weiler, J. H. H. (1994). A Quiet Revolution: "The European Court of Justice and Its Interlocutors". *Comparative Political Studies, 26*(4), 510–534.

Wilkinson, M. (2013). Political Constitutionalism and the European Union. *Modern Law Review, 76*(2), 191–222.

Young, A., & Gee, G. (2016). Regaining Sovereignty, Brexit, the UK Parliament and the Common Law. *European Public Law, 22*(1), 131–147.

Zambrano v Office national de l'emploi (ONEm). [2011, March 8]. Case C-34/09. Judgment of the Court (Grand Chamber).

Ziegler, K. S., Wicks, E., & Hodson, L. (2015). *The UK and European Human Rights—A Strained Relationship?* Oxford: Hart Publishing.

CHAPTER 7

A Great Resettlement? Parliamentary Sovereignty After Brexit

In contrast to the consideration of three case studies in Chapters 4–6 in which EU policies have *unsettled* previous historical constitutional forms of parliamentary sovereignty, the example of the UK's parliamentary power since the EU referendum provides evidence of a *resettling* of past constitutional forms. Where the UK Parliament has become unsettled due to the incremental removal of parliamentary power over policy and law under EU membership, an unsettlement provides an executive-legislature accountability gap.

Episodes following the EU referendum of June 2016 indicate that Parliament's ultimate power to decide on the UK's Brexit strategy and withdrawal agreement could establish a new constitutional resettlement, if MPs choose, to address the historical dilution of parliamentary powers. As the UK seeks to un-incorporate EU-level decision-making by pursuing a policy of leaving the EU, it becomes evident that parliament's potential regaining of its ultimate decision-making power affirms parliament's sovereignty (contra Bogdanor 2019; Mabbett 2017). The magnitude of such a shift indicates a further resettlement of parliament upon a historically precedented basis. The practice of parliament's ultimate decision-making power over substantive decisions was maintained by the Government, through Parliament, on behalf of its electorate (McConalogue 2019, p. 442).

This chapter first begins with an analysis of the historical constitutional forms, as precedents. Past precedent organises the British constitution in a way in which governing at the helm is crucially dependent

J. McConalogue, *The British Constitution Resettled*,
https://doi.org/10.1007/978-3-030-25290-8_7

upon historical custom. The sixth and seventh constitutional forms act as guiding precedents for government by consent in the contemporary constitution. It is both through Dicey's consent of the people in referendums, as with Burke's political parties in elections, which provide for the consent of the governed and enable the (re)alignment of power between the executive and the legislature. Parliament exercises that power in a contemporary British constitution in which governing is frequently dependent upon both: (i) the regularity of party-political representation by parliamentary consent; and (ii) Parliament ruling through external agencies, commissions or bodies, the EU and if parliament wishes, by national referendums. Parliamentary decision-making on substantive issues defers to the contemporary consent-seeking powers of Parliament, including its ability to outsource that decision-making capacity over political decisions. Both of those past constitutional forms are contingent upon Dicey's principle of government by consent—and are central to the constitutional resettlement of parliamentary sovereignty in withdrawal-related votes and legislation when un-incorporating EU decision-making structures.

By rethinking explanatory theories which undermine the relationship of parliamentary decision-making to sovereignty, portraying it instead as subsidiary to elements of popular or judicial power (Bogdanor 2009, 2019), the idea of institutional sovereignty can be redressed by focusing on politics and political constitutionalism more specifically. A series of significant parliamentary developments since the UK's holding of referendum on the EU, particularly in scrutinising Theresa May's 599-page negotiated UK-EU withdrawal agreement, suggest a central resettlement, if not enhanced role, for politics in determining the character of Parliament's sovereignty. Those developments in which parliament has asserted a strengthened degree of accountability upon the Prime Minister and the Government, have included:

- Securing a 'meaningful vote' for parliament on the withdrawal agreement;
- Parliament voting down (on three occasions) and refining the Prime Minister's deal.
- MPs' as Motion-making, agenda-shapers, ensuring a Government Motion would be amendable, so as to enable MPs to propose meaningful motions and thereby shape future direction;

- Parliament holding the Government in contempt and defending the 'will of parliament';
- MPs' twice requesting a delay of Article 50;
- Parliament preventing a 'no deal Brexit'.

It is worth considering that in significant areas, in the referendum aftermath between 2016 and 2019, the Supreme Court's ruling in the *Miller* [2017] judgement and the EU (Notification of Withdrawal) Act 2017 triggering Article 50 as well as the enacting of the EU (Withdrawal) Act 2018 affirms that a referendum is an essential complement (not a substitute of) parliamentary votes and legislation to exercise ultimate parliamentary decision-making over the UK's future EU relationship (McConalogue 2019). It also affirms that the Supreme Court would strive for guardianship of the constitution while confirming Parliament's ultimate decision-making power over EU membership, consistent with some aspects of modern, common law constitutionalism. Overall, since the holding of the EU referendum, the subsequent actions by parliament in relation to Prime Ministerial-led Article 50 negotiations has enhanced, not eroded, the principle of representative government and Parliamentary sovereignty (contra Mabbett 2017; McKibbin 2017, p. 385). Subsequent parliamentary votes and episodes from 2016 through to 2019, following the crystallising of opinion in the EU referendum, have resettled previous historical constitutional forms of parliamentary sovereignty.

7.1 Resettling the Historical Precedent of Ultimate Parliamentary Decision-Making Power

Parliamentary sovereignty is impacted upon by an unsettling of previous historical constitutional forms. In the case of the Government's EU withdrawal policy and legislation pursued since the referendum—and on which parliament has a deep involvement in accepting, rejecting or amending proposals put before it—two significant constitutional forms have been further resettled. Parliament's political authority rests upon historical constitutional forms, as precedents, presenting a British constitution in which governing at the helm is presented as dependent upon Parliament's sovereign capacity to exercise ultimate decision-making power. In particular, Edmund Burke's ordering of historical precedents in the sixth historical mixed constitutional form observes Parliament as a national, deliberative assembly with a common interest, which collectively represents the electorate as a whole. In that arena, competitive political parties exercise their power to form a constitutional bridge between the executive and parliament (Burke 1770, 1774, 1792).

However, a more recent modified precedent develops out of the eighth historical constitutional form in the latter part of the twentieth century (after 1973). That form provides for a British constitution in which the recognised helm is dependent both upon the continuity of party political representation through Parliament in addition to Parliament ruling through external agencies, commissions or bodies, the EU and should it wish, by national referendums. Two previous historical constitutional forms derived from eighteenth and nineteenth century (forms six and seven) have worked as guiding historical precedents. The modern capacity for parties in Parliament to make political decisions on vital issues as a deliberative assembly (Burke) in the recognised helm is enmeshed within a system in which the contemporary powers of Parliament have outsourced that decision-making capacity by referendum (Dicey).

From the standpoint of the present, both historical constitutional forms depend upon Dicey's principle of government by consent of the electorate. Burke himself, in his own tradition and in pre-democratic times, would not have countenanced the proposition of a referendum, or any public instruction or mandate for MPs. For Burke, those direct mechanisms would be irreconcilable with trustee Members, exercising their independent judgements, in the exercise of Parliament's sovereignty and the British constitution (Burke 1774). Yet Dicey's cementing of election with referendums, which permit the consent of the people in a representative system, is relevant to resettling parliamentary sovereignty following the EU referendum. It is the consent of the people in referendum, like Burke's political parties in elections, which enables the seeking of consent of the people. Such consent enables the resettling of parliamentary power since it regains from the EU its centrality of political decision-making and effects a realignment of power between the executive and the legislature.

The previous case studies presented in Chapters 4–6 demonstrated how EU legislation and policies have unsettled previous historical constitutional forms of parliamentary sovereignty. For example, I have argued that parliamentary sovereignty is unsettled by a displacement and marginalising of the sixth of the eight historical constitutional forms, reflected in 'What the Crown-*in*-mixed constitutional Parliament enacts is law' (Chapter 4; Blackstone 1765, pp. i, 50–52). The case study of the EU-level Financial Transaction Tax in Chapter 4 demonstrated that the EU institutions incorporated into the UK's recognised helm have, through the unsettling of the historical precedented mixed constitution model, unsettled parliamentary sovereignty. After all, on the very issue of taxation itself, long-standing constitutional principles since the seventeenth century established for the House of Commons—not the European Commission—the primary capacity to authorise taxation and the level of financial supply to the Crown. Chapter 5 argued that Parliament's sovereignty became effectively unsettled when the European Parliament's high level of specialist 'functional' representation unsettles the precedent of 'collective representation' of the people. It unsettles the Westminster model of representation characterised by both a 'trustee' representative status of its elected Members of Parliament and a collective parliamentary status by which Parliament acts in the common, collective interest. The case study of the Working Time Directive showed that the European Parliament's competition and its shared neo-corporatist emphasis relative to Westminster produces a distortion of the historically precedented capacity to collectively represent its electors, thereby unsettling parliamentary sovereignty. Chapter 6 then proceeded to argue that Parliament's sovereignty has become effectively unsettled because EU-level fundamental rights schemes displace the making of rights through political and parliamentary mechanisms, in favour of the provision offered by the courts. The case study of the EU free movement right, for example, illustrates that EU rights have been incorporated into the recognised helm, enabling a dependency upon such rights. It has ultimately led to the dilution of the domestic legislature's activity as a rights-providing institution. In considering the Prime Ministerial negotiation of the UK's withdrawal subsequent to the EU referendum, two precedented constitutional forms which were unsettled under EU membership have now been further resettled by parliamentary decision-making power.

Historical constitutional forms define the unsettling of precedented sovereignty. In short, when there is an experience of friction between past, historical constitutional forms and the present explanation of the UK's political arrangements, it is helpful to consider the unbalancing of past constitutional conventions as 'unsettling' (consistent with Walker

2014; Young and Gee 2016; Gordon 2017, p. 32). When a present day constitutional form in the eighth stage is in conflict with a feature from within one of the previous seven historical constitutional forms, an unsettling and subsequent resettling can potentially occur. The nature of that unsettling centres on the shift from one constitutional form—or more likely, a shift in a particular feature of the form—to a newer or different one, particularly a past historical form in friction with the contemporary eighth form. A further resettling through a policy of withdrawal as a consequence of the crystallising of opinion in the UK's EU referendum verdict of 2016 itself occurs within the eighth constitutional form.

7.2 The Principle of Consent: Leaving the EU After the 2016 EU Referendum

The UK's EU referendum of June 2016 resulted in the people of the UK voting to leave the EU by a margin of 17.4 million people (52%) to 16.1 million (48%) on a significant 72% turnout. Leave won the majority of votes in England (53.4% Leave, 46.6% Remain) and Wales (52.5% Leave, 47.5% Remain), although not in Scotland (38% Leave, 62% Remain) or Northern Ireland (44.2% Leave, 55.8% Remain). After the referendum, most voters were content with the choice that they made (Curtice 2016, 2017a, b, c) and were committed to the decision they registered at the time of the referendum.

In pursuing a constitutional resettlement, the decision to leave in the 2016 referendum was framed as an attempt to wrest back control over decision-making from EU institutions. 'Vote Leave and take back control' became the leading campaign mantra. Nearly half of those Leave voters surveyed chose to leave in recognition of the "principle that decisions about the UK should be taken in the UK" (Ashcroft 2016). Respondents affirmed a primacy of government where decisions are taken by UK rather than EU decision-making bodies. Sovereignty was considered an overriding factor, expressed as the ability for UK electors to make their own decisions through their elected Parliament and not have those decisions presented to them at the EU-level. As many as 60% agreed in one survey that the EU had "undermined the powers of the UK parliament" while just 17% disagreed (see Curtice 2017a, p. 11). Further polls and studies found that sovereignty had been the main motivating factor for most Leave voters (ComRes 2016; Clarke et al. 2017, p. 448; Swales 2016, p. 13; see also Prosser et al. 2016;

Geddes 2016, p. 266; Menon and Fowler 2016, R6). A strong identity of Eurosceptic Britishness had become politically dominant in the electorate (Bodganor 2019, p. 8; Gifford 2010, 2014) and in British politics, particularly within the Conservative Party (Geddes 2016, p. 265). Given the recognition of the UK as "the most consistently Eurosceptic Member State" (Nugent 2018, p. 59), the relevance of sovereignty to those eventual Leave voters who had been waiting for David Cameron's renegotiation in EU powers was pivotal (Curtice 2017b; Geddes 2016). There had been a doubling between 1992 and 2014 of those supporting EU exit (10–24%) but importantly, a growth in those sceptical and who wanted to see EU powers reduced (30–38%) (The British Election Study 2016; Geddes 2016). By 2015, two thirds opposed the UK's existing relationship with the EU, with 22% saying we should leave, 43% wanting a reduction in EU powers (Swales 2016, p. 5; see also Curtice 2017b). Cameron's renegotiation strategy rested on the need to convince the substantial number of 'Remain but reduce powers' camp that his renegotiation amounted to a substantive change and a reduction in EU power (Geddes 2016, p. 270; Curtice 2017b)—but it did not. It might be expected that if the UK Government is to continue to deliver on a Brexit strategy that satisfies the political preferences of Leave voters, then the final settlement should maximise the sovereignty of a representative UK Parliament (Chalmers 2017; Hix 2018, p. 19).

In the UK constitution, the referendum functions as an additive to representative government, not a compartmentalised aspect of the constitution (Qvortrup 2015). That is primarily because, under the UK referendum procedure, voters do not have the right to initiate legislation—they can merely approve or reject proposals put forward by the legislature (Qvortrup 2015, p. 7). As such, the people's verdict of 23 June is triggered and returned for resolution and implementation by the Government-in-Parliament. The process from triggering that mechanism, through to the consequential impact on Government policy, in Parliament, in implementing the result affirms, rather than challenges, the UK's parliamentary sovereignty (McConalogue 2019, contra Bogdanor 2009, 2019). The referendum is therefore a complement to representative government—not an instance of popular sovereignty. As Dicey put it, a referendum provides formal recognition that the enactment of laws depends on the consent of the nationally, represented electorate (Qvortrup 1999, 2015; Dicey 1911), not a bypassing of that consent. The historical constitutional forms (notably, six and seven) engendering party political representation and representation by referendum reflect Dicey's view of government by consent (Box 7.1).

Box 7.1: UK Referendums

Although referendums are a highly irregular mechanism in the UK constitution, the 2016 referendum on EU membership has some precedents in the past 45 years of British politics not only in relation to a European Community referendum but mostly devolution referendums. Since 1973, there have been only twelve referendums held in the UK, including:

- the first nation-wide referendum on 5 June 1975 on whether the UK should stay in the European Community (yes);
- the Scottish devolution referendum on 11 September 1997 on whether there should be a Scottish Parliament and whether the Scottish Parliament should have tax varying powers (both referendums received a yes vote);
- the second nation-wide referendum on 5 May 2011 on whether to change the voting system for electing MPs to the House of Commons from first past the post to the alternative vote (no) and;
- the referendum on 18 September 2014 on whether Scotland should become an independent country (no).
- the referendum on 23 June 2016 on whether the UK should remain a member of or leave the EU (leave).

However, the first UK-wide referendum held in 1975 on the UK's continued membership of the European Community was the first British precedent for a national referendum on staying in the Community, which was affirmed with 67% of the vote (Swales 2016, p. 4) on a turnout of 64% (Geddes 2013, p. 65). The third UK-wide referendum in 2016 was met with a verdict of leaving the EU.

As well as acting as a 'constitutional safeguard', in terms of legislating for an EU referendum in both 1975 and in 2016, the internal politically constraining factor upon the Prime Minister has been the disagreement between the governing parties in Parliament, which has often provided the main pretext for such a referendum (see Qvortrup 2015, pp. 16–17, type I referendum; Bogdanor 2019, p. 91; Gamble 2018, p. 1226). The impasse faced by the parties in Parliament is essential to providing the pretext in legislating for a referendum on a difficult constitutional issue. That is not to dismiss the deeper, foundational reasons behind the ad hoc use of those constitutional devices increasingly in free states such as the UK, particularly since the 1970s, to perform as a constitutional safeguard—and not (as is often implied) as a means for populists to overturn the status quo (Qvortrup 2015, p. 39; 2018, p. 72). Such a function has some relevance in relation to the UK's experience of continued European integration where, without a written constitution, Parliament has few other constitutional safeguards or institutional safety-valves outside government to protect its own institution or its electors.

7.3 A Resettlement of the UK's Relationship to the EU?

The referendum decision and the proceeding Government withdrawal policy has meant the UK "constitutional settlement is in flux" in relation to that decision (The UK in a Changing Europe Initiative and The Political Studies Association 2016a, b; Smith 2017, pp. 78–79; Young and Gee 2016). Parliament's decision-making power over recasting the agenda and resettling the UK's new EU relationship—led presently by Theresa May's Government—occupies a renewed, elevated and central position in the constitutional resettlement. The subsequent attempt to create a formalised withdrawal agreement cementing a withdrawal settlement from the EU had been negotiated over two years, and yet rejected by the House of Commons on three occasions. The referendum result indicates that the majority of the voting electorate in a UK-wide referendum want to 'Leave' the EU, albeit a significant minority wanted to Remain. Further still, a wide variety of political and economic actors have frustrations and reservations of precisely what the new future settled relationship might look like, politically, legally and economically.

Historically, after 45 years membership of the EU, the UK's withdrawal, if achieved, will mean Parliament regaining from the EU its sovereignty over decision-making in respect of key political decisions. Parliamentary sovereignty, after all, implies the centrality of Parliament to institutional state architecture (Walker 2014, p. 532). The resettlement means Parliament will be called upon to decide on policies as broad in scope as the future UK-EU trading relationship, or the UK remaining bound by EU free movement of people (see House of Commons Library 2016). There remain a whole range of policies that the Government in Parliament must still decide upon which will determine a long-standing future form of UK-EU relationship (Raitio and Raulus 2017, p. 38), including whether to: leave the EU onto WTO rules ('no deal' option); limit the free movement for goods, services, capital and people (e.g. Switzerland); or its ability to make third-party trade deals (e.g. Singapore and Canada) (The UK in a Changing Europe Initiative and Political Studies Association 2016a).

Parliament, in legislating for the referendum through to the repeal of the European Communities Act, has been central to the resettling of constitutional powers. The current Government's policy had been committed 'to leave', having begun the 'Article 50' negotiations in March 2017. The aim had been to reach an agreement about the UK's future partnership by the time the 2-year Article 50 process had concluded on 29 March 2019 (May 2017a, b; Davis 2017; The UK in a Changing Europe Initiative and Political Studies Association 2016a). The Prime Minister Theresa May regularly maintained that since the British people voted to leave the EU, it is the job of the Government and MPs to deliver that "instruction" (May 2017a; see Gamble 2018, p. 1217). Parliament has both passed the Government's key withdrawal legislation and strongly constrained the Prime Minister's agenda throughout the process and particularly with regard to her EU-level renegotiated withdrawal agreement. At the time of writing, Theresa May's negotiated agreement was three times rejected by MPs—in January 2019 (by 432 votes to 202) (BBC News 2019a; UK Parliament 2019a), the worst defeat for a government in more than a century, and twice in March 2019 (391 to 242, and again, 344 to 286), prior to her resignation.

For its part in a potential resettlement, Parliament legislated for the EU referendum through the EU Referendum Act 2015. The House of Commons voted the Bill through by 544 to 53 votes at second reading (a ratio of six to one in the Commons), with only the Scottish National Party (SNP) voting against (House of Commons 2015). If not more fundamentally, electors on 23 June 2016 directly tasked Parliament to exercise its ultimate decision-making powers to implement the majority decision to 'leave the EU' (McConalogue 2019).

The House of Commons held a vote on a Motion calling on the Government to invoke Article 50 by 31 March 2017, which again was supported by 448 to 75 MPs, with again predominantly SNP MPs opposing (House of Commons 2016). The House of Commons also passed the formal European Union (Notification of Withdrawal) Act 2017, formally affirming the triggering of Article 50, by 498 to 114 votes at second reading (House of Commons 2017a; BBC News 2017), despite being asked by the Supreme Court to take the initiative to do so (*Miller* [2017]). The *Miller* judgement in the Supreme Court made Parliament itself the single most fundamental and politically legitimate authority to trigger the UK Government's proposed withdrawal negotiations with the EU (*Miller* [2017]; Eleftheriadis 2017; Eeckhout 2018, p. 168; Chalmers 2017). MPs were not only active but effective in shaping the key withdrawal legislation, namely the European Union (Withdrawal) Act 2018, voting in favour of that Act at its second reading by 326 votes to 290 (House of Commons 2017b). Simultaneously, most Labour, LibDem and SNP MPs voted against the legislation—opposing and deeply scrutinising the Bill's "power grab" Henry VIII provisions which those parties argued gave government ministers broad powers to make legislative changes (rather than Parliament) to remedy the problems arising out of withdrawal. With that legislation having been both passed as well as amended in significant areas (by MPs' negotiating and voting for changes), the current resettlement therefore puts Parliament centre-stage.

7.4 Parliamentary Sovereignty and Resettling the Contemporary Power of Parliament

7.4.1 The Ultimate Decision-Making Power of Parliament over Political Decisions

It is necessary to recognise the contemporary relationship between parliamentary sovereignty and the ultimate decision making-power of Parliament over political decisions as unsettled by EU membership—particularly in contrast to underlying features of Bogdanor's (2009) constitutional state theory and some of his assumptions which rest upon radical common law constitutionalism. Bogdanor's (2009) constitutional state theory appears to underplay the capacity for effective decision-making on EU rules by government. By emphasising public power, it often understates Parliament's institutional capacity with its partisan actors to bring about pressure to accept, reject or change the government's decisions on the terms of EU withdrawal.

Specifically, also, on an alternative radical common law perspective, Bogdanor (2009) and other theorists have partially adopted the radical theory of national common law constitutionalism. The approach directly seeks to affirm the power of a national court-decided, judicial, common law at the expense of the doctrine of parliamentary sovereignty in settling the substantive questions over the UK's EU relationship. The argument is highly apposite when considering the High Court, then Supreme Court, in *Miller* held that an Act of Parliament would be needed before Article 50 could be triggered (*Miller* 2016, 2017). The absence in those explanatory theories draws this concluding chapter towards politics and political constitutionalism more specifically. Such an approach gives sufficient weight to sovereignty as defined by parliamentary decision-making power. It serves as an adaptation of Burke's defence of MPs making the ultimate decisions in the party-political, parliamentary realm because of their ability to collectively represent electors. In that environment, contested issues are reasoned through party competition (including intra-party deliberation), bridging the accountability gap between executive and legislative powers.

In employing the term 'ultimate' decision-making power of Parliament over political decisions relating to the UK's relationship with the EU, the contemporary Parliament has four overarching and general functions defining its powers:

i. To check the work of the Government through questioning ministers, debating and the investigative work of committees pursuing scrutiny of Government's EU policy;
ii. To make and change legislation;
iii. To secure debates in which members discuss (support or oppose) Government policy, legislation and events of the day;
iv. To check and approve Government spending and taxation.

The power is 'ultimate' because Parliament has the highest legal authority in the UK to create or end any law and which courts cannot overrule, nor Parliament bind its future Parliaments.

7.4.2 Constitutional State Theory, Common Law Constitutionalism and the Undermining of Parliamentary Decision-Making Power

From a constitutional state perspective, Bogdanor's (2009) theory has insufficiently reconciled parliamentary sovereignty and the ultimate power to make political decisions over policy and law. Part of the assumed disconnect arises from disregarding the historical precedent of how parliamentary sovereignty derives from decision-making power in support or opposition to law and national referendums. The constitutional state perspective has pointed to a popular power in referendums that equates with popular sovereignty which in turn supposedly trumps Parliament's sovereignty. Bogdanor's (2009, 2019) assumption that Britain's era of constitutional reform after 1997, together with its 1973 entry into the European Communities, has paved the way for a new constitution is particularly concerning. The new arrangement is considered to rest, unconvincingly, upon the shift from parliamentary sovereignty to a constitutional state based upon popular sovereignty (Bogdanor 2009, p. xiii). In its analysis, it underplays the effective power of decision-making on EU membership by the government when:

- Overstating public power in relation to government authority and Parliament's sovereignty.
- Understating Parliament's own capacity to force an executive decision and therefore its implicit political will and power in deciding on EU rules.

Bogdanor achieves this objective by first, insisting, in line with radical common law constitutionalism that the effect of the European Communities Act 1972 is to bind future Parliaments. He holds it is a 'constitutional statute' (Bogdanor 2009, p. 278); it could not simply be repealed. In consequence, Parliament cannot simply repeal the European Communities Act (Bogdanor 2009, p. 278) but now, seemingly it can, armed with the people's instruction. The radical outcome of ultra-common law constitutionalism which Bogdanor relies upon to make his argument is that Parliament cannot decide on EU laws, or its membership, or repeal the European Communities Act. Yet, the Government, after the 2016 EU referendum, promised to repeal that Act (May 2017a) and then enacted that repeal by legislation. Bogdanor (2009) adopts the radical theory of national common law constitutionalism which directly seeks to affirm the primacy of a national, court-decided common law at the expense of politics as settling the final question over the deployment of parliamentary decision-making power in relation to the EU. However, it is possible Bogdanor might accept that the European Communities Act being entrenched in this way in no way affects the ability of a Government to finally decide on EU rules, or categorically, the rules which compose its membership.

Constitutional state theory also sets out to achieve its objective by second, consigning the referendum of the people to an exercise in popular sovereignty. It is said to act as a check upon the 'elective dictatorship' in British politics (Bogdanor 2009, p. 275), rather than a discretionary act of parliamentary sovereignty, outsourcing parliament's decision-making capacity on a narrow question. Bogdanor reaffirms that the referendum on EU membership crystallised the introduction of a new principle, the sovereignty of the people, into the British constitution, which supersedes the sovereignty of parliament (Bogdanor 2016a, b, 2019, pp. 109–110). For Bogdanor, the referendum creates in effect "an extra chamber of parliament comprising in addition to the Queen, the Lords and the Commons, the people" (Bogdanor 2009, p. 280). It resembles Dicey's mischaracterisation of the referendum as an "alternative second chamber" (Dicey 1911). The referendum, however, is not an exercise in popular sovereignty but popular decision-making power, which in turn, instructs the sovereign power. The power is limited only to the question in hand. It is a decision-making power only and it is, as Bogdanor accepts, 'advisory', not prescriptive. For Bogdanor, though, the instrument knowingly removes the centrality of Parliament. That is a difficult conclusion to draw given that Parliament is the only political actor to legislate for one and the joint-in-command (with Government) in deciding policy strategy in light of a referendum outcome (contra Bogdanor 2016a, p. 348). Referendums if anything reinvigorate Parliament's public power. The referendum is an addendum, not a challenge, to representative government (Qvortrup 2015). Accordingly, referendums have been used increasingly by parliament often as a constitutional safeguard, not as a means for populists to realise their objectives (Qvortrup 2018, p. 72).

Parliament occupies a political centrality. Referendums on EU membership or EU rules cannot express the sovereignty of the people. The argument for popular sovereignty (see Bogdanor 2019, p. 110) does not take into account the role of Parliament in triggering, asking the question, and providing a coherent policy after the referendum, consistent with the public instruction to Parliament by referendum. The people at no point have that ultimate decision-making power but they do have the decision-making power to support or oppose a specific policy which has been put before Parliament. This action confirms, not denies, Burke's views of ultimate parliamentary power resting on party competition, exercised between the executive and legislature; yet, contrary to Burke, modern parliamentary power is now more greatly subject to the will of the people.

However, constitutional state theory persuasively identifies mainstream parties in Parliament as central to justifying referendums: the 1975 referendum on the EC was called to reconcile opposition factions in the Labour Party (Bogdanor 2009, pp. 180, 185) in a situation whereby all three mainstream parties were committed to EEC membership. Again, ahead of the 2016 referendum, all mainstream parties in the 2015 general election had been committed to remaining with EU membership (Bogdanor 2016b) but the issue could not be resolved through the normal working of the party system. Furthermore, this impasse in party government advances the legitimacy question: a referendum is necessary on an issue of fundamental importance where the parliamentary vote is insufficient to ensure legitimacy (Bogdanor 2009, p. 185). In making that claim, Bogdanor protects legitimacy as relevant and with good reason. However, Bogdanor chooses to sidestep the referendum question by not addressing Parliament's power in Burke's sense whereby party competition in Parliament is exercised to bridge the executive-legislature divide.

The facets of radical common law constitutionalism and constitutional statism engendered in Bogdanor's view have more broadly overemphasised judicial and people power, respectively, as finalising what constitutes ultimate decision-making power in the British political tradition. Yet the British constitution provides neither the people or the common law court with an *ultimate* decision-making power in respect of making, altering and opposing fundamental political decisions. The dual tendency in this theory has troublingly sought to institutionally bypass the role of ongoing contestation in politics. The way in which decisions are made, resolved and resettled serves to explain how Parliament maintains its sovereignty.

7.4.3 *Political Constitutionalism: Addressing the Vacuum in Explaining Parliamentary Power*

Several explanatory theories understate the relevance of Parliament's decision-making power on political decisions to parliamentary sovereignty. Instead, they have portrayed it often as subsidiary to popular power, or to judicial power (Bogdanor 2009). A focus on politics and political constitutionalism can redress this absence. Such a view enables a sufficient consideration of sovereignty as parliamentary decision-making power by adapting Burke's defence of political representation. In the sixth constitutional form, both (i) a collective parliamentary status by which Parliament acts as a deliberative assembly (Burke 1774); and (ii) competing parties doing the representing are able to act, when effective, as a constitutional bridge, with strength and consistency, between the executive and legislature (Burke 1770).

The model of political constitutionalism on Burke's twin assumptions helps to locate parliamentary sovereignty in the political realm since it assumes, there is an inherent and ongoing disagreement about substantive outcomes that society should achieve, and yet a recognised legitimate and effective parliamentary process for resolving these disagreements (see Bellamy 2007; Waldron 1999). Thus, no parliament may bind its successor. A recognised legitimate process to resolve disagreements and make policy and law requires the recognition of decision-making powers involved in that process.

Political constitutionalism might better address the absence in explanatory theories of Parliament's power in relation to parliamentary sovereignty because it looks beyond law and legal institutions and towards the legitimacy of political institutions as sites of contestation (Waldron 1999; Bellamy 2007). A legitimate process of resolution could not be achieved via an appeal to the legal machinery and the judicial component alone. While Richard Bellamy (2007) persuasively draws that model into a democratic tradition and the political constitutionalist tradition does at the very least inquire into political conditions in relation to Parliament's sovereignty, legal constitutionalists look only to identify judicially enforceable, external substantive limits on Parliament, grounded in the common law or the rule of law (Delaney 2014). The inherent, institutionalised disagreement to seek alternative resettlement, as contained by backbench party competition, has an important part to play in bridging Government and Parliament's decision-making power both in conventional government and when outsourcing and reorienting policy after a referendum.

Under EU membership in which the executive and the demoted legislature are strongly disaligned, thereby softening the legislature's ability to scrutinise the executive (Hix and Goetz 2000, p. 11), it is MPs from their differing political parties which rekindle a constitutional relationship between executive and parliament in the recognised helm. Burke's discerning observation helps to recast Parliament's demoted powers as distinct from the position of the executives across Europe. What matters is the organised independence of party backbencher positions adopted in parliamentary chambers (Raunio and Hix 2000), notably in the UK. The government's majority backbench MPs are (at least) capable of reorienting, as Burke describes, forming an association between the executive and parliament. Dicey's approach to government by consent understands both the preserving of the centrality of parliamentary decision-making, via parties, and of referendums (beyond parties), as providing instruction to Parliament. They are both features which have otherwise been resisted in constitutional state 'popular sovereignty' approaches or the common law tradition.

Where EU institutional membership has lessened the ability of parliaments to regulate executives (Raunio 2011; Raunio and Hix 2000; Schmidt 1999), executives are provided with a policy space far removed from domestic parliamentary scrutiny. The executive holds a near monopoly on information in a significant public policy space (Raunio and Hix 2000, p. 163). By reaction to this deepening trend, the parliaments of Europe since the 1990s established institutions that forced governments to explain their EU policies and actions in the European arena to parliaments. The "driving force" behind this reaffirming power has been the aspiration by backbench parliamentarians to "redress the 'information gap'" between governing elites and the parliamentary rank-and-file (Raunio and Hix 2000, p. 163), in holding the government to account on EU policy. When backbench MPs are met with EU agendas, laws or politics—so often curbed when open parliamentary debates are avoided by the executive as far as possible—they have the power to induce the minister, or Prime Minister, to act as a representative of the electorate, or act via its parliamentary committee (Benz 2004, p. 887), particularly through either the Exiting the EU and European Scrutiny Committees in the House of Commons. MPs, peers and the Select Committees have opportunities to make ministers indirectly aware of their views on EU proposals, albeit *ex ante* controls and which in no way define Government mandates (Benz 2004; Auel 2007). Despite the considerable lack of involvement of Parliaments, backbench MPs and Select Committees in the EU governance process, and their apparent absence of contemporary direct decision-making powers, in Westminster they can still collectively and vigorously supply crucial rationales and articulate policy views to informally require ministers to reorient, or augment, that existing EU policy.

Political constitutionalism can better reformulate the absence in explanatory theories of Parliament's power over political decisions in relation to parliamentary sovereignty through the incorporation of party competition into Parliament. As described in Chapter 5, it is political parties which are the primary vehicles that articulate citizens' policy beliefs and convert them into public policies (Adams 2001, p. 3). Voters' choices of parties then provide them with a method of exercising indirect control over the actions of individual legislators and through these over the affairs of government (Adams 2001, p. 4). Parties invariably vote as a bloc in Parliament—with few regular exceptions—and they exercise control over the government agenda and policy-making process in Parliament. The electorate use party policies as the basis for their voting decisions and provide effective vehicles for representing the electorate's political beliefs (Adams 2001, p. 5). Understanding the relationship between public opinion and party competition on Europe is important for domestic political contestation in the member states (Down and Wilson 2010, p. 62).

The political constitutionalist tradition might better attempt to accommodate the missing link in explanatory theories of Parliament's power over political decisions in relation to parliamentary sovereignty. The tradition does better work of conceiving of the political environment of ***dissensus*** in which the legislature and its electors hold the Prime Minister to account. Hooghe and Marks (2009, p. 5) argue that prior to 1991, EU politics occupied a period of permissive consensus in which negotiated "deals" were "cut by insulated elites" and "public opinion was quiescent". After 1991, EU contemporary politics is occupied by a "constraining dissensus" in which party leaders must look to public opinion when negotiating European issues and where referendums have been able to "disarm party elites" (Katz and Wessels 1999; Hooghe and Marks 2009, p. 20; see also Geddes 2016; de Wilde 2012; Franklin et al.

1994; Copeland and Copsey 2017, p. 709). The assumption that Prime Ministerial executives are constrained through government under EU membership relies upon the dissensus by some public groups and particularly from opposition and government-aligned backbench MPs. The dissensus in the UK-EU context and the role of parties in Parliament, rather than exercised from the viewpoint of the Prime Minister's executive, reinvigorates (rather than denies) the political inter-relationships between the executive, the legislature and the electorate which support parliamentary sovereignty. The exercise of parliamentary sovereignty is now dependent upon the Prime Minister's broad accountability to Parliament and the electorate over all EU negotiations. The Prime Minister's failure to recognise such a dissensus would undermine the accountability of executive policy to the legislature and the electorate and therefore the exercise of parliamentary sovereignty.

7.5 Parliamentary Sovereignty and Resettling Parliamentary Power: The Principle of Leaving the EU After the 2016 EU Referendum

In understanding the resettling of the Parliament's power in deciding the UK's terms of withdrawal from the EU following the referendum in June 2016, the referendum is considered not as an instance of popular sovereignty but as a discretionary exercise of Parliament's outsourcing of its own essential decision-making capacity (to Remain or Leave) (McConalogue 2019). Some three years on from the referendum itself (2016–2019), Parliament has taken several significant steps to resettle its powers in relation to the Prime Minister and her negotiated withdrawal agreement, including:

- Securing a 'meaningful vote' for MPs on that agreement.
- Parliament voting to reject and refine the Prime Minister's deal.
- MPs acting as Motion-making, agenda-shapers, drafting meaningful motions and shaping future direction;
- Parliament holding the Government in contempt and protecting the 'will of parliament';
- MPs' requesting a delay to Article 50 negotiations;
- Parliament preventing a 'no deal Brexit'.

Those episodes highlight how tightly regulated the powers of Prime Minister are by Parliament (Menon 2018). In that constitutional resettlement, MPs were being tasked to pursue their strengthened power (McConalogue 2019), which they had otherwise not fully exercised for 45 years of EU membership. To make it even more difficult, the Prime Minister's negotiated withdrawal agreement was a complex compromise (Cygan 2019; Gamble 2019, p. 178). Certainly, UK citizens in the EU, and EU citizens in the UK, retained specific residency (and related social security rights) after withdrawal. However, the specified transition period which in theory would have begun on 29 March 2019 and last until 31 December 2020 remained contentious among both European Research Group (ERG) MPs—the most hardline, pro-Brexit MP group within the governing Conservative Party—and the Northern Irish Democratic Unionist Party (DUP) MPs. After all, during the transition period, the UK would have no formal say in making or amending EU rules and yet it was required to follow them precisely. No actual payment figure appeared in the document and yet many anticipated at least £39 billion to be paid by the UK—again, far too substantial a cost for Conservative Brexiteer colleagues. It broke a further red line for both classically 'unionist' DUP and ERG colleagues that Northern Ireland was to be placed in a deeper customs and regulatory relationship with the EU than the rest of the UK. Difficult for many of May's Brexiteer Conservative colleagues, the agreement further requested the UK would remain under ECJ jurisdiction during such a transition. As will become clearer, competing parties, with internal factions, tightly constrained the Prime Minister's ability to negotiate an agreement reflecting their desired objectives.

7.5.1 Securing a 'Meaningful Vote' for MPs on the Withdrawal Agreement

The resettlement of parliamentary powers is evident from MPs ability to force Government and the Prime Minister to secure a 'meaningful vote' on the withdrawal agreement (House of Commons 2018). The Government had claimed as early as October 2016 that Parliament would be given a vote on the withdrawal agreement. It remained unsatisfactory for many MPs during the tense period that this commitment was only a stated ministerial intention; far better, for many MPs, it stand as a binding legal duty. During the passage of the EU Withdrawal Act, the

Government therefore agreed to a significant change in order to avoid defeat through a voted on an amendment on the floor of the House and importantly, later through the force of political negotiation (Institute for Government 2018). In any case, MPs have generally been more effective at winning concessions through negotiations prior to votes rather than through defeat of the Government (Caird et al. 2019). As a result, the Prime Minister needed to change the original proposed plans for Parliament's consideration of the agreement. The actions of a small, targeted and influential group of pro-EU Conservative MPs resulted in Section 13 of the Withdrawal Act, finally giving Parliament a 'meaningful vote' on the deal (Institute for Government 2018).

In particular, one Conservative MP, Dominic Grieve had continued to provide leadership for a legally binding meaningful vote and a role for the Commons if and when the negotiated withdrawal deal was rejected. The Government, by accepting changes, brought forward Section 13 of the EU (Withdrawal) Act, which provides the legal framework for the meaningful vote process and provided for a post-rejection role for the Commons (Caird et al. 2019). It could hardly be labelled a mere procedural change. As the UK in a Changing Europe (2018) reported, "Its very existence is a sign of the influence that parliament has been able to exert over the process" (p. 7). It was a result of a fuller political negotiation in which MPs were able to prompt the Government to change its position and offer those concessions (Caird et al. 2019).

Fowler (2018) persuasively identifies parliament's forcing of the 'meaningful vote' procedure over the UK-EU withdrawal agreement as not only "near-unique in 170 years of UK treaty-making" but what "could be the UK treaty with the most parliamentary decision-making involvement ever" (Fowler 2018). The 'meaningful vote' came towards the end of a treaty-making process which itself required parliamentary authorisation to launch. Through the 'meaningful vote', Parliament was being asked to approve the agreement before it was signed. As Fowler suggests, the only one other case where this occurred in the UK acting alone was under the 1984 Sino-British Joint Declaration on Hong Kong (Fowler 2018).

The essential part of the parliament-altered Withdrawal Act (Section 13) specifies that the Government would not be able to ratify the agreement without four significant conditions having been met, namely (i) the documents and an associated statement have been published; (ii) "The negotiated Withdrawal Agreement and the framework for the future relationship have been approved by a resolution of the House of Commons on a motion moved by a minister of the Crown"; (iii) a subsequent debate has taken place in the House of Lords; and (iv) Parliament has passed legislation to implement the withdrawal agreement (Institute for Government 2018). With MPs exercising their powers by proposing pertinent amendments to leading government legislation and through force of negotiation, Parliament itself brought about those fourfold binding conditions. It gave Parliament a far stronger role in the ratification of the agreement than under past precedent of parliamentary procedure for such Treaties (set out in the Constitutional Reform and Governance Act 2010).

It is usually within the remit of a 'reactive' Parliament to debate, amend or reject the proposals put before it by the government of the day. However, by the nature of having triggered the referendum and the Article 50 process—and the withdrawal negotiations having created such disagreement within Parliament, politics and in wider society—there is a status of the parties in disagreement in Parliament, battling for ownership over the debate in response (Glencross 2018, p. 26), at least more so than in regular proposals in Government Bills. The claim to ownership over the Brexit agenda and terms of withdrawal stems from a broader post-2016 resettlement. The claiming of a meaningful vote results from Parliament's ultimate decision-making power on the UK-EU relationship and claiming a strengthened capacity to pass (or reject) a withdrawal agreement. The power defers to Westminster's collective and tribal capacity to represent electors. Electors directly tasked Parliament to thereby resettle that ultimate power of consent by nature of the referendum's majority verdict. The post-2016 'Remain-majority' Parliament on the whole reoriented their position—at least, initially—towards the majority verdict because of Parliament's primary instinct to collectively represent electors.

7.5.2 *Parliament Voting Down and Refining the Prime Minister's Deal*

Parliament's resettling of its ultimate decision-making powers was further evidenced by MPs voting against the Prime Minister's negotiated agreement on three occasions. The Government had published a draft UK-EU level withdrawal agreement by 14 November (together with its protocols and annexes), combined with a Political Declaration on the future framework. It was endorsed weeks later at a European Council meeting on 25 November (Miller 2018) but key parts of its withdrawal terms had isolated the legislature. It was a "compromise", pleasing no individual group in particular, but merely a product of two years of Article 50 negotiations and reflecting that the UK has been an EU member state for 45 years (Cygan 2019).

May's negotiated agreement had, as with David Cameron's renegotiated-Remain package, strongly isolated the legislature. The Conservatives as a governing party rapidly reoriented toward the referendum result itself and thereby in implementing the majority verdict (Menon 2016; Curtice 2017c, p. 13). Whereas 83% of Labour members opted for Remain; 73% of Tory members had voted for Leave (Bale et al. 2019, p. 27). The Conservative government of the day therefore chose to pursue a Leave-oriented withdrawal but through fast-track prerogative-led negotiation. That form of negotiation only exacerbated the executive-legislature rupture which, in the spirit of David Cameron and Theresa May's renegotiations, had characterised their respective EU negotiating strategies and unpopular outcomes.

Even among the MPs she was reliant on for a parliamentary majority, the agreement had marginalised several key 'red lines' among her supporting colleagues. The negotiated agreement could not win over many Remain-centric MPs partly due to its outright rejection of single market and customs union advantages—and yet the campaign for a second referendum (which many of that group began to favour) had gained some political traction inside and outside parliament. The negotiated agreement's Irish border backstop—a kind of binding insurance policy to avoid a hard border between Northern Ireland and the Republic of Ireland after Brexit—was opposed by the DUP MPs. The Prime Minister was broadly dependent upon them for governing through a confidence and supply agreement. Despite May later gaining specific EU assurances and a protocol, the DUP remained opposed to any suggestion of difference in treatment between Northern Ireland and Great Britain, provided in the backstop. The DUP rejected the agreement's regulatory differences in which Northern Ireland would continue to follow some EU rules. The Prime Minister's own colleagues in the Conservative Party, mainly through affiliations with the European Research Group (ERG), could not countenance the deal either. Their objections included handing over £39 billion as part of the deal, the remaining role of the European Court of Justice, the UK remaining a 'rule taker' over large areas of EU law, of locking the UK in a Customs Union without the ability to leave and, in sympathy with the DUP, of undermining the integrity of the Union through the backstop (European Research Group 2018). Since EU-level negotiation rules play a central process in the diminished ability of parliaments to regulate executives (Raunio and Hix 2000) and in which Prime (ministers) attempt to take ever greater ownership of the agenda, the legislature is induced into strongly scrutinising (if not, rejecting) that agreement, crystallising their views and resettling its position.

Parliament's actions to vote down Theresa May's deal were seismic in respect of negotiating an orderly, business-like departure. After a critical deferral of a vote in December 2018, on the first 'meaningful vote' on 15 January, MPs voted down by a very clear 230-strong majority (by 432 to 202) the Government's negotiated agreement and future relationship framework (BBC News 2019a; UK Parliament 2019a). The Prime Minister had spent two years negotiating the deal (BBC News 2019a) and five days of debate had been held on the content of the agreement (UK Parliament 2019a). The next day's newspapers described that first defeat as "crushing", "historic" and "humiliating" (Sparrow 2019a). Given the substantive loss, the opposition were eager to have the Prime Minister removed, along with her deal.

Parliament's strengthened actions were not as uncompromising as for internal factions to immediately displace the Prime Minister from her position. For many months, May retained a weak command of a governing majority (of Conservative and fellow DUP MPs) who still treated their confidence in her as wholly distinct from the issue of what many regarded as a failure to have negotiated an acceptable withdrawal deal. The Labour leader tabled a motion of no-confidence in the Government, for debate on the day after the first meaningful vote in January and which had the potential to trigger a general election (BBC News 2019a). Had the No Confidence motion been agreed to, the Government would have 14 days to form a new government that could command a majority to win a confidence motion in the House of Commons (UK Parliament 2019b). Conservative and fellow DUP MPs nonetheless expressed confidence in Her Majesty's Government, voting against the motion of no confidence, 325 to 306 (UK Parliament 2019b); only four months later did Theresa May announce her resignation.

Following the House of Commons rejecting the agreement in that first meaningful vote and despite pledges to then seek parliamentary consensus (Fox 2019; Sunday Post 2019; UK Parliament 2019a), no genuine consensus materialised at that stage. Party-disaligned factions and broader party anxieties had made such consensus near impossible. Traditional party lines had broken ahead of the first meaningful vote, with some 118 Conservative MPs (both Leave and Remain-advocates) voting with the opposition against the deal and three Labour MPs supporting the deal (BBC News 2019a). Fundamentally, parliament had shown through party competition and its intra-party factional disagreements, its genuine strength in rejecting the government's agreement. It is perhaps to be expected however that in two-party systems, policies that depend on even a temporary consensual, cross-party alliance may often not emerge because such alliances can bring about deep-seated divisions in one or other existing party, thereby weakening its internal cohesion (Quinn 2019).

In terms of shaping and constraining the agenda and thereby refining the Prime Minister's withdrawal agreement, the Opposition's policies were often considered difficult to align with her agreement. The Labour party's alternative proposals—to secure a permanent customs union with the EU, a strong relationship with the single market, and alignment on rights (UK Parliament 2019c; ITV 2019) or a vote on the option to legislate to hold another referendum on the deal (BBC News 2019b; House of Commons 2019a)—were deemed unworkable by governing MPs outside Jeremy Corbyn's party boundaries. For the government, Labour proposals did not merely fail to sit well with the negotiated agreement but bore too weak a relationship with the referendum verdict of June 2016. Nonetheless, after failing to pass the withdrawal agreement, Theresa May entered into negotiations with the Labour leader to attempt to secure the passage of a deal which could suit both leaders. At the time of writing, those negotiations have ended without agreement and within weeks Theresa May announced her resignation.

In taking the initiative to shape the agenda and refine the Prime Minister's deal in 2019, a more practical (albeit, unsuccessful) force in shaping the Prime Minister's future approach had been her own governing party backbenchers. They, along with the DUP, had voted to require the Northern Ireland backstop within the agreement to be replaced with alternative arrangements to avoid a hard border (by 317 to 301)

(House of Commons 2019a). Conservative MPs were ordered to vote for this amendment (BBC News 2019b; ITV 2019). The amendment supported leaving with a deal and that MPs would therefore support the agreement subject to this change on the Northern Ireland backstop (House of Commons 2019a). May subsequently committed to returning to Brussels to reopen negotiations on legally-binding alternatives to the backstop (BBC News 2019b), with less than 60 days until leaving the EU (ITV 2019).

The Prime Minister remained, however, strongly constrained by the parliamentary factions of the Brexiteer bloc—namely, the ERG and DUP—in pursuing her subsequent strategy. She experienced continued defeats within a strengthened House of Commons, when MPs declined supporting her motion (Sparrow 2019b) which had reiterated support for the approach to leaving the EU in renegotiating the backstop, while the discussions between the UK and the EU on the Northern Ireland backstop were still ongoing (House of Commons 2019b). It was a majority of 45 (303 to 258) against her and, although it had little legal effect, it was politically constraining: how could the prime minister seek to negotiate in Brussels when a Commons majority at home could not vote in favour of her own Brexit strategy? After all, a significant number of the ERG Eurosceptics in her own party had abstained, on the basis that the government's motion implied the ruling out of a No Deal Brexit, which many of those MPs in fact desired. The official Opposition held no similar power (at that stage) in attempting to provide an alternative pathway—their own amendment aimed to set a deadline for another 'meaningful vote' but was defeated by 322 to 306 (House of Commons 2019b). Despite the Prime Minister later returning from Brussels with additional hard-won changes clarifying the Northern Irish backstop, MPs voted (391 to 242, on 12 March) to again reject the Government's deal in a second meaningful vote (UK Parliament 2019d). In a third failed vote (not a meaningful vote), on the day the UK had meant to leave the EU (29th March), MPs voted (by 344 to 286) to again reject the negotiated agreement (UK Parliament 2019e).

Competitive party jockeying and factional dealignment within parties had enabled the executive-legislature accountability chasm to be filled, as might be expected in adopting Burke's assumption, to reject the kind of withdrawal terms the Prime Minister had presented. The reasons were significantly founded on the Labour Party's softer 'customs union' option and the ERG-Conservative and DUP MPs harder, clean Brexit alternatives. Each sought to directly enhance their party position vis-a-vis Parliament's political representative role. Inter-party competition and intra-party deliberation and factionalism were key to reconciling political opinion in the process. After all, for Burke, the combined judgement of MPs forms the basis of a mandate for government in which intra-party deliberation enhances this foundation (Burke 1770; Dewan and Squintani 2016, p. 3). Party-disaligned factions became central. The vision of a hypothetical, consensual solution of a cross-party May-Corbyn Brexit deal alliance, which would have marginalised the ERG or DUP support, remains unachievable (at the time of writing). Those analysts who noted such a cross-party solution would potentially be subject to subsequent Conservative fragmentation, ministerial resignations, broken parliamentary discipline, local parties seeking deselection of pro-EU MPs, and Brexit-voters publicly insisting on the prime minister's resignation (Quinn 2019) now appear highly relevant. In the Conservative Party itself, the views of its 124,000 members and 330 MPs had grown increasingly irreconcilable with what is required in a deal that could command a majority in Parliament (Menon and Wager 2019a, p 29).

On the opposition benches, the Labour party remained "in disarray" (Menon 2016; Curtice 2017c, p. 13) as two thirds of its voters voted Remain yet 70% of Labour constituencies voted Leave, many by wide margins (Gamble 2017). The parliamentary party and the membership are strongly pro-Remain but the leadership and key Labour constituencies are not (Hoare 2019). The referendum result and the attempt to formulate a cohesive Brexit policy disoriented the party itself, resulting in a policy orientation characterised by "constructive ambiguity" (Menon and Wager 2019b, p. 32). In electoral terms, whereas Labour embraced the social liberal values of its Remain voters but nearly 70% of Labour seats voted for Brexit, Conservatives had also put at risk the support of liberal, Remain-voting Conservatives (Ford and Goodwin 2017, p. 27; Goodwin 2016). The Labour party therefore pursued a significant strategy in the scrutiny of Government negotiations and agreement reflecting different terms upon which the UK leaves the EU, namely within a customs union and closer relationship with the single market.

7.5.3 MPs as Motion-Making, Agenda-Shapers: Drafting Meaningful Motions, Shaping Future Direction

The resettlement of parliamentary powers was manifest in MPs' and the Speaker's highly unusual ability to force Parliament, government and the Prime Minister to enable amendable Government motions in relation to the negotiated agreement. MPs specifically voted for an amendment (by 320 to 298) to enable debates, and votes on specific motions, in the eventuality MPs had voted down the withdrawal agreement and the future relationship framework (Stewart 2018). Without the Speaker selecting that amendment, MPs would have simply debated and voted on a motion stating they had considered the Government's plans in relation to withdrawal negotiations. The amendment had substantive implications. It meant that if MPs did not approve the agreement, then during future debates on the matter, the Government's Motion under consideration would be amendable. This would then enable meaningful, MP-led motions to be considered rather than only motions proposing to merely note that MPs had considered how the Government proposes to proceed.

By nature of the motion being amendable, MPs were free to amend the motion to add further requirements, including, for example, a second referendum to be held (The UK in a Changing Europe 2018, p. 4). As a crucial point both for parliament and the future course of the Brexit strategy, it carried with it the implication that backbench factions who wanted a different strategy to the Government's own agreement—a softer 'customs union' based Brexit or even a second referendum—would, in principle, be allowed to put their own proposals to a vote in the Commons (Stewart 2018), however non-legally binding those alternative motions were (Maguire 2018). It would be accurate to suggest the successful vote gave MPs a power "to try and influence events" (Isaby 2018), rather than a "right to dictate" a Plan B the government adopted once the Brexit deal was voted down (Maguire 2018). The successful vote to achieve this power through one amendment (by Dominic Grieve, Con) had also meant that 25 Tory MPs rebelled against their own Government, including some considered especially loyal to the Government (Isaby 2018), thus raising the ongoing problematic issue of the Prime Minister's command of a majority during the Brexit process.

Although Parliament (notably, the Speaker) stepped up to obtain broader powers in relation to amendable Government Motions, the majority of governing MPs from the Conservative and DUP proved unwilling to overstate its competence. For example, in January 2019, MPs voted down an important cross-party amendment by 321 to 301 which would have given the Commons the priority to debate Brexit on six days in February and March (House of Commons 2019a). It would have bound the government to make time in parliament for MPs to discuss the different alternatives to the Prime Minister's faltering Brexit plan over six full days. Potentially, MPs could have tabled amendments and voted for alternative Brexit options (BBC News 2019b). As agenda-shapers, MPs chose however not to take Parliament into this agenda-making process at an early stage (a process of indicative votes came months later). Such an outcome had clear pitfalls for MPs in deepening the crisis and in which potentially no majority-backed political solution could even be found.

Nonetheless, sovereignty depends upon parliament which depends upon parties—including major party-disaligned factions—to act as representatives between executive and legislative powers. The enhanced party-elector convergence over EU-leaving and accepting or rejecting a final deal through party realignment brought about by the referendum verdict seeks to potentially bridge the executive-legislature relationship. The referendum choices were broadly crystallised in the party system at the point of the referendum around the most salient political issues—including EU-leaving/remaining, restrictions to EU immigration, preserving or reforming economic trading relationships—on which voters and successful parties then align their issue preferences. Yet, simply because the referendum has a crystallising effect on salient issues can hardly be said to undermine representative government (consistent with Qvortrup 2015, p. 7), or parliamentary sovereignty.

The enhanced role of intra-party factionalised parliamentary groups made it near impossible between 2016 and 2018 to achieve cross-party, majority support on an Opposition-led positive alternative to the Prime Minister's deal; but faction formation proved constructive and efficient in promoting parliamentary decision-making. In Parliament as a whole, specific actions enabled individual motions (MP-amendments to the Government's) to be brought forward by those respective groups to both demonstrate their Brexit legislative counter-proposals (a second referendum, delaying Article 50 or opting for No Deal). It helped to illustrate the presence (and absence) of support in parliament and to the electorate more broadly for their desired objectives. In this sense, factions can increase the aggregate capacity of their party and facilitate intra-party cooperation by regulating internal competition, in so far as they align with the party's broader interests (consistent with Boucek 2009, 2013). While the DUP pact may have kept her party in office after 2017, the Prime Minister's post-election minority status had diminished the government's capacity to manage the developing socio-political cleavages in parliament (Matthews 2017), including powerful factions. In the absence of effective factional management by government, occurring (in some cases) across party disaligned lines, the management of factions fell to a far greater, reinvigorated and fluid parliament as it reacted to the impending Brexit legislation and policy.

The Brexit-inducing party reorientation was not a dynamic for all time and all circumstances—for example, the 2017 general election gave Labour a strengthened confidence in parliament (Cygan 2017, p. 18). In Select Committees, for example, when agreeing reports in the Select Committee on Exiting the EU, Labour MP members voted entirely cohesively on all votes, while Conservatives were much more divided (Lynch and Whitaker 2018). The Conservative party was also seriously divided between eurosceptics who have coalesced around the European Research Group (ERG) and Remain-supporting MPs who mostly seemed to respect the referendum result (Hoare 2019) and many of whom formed around a Brexit Delivery Group (BDG) in support of Theresa May's deal.

The intersection of the Brexit process with the enhanced factionalisation of parliamentary parties could not have been made more clearer than an episode in which eight pro-Remain MPs resigned from the Labour Party in protest at Jeremy Corbyn's approach to Brexit and anti-Semitism (BBC News 2019c, d). Then, three pro-Remain Tory MPs resigned from the party to join their Independent Group, citing the government enabling the "hard-line anti-EU awkward squad" take over the party (BBC News 2019d). The group later formed a party, Change UK. Despite giving various reasons for leaving, the binding glue between them had been their opposition to their respective party's pursuit of a Brexit strategy. Their objectives included voting down the Prime Minister's withdrawal agreement, holding a second referendum (which many Remain campaigners believed would reverse the result of the first) or delay the Article 50 negotiations by a considerable time. They contributed, at least to a small degree, towards the Prime Minister then giving ground to Cabinet and her Conservative parliamentary colleagues in averting a No Deal Brexit; with Jeremy Corbyn then also accepting a shift towards conditional support for a second referendum (Diamond 2019).

Furthermore, the strengthened House of Commons took the unusual step of voting to approve a Motion, strongly constraining the Prime Minister's demands and setting out MPs objectives to hold a series of indicative votes on a way forward in the Brexit process. Given the failure of Theresa May's deal to win support (at that stage) on the second meaningful vote, MPs voted in favour of a self-initiated broad power to hold indicative votes on Brexit-related proposals (UK Parliament 2019f, g). Ministerial power was marginalised since MPs (not Government) were imposing their own agenda in parliament—while ministers were being asked to vote against the motion authorising the whole process as well as abstain on all proposals. Parliament faced an impasse since the Government had lost the second 'meaningful vote' (UK Parliament 2019d, f); there was no other immediate deal available. In this political limbo, MPs voted by 329 to 302, a majority of 27, to approve the 'Oliver Letwin amendment' that effectively took control of the parliamentary schedule to hold a series of indicative votes on a way forward which might secure a majority in the House of Commons. The action specifically led to the suspending of normal parliamentary business rules (Standing Order 14), which usually gave the Government business priority on all sitting days (except Fridays), to allow the House to hold indicative votes. The results of these votes were not be legally binding but would have political weight as the House of Commons debated the terms of withdrawal (UK Parliament 2019f).

The Prime Minister was strongly sceptical of the indicative votes process, it achieved no substantive 'majority' outcome and yet inside parliament, it managed to illustrate (with a show of numbers) the vigorous and determined articulation of rationales and alternatives by MPs in the process. In the first round of indicative votes on eight Brexit-related motions in March 2019, no proposals could command a majority in the House of Commons, each being outvoted by differing degrees: No Deal (400 to 160), Common Market 2.0 'Norway-style' Brexit (283 to 188), European Free Trade Association (EFTA) and European Economic Area (EEA) membership (377 to 65), a preference for a customs union (272 to 264), Labour's alternative plan (307 to 237), a revocation of Article 50 to avoid a No Deal (293 to 184), a second referendum (295 to 268), and contingent preferential arrangements in the absence of a withdrawal agreement, including a 2-year, no-tariff trade agreement covering UK-EU goods (422 to 139) (UK Parliament 2019f). In the second round of indicative votes in the Commons, after Theresa May had lost the third vote on her agreement, again, no proposed Motions could command a majority in the House of Commons. Some were outvoted by only slim margins, including: customs union (276 to 273), Common Market 2.0 (282 to 261), a second referendum (292 to 280), revoking Article 50 notification based on the withdrawal agreement and No Deal being opposed by MPs (292 to 191) (UK Parliament 2019g). Subsequent to the electors having delivering a verdict by referendum, Parliament is instructed with that verdict. Equally, the role of post-referendum party competition proceeds in reconciling their positions (De Vries 2009), not only on EU-leaving but the terms of such a withdrawal. By reaching around the Prime Minister and providing space in the House of Commons for indicative votes and to take control of a longer Article 50 extension, EU leaders were themselves seeking for MPs to (re)'crystallise its own solution' (Islam 2019).

Political parties and factions within the parties jockey between one another by disagreement, debate and opportunity-creation to realign executive as against legislative positions. The result of their competition is to enable decision-making in Parliament to then be exercised (McConalogue 2019). Party competition enables parties to creates positions, concentrated around the terms of 'leaving the EU' in which opportunities are created—on further delaying the endpoint of Article 50 negotiations, on passing or rejecting the Prime Minister's deal, on a 'No Deal' Brexit scenario, voting down immigration legislation, holding of a second referendum or another general election (Bogdanor 2017; Miller et al. 2017; Renwick 2017a; Caird 2017). The broader outcome of this deliberative process is that it enables the ordinary, parliamentary politics of 650 MPs to permit the competition between the separate arms of the constitution and their interests to moderate the risk of one (namely, the Prime Minister) dominating the other (the House of Commons) (consistent with Bellamy 2007).

7.5.4 *Parliament Holding the Government in Contempt and Protecting the 'Will of Parliament'*

Parliament acted rapidly and with devoted scrutiny in finding Government ministers in contempt for their failure to publish the required legal advice by the Attorney General (Geoffrey Cox) on the withdrawal agreement. What is most relevant to the enhancement of parliament's power in this rare context is that 'contempt' of parliament defines any act or omission which obstructs the House of Commons in carrying out its duties (UK Parliament 2018). It was therefore a formal and strong statement of Parliament's power in relation to the executive. The strengthened exercise of such parliamentary power challenges assumptions in the research literature identifying either that Parliament has become isolated from fundamental questions for the executive in relation to the Brexit process or that the Prime Minister dominates parliament in that process (Eeckhout 2018, pp. 169, 172; Eleftheriadis 2017).

After all, an effective parliamentary majority voted in favour of finding ministers in contempt for their failure to publish the final and full legal advice provided by the Attorney General to the Cabinet on the agreement and framework for the future relationship, including to order the immediate publication of the advice (House of Commons 2018; UK Parliament 2018). The Attorney General had made a previous statement in the House of Commons on the legal position but MPs recognised the failure to comply with the fullest terms of the motion. The Speaker conceded "an arguable case that a contempt has been committed" and gave precedence to a motion on the matter (Kirkland 2018; UK Parliament 2018). The Government's own unsuccessful amendment sought to refer to the Committee of Privileges the question of whether the Government's existing response fulfilled the expectations set out in an earlier motion. That motion was voted down by only 311 to 305 MPs (House of Commons 2018). The Leader of the House, Andrea Leadsom, subsequently announced that the legal advice would be made available to MPs the following day (UK Parliament 2018; Elgot et al. 2018). The Attorney-General's advice strongly informed MPs ongoing votes in scrutinising the withdrawal agreement.

As Kirkland (2018) expressed it, "To accuse someone of contempt of parliament is to suggest they have deliberately and knowingly obstructed the will of parliament"—and that 'sovereignty' itself is at stake in such proceedings. After all, as he suggests, if government ministers seek to bypass the will of parliament as expressed in votes, then it seriously questions parliament's sovereignty. But Kirkland falls short of the plausible conclusion that, given MPs did indeed hold Government in contempt of parliament, it strongly implies parliamentary sovereignty was not only protected, but bolstered during that episode. It again questioned the ability of the Prime Minister to directly command a majority in the House of Commons (Elgot et al. 2018; Kirland 2018), particularly given that the DUP, propping up the government's majority, had voted with Labour on the contempt motion.

7.5.5 *MPs' Requesting a Delay to Article 50 Negotiations*

A further resettlement of parliamentary decision-making powers was largely evident from a vote on a motion to extend the Article 50 period. The House of Commons voted 412 to 202 to approve a motion to seek to extend the Article 50 period, only weeks before it was seeking to leave on 29 March 2019 (UK Parliament 2019h). That initially imposed a requested extension until 30 June 2019. The reason for the extension would be for the purpose of passing the necessary EU exit legislation. The politics of extending this period revolved around Article 50 itself of the 2009 Lisbon Treaty setting out how a member state would leave the EU, with a two year period between the member state "triggering" the Article and the day that the state leaves the Union. Since the UK Government had triggered Article 50 on 29 March 2017, it was due to leave the European Union on 29 March 2019. If the Article 50 period was to be extended, the UK would remain a member of the European Union during this period. As such, it made it increasingly problematic for the Government to claim to be pursuing a Brexit strategy in so far as it had not technically left the EU. In any case, even as Theresa May attended Brussels to request a short 3-month extension of Article 50 within a week of the 29 March deadline, the European Council itself chose to put MPs themselves centre-stage. EU leaders agreed a short, initial extension to 22 May on the basis the agreement passed its third meaningful vote, or to leave on 12 April if the agreement did not pass (in a No Deal scenario). It is an issue which essentially put 'MPs in the driving seat' (Islam 2019).

Until at least early February 2019, it was not always considered credible by the governing party MPs to delay the Article 50 process as a seriously realistic option, having voted down the proposal in January (House of Commons 2019a; BBC News 2019b). Yet, it became more necessary as the clock was running down up to 29th March and then subsequently 12 April, without an agreement in place, that parliament felt compelled to act. The Prime Minster was constrained by parliament to request a short extension of Article 50. The underlying logic in the weeks preceding the withdrawal date illustrated that an extension to the Article 50 process would itself help to avoid a No Deal withdrawal. For example, a second, subsequent and successful cross-party EU (Withdrawal) (No. 5) Bill initiated by Yvette Cooper (Lab), passed by only 313 votes to 312 (at third reading), was then passed by a fast-track procedure in order to force the Prime Minister to request from the EU an extension to the Article 50 process beyond 12 April (Institute for Government 2019). The European Council subsequently agreed a further extension until 31 October 2019 for the purpose of ratifying the withdrawal agreement. Both Article 50 extensions derived from Parliament—on the first occasion, by an MP-initiated Motion, on the second occasion by MP-initiated legislation.

7.5.6 Parliament Preventing a No Deal Brexit

The resettlement of parliamentary powers became apparent from the widespread anxiety and parliamentary actions across most parties in forcing the government and the Prime Minister to not leave the EU on 29 March without a satisfactory agreement in place. Although MPs have so far prevented No Deal essentially by requesting an Article 50 extension (as above), Parliament also asserted itself against the government in preventing a No Deal Brexit scenario. While delivering a withdrawal agreement remained the Government's priority, the Prime Minister continuously told MPs that they either accept her deal or face a No Deal scenario on 29 March. The Prime Minister therefore requested extensive and costly governmental preparations were made across the UK for all scenarios, including for No Deal, in anticipation of the March 2019 withdrawal deadline. Until an alternative outcome was legislated for, it remained the legal default. In the absence of an agreement ratified by both the House of Commons (and the EU 27), May assured, the UK would exit without a deal. This situation made it concerning for MPs that, without Prime Ministerial backing, they could not seem to legislate or to vote in order to prohibit a No Deal scenario.

In Parliament, there had therefore been significant attempts made by MPs to prevent that scenario. One successful Commons amendment in January had already rejected the UK leaving the EU without an agreement and which received majority support by 318 to 310 votes (House of Commons 2019a). It was a non-legally binding vote but the political point had been made. Seventeen pro-EU Conservatives significantly voted with the opposition against the No Deal option. The House of Commons voted again in March to reject leaving the UK without a deal by 321 to 278 (on a margin of 43) (UK Parliament 2019i). Again, the move was not legally binding but strongly reflected the will of the House of Commons.

Throughout the Prime Minister's three unsuccessful attempts to steer a withdrawal agreement through parliament, it had become commonplace for Opposition MPs—the SNP in particular—to attempt to block any form of No Deal scenario, combined with extensions of the Article 50 period, in several unsuccessful votes (BBC News 2019b; House of Commons 2019a, b). Even prior to Theresa May returning to parliament with an agreement, MPs had made multiple but ultimately unsuccessful efforts to amend the Finance Bill, to help force the No Deal option off the table. Then, finally, in January 2019, MPs effectively voted to amend tax legislation as a means of averting a No Deal Brexit, a scenario which seemed to lack majority support across Parliament. MPs eventually voted (by 303 to 296) to limit Treasury powers in the Finance Bill (House of Commons 2019c). The amendment effectively prevented the Government implementing the No Deal provisions (in Clause 89 of the Finance Bill) without the explicit consent of Parliament for such an outcome. Nonetheless, it was the first, real, majority-backed move to take the No Deal scenario off the table.

7.6 Conclusion

The UK's commitment to leaving the EU and Parliament's constitutional resettlement within that decision-making process is unfinished. Theresa May, as Prime Minister, had negotiated a withdrawal agreement which the House of Commons has rejected on three occasions. Parliament's ultimate decision-making power in holding to account the Prime Minister during the negotiation of a satisfactory agreement and the UK's official departure remains dependent upon the capacity for party competition to exploit the executive-legislative accountability gap on policy and legislation. Some emphasis has been placed on the role of intra-party deliberation and factionalisation of the governing party in this chapter but that is not to ignore the ongoing role of the deployment of Select Committee scrutiny in party competition. The intensely rigorous process of MPs' and peers' in pursuing scrutiny through their memberships of Select Committees has championed Parliament's sometimes problematic 'corporate spirit' (McConalogue 2019; Renwick 2017a, p. 2; Smith 2017, p. 94–95; EU Committee 2016). Backbench MPs, reliant on those committees, worked to redress the accountability gap between Government and Parliament on complex, multi-layered, EU withdrawal policies (consistent with Winzen 2012; Raunio and Hix 2000, p. 163).

When it came to MPs imposing conditionality on a No Deal scenario or delaying Article 50, the articulation of Labour and SNP party competition with the governing party on the floor of the House produced significant results. Where those results were political demands, such as in an amended Motion, they were often not legally binding on the government and were without overtly direct constraints upon the Prime Minister. Even more resourceful, if not unusual, were MPs' holding of a non-binding 'indicative votes' exercise, leading the way in the articulation of Brexit alternative proposals. While the scrutineers were not able to directly mandate the Government's policy agenda preceding Article 50 negotiations (beyond the original 'notification') or for a second referendum, MPs did partially mandate to a more successful degree, the Government's initial request of two Article 50 extensions in March and April 2019. The vigorous supply of policy and legislative views by MPs on Theresa May requesting such an extension at the European Council directly moderated, conditioned and nuanced the government's policy—to otherwise leave on 'No Deal' terms after 29 March—and enhanced the parliament's own corporate view in attempting to modify as well as reject the withdrawal agreement. Through party competition, Labour had begun to reorient its Brexit policy away from both the referendum result and the Conservative Government's agenda. The party, notably following the 2017 election, moved towards UK membership of an EU customs union and a stronger form of relationship with the single market. For the Conservative leadership, if either the commencement of Article 50 proceedings in the *Miller* [2017] judgement and the passage of the agreement towards the end of Article 50 process (up to 29 March) provided any stark lessons for the government, it is that agreement by ministerial power in altering EU law or membership is absent of political legitimacy, accountability and consent, whereas the agreement by Parliament and statute is not.

A significant series of major realignments have developed in the party system during the withdrawal agreement debates. During deliberations, voters with already strong Brexit identities (Evans and Schaffner 2019, p. 19; Hobolt and Tilley 2019, p. 20) may potentially after time seek to (re)task parliamentary parties to align with, or review the deal, hold a second referendum, delay the Article 50 negotiations or consider No Deal preferences. At least a significant part of division over the negotiation of the withdrawal agreement stems from the 2017 election. The outcome of the 'Brexit election' led to an amplified power of accountability influence and scrutiny of Parliament over the Brexit negotiating policy of the Conservative Government of the day (Cygan 2017, p. 18). Equally, it led to nine tenths of elected MPs in the House of Commons to have pledged their party's position of respecting the referendum result (Rose 2017). In public opinion on Brexit, liberal-authoritarian value orientations have substantially modified party choices within left-right attitude positions (Surridge 2019, p. 8). The election itself left the Prime Minister in an exposed situation with only a wafer-thin parliamentary majority of 13. Her entire authority rested upon a Conservative-Democratic Unionist Party agreement, which whilst preserving her position in the Commons wholly undermined her attempts to pass the Northern Ireland backstop insurance policy specified within the agreement.

Theresa May's three-time-opposed negotiated agreement—broadly at odds with positions expressed by all opposition parties, the approximate 80 ERG governing party members and 10 DUPs in Parliament—demonstrated a challenge to her marginalising of the legislature in relation to negotiations led by the Prime Ministerial executive. The demotion of parliament, evidenced by a broad lack of consultation during negotiation, can be understood as a Prime Ministerial exercise in permissive consensus (Hooghe and Marks 2009, p. 5; Geddes 2016; Franklin et al. 1994). Prime Ministerial executives can nowadays be constrained in negotiation under EU membership by a dissensus from both opposition and government-aligned backbench MPs. The awaiting dissensus in Westminster and the role of parties (and intra-party factions) in Parliament affirms a heightened state of political accountability between the executive, the legislature and the electorate, which support parliamentary sovereignty.

Voters in the referendum on 23 June directly tasked Parliament to resettle its ultimate decision-making power to implement the majority decision to 'leave the EU'. This tasking of Parliament has had the effect, evidenced by the 'Article 50 votes' in 2017, the Withdrawal Act votes in 2018 and subsequently during the passage of the withdrawal agreement in 2019, of creating cleavages in the party system, crystallised foremost at the point of the referendum result. The process indicates a constitutionally enhanced role for Parliament in making political decisions and thereby in resettling parliamentary sovereignty. This resettling indicates the holding of a referendum on the UK's membership of the EU has enhanced, not eroded, the principle of representative government and Parliamentary sovereignty (contra Bogdanor 2019, p. 261; McKibbin 2017, p. 385; Mabbett 2017, p. 169). After 45 years of EU membership, the UK's withdrawal will mean the Parliament regaining from the EU its centrality of decision-making over key political decisions. Whereas Kirkland (2019) refers to a power grab rivalry between the executive and legislature within the Brexit process and Baldini et al. (2018) theorise a potential strengthening of the executive over the legislature, I reinterpret such votes and episodes (both in and outside traditional party competition) as inducing a potential resettlement, strongly enhancing parliamentary power (consistent with Loughlin and Tierney 2018, p. 1010) in relation to the Prime Ministerial executive.

There are clear implications of the approach taken. The view presented of the 'rule of the recognised helm' contrasts with other leading legal and political theories placing popular and legal limitations upon Parliament's sovereignty. The rule of the recognised helm is both a fundamental rule of government and a helm which defines the settlement and resettlement of multiple political actors at the helm. It explains the unsettling and resettling of uncodified relations and conventions between the executive, the legislature, the judiciary and the electorate in their tacit consent/recognition of a rule having the capacity to steer and direct. Other approaches within a popular sovereigntist and common law paradigm have accorded inconsiderable significance and weight to the eight historical constitutional forms defining Parliament's political supremacy, institutional relationships and inter-linkages. By attaching less significance to the eight historical constitutional forms, the gravity of the impact of EU membership on the unsettling of the UK constitution has often been misunderstood if not underestimated.

The identification of eight innovative developmental, historical constitutional forms enable political and constitutional theories to more widely rethink the shifting and unsettling that occurs between those forms. That experience of a further resettling is particularly relevant to today's understandings of constitutional change. Through the incorporation of the EU at the realigned recognised helm, the sovereignty formed in Parliament incorporates the inter-relationships between the other constitutional actors. Those complex inter-relationships have intensified under EU membership, unsettling the powers at the helm, including the concentration of powers within the helm itself. In the final case study, events since the EU referendum illustrate that Parliament's ultimate power can be potentially resettled, namely by addressing the historical dilution of its powers. Walker's (2014) assumption that the modern period of constitutional unsettlement, in which parliamentary sovereignty is modified or challenged and occurs because its end-phase offers neither a return to a settled constitution nor arrival to a newer one, remains persuasive (see Young and Gee 2016; Gordon 2017, p. 32). The character of the current, eighth constitutional form is an institutional expression of a fusion of the executive with EU machinery, a part-synthesis of the strengthened judiciary with the Luxembourg court system, but which has ultimately diluted the strength of the domestic legislature. The process unsettles the previous historical precedents of parliamentary sovereignty.

This analysis throughout Chapters 4–7 has tended more broadly to concentrate on the EU's unsettling of the features belonging to 'What the Crown-*with*-magnates enacts is law' (1200–1350), 'What the Crown-*in*-regulating Parliament enacts is law' (1688–1689), 'What the Crown-*in*-mixed constitutional Parliament enacts is law' (1690–1790s) and 'What the Crown-*through*-Parliamentary political elite with external bodies enacts is law' (1973–Present). It is certainly plausible that potential further examination of constitutional unsettlement need not be restricted to those constitutional forms, nor the role of the EU itself, but other challenges to UK parliamentary sovereignty including the growth of the devolved bodies and the introduction of the Supreme Court.

Today, an executive-led Parliament delegates its law-making capacity to other institutions. Other institutions are then able to impose a degree of steerage upon legislation and policy, meaning those representatives who are elected to the House of Commons by the political community to do that precise role no longer have that practical capacity. That is because their everyday competency, but not ultimate right, was voluntarily transferred under the European Communities Act 1972 to navigate the ship of state with a new hand on the helm. Parliament retains its ultimate sovereignty because it has the power to alter that membership—Theresa May's government having passed the legislation to repeal the European Communities Act 1972 from 'exit day'—despite the 45-year practice of choosing not to end or alter substantial aspects of its Parliament-diminishing EU membership. This final chapter indicates that a sovereignty once shared with the EU does not mean it could not be resettled; to the contrary, it has voluntary and politically shared sovereignty which can be returned if it so chooses.

The constitutional 'unsettling' occurs when new events transgress the rules set out in previous precedented relationships as understood through historical constitutional forms. The EU contributes, with its competitive hand on the helm, to steering and directing the Government and Parliament, giving it a greater role in navigating state policies. At the recognised helm, successive governments, through Parliaments, have adopted practices which whilst preserving the fundamental rule, are at odds with past historical precedents. This process has led to strengthened roles for the executive (within the EU decision-making architecture), and the judiciary (with the European Court system) but which unsettles the historical precedents of parliamentary sovereignty. Parliament can, if it so chooses, place a stronger hand at the helm.

Bibliography

Adams, J. F. (2001). *Party Competition and Responsible Party Government: A Theory of Spatial Competition Based Upon Insights from Behavioral Voting Research.* Ann Arbor: University of Michigan Press.

Allan, T. R. S. (2013). *The Sovereignty of Law: Freedom, Constitution and Common Law.* Oxford: Oxford University Press.

Auel, K. (2007). Democratic Accountability and National Parliaments: Redefining the Impact of Parliamentary Scrutiny in EU Affairs. *European Law Journal, 13*(4), 487–504.

Baldini, G., Bressanelli, E., & Massetti, E. (2018). Who Is in Control? Brexit and the Westminster Model. *The Political Quarterly, 89*(4), 537–544.

Bale, T., Webb, P., & Poletti, M. (2019, January 22). Party Members. In The UK in a Changing Europe, *Brexit and Public Opinion 2019* [Online]. Available at https://ukandeu.ac.uk/wp-content/uploads/2019/01/Public-opinion-2019.pdf. Accessed 5 February 2019.

BBC News. (2017, February 1). Brexit: MPs Overwhelmingly Back Article 50 Bill. *BBC News* [Online]. Available at http://www.bbc.co.uk/news/uk-politics-38833883. Accessed 1 February 2017.

BBC News. (2019a, January 15). Brexit: Theresa May's Deal Is Voted Down in Historic Commons Defeat. *BBC News* [Online]. Available at https://www.bbc.co.uk/news/uk-politics-46885828. Accessed 15 February 2019.

BBC News. (2019b, January 29). Brexit Amendments: What Did MPs Vote on and What Were the Results? *BBC News* [Online]. Available at https://www.bbc.co.uk/news/uk-politics-46959545. Accessed 14 February 2019.

BBC News. (2019c, February 20). Independent Group: Three MPs Quit Tory Party to Join. *BBC News* [Online]. Available at https://www.bbc.co.uk/news/uk-politics-47278902. Accessed 25 February 2019.

BBC News. (2019d, February 12). Brexit: Theresa May Promises Meaningful Vote After More Talks with EU. *BBC News* [Online]. Available at https://www.bbc.co.uk/news/uk-politics-47206286. Accessed 27 February 2019.

Bellamy, R. (2007). *Political Constitutionalism: A Republican Defence of the Constitutionality of Democracy*. Cambridge: Cambridge University Press.

Benz, A. (2004). Path-Dependent Institutions and Strategic Veto Players: National Parliaments in the European Union. *West European Politics, 27*(5), 875–900.

Blackstone, W. (1765). *Commentaries on the Laws of England (1765–1769)*. Chicago, IL: University of Chicago Press (this edition 1979).

Bogdanor, V. (2009). *The New British Constitution*. Oxford: Hart Publishing.

Bogdanor, V. (2016a). Europe and the Sovereignty of the People. *Political Quarterly, 87*(3), 348–351.

Bogdanor, V. (2016b, December 9). After the Referendum, the People, Not Parliament, Are Sovereign. *Financial Times* [Online]. Available at https://www.ft.com/content/9b00bca0-bd61-11e6-8b45-b8b81dd5d080. Accessed 20 December 2016.

Bogdanor, V. (2017, August 20). Why Britain's Voters Must Have a Second Referendum on Brexit. *The Guardian* [Online]. Available at https://www.theguardian.com/commentisfree/2017/aug/19/british-voters-second-referendum-on-brexit?CMP=Share_iOSApp_Other. Accessed 20 August 2017.

Bogdanor, V. (2019). *Beyond Brexit: Towards a British Constitution*. London: I.B. Tauris.

Boucek, F. (2009). Rethinking Factionalism: Typologies, Intra-party Dynamics and Three Faces of Factionalism. *Party Politics, 15*(4), 455–485.

Boucek, F. (2013, September 4–7). *The Dilemmas of Intra-party Democracy: Lessons from Italy, Japan and Elsewhere*. 7th European Consortium for Political Research (ECPR) General Conference, Bordeaux, France [Online]. Available at https://ecpr.eu/filestore/paperproposal/32542a0c-8aca-4dff-a52f-3cd7f169beec.pdf. Accessed 21 January 2019.

British Election Study. (2016). *Brexit Britain: British Election Study Insights from the Post-EU Referendum Wave of the BES Internet Panel* [Online]. Available at http://www.britishelectionstudy.com/bes-resources/brexit-britain-british-election-study-insights-from-the-post-eu-referendum-wave-of-the-bes-internet-panel/#.WY2VN1GGPIU. Accessed 6 December 2016.

Burke, E. (1770). Thoughts on the Cause of the Present Discontents. In E. J. Payne (Ed.). (1999), *Select Works of Edmund Burke* (Vol. 1). Indianapolis, IN: Liberty Fund. Available at http://oll.libertyfund.org/titles/burke-select-works-of-edmund-burke-vol-1–5. Accessed 3 December 2013.

Burke, E. (1774). Speech to the Electors of Bristol. In E. J. Payne (Ed.). (1999), *Select Works of Edmund Burke* (Vol. 4). Indianapolis, IN: Liberty Fund. Available at http://oll.libertyfund.org/titles/burke-select-works-of-edmund-burke-vol-4. Accessed 17 December 2013.

Burke, E. (1792). A Letter to Sir Hercules Langrishe on the Catholics of Ireland. In E. J. Payne (Ed.). (1999), *Select Works of Edmund Burke* (Vol. 4). Indianapolis, IN: Liberty Fund. Available at http://www.econlib.org/library/LFBooks/Burke/brkSWv4c6.html. Accessed 16 January 2014.

Caird, J.-S. (2017). *Legislating for Brexit: The Great Repeal Bill* (House of Commons Briefing Paper No. 7793) [Online]. Available at http://research-briefings.parliament.uk/ResearchBriefing/Summary/CBP-7793. Accessed 10 April 2017.

Caird, J. S., Wager, A., & Bevington, M. (2019, March 11). *Brexit Votes Explained.* The UK in a Changing Europe Initiative [Report]. Available at https://ukandeu.ac.uk/how-parliament-can-shape-brexit/.

Chalmers, D. (2017). Brexit and the Renaissance of Parliamentary Authority. *The British Journal of Politics and International Relations, 19*(4), 663–679.

Clarke, H. D., Goodwin, M., & Whiteley, P. (2017). Why Britain Voted for Brexit: An Individual-Level Analysis of the 2016 Referendum Vote. *Parliamentary Affairs, 70*(3), 439–464.

ComRes. (2016, June 25). *Sunday Mirror Post Referendum Poll* [Online]. Available at http://www.comresglobal.com/polls/sunday-mirror-post-referendum-poll/. Accessed 27 June 2016.

Copeland, P., & Copsey, N. (2017). Rethinking Britain and the European Union: Politicians, the Media and Public Opinion Reconsidered. *Journal of Common Market Studies, 55*(4), 709–726.

Curtice, J. (2016). Public Opinion. In The UK in a Changing Europe Initiative and the Political Studies Association, *Brexit: Six Months On* [Report]. Available at http://www.ukandeu.ac.uk/wp-content/uploads/2016/12/Brexit-Six-months-on.pdf. Accessed 11 April 2017).

Curtice, J. (2017a). Why Leave Won the UK's EU Referendum. *Journal of Common Market Studies, 55*(Suppl. 1), 19–37.

Curtice, J. (2017b). The Vote to Leave the EU, Litmus Test or Lightning Rod? *British Social Attitudes 34* [Online]. Available at http://www.bsa.natcen.ac.uk/media/39149/bsa34_brexit_final.pdf. Accessed 30 July 2017.

Curtice, J. (2017c, April 11). *On Brexit, Theresa May Is Giving the Public What They Want*. The UK in a Changing Europe Initiative [Blog]. Available at http://www.ukandeu.ac.uk/on-brexit-theresa-may-is-giving-the-public-what-they-want/. Accessed 11 April 2017.

Cygan, A. (2017). The Role of Parliament. In The UK in a Changing Europe Initiative and The Political Studies Association (Eds.), *EU Referendum: One Year On* [Report]. Available at http://www.ukandeu.ac.uk/wp-content/uploads/2017/06/One-year-on.pdf. Accessed 30 June 2017.

Cygan, A. (2019, March 12). *The EU Withdrawal Agreement: Unpopular, Yes, but Things May Get a Whole Lot Worse*. The UK in a Changing Europe [Online]. Available at https://ukandeu.ac.uk/the-eu-withdrawal-agreement-unpopular-yes-but-things-may-get-a-whole-lot-worse/. Accessed 15 March 2019.

Davis, D. (2017, January 17). *Statement on a New Partnership with the EU*. [Online]. Available at https://www.gov.uk/government/speeches/statement-on-a-new-partnership-with-the-eu. Accessed 29 June 2017.

De Vries, C. E. (2009). The Impact of EU Referenda on National Electoral Politics: The Dutch Case. *West European Politics, 32*(1), 142–171.

de Wilde, P. (2012). Politicisation of the EU Budget: Conflict and the Constraining Dissensus. *West European Politics, 35*(5), 1075–1094.

Delaney, E. F. (2014). Judiciary Rising: Constitutional Change in the United Kingdom. *Northwestern University Law Review, 108*(2), 543–605.

Dewan, T., & Squintani, F. (2016). In Defense of Factions. *American Journal of Political Science, 60*(4), 860–881.

Diamond, P. (2019, March 6). *Brexit Is the Catalyst for a Rupture in UK Politics That Has Been a Long Time in the Making*. The UK in a Changing Europe [Online]. Available at https://ukandeu.ac.uk/brexit-is-the-catalyst-for-a-rupture-in-uk-politics-that-has-been-a-long-time-in-the-making/. Accessed 15 March 2019.

Dicey, A. V. (1885/1964). *An Introduction to the Study of the Law of the Constitution*. London: Macmillan.

Dicey, A. V. (1911). *A Leap in the Dark* (2nd ed.). London: John Murray.

Down, I., & Wilson, C. J. (2010). Opinion Polarization and Inter-Party Competition on Europe. *European Union Politics, 11*(1), 61–87.

Eeckhout, P. (2018). The Emperor Has No Clothes: Brexit and the UK Constitution. In B. Martill & U. Staiger (Eds.), *Brexit and Beyond: Rethinking the Futures of Europe* (pp. 165–172). London: UCL Press.

Eleftheriadis, P. (2017). Constitutional Illegitimacy over Brexit. *Political Quarterly, 88*(2), 182–188.

Elgot, J., Syaland, R., & Stewart, H. (2018, December 4). Full Brexit Legal Advice to be Published After Government Loses Vote. *The Guardian*. https://www.theguardian.com/politics/2018/dec/04/mps-demand-for-brexit-legal-advice-too-vague-says-geoffrey-cox. Accessed 15 January 2019.

EU Committee. (2016, October 20). *Brexit: Parliamentary Scrutiny* (HL Paper 50) [Online]. Available at https://publications.parliament.uk/pa/ld201617/ldselect/ldeucom/50/50.pdf. Accessed 2 November 2016.

European Research Group. (2018). *Your Right to Know: The Case against Chequers and the Draft Withdrawal Agreement in plain English* [Report], 18 November. Available at https://brexitcentral.com. Accessed 25 November 2018.

European Union (Notification of Withdrawal) Act 2017. Available at http://www.legislation.gov.uk/ukpga/2017/9/contents/enacted/data.htm. Accessed 1 April 2017.

Evans, G., & Schaffner, F. (2019, January 22). Brexit Identity vs Party Identity. In The UK in a Changing Europe, *Brexit and Public Opinion 2019* [Report]. Available at https://ukandeu.ac.uk/wp-content/uploads/2019/01/Public-opinion-2019.pdf. Accessed 5 February 2019.

Ford, R., & Goodwin, M. (2017). A Nation Divided. *Journal of Democracy, 28*(1), 17–30 [Online]. Available at http://www.ukandeu.ac.uk/wp-content/uploads/2017/01/Britain-after-Brexit.pdf. Accessed 11 April 2017.

Fowler, B. (2018, December 10). Six Ways the 'Meaningful Vote' Is Noteworthy: The Withdrawal Agreement & Parliament's Role in Treaty-Making. *Hansard Society* [Blog]. Available at https://www.hansardsociety.org.uk/blog/https:/www.hansardsociety.org.uk/blog/six-ways-the-meaningful-vote-is-noteworthy-the-withdrawal-agreement-and.

Fox, R. (2019, January 21). 'Plan B for Brexit': What Will Happen in the Week Ahead? *Hansard Society* [Blog]. https://www.hansardsociety.org.uk/blog/plan-b-for-brexit-what-will-happen-in-the-week-ahead.

Franklin, M., Marsh, M., & McLaren, L. (1994). Uncorking the Bottle: Popular Opposition to European Unification in the Wake of Maastricht. *Journal of Common Market Studies, 32*(4), 455–472.

Gamble, A. (2017, March 16). British Politics After Brexit. *Political Insight* [Online]. Available at http://journals.sagepub.com/doi/full/10.1177/2041905817702715. Accessed 15 April 2017.

Gamble, A. (2018). Taking Back Control: The Political Implications of Brexit. *Journal of European Public Policy, 25*(8), 1215–1232.

Gamble, A. (2019). The Realignment of British Politics in the Wake of Brexit. *The Political Quarterly, 90*(S2), 177–186.

Geddes, A. (2013). *Britain and the European Union*. London: Palgrave Macmillan.

Geddes, A. (2016). Britain Beyond the European Union? In R. Heffernan, C. Hay, M. Russell, & P. Cowley (Eds.), *Developments in British Politics 10* (10th ed., pp. 264–286). London: Palgrave.

Gifford, C. (2010). The UK and the European Union: Dimensions of Sovereignty and the Problem of Eurosceptic Britishness. *Parliamentary Affairs, 63*(2), 321–338.

Gifford, C. (2014). The People Against Europe: The Eurosceptic Challenge to the United Kingdom's Coalition Government. *Journal of Common Market Studies, 52*(3), 512–528.

Glencross, A. (2018). Cameron's European Legacy: How Brexit Demonstrates the Flawed Politics of Simple Solutions. In B. Martill & U. Staiger (Eds.), *Brexit and Beyond: Rethinking the Futures of Europe* (pp. 22–27). London: UCL Press.

Goodwin, M. (2016). Electoral Dynamics. In The UK in a Changing Europe Initiative and The Political Studies Association (Eds.), *Brexit: Six Months On* [Online]. Available at http://www.ukandeu.ac.uk/wp-content/uploads/2016/12/Brexit-Six-months-on.pdf. Accessed 11 April 2017.

Gordon, M. J. (2017). Brexit: The Relationship Between the UK Parliament and the UK Government. In M. Dougan (Ed.), *The UK After Brexit Legal and Policy Challenges* (pp. 15–33). Cambridge: Intersentia.

Hart, H. L. A. (1997). *The Concept of Law* (2nd ed.). Oxford: Clarendon Press.

Hix, S. (2018). Brexit: Where Is the EU–UK Relationship Heading? *Journal of Common Market Studies, 56*, 11–27.

Hix, S., & Goetz, K. H. (2000). Introduction: European Integration and National Political Systems. *West European Politics, 23*(4), 1–26.

Hoare, G. (2019, February 18). *Brexit Chaos Has Exposed the Effects of European Integration on British Politics.* The UK in a Changing Europe [Online]. Available at https://ukandeu.ac.uk/brexit-chaos-has-exposed-the-effects-of-european-integration-on-british-politics/. Accessed 15 March 2019.

Hobolt, S., & Tilley, J. (2019, January 22). The Brexit Identity Divide. In The UK in a Changing Europe. *Brexit and Public Opinion 2019* [Report]. Available at https://ukandeu.ac.uk/wp-content/uploads/2019/01/Public-opinion-2019.pdf. Accessed 5 February 2019.

Hooghe, L., & Marks, G. (2009). A Postfunctionalist Theory of European Integration: From Permissive Consensus to Constraining Dissensus. *British Journal of Political Science, 39*(1), 1–23.

House of Commons. (2015, June 9). *Hansard*, Column 1060 [Online]. Available at https://publications.parliament.uk/pa/cm201516/cmhansrd/cm150609/debtext/150609-0001.htm#15060939000944. Accessed 12 June 2015.

House of Commons. (2016, December 7). *Hansard*, Column 220 [Online]. Available at https://hansard.parliament.uk/Commons/2016-12-07/debates/CA09D9B2-9634-41C8-8979-8B9CD82DBB8F/TheGovernmentSPlanForBrexit. Accessed 12 December 2016.

House of Commons. (2017a, February 1). *Hansard*, Division No. 135 [Online]. Available at https://hansard.parliament.uk/Commons/2017-02-01/debates/5B0251FC-94E6-4216-8830-4F85E0EC2250/EuropeanUnion(NotificationOfWithdrawal)Bill. Accessed 9 February 2017.

House of Commons. (2017b, September 11). *Hansard*, Column 1030 [Online]. Available at https://hansard.parliament.uk/commons/2017-09-11/debates/B10868CD-F096-47A2-84EE-A902C8A271BE/EuropeanUnion(Withdrawal)Bill. Accessed 12 September 2017.

House of Commons. (2018, December 4). *Hansard*, Column 723–745.

House of Commons. (2019a, January 29). *Hansard* (debate), Column 756.

House of Commons. (2019b, February 14). *Hansard* (debate), Column 1146, Division No. 333.

House of Commons. (2019c, January 8). *Hansard* (debate), Column 277.

House of Commons Library. (2016, August 26). *Brexit: Impact Across Policy Areas* (Briefing Paper CBP-7213) [Online]. Available at http://research-briefings.parliament.uk/ResearchBriefing/Summary/CBP-7213. Accessed 5 September 2016.

Institute for Government. (2018). *Parliament's 'Meaningful Vote' on Brexit.* https://www.instituteforgovernment.org.uk/explainers/parliament-meaningful-vote-brexit.

Institute for Government. (2019). *Parliament's Next Steps on Brexit.* https://www.instituteforgovernment.org.uk/explainers/parliament-next-steps-brexit.

Isaby, J. (2018, December 5). What the Grieve Amendment Means and How MPs Voted on It. *Brexit Central* [Online]. Available at https://brexitcentral.com/grieve-amendment-means-mps-voted/. Accessed 25 March 2019.

Islam, F. (2019, March 22). EU Has Put MPs in the Driving Seat for Brexit. *Sky News* [Online]. Available at https://news.sky.com/story/eu-has-put-mps-in-the-driving-seat-for-brexit-11672338. Accessed 25 March 2019.

ITV News. (2019, January 29). PM Enjoys Good Night as MPs Back Brady Amendment and Reject Five Out of Six Others—But EU Block Renegotiation. *ITV News* [Online]. Available at https://www.itv.com/news/2019-01-29/brexit-amendment-vote/. Accessed 25 March 2019.

Joint Committee on Human Rights. (2016, December 19). *The Human Rights Implications of Brexit* (HL Paper 88 / HC 695) [Online]. Available at https://www.publications.parliament.uk/pa/jt201617/jtselect/jtrights/695/695.pdf. Accessed 11 April 2017.

Katz, R., & Wessels, B. (1999). Parliaments and Democracy in Europe in the Era of the Euro. In R. Katz & B. Wessels (Eds.), *The European Parliament, National Parliaments, and European Integration* (Chapter 6). Oxford: Oxford University Press.

Kirkland, C. (2018, December 4). Ministers Found in Contempt of Parliament Over Legal Advice—Why It Matters for Brexit. *The Conversation* [Online]. Available at https://theconversation.com/ministers-found-in-contempt-of-parliament-over-legal-advice-why-it-matters-for-brexit-108199. Accessed 15 January 2019.

Kirkland, C. (2019, 19 January). *The Constitutional Issues That Underlie the Brexit Negotiations.* The UK in a Changing Europe [Online]. Available at http://ukandeu.ac.uk/the-constitutional-issues-that-underlie-the-brexit-negotiations/. Accessed 15 March 2019.

Lord Ashcroft. (2016, June 24). *How the United Kingdom Voted on Thursday… and Why.* Available at http://lordashcroftpolls.com/2016/06/how-the-united-kingdom-voted-and-why/. Accessed 11 July 2016.

Loughlin, M., & Tierney, S. (2018). The Shibboleth of Sovereignty. *The Modern Law Review, 81*(6), 989–1016.

Lynch, P., & Whitaker, R. (2018, April 30). *Divided but Influential? The Exiting the European Union Select Committee.* The UK in a Changing Europe [Online]. Available at https://ukandeu.ac.uk/divided-but-influential-the-exiting-the-european-union-select-committee/.

Mabbett, D. (2017). Parliamentary Sovereignty and Brexit. *Political Quarterly, 88*(2), 167–169.

Maguire, P. (2018, December 4). Dominic Grieve's Brexit Amendment Gives Control Back to MPs—But What Will They Do with It? *New Statesman* [Online]. Available at https://www.newstatesman.com/politics/uk/2018/12/dominic-grieve-s-brexit-amendment-gives-control-back-mps-what-will-they-do-it.

Matthews, F. (2017). Whose Mandate Is It Anyway? Brexit, the Constitution and the Contestation of Authority. *Political Quarterly, 88*(4), 603–611.

May, T. (2017a). *The Government's Negotiating Objectives for Exiting the EU* [Online]. Available at https://www.gov.uk/government/speeches/the-governments-negotiating-objectives-for-exiting-the-eu-pm-speech. Accessed 18 January 2017.

May, T. (2017b). *The United Kingdom's Exit from and New Partnership with the European Union* (Cm 9417) [Online]. Available at https://www.gov.uk/government/uploads/system/uploads/attachment_data/file/589189/The_United_Kingdoms_exit_from_and_partnership_with_the_EU_Print.pdf. Accessed 5 July 2017.

McConalogue, J. (2019). The British Constitution Resettled? Parliamentary Sovereignty After the EU Referendum. *The British Journal of Politics and International Relations, 21*(2), 439–458.

McKibbin, R. (2017). In the Shadow of the Referendums. *The Political Quarterly, 88*(3), 382–385.

Menon, A. (2016). The Politics of Brexit. In The UK in a Changing Europe Initiative and The Political Studies Association (Eds.), *Brexit: Six Months On* [Report]. Available at http://www.ukandeu.ac.uk/wp-content/uploads/2016/12/Brexit-Six-months-on.pdf. Accessed 11 April 2017.

Menon, A. (2018, September 29). Forget Salzburg: The Real Brexit Battleground Will Be Westminster; Even If Theresa May Gets a Brexit Deal on the Table, It Will Still Have to Face a Febrile, Unpredictable Parliament. *The Guardian*.

Menon, A., & Fowler, B. (2016). Hard or Soft? The Politics of Brexit. *National Institute Economic Review, 238*(1), R4–R12. (R6).

Menon, A., & Wager, A. (2019a, January 22). Will the Conservative Party Split. In The UK in a Changing Europe. *Brexit and Public Opinion 2019* [Report]. Available at https://ukandeu.ac.uk/wp-content/uploads/2019/01/Public-opinion-2019.pdf. Accessed 5 February 2019.

Menon, A., & Wager, A. (2019b, January 22). Labour's Brexit Dilemma. In The UK in a Changing Europe. *Brexit and Public Opinion 2019* [Report]. Available at https://ukandeu.ac.uk/wp-content/uploads/2019/01/Public-opinion-2019.pdf. Accessed 5 February 2019.

Miller, V. (2018, Friday, December 7). *The UK's EU Withdrawal Agreement* (House of Commons Briefing Papers, CBP-8453). https://researchbriefings.parliament.uk/ResearchBriefing/Summary/CBP-8453#fullreport.

Miller, V., Lang, A., & Simson-Caird, J. (2017, January 16). *Brexit: How Does the Article 50 Process Work?* (House of Commons Briefing Paper CBP-7551) [Online]. Available at http://researchbriefings.parliament.uk/ResearchBriefing/Summary/CBP-7551. Accessed 30 January 2017.

Miller v Secretary of State for Exiting the European Union. [2016, November 3]. EWHC 2768 (Admin), Case No. CO/3809/2016 and CO/3281/2016 (2016) [Online]. Available at https://www.judiciary.gov.uk/wp-content/uploads/2016/11/r-miller-v-secretary-of-state-for-exiting-eu-amended-20161122.pdf. Accessed 22 December 2016.

Miller v Secretary of State for Exiting the European Union. [2017, January 24]. Supreme Court Judgement [Online]. Available at https://www.supremecourt.uk/cases/docs/uksc-2016-0196-judgment.pdf. Accessed 26 January 2017.

Nugent, N. (2018). Brexit: Yet Another Crisis for the EU. In B. Martill & U. Staiger (Eds.), *Brexit and Beyond: Rethinking the Futures of Europe* (pp. 54–62). London: UCL Press.

Prosser, C., Mellon, J., & Green, J. (2016, July 11) *What Mattered Most to You When Deciding How to Vote in the EU Referendum?* British Election Study [Blog]. Available at http://www.britishelectionstudy.com/bes-findings/what-mattered-most-to-you-when-deciding-how-to-vote-in-the-eu-referendum/#.WPAZl9QrKt8. Accessed 16 July 2016.

Quinn, T. (2019, February 20). *The Brexit Deal and Party Divisions*. The UK in a Changing Europe [Online]. Available at https://ukandeu.ac.uk/the-brexit-deal-and-party-divisions/. Accessed 15 March 2019.

Qvortrup, M. (1999). A.V. Dicey: The Referendum as the People's Veto. *History of Political Thought, 20*(3), 531–546.

Qvortrup, M. (2015). *A Tale of Two Referendums Elite Manipulation or Civic Engagement?* London: The Constitution Society [Online]. Available at https://consoc.org.uk/wp-content/uploads/2015/09/COSJ3706_Referendum_report_COMPLETE_18.09.15.pdf. Accessed 15 June 2016.

Qvortrup, M. (2018). *Government by Referendum*. Manchester: Manchester University Press.

Raitio, J., & Raulus, H. (2017). The UK EU Referendum and the Move Towards Brexit. *Maastricht Journal of European and Comparative Law, 24*(1), 25–42.

Raunio, T. (2011). The Gatekeepers of European Integration? The Functions of National Parliaments in the EU Political System. *Journal of European Integration, 33*(3), 303–321.

Raunio, T., & Hix, S. (2000). Backbenchers Learn to Fight Back: European Integration and Parliamentary Government. *West European Politics, 23*(4), 142–168.

Renwick, A. (2017a, January). *The Process of Brexit: What Comes Next?* (UCL European Institute Working Paper) [Online]. Available at http://www.ucl.ac.uk/european-institute/ei-publications/renwick-brexit-process.pdf. Accessed 1 February 2017.

Renwick, A. (2017b). Public Debate. In The UK in a Changing Europe Initiative and the Political Studies Association (Eds.), *EU Referendum: One Year On* [Report]. Available at http://ukandeu.ac.uk/wp-content/uploads/2017/06/One-year-on.pdf. Accessed 30 June 2017.

Rose, R. (2017, June 13). *Voters Endorse an Alice-in-Wonderland Brexit*. The UK in a Changing Europe Initiative [Online]. Available at http://www.ukandeu.ac.uk/voters-endorse-an-alice-in-wonderland-brexit/. Accessed 12 July 2017.

Schmidt, V. A. (1999). European "Federalism" and Its Encroachments on National Institutions. *Publius: The Journal of Federalism, 29*(1), 19–44.

Secretary of State for the Home Department. (2017). *The United Kingdom's Exit from the European Union: Safeguarding the Position of EU Citizens Living in the UK and UK Nationals Living in the EU* (Cm 9464) [Online]. Available at https://www.gov.uk/government/uploads/system/uploads/attachment_data/file/621848/60093_Cm9464_NSS_SDR_Web.pdf. Accessed 5 July 2017.

Smith, J. (2017). National Parliaments and the European Union—A View from Westminster. In D. Jancic (Ed.), *National Parliaments After the Lisbon Treaty and the Euro Crisis: Resilience or Resignation?* Oxford: Oxford University Press.

Sparrow, A. (2019a, January 17). May Calls on MPs from All Parties to 'Put Self-Interest Aside'—As It Happened. *The Guardian* [Online]. Available at https://www.theguardian.com/politics/live/2019/jan/16/brexit-vote-theresa-may-faces-no-confidence-vote-after-crushing-defeat?page=with%3Ablock-5c3ed307e4b03740e8745ba8.

Sparrow, A. (2019b, February 14). Brexit: Blow to May's Authority as MPs Reject Her Motion by 303 Votes to 258—As It Happened. *The Guardian* [Blog]. Available at https://www.theguardian.com/politics/live/2019/feb/14/brexit-latest-news-developments-debate-vote-amendments-fox-tells-potential-tory-rebels-they-will-undermine-pms-negotiation-if-she-loses-key-vote-politics-live.

Stewart, H. (2018, December 4). What Does Dominic Grieve's Amendment Mean for Brexit? *The Guardian* [Blog]. Available at https://www.theguardian.com/politics/2018/dec/04/what-does-dominic-grieves-amendment-mean-for-brexit.

Sunday Post. (2019, January 16). Theresa May Calls for Cross-Party Talks After Government Survives Vote of No Confidence. *Sunday Post* [Online]. Available at https://www.sundaypost.com/fp/theresa-may-calls-for-cross-party-talks-after-government-survives-vote-of-no-confidence/.

Surridge, P. (2019, January 22). The Left-Right Divide. In The UK in a Changing Europe. *Brexit and Public Opinion 2019* [Report]. Available at https://ukandeu.ac.uk/wp-content/uploads/2019/01/Public-opinion-2019.pdf. Accessed 5 February 2019.

Swales, K. (2016). *Understanding the Leave Vote*. London: NatCen Social Research [Online]. Available at http://www.natcen.ac.uk/media/1319222/natcen_brexplanations-report-final-web2.pdf. Accessed 11 April 2017.

The UK in a Changing Europe. (2018, September 29). *The Brexit Endgame: A Guide to the Parliamentary Process of Withdrawal from the European Union* [Report]. Available at https://ukandeu.ac.uk/wp-content/uploads/2018/09/Brexit-endgame-A-guide-to-the-parliamentary-process.pdf. Accessed 5 January 2019.

The UK in a Changing Europe. (2019, January 22). *Brexit and Public Opinion 2019* [Report]. Available at https://ukandeu.ac.uk/wp-content/uploads/2019/01/Public-opinion-2019.pdf. Accessed 5 February 2019.

The UK in a Changing Europe Initiative and Political Studies Association of the UK (Eds.). (2016a). *Brexit and Beyond: How the United Kingdom Might Leave the European Union* [Online]. Available at http://www.ukandeu.ac.uk/wp-content/uploads/2016/11/Brexit-and-Beyond-how-the-UK-might-leave-the-EU.pdf. Accessed 11 April 2017.

The UK in a Changing Europe Initiative and the Political Studies Association (Eds.). (2016b). *Brexit: Six Months On* [Online]. Available at http://www.ukandeu.ac.uk/wp-content/uploads/2016/12/Brexit-Six-months-on.pdf. Accessed 11 April 2017.

Tomkins, A. (2010). *Written Evidence to the European Scrutiny Committee, Clause 18 of the Bill: Parliamentary Sovereignty and EU Law*. The EU Bill and Parliamentary Sovereignty. Available at https://publications.parliament.uk/pa/cm201011/cmselect/cmeuleg/633ii/633we02.htm. Accessed 5 December 2010.

UK Parliament. (2018, December 4). *'Contempt Motion' on Publishing of Legal Advice*. UK Parliament [Online]. Available at https://www.parliament.uk/business/news/2018/december/contempt-motion-on-publishing-of-legal-advice/. Accessed 8 December 2018.

UK Parliament. (2019a, January 16). *Government Loses 'Meaningful Vote' in the Commons*. UK Parliament [Online]. Available at https://www.parliament.uk/business/news/2019/parliamentary-news-2019/meaningful-vote-on-brexit-resumes-in-the-commons/. Accessed 18 January 2019.

UK Parliament. (2019b, January 16). *MPs Have Confidence in Government: No Confidence Motion Defeated*. UK Parliament [Online]. Available at https://www.parliament.uk/business/news/2019/parliamentary-news-2019/commons-debate-motion-of-no-confidence-in-hm-government/. Accessed 19 January 2019.

UK Parliament. (2019c, January 29). *House of Commons Debates Brexit Next Steps*. UK Parliament [Online]. Available at https://www.parliament.uk/business/news/2019/parliamentary-news-2019/house-of-commons-debates-brexit-next-steps/. Accessed 29 January 2019.

UK Parliament. (2019d, March 12). *Government's Brexit Deal Defeated Again in 'Meaningful Vote'*. UK Parliament [Online]. Available at https://www.parliament.uk/business/news/2019/march/key-brexit-vote-as-meaningful-vote-returns-to-the-commons/. Accessed 15 March 2019.

UK Parliament. (2019e, March 29). *Commons Votes to Reject Government's EU Withdrawal Agreement*. UK Parliament [Online]. Available at https://www.parliament.uk/business/news/2019/march/mps-debate-and-vote-on-the-withdrawal-agreement-with-the-european-union/. Accessed 5 April 2019.

UK Parliament. (2019f, March 27). *What's Next for Brexit? No Commons Majority in Indicative Votes*. UK Parliament [Online]. Available at https://www.parliament.uk/business/news/2019/march/whats-next-for-brexit-house-of-commons-holds-indicative-votes/. Accessed 29 March 2019.

UK Parliament. (2019g, April 1). *House of Commons Holds Second Round of Indicative Votes*. UK Parliament [Online]. Available at https://www.parliament.uk/business/news/2019/april/house-of-commons-holds-second-round-of-indicative-votes/. Accessed 5 April 2019.

UK Parliament. (2019h, March 14). *House of Commons Votes to Seek Article 50 Extension*. UK Parliament [Online]. Available at https://www.parliament.uk/business/news/2019/march/house-of-commons-to-vote-on-article-50-extension/. Accessed 17 March 2019.

UK Parliament. (2019i, March 13). *House of Commons Vote on No-Deal Brexit*. UK Parliament [Online]. Available at https://www.parliament.uk/business/news/2019/march/house-of-commons-to-vote-on-no-deal-brexit/. Accessed 17 March 2019.

Waldron, J. (1999). *Law and Disagreement*. Oxford: Oxford University Press.

Walker, N. (2014, July). Our Constitutional Unsettlement. *Public Law*, 529–548.

Winzen, T. (2012). National Parliamentary Control of European Union Affairs: A Cross-National and Longitudinal Comparison. *West European Politics*, *35*(3), 657–672.

Young, A., & Gee, G. (2016). Regaining Sovereignty, Brexit, the UK Parliament and the Common Law. *European Public Law*, *22*(1), 131–147.

Index

J. McConalogue, *The British Constitution Resettled*,
https://doi.org/10.1007/978-3-030-25290-8

The manufacturer's authorised representative in the EU is Springer Nature Customer Service Centre GmbH, Europaplatz 3, 69115 Heidelberg, Germany. If you have any concerns regarding our products, please contact ProductSafety@springernature.com

Printed and bound by CPI Group (UK) Ltd, Croydon, CR0 4YY
06/10/2026
02228468-0003